GUIDING TO A BLESSED END

Eugenia Scarvelis Constantinou

GUIDING TO A BLESSED END

ANDREW OF CAESAREA AND HIS APOCALYPSE COMMENTARY IN THE ANCIENT CHURCH

The Catholic University of America Press | Washington, D.C.

Copyright © 2013
The Catholic University of America Press
All rights reserved

Design and typesetting by Kachergis Book Design

Library of Congress Cataloging-in-Publication Data
Constantinou, Eugenia Scarvelis.
 Guiding to a blessed end : Andrew of Caesarea and His Apocalypse
Commentary in the Ancient Church / Eugenia Scarvelis Constantinou.
  p. cm
 Includes bibliographical references and index.
 ISBN 978-0-8132-2114-4 (cloth)
 1. Bible. N.T. Revelation—Commentaries.   I. Title.
 [DNLM: 1. Andrew, Archbishop of Caesarea. Hermeneia eis ten
Apokalypsin.]
 BS2825.53.C66 2012
 228'.07—dc23   2012036759

To

the One who is Alpha and Omega,
the Beginning and the End,

and

to my noble father with inexpressible gratitude
for his life of love and sacrifice
γιά τά παιδιά!

He who overcomes, I will make him a pillar
in the temple of my God

Rev. 3:12

CONTENTS

Preface ix | Abbreviations xi | Introduction xiii

1 The Trajectory of Early Apocalypse Commentaries 1
The Earliest Latin Apocalypse Commentaries 2 | Other Early Latin Commentaries 6
Greek Commentaries Emerge 7 | The Duality of the Apocalypse Interpretive
Tradition 9 | Independence of the Eastern Apocalypse Interpretive Tradition 10

2 The Apocalypse in the Ancient East: From Acceptance to Rejection 14
Early Acceptance of the Apocalypse 17 | The Third Century: Opposition
Appears 22 | The Fourth Century: Erosion of Support 27

3 Later Eastern Developments: From Rejection to Acceptance 35

4 Dating Andrew of Caesarea and Oikoumenios 47
Dating Andrew's Episcopal Reign 48 | Dating the Oikoumenios Commentary 50
Dating Andrew of Caesarea's Apocalypse Commentary 61

5 Andrew's Recipient: "Makarios" and the Historical Milieu 72
Motivation and Historical Milieu 77

6 Why the Oikoumenios Commentary Failed 86
Andrew of Caesarea's Assessment 86 | Presentation: Philosophical and Learned,
but Unskilled and Unorthodox 93 | Theology: Non-Chalcedonian 99

7 Andrew's Commentary: Purpose and Motivation 104
Expressed Purpose and Motivation 104 | Unexpressed Purpose and Motivation 106

8 Orientation, Structure, and Characteristics 112
A Pastoral Orientation 112 | A Liturgical Orientation 114 | A Sacramental
Orientation 117 | The Structure of the Commentary 120 | Style and Characteristics
of the Commentary 121

9 Andrew's Exegetical Education and Skill 126

Knowledge of Manuscript Variations 128 | Knowledge of the Canonical Status of Revelation 131 | Knowledge of Other Traditional Scripture Interpretations 131 | Andrew's Limitations 135 | The Three Levels of Scripture Interpretation 136 | The Literal Sense: *Historia* 137 | Typology 140 | The Moral Sense: *Tropologia* 141 | The Spiritual Sense: *Theoria* and *Anagoge* 143

10 Andrew's Technique and Sources 152

Purpose—*Skopos* 152 | Context—*Ta symphrazomena* 154 | Sequence—*Akolouthia* 155 | Word Association 162 | Andrew's Use of Scripture 168 | Andrew's Use of Sources 169

11 Andrew's Dogmatic Theology 181

Doctrine 181 | View of Prophecy 187 | View of History 189 | Ecclesiology 194 | The Apostles 197 | Angelology 201 | Sin and Salvation 205 | Free Will 209

12 Afflictions and the Love of God 215

The Purpose of the Afflictions 215 | The Nature of the Afflictions 218 | The Extent of the Afflictions 221 | The Suffering of the Saints 223 | The Love of God: *Philanthropia* 226

13 Andrew's Eschatology 232

The End Is Not Near 232 | The Millennium 234 | Babylon and the Successive Kingdoms 238 | The Devil 244 | The Antichrist and the False Prophet 250 | The Mark of the Beast and the Name of the Antichrist 256

14 Death, Judgment, Punishment, and Reward 259

Death and the Soul 259 | Armageddon, Parousia, and Judgment 265 | Resurrection and the Renewal of Creation 267 | Oikoumenios and *Apokatastasis* 271 | Andrew on Eternal Punishment 278 | The Kingdom of Heaven 282

15 Andrew and the Greek Apocalypse Text 288

16 Andrew's Posterity and Contributions 298

Subsequent Commentaries 298 | Translations of the Commentary 300 | Artistic Depictions of the Apocalypse 303 | Preservation of Early Traditions 304 | Facilitating Acceptance of Revelation into the Canon 306

17 Conclusion 311

Selected Bibliography 319 | Scripture Index 333 | General Index 337

PREFACE

Revelation's shaky canonical status and association with heresy caused the East to lag behind the West by three hundred years before producing a commentary on Revelation. Not until the end of the sixth century did the first Greek commentary appear, authored by Oikoumenios, a Miaphysite philosopher. Serious crises in the empire contributed to popular sentiment that the end of the world might be near, renewing interest in apocalyptic writings. As the only Greek commentary on Revelation, Oikoumenios's interpretation would have found a ready readership. But due to his philosophical background and obvious lack of exegetical training, Oikoumenios's quirky commentary expressed theological, eschatological, and exegetical conclusions that were unacceptable in mainstream ecclesiastical circles.

Not long afterward, a second Greek commentary appeared to respond to Oikoumenios. This second commentary was composed by Andrew, Archbishop of Caesarea, Cappadocia, a well-known and respected exegete during his time. Andrew's superior skill and exegetical training produced a commentary that quickly eclipsed the work of Oikoumenios to become predominant and the standard patristic commentary for the East, including the Greek, Slavic, Armenian, and Georgian Churches.

Andrew demonstrated that he stood in the stream of patristic tradition, even if it amounted to no more than a trickle. Although composed in 611 (a specific date proposed here for the first time), Andrew refers to many interpretations of Revelation found in passages by earlier Fathers as well as citing the opinions of anonymous teachers, pointing to a heretofore unexplored rich oral tradition of interpretation of the Apocalypse in the Greek East reaching back into the centuries preceding Andrew's time.

The English translation completed by the present author has been published as volume 123 in the Fathers of the Church series, published by the Catholic University of America Press (2011). Prior to my English translation and study of the commentary as part of my doctoral dissertation at Université Laval, Québec City (2008), no translation of Andrew's commentary had been produced in any modern language and no significant amount of scholarship had been devoted to this commentary.

The Apocalypse Commentary of Andrew of Caesarea is undoubtedly the most important ancient Greek patristic commentary on Revelation. The totality of the ancient Greek tradition for the interpretation of the Apocalypse was preserved in the commentary of Andrew of Caesarea, who succeeded in drawing together the various strands of ancient tradition. His thoughtful, balanced, and well-written commentary was quickly embraced and became extremely important. His accomplishment was widely recognized and is evidenced by the existence of eighty-three complete manuscripts of Andrew's commentary, along with countless abbreviated versions.

Andrew's commentary also influenced the textual transmission of the Apocalypse and created a unique text type. Moreover, the commentary is responsible for the eventual acceptance of Revelation into the canon of the Oriental and Eastern Orthodox Churches as well as influencing Eastern Christian eschatology. Translations of the commentary in a modified or condensed form were produced in the eleventh, twelfth, and thirteenth centuries in the Georgian, Armenian, and Old Slavonic languages respectively, where the commentary contributed toward the acceptance of Revelation into the New Testament canon in those churches.

ABBREVIATIONS

ANF	*Ante-Nicene Fathers*
Chap.	Chapter designation according to Andrew's original divisions
Comm.	Andrew's Commentary, with page numbers from FOTC 123
Dial.	Justin Martyr, *Dialogue with Trypho*
E.H.	Eusebius of Caesarea, *Ecclesiastical History*
Ep.	Epistle
FOTC	Fathers of the Church series
FOTC 112	*Oecumenius: Commentary on the Apocalypse*, trans. John Suggit
Heres.	Irenaeus, *Against Heresies*
Hom.	Homily
LF	Library of the Fathers
LCL	Loeb Classical Library
n	footnote
NPNF[1]	*Nicene and Post-Nicene Fathers*, Series 1
NPNF[2]	*Nicene and Post-Nicene Fathers*, Series 2
Oik.	Oikoumenios, *Commentary on the Apocalypse*
PG	*Patrologiae cursus completus: Series graeca*, edited by J.-P. Migne.

INTRODUCTION

No patristic composition has exerted more influence over the canonical acceptance and continuous interpretation of any biblical book as Andrew of Caesarea's commentary has of the Apocalypse of John for the Orthodox Church. Andrew's commentary stands alone as the most important ancient commentary on the Book of Revelation produced by the Greek East. It became the standard patristic commentary in the Eastern Christian tradition, significantly influenced most subsequent Eastern commentaries, and decisively influenced the reception of the Book of Revelation into the canon of the Orthodox Church.

Long after the biblical canon was fixed in the West, the Christian East wavered in its attitude toward the Apocalypse. Certain councils, bishops, and patriarchs might accept it, but in the main it remained rejected, viewed skeptically, even suspiciously. This seemingly odd treatment of one of the most extraordinary books in the Bible has roots in doubts regarding the apostolic authorship of Revelation. Raised during the fourth and fifth centuries by influential Eastern bishops, these doubts resulted in the book's exclusion from the Orthodox lectionary and from the canon of scripture in the view of most Orthodox Christians for many centuries.

While the invention of the printing press may have contributed in some degree toward the acceptance of the Apocalypse in the biblical canon, because of its appearance within printed Greek New Testaments, this uncertain canonical status continued well into the modern era. During the course of the intervening centuries, Revelation had slowly gained acceptance in the Orthodox world. Muslim conquests and occupation of many traditionally Orthodox lands had renewed eastern interest in Revelation. The fall of Constantinople in 1453 and the experience of daily life under sometimes-hostile Islamic rulers, including persecution and martyrdom, advanced Eastern Christian interest in John's apocalyptic vision. The eventual reception of Revelation into the Orthodox New Testament canon occurred in large measure due to the commentary penned by Andrew, a respected ancient bishop and thoughtful orthodox interpreter of the Scriptures, who occupied the celebrated see of Caesarea, Cappadocia.

Composed against a backdrop of epic calamities, disease and famine, barbarian invasions, and wholesale destruction of cities, Andrew's commentary provided the first patristic Eastern Christian insight to the most challenging and problematic book of the Bible. Even though his commentary was not the first in the Greek language (that honor must go to a philosophically trained writer, Oikoumenios), it can truly be said that Andrew wrote the first Greek patristic commentary since he alone stood squarely in the stream of Eastern Church tradition. He summarized virtually all of the Eastern ecclesiastical tradition of Apocalypse interpretation and expanded upon the interpretation in a manner which encapsulated a classic Eastern Christian approach to Revelation in every aspect: exegesis, theology, spirituality, patrology, liturgy, sacraments, and ecclesiology. The commentary so resonated with the faithful that it outshone the earlier commentary by Oikoumenios and found an enduring home within the Eastern Church tradition, not only for itself but for the Book of Revelation.

Commentary on the Apocalypse exists in eighty-three complete Greek manuscripts, thirteen abbreviated versions and fifteen manuscripts with scholia from Andrew. It was published in Migne's Patrologia graeca, vol. 106 (Paris 1863), 215–457, however, the first critical edition of the *Apocalypse Commentary of Andrew of Caesarea* was published in 1955 by Josef Schmid.[1] Before the commentary ever appeared in print

---

1. Josef Schmid, *Der Apokalypse-Kommentar des Andreas von Kaisareia*, vol. 1 of *Studien zur Geschichte des griechischen Apokalypse-Textes*, 3 parts (München: Karl Zink Verlag, 1955–56).

in the Greek original text, Theodore Peltanus, a Jesuit scholar and professor at the University of Ingolstadt in the mid-sixteenth century, published his own free Latin translation in Ingolstadt in 1584 which is reprinted in the same Patrologia Graeca volume. Several additional Latin editions were also subsequently printed.[2]

I would like to thank Dr. Paul-Hubert Poirier for his encouragement and guidance during the research and writing of this book. I extend many thanks to CUA Press for deciding to publish a book on a subject not very well known but which deserves more attention. Special thanks go to my brother, George Scarvelis, who spent many hours reading the manuscript and suggesting stylistic improvements. I also thank Dr. John Fendrick of the University of San Diego, for his time, help, and especially his good humor, as we worked through some challenging German passages. Finally, I especially acknowledge the support and understanding of my husband, Costas, and our son, Christopher.

The three sections are (1) *Der Apokalypse-Kommentar des Andreas von Kaisareia, Text* (1955), the Greek critical text, hereinafter *Text* (2) *Die alten Stämme* (1955), Schmid's study of the textual tradition of the Apocalypse itself and the relationship of Andrew's commentary to the textual history of the Apocalypse, hereinafter *Alten Stämme*, and (3) *Historische Abteilung Ergänzungsband, Einleitung,* (1956) Schmid's study of the manuscript tradition and reception of the commentary itself, hereinafter *Einleitung*.

2. Josef Schmid, *Einleitung*, 122. The commentary was most likely rendered into Latin long before Peltanus's translation, because Nerses of Lampron, the famous Armenian Archbishop who is responsible for the twelfth century translation of the commentary, described how he had first discovered the commentary in a Latin monastery in the city of Antioch. However, the commentary was "in the Lombard language," and he could not to find anyone to translate it into Armenian. He later found it in Greek. Josef Schmid, *Einleitung*, 107–8. See also chap. 16.

GUIDING TO A BLESSED END

1

THE TRAJECTORY OF EARLY APOCALYPSE COMMENTARIES

Every important book of the Bible became the focus of a commentary by one or more of the early Fathers of the Church. Yet not a single major patristic figure, East or West, wrote a commentary on the Book of Revelation. To the modern reader this absence of commentary on such a significant and portentous book is startling. The Apocalypse of John, with all its prophetic significance seems to us an immediate candidate for commentary. But this was not the case for the early Fathers. Without a doubt, the lack of commentaries can be attributed to the unusual subject matter and the great difficulty in interpreting such a challenging text.

Numerous early Christian writers did cite and comment on various passages of Revelation, including Justin Martyr (d. c. 165), Melito of Sardis (d. c. 190), Theophilos of Antioch (d. c. 183), Cyprian of Carthage (d. 258), Methodios of Olympus (d. 311), Clement of Alexandria (d. c. 210), Tertullian (d. c. 220), Irenaeus (d. c. 202), Origen (d. 253), and Hippolytus (d. 236). These patristic authors of the second and third centuries appealed to the Apocalypse to respond to heresy, to support theological positions, to encourage the faithful during persecution, and to correct misinterpretations and misuse of the book.

2 TRAJECTORY OF EARLY COMMENTARIES

However, by the time actual commentaries on the Apocalypse appeared in the West, the book was losing favor in the East. It had become associated with Montanism and millennialism in the second century. Then in the mid-third century efforts were launched to discredit it, first by Dionysios of Alexandria and again later by Eusebius of Caesarea in the fourth century. Thus, the earliest Apocalypse commentaries were composed in the Latin West, where acceptance of the book had never seriously wavered. For the East, the ambiguous and tenuous position of the Apocalypse in the canon of Scripture contributed to the absence of a Greek commentary. Indeed, the first Greek Apocalypse commentary did not appear until the end of the sixth century, approximately 300 years after the first Latin commentary.

The Earliest Latin Apocalypse Commentaries

Credit for composing the first commentary on the Apocalypse is usually given to Victorinus, Bishop of Pettau (modern city of Ptuj, Slovenia), the first biblical exegete in the Latin language. He died as a martyr, probably in 304 under Diocletian. Victorinus may have been a Greek by birth and later learned Latin.[1] He wrote several commentaries, but only his commentary on the Apocalypse remains.[2] Although he is described as having written a "commentary" on Revelation, in fact it is not a complete commentary but rather consists of explanations of selected key passages throughout the book. Still, Victorinus is credited with the first commentary because previous patristic use of the Apocalypse was limited to allusions, brief citations, or the explanation of a single passage in the context of a theological treatise.

Victorinus was the first to offer an exposition of the book as a

---

1. This is only speculation. Scholars have arrived at this conclusion based primarily on Jerome's observation that Victorinus's Greek was better than his Latin. Jerome, *Illustrious Men*, in *Theodoret, Jerome, Gennadius & Rufinus: Historical Writings*, ed. Philip Schaff and Henry Wace, NPNF[2] 3 (Grand Rapids, Mich.: Eerdmans, repr. 1989), 74.

2. Victorinus, *Commentary on the Apocalypse*, in *Victorin de Poetovio Sur l'Apocalypse*, trans. M. Dulaey, Sources chrétiennes 423 (Paris: Les Éditions du Cerf, 1997), 20.

whole. He attempted to base his interpretation on Papias, Irenaeus, Hippolytus, and especially Origen, upon whom he relied heavily for inspiration.[3] Although Victorinus provided allegorical interpretations of many passages of Revelation, unlike Origen he was a chiliast and promoted a literal interpretation of Christ's millennial reign and the New Jerusalem.

Victorinus is especially remembered as the first to use the theory of recapitulation to explain the sequence of events described in Revelation.[4] According to this theory, the Apocalypse does not proceed in a linear fashion but repeats the same events using different imagery. For example, the bowl visions[5] are the same events described in the trumpet visions, but with different descriptions.[6] The vision of the New Jerusalem[7] recapitulates the vision of the millennium.[8] Victorinus justified his theory by asserting that

although the same thing recurs ... still it is not said as if it occurred twice.... We must not regard the order of what is said, because frequently the Holy Spirit, when he has traversed even to the end of the last times, returns again to the same times, and fills up what He had before failed to say.[9]

The theory of recapitulation was later adopted by the Donatist exegete Tyconius in his *Book of Rules*.[10]

---

3. Jerome makes this observation. In *Ep.* 61.2, Jerome specifically says that Victorinus was an imitator of Origen. *The Principle Works of St. Jerome*, trans. W. H. Fremantle, edited by Philip Schaff and Henry Wace, NPNF² 6 (Grand Rapids, Mich.: Eerdmans, repr. 1989). See also Henry Barclay Swete, *The Apocalypse of St. John* (London: MacMillan, 1906), cxcvii.

4. Kenneth B. Steinhauser, *The Apocalypse Commentary of Tyconius: A History of Its Reception and Influence* (Frankfurt am Main: Peter Lang, 1986), 30. Although Victorinus used the technique, he did not employ the terminology.

5. Rev. 16.

6. Rev. 8 and 9. Victorinus, *Comm. on the Apoc.* 8.2, trans. M. Dulaey, Sources chrétiennes 423 (Paris: Les Éditions du Cerf, 1997): 87. ANF 7:352 (ANF cites it as Rev. 7:2).

7. Rev. 21:2.

8. Rev. 20:4. Victorinus, *Comm. on the Apoc.* 21.2, Sources chrétiennes 423:117.

9. Victorinus, *Comm. on the Apoc.* 8.2, Sources chrétiennes 423:87. ANF 7:352 (ANF cites it as Rev. 7:2).

10. *Tyconius, Le Livre de Règles*, trans. Jean-Marc Vercruysse, Sources chrétiennes 488 (Paris: Les Éditions du Cerf, 2004). See also *Liber Regularum*, in *Tyconius: the Book of Rules*,

4   TRAJECTORY OF EARLY COMMENTARIES

Writing in the fourth century, Jerome described Victorinus's life in *Illustrious Men*.[11] So impressed was he with Victorinus's work that he edited and republished Victorinus's interpretation. Jerome corrected Victorinus's Latin, introduced an improved Latin biblical text for quotations, removed whatever he did not agree with (especially the chiliastic portions), rearranged sections, and finally added his own comments and selections from Tyconius.[12] This improved Victorinus commentary is often referred to as the "Victorinus-Jerome commentary" (sometimes as "Jerome-Victorinus"), and proved to be extremely popular in the West.

Eventually, Victorinus-Jerome was to exert the greatest influence on subsequent Latin commentators and Jerome's reworking of Victorinus proved so successful that manuscripts of Victorinus's original work—free of Jerome's editing—essentially disappeared.[13] His work was only known through the lens of Jerome's recension. Indeed, an unedited Victorinus manuscript was not discovered until the modern era and then only published in 1916.[14]

Jerome's revision of the Victorinus commentary reflected the pre-

---

trans. William S. Babcock (Atlanta: Scholars Press, 1989). For a succinct list of the rules, see Manlio Simonetti, *Biblical Interpretation in the Early Church*, trans. John A. Hughes (Edinburgh: T. & T. Clark, 1994), 95–96. Recapitulation is the sixth rule.

11. Jerome, *Illustrious Men*, 74.

12. Kenneth B. Steinhauser, *Apocalypse Commentary of Tyconius*, 32.

13. Including Caesarius of Arles (early sixth century), Primasius (early sixth century), Cassiodorus (mid-sixth century), Ambrosius Autpertus (second half of the eighth century), Beatus of Liébana (second half of the eighth century), and the Venerable Bede (late seventh to early eighth centuries).

14. Published by Johannes Haußleiter, Corpus scriptorum ecclesiasticorum latinorum 49 (reprint, New York: Johnson Reprint Corporation, 1965). See also Johannes Haußleiter, "Der chiliastische Schlussabschnitt im echten apocalypsekommentar des Bischofs Victorinus von Pettau," *Theologisches Litteraturblatt* 26 (1895): 193–99. The original commentary is preserved in the Codex Ottobonianus latinus 3288A. However, E. Ann Matter believes that the Victorinus text is still essentially lost since Haußleiter establishes the Victorinus text from fifteenth and sixteenth century manuscripts "which are in any case not overwhelmingly different. The three recensions of Jerome's version show that this text was as unstable as it was popular and that the original is essentially lost." E. Ann Matter, "The Apocalypse in Early Medieval Exegesis," in *The Apocalypse in the Middle Ages*, ed. Richard Emmerson and Bernard McGinn (Ithaca: Cornell University Press, 1992), 38, n. 1.

vailing fourth century attitude repudiating millennialism. In the West, the Apocalypse was never threatened with complete rejection from the canon. Western writers simply replaced unacceptable chiliastic explanations with spiritual interpretations. The story was different in the East. Among Eastern Christians who opposed chiliasm a few accepted a spiritual interpretation of Revelation, however most simply rejected the book altogether.

The fourth century North African Donatist writer Tyconius, who flourished around 390, wrote a commentary on the Apocalypse that followed a spiritual rather than literal interpretation.[15] Augustine of Hippo, who had once embraced a chiliastic interpretation of Revelation 20,[16] was highly influenced by Tyconius and eventually rejected both chronological and sensual interpretations of the passage.[17] Tyconius's commentary on the Apocalypse was important as "the first attempt in the Western Church to apply a system of exegetical rules to the interpretation of a single biblical book."[18] Despite his Donatism, the Tyconius commentary had a profound and sustained influence on Revelation commentaries in the West. Together with the commentary of Victorinus-Jerome, it formed the foundation for nearly all Latin commentaries well into the second millennium. In fact, Tyconius was so heavily quoted by subsequent Latin writers that even though his original commentary no longer survives, remarkably, his entire work can be reconstructed.[19]

---

15. *Tyconius, Le Livre de Règles*, trans. Jean-Marc Vercruysse, Sources chrétiennes 488, 26–27. Ned Bernard Stonehouse, *The Apocalypse in the Ancient Church* (Goes, Holland: Oosterbaan and Le Cointre, 1929), 47.

16. See Augustine, *City of God*, 20.7.

17. Ned Bernard Stonehouse, *Apocalypse in the Ancient Church*, 148. Augustine listed his canon of Scriptures in *De doctrina christiana* and it corresponds to our present canon. The issue of the canon was raised at a synod in Hippo in 393 and Augustine's canon was adopted. This was later confirmed by synods at Carthage in 397 and 419. The influence of Augustine at these councils cannot be overstated.

18. Kenneth B. Steinhauser, *Apocalypse Commentary of Tyconius*, 2.

19. By extensive analysis and comparison of subsequent Latin commentators, Steinhauser was able to reconstruct Tyconius's commentary. A few extant fragments of Tyconius's work have been published in *The Turin Fragments of Tyconius' Commentary on Revelation*, ed. Francesco Lo Bue (Cambridge, England: University Press, 1963).

Other Early Latin Commentaries

In the early sixth century, Caesarius, Bishop of Arles, wrote a commentary on the Apocalypse which for centuries was erroneously attributed to Augustine.[20] Caesarius's two main sources were the commentaries of Victorinus and Tyconius, and he depended on both heavily.[21] During the mid-sixth century, three Latin writers offered commentaries on the Apocalypse: Primasius, Apringius, and Cassiodorus. Primasius of Hadrumentum, a bishop in North Africa from 527 to 565, wrote a very influential commentary which followed Jerome, Victorinus, and Tyconius in many respects, but also made a few original contributions.[22] Despite its comprehensive quality, it offered little that was new since it consisted almost entirely (and often word for word), of passages from Tyconius and Augustine.[23] Apringius, the Bishop of Béja, Portugal, also wrote a commentary during the mid-sixth century.[24] The sole surviving manuscript of his work covers only the first five chapters and the last three chapters of Revelation.[25] Cassiodorus was a politician and statesman in Ravenna who left politics to study theology. While he probably never became an actual monk, he wrote several commentaries and brief notes *(Complexiones)* on the Acts, Epistles, and the Apocalypse. His work also shows the influence of Victorinus and Augustine and refers the reader specifically to Tyconius.[26]

---

20. He became bishop in 502 and ruled his diocese for 40 years. Kenneth B. Steinhauser, *Apocalypse Commentary of Tyconius*, 45.

21. Kenneth B. Steinhauser, *Apocalypse Commentary of Tyconius*, 49–51.

22. E. Ann Matter, "Apocalypse in Early Medieval Exegesis," 44. Arthur Wainwright, *Mysterious Apocalypse* (Nashville: Abingdon Press, 1993), 39.

23. Kenneth B. Steinhauser, *Apocalypse Commentary of Tyconius*, 69. Henry Barclay Swete, *Apocalypse of St. John*, cxcviii.

24. Kenneth B. Steinhauser, *Apocalypse Commentary of Tyconius*, 153. Its influence seems to have been limited to the Iberian peninsula, since the only author to refer to Apringius is the Spanish writer, Beatus of Liébana. E. Ann Matter, "Apocalypse in Early Medieval Exegesis," 44.

25. E. Ann Matter, "Apocalypse in Early Medieval Exegesis," 43. Arthur Wainwright, *Mysterious Apocalypse*, 39.

26. Kenneth B. Steinhauser, *Apocalypse Commentary of Tyconius*, 89.

Greek Commentaries Emerge

Oikoumenios ⸺ Five centuries passed from the time that John composed the Apocalypse until a commentary appeared in the Greek language. Long after the controversies of chiliasm and Montanism had waned, the Book of Revelation lingered under a cloud of suspicion in the East, rarely quoted, due to doubts reinforced by its close association with disfavored forms of Christianity and by suspicions fueled by Eusebius of Caesarea.[27] And so it is that the distinction of writing the first Greek commentary on the Apocalypse goes to a man whose precise identity eludes us: Oikoumenios.[28] Virtually nothing is known about the man, which only fuels conjecture and speculation. Oikoumenios has been frequently misidentified as the bishop of Trikki in Thessaly,[29] but this is certainly incorrect, the result of an erroneous attribution of the Apocalypse commentary to another Oikoumenios, a tenth century exegete and bishop of Trikki. From internal evidence in the commentary of Oikoumenios itself—and from Andrew's familiarity with the text—we know with certainty that the commentary is dated near the end of the sixth century and could not have therefore been composed by the tenth century Oikoumenios. Clues to Oikoumenios's possible identity, and the problems with his exegesis and theology, are discussed below. These problems and other concerns prompted the composition of Andrew's commentary.

Andrew of Caesarea ⸺ Andrew of Caesarea composed his commentary, Ἑρμηνεία εἰς τὴν Ἀποκάλυψιν, shortly after Oikoumenios's com-

---

27. Manlio Simonetti, *Biblical Interpretation*, 111.
28. The commentary, Ἑρμηνεία τῆς Ἀποκαλύψεως Οἰκουμενίου was first published by H.C. Hoskier, *The Complete Commentary of Oecumenius*, University of Michigan Humanistic Studies 22 (Ann Arbor: University of Michigan Press, 1928). A critical edition was published, *Oecumenii Commentarius in Apocalypsin*, Traditio Exegetica Graeca 8, ed. Marc De Groote (Louvain: Peeters, 1999), and it was recently translated into English in *Oecumenius: Commentary on the Apocalypse*, trans. John Suggit, FOTC 112 (Washington, D.C.: The Catholic University of America Press, 2006), hereinafter FOTC 112.
29. Most recently by Charles Kannengiesser, *Handbook of Patristic Exegesis*, 2 vols. (Brill: Leiden, 2004), 2: 937–38.

mentary appeared. It is clear that Andrew wrote largely in response to Oikoumenios, who in any case preceded Andrew by only a few years.[30] This suddenness is striking: after a span of five centuries without an Eastern Christian commentary on Revelation, the Eastern Church had two in short order. It cannot be said that Andrew stepped into a Greek Apocalypse commentary tradition in the same manner as his near-contemporaneous sixth century Latin Apocalypse commentators. His only predecessor was Oikoumenios, essentially an historical contemporary. Nonetheless, the Oikoumenios commentary frames and forms the context for Andrew's interpretative effort, especially since Andrew unquestionably had the Oikoumenios commentary before him as he composed his own. It is our contention that the deficiencies in the Oikoumenios commentary—perceived or actual—prompted Andrew's commentary and influenced both its content and emphases.

Both Oikoumenios and Andrew used the opinions of earlier Greek authorities to support their views. A huge gap existed, however, between the time period of Andrew and Oikoumenios, in the late sixth or early seventh centuries, and the time period of most of the Greek Fathers who had made comments about the Apocalypse in the second and third centuries, to whom both Andrew and Oikoumenios looked back for guidance. References to Revelation among the fourth, fifth, and sixth century Greek Fathers were even more meager and far less helpful.

There are numerous reasons for this. During the centuries preceding the composition of these commentaries, little effort had been expended toward understanding the Apocalypse in the East. At the time Oikoumenios and Andrew composed their commentaries, the resources available to a Greek expositor were extremely limited. Most passages in the Apocalypse had not been discussed by those earlier authorities, and therefore, a great deal of groundbreaking work remained for both men to do. Nonetheless, both of them felt the need

---

30. Andrew's motive for writing his commentary will be thoroughly discussed below in chapter 7.

to demonstrate that they stood within the stream of tradition, even if that stream amounted to a mere trickle. Oikoumenios relied greatly on his imagination to explain difficult passages and had a tendency to cite patristic authorities primarily for theological points rather than exegetical ones. Andrew of Caesarea rejected this approach, and composed instead a commentary based on sound exegetical technique and ecclesiastical traditions. It was Andrew's commentary which was responsible for preserving basically the entire Greek interpretive tradition for the Apocalypse.

The Duality of the Apocalypse Interpretive Tradition

The Book of Revelation holds a unique position in the New Testament manuscript tradition. It is the only New Testament book with a bifurcated history of transmission: ecclesiastical and nonecclesiastical. Revelation did not simply circulate as a church text through ecclesiastical avenues, but was also copied and transmitted alongside profane literature through secular channels because it was mostly rejected from the Eastern canon of Scripture and never utilized in the Orthodox lectionary.[31] This dual stream of tradition also mirrors the history of early Apocalypse commentaries: Greek and Latin. These two interpretive traditions developed and coexisted independently of one another. Hippolytus, who lived in the third century, was the last Western Father to write in Greek.[32] By the third century, Latin had entirely supplanted Greek as the common spoken language in the West.[33] Numerous Latin translations of the Bible appeared and many ecclesiastical works began to be composed in Latin. Writers such as Tertullian,

---

31. The contribution of the Andreas Commentary to the text of the Apocalypse itself and the unique characteristics of the Apocalypse text in the manuscript tradition are discussed in chapter 15.

32. F. L. Cross, ed. "Hippolytus," in *The Oxford Dictionary of the Christian Church*, 3rd ed., rev. (Oxford: Oxford University Press, 2005).

33. Johannes Quasten, *Patrology*, 4th ed., 4 vols. (Westminster, Md.: Christian Classics, 1988), IV: 4–5.

Ambrose, Hilary, Jerome, and Augustine rapidly created an impressive Latin patristic tradition. The Latin Fathers of the third and fourth centuries had read and depended upon the Greek tradition.[34] Some Greek Fathers had been translated, but educated men of the West were expected to know Greek in order to access the writings of the outstanding Greek Fathers as well as philosophical and other classical Hellenic secular works of earlier eras.

But the reverse was not true: Greek patristic writers indicate no knowledge of Latin nor apparently did they feel a need to learn it. Once eminent Latin writers produced their own works, it was natural that Western Christians who lived after the time of the great Latin Fathers would turn to them and depend upon them, since their works required no translation and no knowledge of Greek. Latin writers became the theological standard for the West and were unparalleled in their influence, especially Augustine.

Independence of the Eastern Apocalypse Interpretive Tradition

With a new wealth of Latin material, Western Christians of the fifth century were no longer dependent on Greek authors. The absence of necessity to learn Greek, coupled with the fall of Rome and deteriorating conditions, led to a dramatic decline in Greek literacy in the West. Meanwhile, in the East widespread knowledge of Latin, even among the most highly educated, had never existed[35] and as a consequence

---

34. "The principal Western theologians, Hilary, Ambrose, and Jerome, formed part of a spiritual elite, which moved at ease in Greek culture.... This was, however, a one-way street. There was not to be found in the East the same curiosity with regard to the West, even the Christian West. The imperial court established at Constantinople, instead of introducing Latin, was itself Hellenized. Only official documents and works of hagiography came to be translated into Greek. Augustine himself was little known in the East." Johannes Quasten, *Patrology*, IV: 5.

35. George Every explains that even in Constantinople, knowledge of Latin was not common. Although "some attention was paid to Latin, this was apparently limited to what was required for official and legal business. It was not difficult to find a translator for a Latin letter or a controversial treatise, but few if any citizens of Constantinople had any wide knowledge of Latin theological or secular literature before the thirteenth century, when the impact

the two branches of the Church eventually no longer spoke each other's language.³⁶ While of little significance perhaps to daily life or to the administrative functions of church or government, this growing language gulf resulted in a narrowing of sources. Western commentators read Latin sources and Eastern commentators read Greek sources. While they may have occasionally arrived at the same interpretation or explanation for a particular passage in Revelation or other biblical books, it cannot be presumed that this is the result of direct influence. In many instances interpretive commonalities reflect the earliest Christian traditions, shared by both East and West. Otherwise, it is more likely that similar ideas were arrived at independently, due to a commonly rooted ecclesiastical perspective, a common Bible corpus, and common exegetical techniques. This must be the conclusion absent direct evidence to the contrary.

Arthur Wainwright makes a rather cynical comment that completely ignores the reality of the state of communication between East and West during these centuries. He observes that the thousand-year reign of Christ is interpreted as the period between the two advents of Christ by both Augustine and Tyconius in the West and by Andrew and Arethas in the East.³⁷ Wainwright lauds the long string of Latin

---

of the Latin conquest made it absolutely necessary to understand the enemy. Only in the fourteenth century was S. Augustine translated into Greek." George Every, *Misunderstandings Between East and West* (Richmond, Va.: John Knox Pres, 1966), 35. See Warren Treadgold, who also concludes that after Justinian, who reigned in the mid-sixth century, knowledge of Latin was rare in the East. *A History of Byzantine State and Society* (Stanford: Stanford University Press, 1997), 266.

36. A future pope, Gregory I, when serving in Constantinople as the representative for Pope Pelagius at the end of the sixth century, complained about the difficulty of finding a good Latin interpreter. Andreas Stratos, *Byzantium in the Seventh Century*, trans. Marc Ogilvie-Grant, 5 vols. (Amsterdam: Hakkert, 1968), 1: 345. On the decline of Latin knowledge after the time of Justinian, see Andreas Stratos, *Byzantium*, 1: 344–49.

37. Arethas was the Archbishop of Caesarea Cappadocia in the ninth century and also wrote a commentary on the Apocalypse, Συλλογὴ ἐξηγήσεως ἐκ διαφόρων ἁγίων ἀνδρῶν, or according to another manuscript Ἐκ τῶν Ἀνδρέα ... πεπονημένων σύνοψις σχολική, παρατεθεῖσα ὑπὸ Ἀρέθα. Henry Barclay Swete, *Apocalypse of St. John*, cxcix. Arethas is printed in J.-P. Migne, ed., PG 106: 487–806. See also Josef Schmid, *Untersuchungen zur Geschichte des griechischen Apokalypsetextes 1. Der Apokalypse-text des Arethas von Kaisareia und einiger anderer*

commentators who "freely attribute their ideas to Augustine" and even "somewhat grudgingly recognize Tyconius's contributions," even though he was a Donatist.[38] Wainwright insinuates that since the two Greek writers chronologically followed Augustine and Tyconius, the Greeks must have taken the idea from the Latins but grudgingly refused to give credit to the Latins because of "parochialism" and a "reluctance to recognize any dependence on Western Christianity."[39]

Wainwright fails to establish any actual connection between a single Western patristic Apocalypse commentary and an Eastern one which would indicate a direct dependence or even indirect influence. Wainwright also cannot support his claims that Andrew refused to credit his sources; on the contrary, Andrew freely acknowledged his sources, except for Oikoumenios, whom he clearly did not recognize as an authority. Wainwright furthermore fails to cite even a single example of any Greek Father who shows knowledge of Latin or cites a Latin source. No cross-influence between East and West can be found in Apocalypse interpretation: Greek interpreters after the third century show no effect upon the Latins and Latin Apocalypse interpretation had no effect upon the Greeks. The only writers who influenced both Greek and Latin commentators were the earliest Greek writers, such as Irenaeus and Hippolytus, none of whom produced complete commentaries but only commented on a few key passages. Their influence on both the Eastern and Western sides of the Church is obvious.

---

jüngerer Gruppen. Texte und Forschungen zur byzantinisch-neugriechischen Philologie 27 (Athens: Verlag der Byzantinisch-neugriechischen Jahrbücher, 1936). The Arethas commentary is highly dependent on Andrew.

38. Arthur Wainwright, *Mysterious Apocalypse*, 44.

39. Arthur Wainwright, *Mysterious Apocalypse*, 44. Andrew repeatedly demonstrated that he was not averse to crediting his sources and undoubtedly would have used Augustine had Augustine been available in Greek. But in fact, Augustine was not translated into Greek until the fourteenth century, according to George Every (*Misunderstandings*, 35). By Andrew's time, few people in the Eastern parts of the empire had knowledge of Latin, with the exception of those holding imperial offices. Wainwright mistakenly presumes that post-Schism attitudes prevailed in seventh-century relations between the Christian East and West and that hostilities and biases between the two branches of Christendom existed at that time, when in fact such negative feelings were centuries away from developing.

The first complete commentaries on the Apocalypse in the West appeared after the rise of Latin ecclesiastical literature. This inaugurated the Latin branch of Apocalypse exegesis, the full flower and fruit of which would never find its way to the East. As we have seen, Tyconius and Victorinus, the first to offer systematic expositions on the Apocalypse, became the foundation and primary resource for subsequent Latin commentators. In the East, Oikoumenios was entirely eclipsed by Andrew, his commentary having surprisingly little impact or lasting influence. It is therefore Andrew of Caesarea who truly begins and shapes the Eastern ecclesiastical tradition of Apocalypse interpretation.

2

THE APOCALYPSE IN THE ANCIENT EAST

From Acceptance to Rejection

Among all the New Testament books, only Revelation claims divine inspiration.[1] Self-described as prophecy in its opening and closing,[2] the book blesses those who read it,[3] curses those who alter it,[4] and instructs that it be read aloud in the Church.[5] No other New Testament book makes such bold declarations, expressing the clear intent and expectation that it be regarded as Scripture. And yet, for well over a

---

1. Revelation appears to be the exception to the general rule that books of the New Testament were not immediately recognized as inspired and authoritative. "Only the book of Revelation claims for itself such a lofty position that would come close to the notion of inspiration and Scripture.... Even the Gospels do not in themselves claim final authority." Lee McDonald, *The Formation of the Christian Biblical Canon* (Peabody, Mass.: Hendrickson, 1995), 9.

2. Rev. 1:3, 22:6, 10, 19.

3. Rev. 1:3.

4. Rev. 22:18. "The writer, John, is evidently a prophet, and if his prophetic vocation be acknowledged, it is a natural conclusion that his book is inspired prophecy and therefore Scripture. The striking thing is that it is so intended, and by virtue of this fact claims for itself a place of permanent authority, side by side with the Jewish Scriptures. In this new type of Christian literature we see the welding of the new prophetic sense of inward spiritual endowment with the old Jewish idea of inspired books. It thus foreshadows a Christian Scripture. Alone among the books of the New Testament the Revelation claims for its whole contents the authority of divine inspiration." Edgar J. Goodspeed, *The Formation of the New Testament* (Chicago: University of Chicago Press, 1926), 14–15.

5. Rev. 1:3.

thousand years, even those claims and assertions did not suffice to secure a place for the Apocalypse in the canon of the Eastern Church.

The process by which the Apocalypse was ultimately accepted into the canon of Eastern Christianity is also unique among all New Testament books. In general, three broad patterns can be identified for books contending for a place in the New Testament canon: overwhelmingly accepted, overwhelmingly rejected, or initially disputed then gradually accepted. Generally speaking, well-established books, traditionally regarded by the Church as ancient, apostolic, and orthodox, faced no challenge and easily found a place in the New Testament canon. A long-held consensus had recognized a core canon of four gospels, Acts of the Apostles, thirteen epistles of Paul (the traditional Pauline corpus minus Hebrews), 1 John and 1 Peter.[6] At the other extreme, most apocryphal works were universally rejected and were never considered for inclusion in the canon. Occupying a position between these two extremes were books initially disputed but which eventually gained acceptance during the course of the fourth century, namely Hebrews, James, 2 and 3 John, Jude, and 2 Peter.

Revelation did not fit any of those patterns. It presents a fourth pattern, curious and entirely unique, of acceptance followed by rejection. As in the case of the gospels and the Pauline epistles, Revelation was initially *un*disputed and widely accepted as apostolic early in the second century. It remained recognized as Scripture almost universally throughout the third century. But during the fourth century, the Apocalypse of John suffered a dramatic fall from grace from overwhelming acceptance to widespread rejection. What was undisputed became disputed and eventually fell out of favor. The story is a surprising one and illustrates the different circumstances of Western and Eastern Christianity in settling the New Testament canon.

The well-worn and simplistic conclusion that the New Testament canon was conclusively established in the fourth century is not defensible, certainly with regard to the Apocalypse in the Eastern Church.

---

6. Although it was widely accepted in the East, Hebrews was mostly rejected in the West.

The traditional benchmark typically cited for a completely settled canon is the Paschal Encyclical of Athanasius in 367. But this is misleading. Athanasius's canon is noteworthy because it is the first canon that exactly reflects our present twenty-seven book collection. Yet Athanasius's list did not conclude discussion on the canon, not even for the Church of Alexandria, and indeed his canon was only one opinion among many. Far from settling the matter, the canon debate continued long after he had issued his encyclical.[7]

Earlier opportunities to establish the canon as we know it today were missed, often because of other pressing matters. The Council at Nicaea had not taken up the issue of the canon in 325, even though the canon was increasingly becoming a subject of discussion among Church leaders at the time. This is not surprising. The pressing concern of the day was Arianism and since the canon was neither a divisive issue nor a dogmatic question, participants at Nicaea turned their attention to the thornier issue of heresy. Assuming that one's canon fell within the parameters of recognized orthodox writings, individual locales and bishops formed their own opinion and exercised their own choice among disputed works. In the East the Christian communities apparently felt no immediate need for a defined canon. In the West, the canon was closed far earlier than in the East, certainly by the fifth century. Bruce Metzger believed that the Latin Church "had a stronger feeling than the Greek for the necessity of making a sharp delineation with regard to the canon" and that "it was less conscious than the Greek Church of the gradation of spiritual quality among the

---

7. The erroneous opinion that Revelation gained acceptance in the East during the fourth century either by the time of or because of Athanasius's paschal encyclical persists. See Eldon Jay Epp, "Issues in the Interrelation of New Testament Textual Criticism and Canon," in *The Canon Debate*, edited by Lee Martin McDonald and James Sanders (Peabody, Mass.: Hendrickson, 2002, 2nd ed., 2004), 485–515. Epp writes: "[T]he place of the Revelation to John in the canon of Eastern Christianity was not certain until the late fourth century, and even later in some places" (505), citing Harry Gamble "Canon: New Testament," *Anchor Bible Dictionary*, ed. Noel David Freedman, 6 vols. (New York: Doubleday, 1992), 1:853–56. See also Helmut Koester, *Introduction to the New Testament: History and Literature of Early Christianity*, 2nd ed., 2 vols. (New York: de Guyter, 1995–2000), 2:6–12.

books that it accepted."[8] It appears the weight of Augustine's opinions and the widespread acceptance of Jerome's Vulgate not only standardized the New Testament text but also the canon itself. In the Greek-speaking East, reproduction of established lectionaries and texts continued, uninterrupted and unchanged, preserving the status quo since Greek manuscripts were simply recopied with no effect on the canon.

Early Acceptance of the Apocalypse

Why, then, given the unusual nature of the book, did the Apocalypse of John meet with such widespread acceptance? Various factors have been cited by many scholars to explain the early appeal of the Apocalypse within the Church. These include the factor of prophecy,[9] Revelation's appeal in times of persecution,[10] its epistolary format,[11] and the fact that it contains actual "words of the Lord."[12] More recently, four primary factors have been proposed: apostolicity, orthodoxy, antiquity and use, and possibly also a book's adaptability and inspiration.[13] However, absent an apostolic provenance, even all of the other factors together would not have resulted in the extraordinary approval the Apocalypse enjoyed throughout the second century. It is evident that Revelation's universal acceptance within the early Church was

---

8. Bruce Metzger, *The Canon of the New Testament: Its Origin, Development and Significance* (Oxford: Clarendon Press, 1987), 229. Arthur Darby Nock agreed that the Greeks were more flexible in their attitudes toward the canon, whereas in the West there was "a tendency to define, not only *de facto*, but also *de iure*, what is permissible." "A Feature of Roman Religion," *Harvard Theological Review* 32, no. 1 (1939): 83–96, 95.

9. This was Adolph von Harnack's opinion. See *The Origin of the New Testament*, trans. J. R. Wilkinson (London: Williams and Norgate, 1925).

10. William Farmer expresses this opinion in his book coauthored with Denis Farkasfalvy, *The Formation of the New Testament Canon* (New York: Paulist Press, 1983).

11. Denis Farkasfalvy's opinion. William Farmer and Denis Farkasfalvy, *The Formation of the New Testament Canon*, 156–57.

12. John Elliotson Symes, *The Evolution of the New Testament* (London: John Murray, 1921), 331.

13. Lee Martin McDonald, "Identifying Scripture and Canon in the Early Church: The Criteria Question," in *The Canon Debate*, ed. Lee Martin McDonald and James Sanders (Peabody, Mass.: Hendrickson, 2002), 416–39.

based on the established tradition which attributed the book to the Apostle John.

Andrew of Caesarea's commentary indirectly provides the earliest evidence for the tradition of Revelation's apostolic authorship. In his preface, Andrew cites Papias as one patristic authority who confirmed the "trustworthiness" of the book, assuring its divinely inspired character.[14] A well-known ecclesiastical author in the ancient world, Papias was the bishop of Hierapolis, a city in Asia Minor near Laodicea and Colossae. Only a few fragments remain of his monumental and famous treatise, *Exposition of Dominical Oracles*, a five volume composition from the first quarter of the second century. Andrew's commentary preserved one extant fragment, however none of the remaining fragments contains any quotations from or allusions to Revelation.[15] Papias's objective in writing *Dominical Oracles* was to preserve oral apostolic traditions. Even though Papias's precise statements about the Apocalypse have not survived, Andrew's citation strongly signifies that Papias accepted Revelation as apostolic, especially since the other patristic authorities which Andrew cited as testifying to the "trustworthiness" of the book also referred to John the Apostle as the author.[16]

From the mid-second century, Justin Martyr, who had been catechized in Asia, offers the earliest direct reference to the Apocalypse in an existing work as well as the earliest extant reference to its authorship by the apostle John.[17] Justin was a millennialist, just as Papias and

---

14. Andrew, Prologue, *Commentary of Andrew of Caesarea*, 54. Andrew of Caesarea divided his commentary into a Prologue followed by 72 chapters, hereinafter abbreviated as Chap. Page numbers for the English translation of the commentary, cited hereinafter as *Comm*. refer to the translation published in FOTC 123, trans. Eugenia Scarvelis Constantinou (Washington, D.C.: The Catholic University of America Press, 2011).

15. Extant Papias fragments have been recently retranslated and republished in *The Apostolic Fathers*, trans. Bart Ehrman, ed. Jeffrey Henderson, 2 vols., LCL 24 and 25 (Cambridge, Mass.: Harvard University Press, 2003), 92–119.

16. Hence, Andrew serves indirectly as a witness to the acceptance of Revelation as apostolic in the early second century by an Asiatic Father. Andrew would have had first-hand knowledge of *Dominical Oracles* since he quotes from Papias at a later point in the commentary. Andrew, Chap. 34, *Comm*. 142–43.

17. Justin Martyr, *Dialogue with Trypho* (hereinafter *Dial*.), 81.

numerous Christians at the time, expecting Christ to return and reign over an earthly kingdom for one thousand years. His belief rested on the authority of the Apocalypse, bolstered by its apostolic pedigree. The John who prophesied the millennium, Justin wrote, was "one of the apostles of Christ."[18] Similarly, although somewhat later in the second century, the *Letter of the Churches of Lyon and Vienne*, which described the martyrdom of many Christians in Gaul during the reign of Marcus Aurelius in 178 CE, contains the earliest direct quote of the Apocalypse and the first reference to it as "Scripture" by introducing the quotation with the formula, "that the Scripture might be fulfilled."[19]

At the end of the second century, Irenaeus of Lyon stressed apostolic authorship as the basis for placing certain Christian writings nearly on par with the Jewish Scriptures. Irenaeus's alarm over the proliferation of apocryphal gospels which were falsely attributed to apostles, confirms the role of apostolic authorship as the primary criterion for the inclusion of a book into a new Christian Testament. Irenaeus had experienced various local Church traditions in different parts of the empire. He had spent his youth in Asia, then a period of time in Rome, and finally became the bishop of Lyon in Gaul. In his famous work *Against Heresies*, Irenaeus associated false scriptures with heresy. He consistently attributed the Apocalypse to the apostle John[20] and cited it alongside other eschatological scripture passages in such prophets as Isaiah and Daniel.[21]

Irenaeus insisted that the number which the Holy Spirit revealed as the name of the Antichrist in Revelation is 666, not 616. The presence of 616 in some manuscripts was not a scribal error but a variation found in some Latin manuscripts as the Latin equivalent of 666, which represented "Nero Caesar" according to popular number symbolism. The presence of this early change suggests that the Apocalypse

---

18. Justin Martyr, *Dial.* 81.
19. Eusebius of Caesarea, *Ecclesiastical History* (hereinafter *E.H.*) 5.1.58.
20. In *Against Heresies* (hereinafter *Heres.*) 5.35.2 and 5.26.1, Irenaeus quotes many passages from the Apocalypse, which he asserts was written by "John, the Lord's disciple."
21. Irenaeus, *Heres.* 5.34.2.

enjoyed popularity among Latin readers during the second century to the extent that the 666 was altered to 616 to preserve the meaning of the numeric symbol. But no such change ought to be made, Irenaeus asserted, and he warned that anyone who altered "Scripture" for his own purposes would be punished. "There shall be no light punishment inflicted upon him who either adds or subtracts anything from the Scriptures."[22]

Perhaps the most striking evidence of the universal acceptance of the Apocalypse in the early Church was Irenaeus's use of the Apocalypse of John to secure a place for the *Gospel* of John in the canon of Scripture. The Fourth Gospel was under attack by some Christians who questioned its reliability and its apostolic authorship. Irenaeus vigorously defended the gospel and explained that four gospels were always intended by God, just as there are four zones in the world and four corners of the earth.[23] Drawing upon the image of the four creatures by the throne of God in Revelation 4, Irenaeus was the first to associate each creature with one of the four gospels.[24] This compels a startling conclusion: that initially the Apocalypse enjoyed a wider reception than even the Fourth Gospel, since Irenaeus appealed to a passage in Revelation to support the inclusion of the Gospel of John in the canon.

Other late second century writers appear to have accepted the Apocalypse as apostolic and authoritative, including Melito of Sardis, who penned a work entitled Τὰ περὶ τοῦ διαβόλου καὶ τῆς Ἀποκαλύψεως Ἰωάννου.[25] Apollonius supported it in his anti-Montanist writings[26] and Theophilos of Antioch, the sixth bishop of Antioch and a contemporary of Irenaeus, had quoted "testimonies from the book of Revelation" to refute the heretic Hermogenes.[27] The work has since been lost. No

---

22. Irenaeus, *Heres.* 5.30.1, based on Rev. 22:19.
23. Irenaeus, *Heres.* 3.11.8   24. Rev. 4:7.
25. Eusebius, *E.H.* 4.26.1–2.
26. Eusebius, *E.H.* 5.18.12. Apollonius was a Greek ecclesiastical writer who flourished c. 200 CE and may have been from Ephesus. He was particularly known for his anti-Montanist writings.
27. See Eusebius, *E.H.* 4.24.

opposition to Revelation was raised in orthodox ecclesiastical circles during the second century, nor does any group appear to have rejected Revelation or doubted the tradition of apostolic authorship.

Two controversial movements at the end of the second century help shed some additional light on the position of Revelation in the Church at that time. First, objections to the Apocalypse had arisen among the followers of Marcion. This was not surprising since his camp objected to most of the books widely regarded as apostolic. Tertullian sharply criticized Marcion's rejection of accepted apostolic books and his drastic alterations of even those writings which Marcion accepted as apostolic. Tertullian's defense of the Apocalypse against Marcion's truncated canon expressed the traditional belief in Revelation's apostolic authorship: "We have also John's foster churches. For, although Marcion rejects his Apocalypse, the order of their bishops when traced back to the beginning rests on John as the author."[28] Tertullian defends the Apocalypse against Marcion on the basis of apostolic authorship.

Secondly, features of the Montanist movement also indicate that early Christians held the Apocalypse in high esteem. Montanism had divided the Church over the authenticity of the "New Prophecy." The Montanists appear to have been mostly orthodox in doctrine, although some practices were extreme, especially with regard to fasting and marriage.[29] Many of their eschatological prophetic messages relied on the Revelation of John, such as the promise of a New Jerusalem coming down to earth and a literal millennium. Some orthodox Christians were hesitant to accept the New Prophecy while others actively opposed the Montanists as false prophets due to their unusual style of ecstatic prophecy and their claims to be the final prophetic outpouring upon the Church. But even those Christians who doubted or rejected the Montanist claims outright did not reject all prophecy in an overreaction against Montanism. Apollonius opposed Montanism but did not disavow prophecy altogether since he emphasized the need to test

---

28. Tertullian, *Against Marcion* 4.5, translation in Ned Bernard Stonehouse, *Apocalypse in the Ancient Church* (Goes, Holland: Oosterbaan and Le Cointre, 1929), 12.

29. Eusebius, *E.H.* 5.18.2.

prophecy.[30] Likewise, Irenaeus also considered the Montanists false prophets but this did not lead to misgivings about prophecy in general. In fact Irenaeus acknowledged the role of prophecy in Christian congregations.[31]

The prophetic and eschatological character of the Apocalypse had undoubtedly inspired the Montanists. Their use of Revelation indicates that their message benefited from the stature of Revelation within the Church. Montanist appropriation of images from Revelation and their assertions that its prophecies were about to be fulfilled were persuasive to many, which again confirms that Christians already recognized the Apocalypse as established apostolic authority. Montanism eventually fizzled and died. It had associated the Apocalypse with controversy and schism, yet the Apocalypse remained universally accepted. With no real opposition in the second century, one would have expected an easy progression toward inclusion in the newly emergent Christian collection of Scripture. But in the third century Revelation faced its first serious opposition.

The Third Century: Opposition Appears

Montanism had ruptured the Church. Orthodox defenders of traditional Christianity expended great effort to oppose the movement and mend the schism. Some writers were content to present arguments against Montanist teachings, their severe practices, prophetic style and outlandish claims but others within the Church chose to attack the Johannine writings from which Montanism drew its inspiration and vigor. This approach was taken by a third century cleric named Gaius and later by a group who would be labeled as the "Alogoi."[32]

---

30. Eusebius, *E.H.* 5.18.2–11.
31. Eusebius, *E.H.* 5.7.6.
32. This group was labeled the "Alogoi" by Epiphanios in the fourth century due to their opposition to the Johannine writings because the term "Logos" was used in the prologue of the Fourth Gospel for the Son of God. Because "logos" also means "reason," the name "Alogoi" was also a sarcastic pun, meaning "irrational ones." *Panarion* 51.3.1.

Gaius and the Alogoi rejected all of the Johannine writings, which by now formed a recognized corpus within the emergent canon.[33] Gaius insisted that the books attributed to John could not possibly be apostolic, but must be the work of Cerinthus, a heretic, forger, and the notorious archenemy of the Beloved Disciple.[34] Similarly, in the previous century, Irenaeus had taken issue with anti-Montanists who were so opposed to the movement that they were prepared to sacrifice all of the Johannine writings to stop it.[35] It was within this context that Irenaeus had argued for the four-fold gospel corpus, using the imagery of the four creatures around the throne of God.

In spite of Irenaeus's efforts, many third century anti-Montanists continued to believe that discrediting the apostolic authorship of the entire Johannine corpus was the most convenient and expedient means to undermine Montanist claims. Gaius opposed Montanism by asserting that the Synoptic Gospels contradicted the Gospel of John and that the eschatological scenario in Revelation contradicted the Synoptic Gospels. He vigorously attacked the prophecies and descriptions in Revelation, such as a millennial kingdom of Christ on earth, and he quoted from Revelation to generally ridicule it as bizarre and preposterous, capitalizing on the distorted literal and grossly sensual interpretation of the millennium which had long enthralled so many early Christians[36] Fortunately, Gaius and other anti-Montanists were not very successful in turning the Church completely away from the writings of John.

But as time passed and the Church drifted farther away from the

---

33. With the exception of 2 and 3 John. Charles Hill exhaustively examined all of the historical sources to determine the status of the Johannine corpus in the second century. He concludes with "no hesitation" that "the Johannine works were indeed a 'corpus' throughout the second century ... [T]hese books existed as a definite conceptual corpus, for writers use them as if they belong together and emanated from a single, authoritative source." Charles E. Hill, *The Johannine Corpus in the Early Church* (New York: Oxford University Press, 2004), 461.

34. Eusebius, *E.H.* 3.28.1–6, 4.14.6. Irenaeus, *Heres.* 3.11.1.

35. Irenaeus, *Heres.* 3.11.9.

36. Eusebius, *E.H.* 3.28.2. Epiphanios also reports that Gaius's primary tactic was to make the Apocalypse appear ridiculous. *Panarion* 51.3.1–2, 51.3.5, 51.17.11–18.1, 51.4.5–10, 51.32.2 and 51.34.2.

historical *Sitz-im-Leben* of Revelation, the book's message and its imagery became increasingly foreign and incomprehensible. Most Christians had no understanding of the apocalyptic genre or that utopian expectations were actually rooted in the prophets of the Hebrew Bible and Jewish apocalyptic interpretation. The idea of a super-fertile, peaceful, and bountiful earthly kingdom as a reward for their suffering was appealing to Christians under persecution. With no alternative explanations for the fantastic descriptions in the book, literalism continued to dominate Apocalypse interpretation at the start of the third century, and these literal interpretations continued to draw fire from Revelation's anti-Montanist and antimillennialist opponents. Revelation, in short, had become an easy target.

But Revelation also had numerous defenders in the third century, among them Hippolytus, the Roman presbyter who wrote in Greek and composed many exegetical and theological works. Hippolytus was very familiar with the Apocalypse, regarded it as Scripture and considered the apostle John to be the author. He wrote a treatise entitled *On Christ and Antichrist* (c. 200), a *Commentary on Daniel* (c. 204), and a lost work, *On the Gospel of John and the Apocalypse*.[37] Hippolytus opposed Gaius and demonstrated that Cerinthus could not have been the author of the Johannine corpus, that the Synoptics neither contradict the Gospel of John nor do their end-time scenarios contradict the Apocalypse.[38] Hippolytus also offered a nonliteral and antichiliastic interpretation of Revelation.

Origen also made an enormous (though indirect) contribution to

37. Pierre Nautin, "Hippolytus," *Encyclopedia of the Early Church*, ed. Angelo Di Berardino, trans. Adrian Walford, 2 vols. (New York: Oxford University Press, 1992).

38. *Heads against Gaius* or *Chapters against Gaius*. Five fragments from this work have been preserved by Dionysios Bar Salibi's Syriac Apocalypse commentary. "Hippolytus of Rome says that a certain man by the name of Gaius appeared, who said that the Gospel was not of John nor the Apocalypse, but that they are of the heretic Cerinthus. And against this Gaius, the blessed Hippolytus protested and proved that the teaching of John in the gospel and in the Apocalypse is different from that of Cerinthus." Dionysios Bar Salibi *On the Apocalypse*, trans. I. Sedlacek, Corpus scriptorum christianorum orientalium, Scriptores Syri 101 (Rome: de Luigi, 1910), 4.

the interpretation of the Apocalypse and its eventual reception into the canon of Eastern Christianity. Origen was among the first Christians to compose a "canon" in the true sense of the word: a list of books recognized as Scripture. Origen had also traveled widely and was familiar with writings in use by various Christian congregations throughout the eastern Empire. Origen divided the books into two groups: books which were acknowledged by all (ὁμολογούμενα) and those which were disputed and not universally acknowledged as genuine (οὐ πάντες φασὶνκ γνησίους).[39] Origen's list of disputed books contained books which he personally accepted but others did not.

According to Origen, John wrote the gospel, the Apocalypse, an epistle, and possibly two other epistles, although he reports that not all agreed that those additional two epistles were genuine.[40] This statement indicates that the Apocalypse was still universally accepted as genuine, in spite of being associated with Montanism. Origen's great contribution was providing an alternative to the literal and chiliastic interpretation of Revelation so popular at the time. He allegorized objectionable passages, replacing the fleshy and materialistic explanations with a spiritual interpretation. Origen's approach provided a thoughtful and intelligent alternative to literalism, and his spiritual vision recast Revelation in such a way that it could eventually be rescued for the Eastern canon.

Also rejecting literalism and chiliasm in favor of a spiritual approach was one of the most important theologians of the late third and early fourth centuries, Methodios of Olympus in Lycia, who was martyred in 311. Methodios became an important patristic resource for Andrew of Caesarea's commentary. Similar to Origen, Methodios employed allegory and treated Revelation's imagery as poetry and symbol in his book, *The Symposium*, but Methodios successfully avoided Origen's mistakes and opposed his theological errors.[41]

39. Eusebius, *E.H.* 6.25.8–10.   40. Eusebius, *E.H.* 6.25.7, 9–10.
41. For example, he interpreted the seven heads of the beast in Rev. 13 as seven sins. Methodios, *Symposium* 8.13.

But despite the efforts of Origen and Methodios, less intellectual Christians continued to interpret Revelation in such an embarrassingly literal manner that subsequently two well-intentioned bishops resolved to destroy the reputation of Apocalypse of John in the Church. The first was a pupil of Origen, Dionysios, who became the bishop of Alexandria in 248. Like Origen, Dionysios preferred the allegorical interpretation of Scriptures which had been promoted by the school of Alexandria. But enthusiasts of chiliasm depended upon a literal interpretation of such eschatological biblical passages. A harsh critic of allegory at the time was an Egyptian bishop, Nepos of Arsinoe, who had composed a treatise entitled *Refutation of the Allegorists*, which argued for the literal interpretation of prophecy, especially the Apocalypse. Conflict broke out in the Egyptian Church between the literalists and the allegorists and Dionysios paid a visit to Nepos for a three day conference to debate the matter. Dionysios's concern was not primarily the methodology of interpretation but millennialism, a teaching which depended on a literal interpretation of Revelation (20:2–5). According to Eusebius of Caesarea, Dionysios successfully persuaded the literalists that their interpretation of eschatological prophecy was unsupportable and the controversy was resolved in favor of allegory.[42]

Just as the anti-Montanists had sought to defeat Montanism by undermining the apostolicity of Revelation, Dionysios also found it expedient to combat millennialism by undermining the Apocalypse. Other than Gaius, the Alogoi, and anti-Montanists, Dionysios appears to be the only individual prior to the fourth century to explicitly dispute the apostolic authorship of Revelation. Dionysios wrote a treatise on chiliasm, *On Promises*, in which he analyzed the Revelation of John, comparing its style and vocabulary to that of the gospel and he concluded that the two books could not have been written by the same person.[43] Unlike Gaius, Dionysios did not attribute Revelation to Cerinthus because its theology differed considerably from that of Cer-

---

42. Eusebius, *E.H.* 7.24.6ff.
43. Eusebius, *E.H.* 7.24.3.

inthus. Dionysios also claimed that he did not reject the Apocalypse entirely, because "many of the brethren take it seriously" and he half-heartedly stated that perhaps it contained a deeper mystical meaning which he did not comprehend.[44] Dionysios conceded that the author's name was John, that he had a revelation and that he prophesied, but Dionysios maintained that the Apocalypse could not have been written by the author of the Fourth Gospel.[45] Then Dionysios casually reported a rumor which he had heard that in Asia there were two tombs bearing the name "John." Therefore, he concluded, the author of Revelation must have been this "other John."[46]

The two prongs of Dionysios's strategy—highlighting the differences between the Apocalypse and the Gospel and suggesting the existence of some "other John"—did not immediately dampen enthusiasm for the Apocalypse. Dionysios clearly did not believe the book belonged in the canon since he did not accept it as apostolic, but Alexandrian bishops who followed after him, such as Athanasius and Cyril, would regard it as canonical. However, Dionysios did convince one very influential Christian: Eusebius of Caesarea. It was Eusebius who later promoted Dionysios's opinions and succeeded in nearly turning the entire Eastern Church against the Revelation of John forever.

The Fourth Century: Erosion of Support

By the fourth century, discussion about the biblical canon was in full swing. Whereas writers and thinkers of earlier eras had made ca-

---

44. Eusebius, *E.H.* 7.25.4. Dionysios's reluctance to reject the book outright was probably not for the reason he expressed: that the Apocalypse contained some incomprehensible mystical meaning. It was more likely a calculated decision on his part not to be overly critical of a book which enjoyed great popularity and which was universally regarded as apostolic. Dionysios's sole objective was to instill doubts about Revelation's apostolic origins, which he did quite successfully.

45. Eusebius, *E.H.* 7.25.7–15. Robert Grant, *Heresy and Criticism: The Search for Authenticity in Early Christian Literature* (Louisville, Ky.: John Knox Press, 1993), 104ff; Ned Bernard Stonehouse, *Apocalypse in the Ancient Church*, 125; Edgar J. Goodspeed, *Formation*, 99.

46. Eusebius, *E.H.* 7.25.16.

sual comments or observations about the state of the canon, leading clerics of the fourth century composed specific lists of sacred Scripture.[47] Among those offering their own canons to the mix were Gregory the Theologian of Nazianzus, Athanasius of Alexandria, Cyril of Jerusalem, Epiphanios of Salamis, Amphilochios of Iconium, and Didymus the Blind. By the mid-fourth century the shift in attitude against Revelation can be seen in its omission from the canon promulgated in association with the Council of Laodicea which met in 363 C.E. The council issued its fifty-ninth canon which forbade the reading of non-canonical books in Church, however, the council itself did not provide a list of books which formed the canon. At some point later, this problematic omission was remedied by the addition of a sixtieth canon which listed twenty-*six* New Testament books, with Revelation being omitted. However, since the sixtieth canon is missing from most of the Latin and Syriac translations of that council's decisions, many believe that the list was not originally promulgated by the council and may not even reflect the opinions of the council's participants, since it is not known when or by whom that canon of Scripture was created.[48] However, the later-added list is routinely considered to be the scriptural canon of the Council of Laodicea even though its origins and a fourth century date for the list are uncertain.[49]

As we have seen, the individual most responsible for the decline of the Apocalypse in popular opinion during the fourth century was Eusebius, the bishop of Caesarea in Palestine. Eusebius authored several books, most notably *Ecclesiastical History*, a monumental work in which

---

47. Bruce Metzger, *Canon*, 209.

48. Alexander Souter, *The Text and Canon of the New Testament* (New York: Charles Scribner, 1913), 195, n. 1.

49. Three early Western synods issued canons: The Council of Hippo, 393, and two synods at Carthage 397 and 419, all of which listed our twenty-seven New Testament books as Scripture. No doubt the last two councils were greatly influenced by Augustine. Edgar J. Goodspeed, *Formation*, 126. Although a canon of Scripture was supposedly promulgated at the council held by Pope Damasus in Rome, 382 CE, which Souter mistakenly considered to be the earliest synodal canon (Alexander Souter, *Text and Canon*, 195), the so-called Damasian Canon is now believed to be a non-papal canon from the sixth century.

he chronicled the history of the Church from the time of the apostles up to his day. In *Ecclesiastical History*, Eusebius reported on the lives, contributions, writings, and controversies of the most prominent Church leaders of the past, often quoting works of earlier Christian writers. In so doing, Eusebius preserved oral traditions and many fragments of documents which have since been lost.

Eusebius opposed millennialism and firmly believed that the Apocalypse of John was spurious, however he sought to maintain the appearance of an unbiased recorder. *Ecclesiastical History* was so widely read and influential that he was able to subtly undermine the reputation of the Apocalypse in the Eastern Church. The result was nothing less than a gradual but steady decline in the book's standing among theologians and clergy in the East. The transformation of popular opinion from universal acceptance to nearly unanimous rejection would occur within just a few decades but the effect would last for more than a thousand years.

A careful reading of his *History* reveals numerous clues to Eusebius's bias against the Book of Revelation. The state of the canon was among his primary interests and he often took note of an ecclesiastical writer's use of the Scriptures. The writer's opinion about the canon, including opinions regarding the Apocalypse of John, would be noted specifically. Eusebius observed that Papias mentioned two different men named John "in Asia," the apostle and a presbyter. He seized on this and suggested the possibility of the presbyter John as the author of Revelation.[50] He insulted Papias's intelligence (a result of the latter's millennialist leanings), to discredit his statement of the apostolic origins of Revelation.[51] Later in the book, while reviewing the work of Dionysios of Alexandria, Eusebius emphasized Dionysios's criticism of the Apocalypse. He repeated Dionysios's rumor about two tombs in Ephesus with the name John. He then devoted an entire chapter of *Ecclesiastical History* to the conference with Nepos, detailing Dionysios's

50. Eusebius, *E.H.* 3.39.6.
51. Eusebius, *E.H.* 3.39.13.

conclusions that John the Apostle did not compose the Apocalypse.[52] Eusebius also praised another antichiliast, Gaius, while never mentioning that Gaius had opposed the Gospel of John or that Hippolytus had responded Gaius's criticisms and refuted them.[53] Finally, Eusebius never mentions Methodios in *Ecclesiastical History*, an important third-century theologian who accepted Revelation as apostolic and effectively interpreted its imagery in an orthodox manner. Was this a mere oversight, or did Eusebius intentionally omit Methodios?

Egregious though these examples may be, Eusebius's most obvious attempt to sway public opinion against the Apocalypse can be seen in his own assessment of the current state of the New Testament canon during his day.[54] Offering an overview of general opinion, Eusebius separated the various books under consideration into three groups. First he listed the "universally acknowledged" books, *homologoumena* (ὁμολογούμενα) those which were unanimously considered inspired, apostolic and genuine according to unbroken Church tradition. These books were the four gospels, Acts, fourteen Pauline epistles (including Hebrews), 1 John and 1 Peter.[55] Then Eusebius added, "After these must be put, if it really seems right, the Apocalypse of John.... These then [are to be placed] among the recognized books."[56] Next, Eusebius listed the "disputed" books, the *antilegomena* (ἀντιλεγόμενα) those accepted by most Christians but not all, since some doubted that they are indeed apostolic. These were James, Jude, 2 Peter, and 2 and 3 John.[57]

The third group consisted of the overwhelmingly rejected books which Eusebius described as *notha* (νόθα), meaning "illegitimate," "counterfeit," or "spurious." On this list Eusebius placed *Acts of Paul*, *Shepherd of Hermas*, *Revelation of Peter*, *Epistle of Barnabas*, the *Didache*,

---

52. Eusebius, *E.H.* 7.24.   53. See n. 38.
54. Eusebius, *E.H.* 3.25.1ff.

55. By this detail, it is obvious that Eusebius's assessment is not truly of the *entire* Church, as he claims, but only for the East, since Hebrews was overwhelmingly rejected in the West at that time.

56. ἐπὶ τούτοις τακτέον, εἴ γε φανείη, τὴν Ἀποκάλυψιν Ἰωάννου ... καὶ ταῦτα μὲν ἐν ὁμολογουμένοις. Eusebius, *E.H.* 3.25.2. Translation by Bruce Metzger, *Canon*, 309.

57. Eusebius, *E.H.* 3.25.3.

the *Gospel According to the Hebrews*, and the *Apocalypse of John*. "Among the spurious books must be reckoned ... in addition, as I said, the Apocalypse of John, if it seems right. (This last, as I said, is rejected by some, but others count it among the recognized books.)"[58]

The double classification of the Apocalypse in two fundamentally incompatible categories, simultaneously placed by Eusebius with the "universally acknowledged" books *and* the "spurious" books, has led to a great deal of scholarly discussion and analysis over the years.[59] The

---

58. Eusebius, *E.H.* 3.25.4. Translation by Bruce Metzger, *Canon*, 309. Eusebius also included a fourth list consisting of works which were not only spurious but heretical and which were never considered for inclusion in the canon, including the *Gospels of Peter, Thomas*, and *Matthias*, the *Acts of Andrew*, and the *Acts of John*.

59. Goodspeed believed that Eusebius regarded some of the disputed books canonical because of the prevailing opinion in the East. Edgar J. Goodspeed, *Formation*, 101. F. F. Bruce merely states that since Eusebius did not consider the book apostolic he placed it with the spurious writings. "The 'spurious' books were not generally included in the canon, yet they were known and esteemed by many churchmen. If not canonical, they were at least orthodox." F. F. Bruce, *Canon of Scripture* (Downers Grove, Ill.: InterVarsity Press, 1988), 199. This is true, but that does not explain why Eusebius included Revelation on two mutually incompatible lists. Charles Hill also wrote that for Eusebius if the Apocalypse was apostolic, it was canonical," otherwise it would be a forgery and spurious. *Johannine Corpus*, 462. Hill believes that Eusebius's dual categorization reflects Eusebius's inability to "adjudicate in a definitive way the matters of authorship and canonicity." *Johannine Corpus*, 462. But Eusebius had already concluded that it was not apostolic, so the conflicting classification was not due to Eusebius's inability to make a decision. Bruce Metzger believed that the conflicting statements arose out of Eusebius's dual role as a historian and a churchman. First Eusebius divided books according to whether they were canonical or not, then according to their orthodoxy. Only orthodox books were placed into the *homologoumena* and *antilegomena* categories, but the *notha* though uncanonical, were not necessarily unorthodox in character. "As a historian, Eusebius recognizes that it is widely received, but as a churchman he has become annoyed by the extravagant use made of this book by the Montanists and other millenarians, and so is glad to report elsewhere in his history that others considerate it to be not genuine." Bruce Metzger, *Canon*, 204. Metzger follows the opinion of Ernst von Dobschütz in this matter, and cited "The Abandonment of the Canonical Idea," *American Journal of Theology* 19 (1915): 416–29. Stonehouse concludes that Eusebius was at odds with the Church as a whole, which regarded the Apocalypse as apostolic when he himself did not. Ned Bernard Stonehouse, *Apocalypse in the Ancient Church*, 132. David Dungan believes that Eusebius considered the Apocalypse as a "subset of the *disputed* writings." However, Eusebius did not place the Apocalypse in the "disputed" category. Dungan provides no explanation for his conclusion that Eusebius considered it "disputed," especially when Eusebius mentions no one who rejected it except for Gaius and Dionysios. David Dungan, *Constantine's Bible* (Minneapolis: Fortress Press, 2007), 56. Dungan also believes that the Apocalypse came to be debated and contested during the fourth cen-

simplest and most sensible explanation, which also takes into consideration the totality of Eusebius's comments on the Apocalypse, is that as a historian reporting the current state of the canon, Eusebius was compelled to place the Apocalypse with the first group because it was indeed universally acknowledged as Scripture at that time. However, as he *personally* regarded the Apocalypse as illegitimate and spurious, he also placed it among the rejected books. There is no mistaking his bias: it is clear from the beginning. From the very first time Eusebius mentions Revelation, he refers to the book as "the so-called Apocalypse of John."[60]

By classifying the Apocalypse among the rejected books, referring to it as "the so-called Apocalypse," extensively reporting Dionysios's analysis and the "two tombs" rumor along with Papias's statements about "two Johns" in Asia, it is abundantly evident that Eusebius hoped to move future ecclesiastical opinion against the Apocalypse. Today we might expect Eusebius to list the Apocalypse among the "disputed" books because its apostolic authorship is widely disputed currently. But during Eusebius's era, the Apocalypse was universally acknowledged as apostolic in both the East and the West, even though Eusebius tried to minimize that acceptance by writing that "with regard to the Apocalypse still at the present time opinion is generally divided."[61] Eusebius blatantly misrepresented the situation. Opinion about Revelation was clearly *not* divided at the time. If opinion were indeed "divided," Eusebius would have classified the Apocalypse among the "disputed" books, which he did not do because everyone knew it was not disputed. If he categorized it as "disputed" Eusebius would have appeared ridiculous to his readership and would have betrayed his personal bias. Furthermore, if opinion were divided, Eusebius would have reported the opinion of clerics who rejected the apostolicity of

---

tury because of the transformation of the empire from pagan to Christian because "it simply would not do to speak of Christ coming back to destroy the evil Roman empire." David Dungan, *Constantine's Bible*, 57.

60. Eusebius, *E.H.* 3.18. 2. ἐν τῇ Ἰωάννου λεγομένῃ.
61. Eusebius, *E.H.* 3.24.18.

Revelation in his multivolume *History*, but he mentions none except for Dionysios and Gaius. Clearly, Eusebius wished to turn Christians against the Revelation of John, but he could not persuade them to reject the Apocalypse so long as it was considered apostolic. His comments, which worked to persistently raise doubts as to its apostolicity, reveal Eusebius's true intent.

After Eusebius's death, the Church of Alexandria generally continued to accept the Apocalypse as canonical, including Athanasius,[62] Didymus the Blind,[63] and Cyril of Alexandria.[64] Elsewhere in the Eastern empire of the late fourth century, support for the Apocalypse was rapidly eroding. It was unanimously rejected in the Antiochean school, which had traditionally embraced a smaller canon.[65] John Chrysostom did not recognize it and by all evidence neither did Theodore of Mopsuestia, although Theodoret of Cyrus seems to have accepted it. In particular, Chrysostom's stance may have indirectly delayed Revelation's place in the Eastern canon since Chrysostom was the most prolific and widely read Greek Father and remains the most influential patristic authority in biblical studies for the East. The Apocalypse was rejected in the fourth century by Cyril of Jerusalem,[66] but accepted by Epiphanios of Salamis.[67]

When Basil the Great quoted Revelation 1:18, "I am the Alpha and the Omega, says the Lord God, who is, who was and who is to come, the Almighty," it was exceptional.[68] Revelation was not often quoted in the East during the fourth century, and when it was employed it was usually to support the full divinity of the Son during Christological debates

---

62. Athanasius, *Ep. 39*, his famous Pascal Encyclical of 367.
63. Bruce Metzger, *Canon*, 213.
64. Cyril of Alexandria, *On Worship in Spirit and Truth*, 6. Andrew, Prologue, *Comm.* 53–54.
65. The Antiocheans typically rejected 2 and 3 John, 2 Peter, Jude and Revelation.
66. Cyril of Jerusalem, *Catechetical Lectures* 4.31. See also Henry Barclay Swete, *Apocalypse of John*, cxi, and Ned Bernard Stonehouse, *Apocalypse in the Ancient Church*, 135.
67. Epiphanios of Salamis, *Panarion* 76. But more important than his personal opinion is the fact that Epiphanios identifies the rejection of John's books, including Revelation, as characteristic of a heresy.
68. Basil the Great, *Against Eunomius* 2.14, and 4.2.

at the time. One may suppose that if Revelation had more Christological content which patristic authorities could have used during doctrinal controversies of the fourth and fifth centuries, it might have been accepted into the Eastern canon more readily. However, even as the book enjoyed acceptance by Basil and his brother, Gregory of Nyssa,[69] it was rejected by Gregory the Theologian of Nazianzus in his poetic rendering of the canon, this despite the fact that Gregory had quoted from Revelation twice.[70]

As the century drew to a close, Amphilochios of Iconium (d. c. 394) composed his own canon as part of a poetic composition known as the *Iambics of Seleucus*, in which he advised Seleucus to study the Scriptures. The mere fact that Amphilochios appeared compelled to evaluate *which* books ought to be considered Scripture indicates that the canon was still not fixed. Amphilochios discussed, evaluated, accepted, and rejected various books. Regarding Revelation, he remarked: "And again, the Revelation of John, some approve, but the most say it is spurious."[71] Amphilochios did not express his own personal opinion about the Apocalypse but his comment reveals the dramatic shift in attitude against the Apocalypse which had taken place in just a few short decades since Eusebius had attempted to destroy Revelation's reputation by convincing Christians that it was spurious.

In the West, the New Testament was settling into the canon we recognize today. The Apocalypse had never lost acceptance and prominent support there. Not so in the East. Controversial in its millennialism and unusual in its message and imagery, the seeds of doubt about its apostolicity planted and nurtured by Eusebius gradually unhinged the standing of the Book of Revelation in the Eastern canon.

Eusebius had been remarkably successful.

---

69. Gregory of Nyssa, *On the Inscriptions of the Psalms* 10, Basil the Great, *Against Apollinarius* 37, *Concerning his own Ordination* 1.

70. Gregory the Theologian of Nazianzus, *Orations* 29.17 and 40.45.

71. Bruce Metzger, *Canon*, 314. See also, Edgar J. Goodspeed, *Formation*, 130. Metzger surmises that he appears to reject 2 Peter, 2 and 3 John, Jude and "almost certainly rejects Revelation." Bruce Metzger, *Canon*, 213.

3

LATER EASTERN DEVELOPMENTS

From Rejection to Acceptance

Disagreement among ecclesiastical writers over the canon continued into later centuries. Eminent Eastern theologians and hierarchs differed over the canonical status of Revelation, which was usually denied. As the Church passed the first millennium, the vicissitudes of Muslim and Christian conflict and the decline of the Byzantine empire brought new meaning to the Book of Revelation.

The reception history of the Apocalypse in the East indicates some ambivalence as scholars and writers of great prominence differed on the canon, and especially the status of the Apocalypse. Pseudo-Dionysios, in the early sixth century may have accepted the book but Maximos the Confessor (d. 662) certainly rejected it.[1] In the eighth century John of Damascus accepted it, but Nikephoros, the Patriarch of Constantinople

---

1. The only direct quote is Rev.1:8, "I am the Alpha and the Omega, who was, and who is and who is to come, the Almighty." (Pseudo-Dionysios, *The Divine Names*, 2.) Numerous possible allusions to the Apocalypse can be found in Pseudo-Dionysios, but it is difficult to determine whether they are indeed allusions to Revelation or allusions to images and language found in various Old Testament prophets which are similar to language in Revelation. The single quotation may not indicate that Dionysios considered Revelation canonical scripture since Gregory Nazianzus also quoted the same verse but did not include the Apocalypse in his canon.

in the ninth century, did not.² Nikephoros composed an actual canon of Scripture to identify which books were canonical and which disputed and listed Revelation as disputed and non-canonical.³ But later in that same century, Photios the Great, who also served as Patriarch of Constantinople, accepted Revelation as canonical.⁴ Also recognizing and promoting the Apocalypse with his own commentary during this era was Arethas, who some three centuries after Andrew occupied the same episcopal see as bishop of Caesarea, Cappadocia. The Arethas commentary, which greatly depends on Andrew, became the second most important patristic commentary in the Greek East, but never rivaled Andrew's commentary in impact or importance.⁵

This canonical uncertainty continued through the Middle Ages and beyond, with canons being composed by church leaders in order to delineate the boundaries of the New Testament. This topsy-turvy history indicates the matter had never been resolved by an ecumenical council, the highest ecclesiastical authority in Eastern Christianity. The result was canons of Scripture promulgated by local councils and various patristic authorities which were not in agreement. The Council in Trullo, also known as the Quinisext Council, which was convened in Constantinople in 691 and 692 to complete the work of the Fifth and Sixth Ecumenical Councils, might have resolved the status of Revelation.⁶ Indeed, some point to this council as having conclusively resolved the biblical canon for the Orthodox. However, the Trullo council not only failed to resolve the status of Revelation, it further hopelessly confused the situation when it ratified the scriptural canons of all of the preceding local councils and Fathers. These canons disagreed, not only with respect to Revelation but as to other books as well. Thus, rather than resolving the question of the canon, Trullo's complete and

---

2. Nikephoros, *Exposition of the Orthodox Faith* 4.17.

3. Also known as *The Stichometry of Nikephoros*. Edgar J. Goodspeed, *The Formation of the New Testament* (Chicago: University of Chicago Press, 1926), 140.

4. Edgar J. Goodspeed, *Formation*, 140.   5. See chapter 1, n. 37.

6. "Trullo" is the Greek word for "dome" and this council has been dubbed "Trullo" because the participants met in a large domed room. The Council of Trullo is sometimes incorrectly cited as having settled the canon for the East.

indiscriminate ratification preserved the status quo, leaving the matter open to individual persons, local bishops, and regional preferences.

Puzzling though it may appear, there are reasons for this continued ambiguity. The Orthodox Church typically refrains from addressing issues in a preemptive or anticipatory manner. The Orthodox Church does not promulgate new dogmas, issue proclamations or disciplinary canons absent a concrete necessity arising from an actual conflict within the Church. Even though unresolved, the canon was not an issue since the lack of a resolution did not create a problem. Unlike the Roman Catholic Church, the Orthodox Church never experienced a Reformation as had occurred in the West, and as a result, the canon was never forced to a conclusion. In contrast, the Reformation compelled the Roman Catholic Church to officially define its canon at the Council of Trent (1546). Since the highest level of authority for the Eastern Orthodox is an ecumenical council, and none of the ecumenical councils wrote its own canon, it can be argued that the canon *still* has not been conclusively resolved for the Orthodox. However, it would also be true that the canon has been resolved de facto, in the typical Orthodox manner: by consensus within the Church over a long period of time.

No other Orthodox commentaries on the Apocalypse appeared after Arethas until the Ottoman empire and the canonical status of Revelation remained uncertain.[7] Now came new threats and a new chapter in the history of the Apocalypse. The continued ascent of Islam in the eighth and ninth centuries placed even greater pressure on the Eastern Church. Lands which had for centuries been secure within the protection of the formidable Byzantine military slowly fell to Arab and then Ottoman armies. Weakened by centuries of pressure by Arab and Christian rivals, Constantinople fell to wayward Crusaders in 1204, cementing the schism between the Western and Eastern Churches. The greatest city of Europe was subjected to indescribable savagery as libraries, monasteries, churches, and homes were looted, burned, and destroyed.

---

7. Savvas Agourides, Ἡ Ἀποκάλυψις τοῦ Ἰωάννου, Ἑρμηνεία Καινῆς Διαθήκης 18 (Thessalonika: Pournaras Press, 1994), 60–65.

38 LATER EASTERN DEVELOPMENTS

The accumulated treasures of a thousand years of Christian history were obliterated or stolen within a three-day orgy of destruction. The trauma was never forgotten and it impacted Revelation in the Orthodox Church.

Although the empire expelled the Crusaders after several decades, the effect on Eastern Christendom and the Apocalypse were complete. As the Byzantine empire slowly shrank and the Ottoman Turks advanced, interest in the Apocalypse revived. The number of manuscript copies of the Apocalypse gradually increased during this period. The great patristic luminary of the fourteenth century, Gregory Palamas, used Revelation and cited it as "composed by John, the greatest theologian among the evangelists."[8] A fourteenth-century ecclesiastical historian of Byzantium, Nikephoros Kallistos, also signaled that the Apocalypse was gaining acceptance as a canonical book.[9] Even before the final end of the empire, most Eastern Christians found themselves living under non-Christian rule, often facing persecution and martyrdom just as the early Christian communities first receiving Revelation had experienced centuries before. Apocalyptic expectations were widespread, reaching an apex with the fall of Constantinople in 1453. Byzantine tradition had long held that the Christian Roman empire (of which Byzantium was the direct continuation) would be the last empire before the end times. Copying of Revelation manuscripts increased significantly during the fifteenth and sixteenth centuries[10] and several new commentaries on the Apocalypse were composed during this period.[11] This era also produced the first known scenes from the Apocalypse on Eastern Church frescoes and icons.[12]

---

8. Gregory Palamas, Homily 34, *On the Transfiguration*, in *The Homilies*, ed. and trans. Christopher Veniamin (Waymart, Pa.: Mt. Thabor Publishing, 2009), 272.

9. Nikephoros Kallistos, *Ecclesiastical History* 2.45.

10. Ernest Cadman Colwell and H. R. Willoughby, *The Elizabeth Day McCormick Apocalypse*, 2 vols., vol. 1, *A Greek Corpus of Revelation Iconography*, H. R. Willoughby, and vol. 2, *History and Text*, Ernest Cadman Colwell (Chicago: University of Chicago Press, 1940), 2:143.

11. See Asterios Argyriou, *Les exégèses grecques de l'Apocalypse à l'epoque turque (1453–1821)*, Seira Philologike kai Theologike 15, (Thessalonika: Hetaireia Makedonikon Spoudon, 1982).

12. Ernest Cadman Colwell and H. R. Willoughby, *McCormick Apocalypse*, 2:13–4.

Not surprisingly, interest in Andrew of Caesarea's commentary also grew. Manuscript copies of Andrew's commentary dramatically increased as did the number of Revelation manuscripts. Approximately one-third of the manuscript copies of Revelation contain Andrew of Caesarea's commentary.[13] The commentary was influential in the transmission of the text of Revelation itself, resulting in a unique text type.[14] The commentary was frequently copied along with the text of the Apocalypse because it provided a highly useful and desirable explanation for the enigmatic book. The number of Andreas manuscripts produced in the fourteenth century spiked sharply compared to the preceding centuries, reaching a peak in the fifteenth and sixteenth centuries. In fact, two-thirds of all Andreas manuscripts are dated between the fourteenth and sixteenth centuries.[15]

Toward the end of the empire, as threats to the survival of Constantinople worsened, many Greeks fled to the West for refuge. Among these refugees were scholars, educated elites, and wealthy citizens of the formerly grand Byzantine empire, now little more than a walled city. The refugees had considerable impact on European culture emerging from the Middle Ages, bringing with them the full fruits of Byzantine scholarship and the collected treasure of not only Eastern Christian theology, but Greek philosophy, literature, and history. The effect sparked the Renaissance and stimulated interest in the classics and—importantly—the Greek text of the New Testament. The near simultaneous invention of the printing press made the dissemination of these works widespread. No longer the long, slow work of scribes, it was now possible to manage the physical production of many copies of the New Testament as a defined collection in one volume. This also may have contributed to some degree toward moving the East to a greater acceptance of Revelation.[16]

---

13. David E. Aune, *Revelation* 52A: cxxxix–cxl. See cxxvi–cxlvii for a complete listing of Revelation manuscripts.

14. Discussed in chapter 15.   15. Josef Schmid, *Einleitung*, 1–85.

16. "[T]he printing of the Greek New Testament formed the most important step for the practical association of the Revelation with the other books of the New Testament." Caspar René Gregory, *Canon and Text of the New Testament* (New York: Charles Scribner, 1907), 292.

But evidence demonstrates that among the Greek Orthodox, the Apocalypse continued to occupy a position somewhere between the obviously canonical and the clearly noncanonical books, a situation which persisted almost into the modern era.

Most Byzantine New Testaments did not contain the Apocalypse. It had never been part of the Church lectionary, and there seemed no reason to print it. During the seventeenth century Swiss and Dutch Protestants circulated many copies of the New Testament in vernacular Greek.[17] Although the clear objective was to convert the Greeks to Protestant Christianity, the distribution of the New Testament in modern Greek was not opposed by the Patriarch of Constantinople, Cyril Loukaris (d. 1638), an educated man who believed that Greeks should be able to read the Scriptures in the vernacular.[18] The efforts by Protestants and Jesuit missionaries to convert the Greeks failed, along with the promulgation of the Bible in demotic Greek, despite strenuous efforts on the part of the missionaries, and later, by the British Bible Society and other groups. These activities were offensive and resented by the Greek Orthodox, who consider themselves preservers of apostolic Christianity in an unbroken connection with the ancient Church.[19] The translation of the Bible into the vernacular Greek came to be associated with foreign and heretical elements since it had been promoted by Protestants, as well as by Catholics who were actively seeking to undermine the Ecumenical Patriarchate.[20]

---

17. Ernest Cadman Colwell and H. R. Willoughby, *McCormick Apocalypse*, 2:26–33.

18. N[omikos] M[ichael] Vaporis, *Translating the Scriptures into Modern Greek* (Brookline, Mass.: Holy Cross Orthodox Press, 1994), 2.

19. Translations promoted by the British Bible Society, which initially had the backing of the Patriarch of Constantinople, were rejected because the British insisted on using the Hebrew text as the basis for the Old Testament, rather than the Septuagint, which has been the unbroken tradition among the Orthodox. Nomikos Michael Vaporis, *Translating*, 59.

20. Vaporis notes that Loukaris's friendliness toward the Protestants was due to political circumstances at the time, including "papal aggression." "Loukaris looked upon the activities of papal agents with mistrust and continued his efforts to counter Papal ambitions in Eastern Europe and the near East." Nomikos Michael Vaporis, *Translating*, 3. "This was the first time in its history that the Orthodox Church was confronted simultaneously by an aggressive and militant Roman Catholic Church led by the Society of Jesus ... and by an equally militant and aspiring Protestant challenge"(4).

Elsewhere in Europe the most popular book to translate into the vernacular at the time was the Bible. Translations in numerous versions and various languages were produced. But this remained controversial among the Greeks who continued to read the Septuagint and the New Testament in the original, and maintain that practice even today in the services of the Greek Orthodox Church. Far from popularizing the Bible, a translation into demotic Greek was seen by conservatives as a corruption of the text.[21] Efforts to produce a translation of the Scriptures into colloquial Greek were continually met with strong resistance among many Greeks from the seventeenth and into the twentieth century since the production of modern Greek translations continued to be associated with Protestant proselytizing and other Western influences. These efforts only fueled opposition by conservative Orthodox Christians who interpreted the translations as an effort to destroy the purity of the faith and introduce heresy. Since Greek Orthodoxy and ethnic identity are inextricably bound together in the Hellenic mind, not surprisingly a sense of nationalism also became a component of the controversy. Proponents of translation were depicted as traitors while opponents were typically presented as patriots and defenders of the faith and the nation.[22]

---

21. Today, the continued usage of the original Greek text in liturgical and ecclesial settings is considered an important tradition and responsibility among the Greek Orthodox. There is still no "official" translation of the New Testament in modern Greek for the Greek Orthodox Church.

22. Nomikos Michael Vaporis, "The Last Phase of the Translation Controversy," *Rightly Teaching the Word of Your Truth: Studies in Faith and Culture, Church and Scriptures, Fathers and Worship, Hellenism and the Contemporary Scene*, ed. Nomikos Michael Vaporis (Brookline, Mass.: Holy Cross Orthodox Press, 1995), 227–35. When a vernacular translation was published in 1901 by Alexander Pallis, a Greek merchant from Liverpool, England, it was condemned by the Patriarch Joachim II and the Synod in Constantinople on October 8, 1901 for its extremely casual vernacular language, described as "philological vandalism, a distortion and desecration of the sacred original." Nomikos Michael Vaporis, 235, citing Emmanuel Konstantinides, *Τὰ Εὐαγγελικά· Τὸ πρόβλημα τῆς μεταφράσεως τῆς Ἁγίας Γραφῆς εἰς τὴν Νεοελληνικὴν κατὰ τὰ αἱματηρὰ γεγονότα τοῦ 1901*. (Athens, 1976), 165. The Pallis translation was also condemned in the press and violent demonstrations broke out in furious opposition to the translation. Nomikos Michael Vaporis, "Last Phase," 235. Eighty people were killed in the streets of Athens during what were dubbed the "Gospel riots" of November 8–12, 1901. The dead included high school and university students, craftsmen, sailors and soldiers. Nomikos

During this period Maximos Kalliopolites (d. 1633) translated numerous works into the vernacular Greek including patristic treatises, sermons, a medical encyclopedia and the Apocalypse.[23] Other ancient Greek works had been translated into everyday Greek by Orthodox predecessors and contemporaries of Maximos, but never the Bible.[24] At the request of Cyril Loukaris, Maximos produced a Bible translation in vernacular Greek which for the first time included the entire New Testament canon. This translation was accepted by some hierarchs, however many opposed it.[25] Maximos Kalliopolites not only translated the text of Revelation but he may also have been the Maximos who offered a demotic Greek commentary on Revelation. The author of the commentary originally intended to combine the commentaries of Andrew of Caesarea and Arethas. As Maximos progressed with his commentary it became less a combination of Andrew and Arethas and eventually developed into a restatement of Andrew with very little taken from Arethas.[26] Maximos's translation of the Apocalypse and the creation of an accompanying commentary does not appear to have ignited controversy, which Ernest Colwell believes signals that the book

---

Michael Vaporis, "Last Phase," 237 and 239, n. 54. Arnold Toynbee commented: "Greece is perhaps the only country in Christendom—either Orthodox or Western—in which popular disturbances over the question of translating the bible out of a classical language into a vulgar tongue have been excited, not against a veto upon the project of translation but against a threat to carry the project into effect!" *A Study of History*, 2nd ed., 12 vols. (London: Oxford University Press, 1935–61), 70, n. 1.

23. There are numerous variations on the spelling, including "Kallipoli," or even "Galliopolite." Some believe him to be the individual also known as Maximos the Peloponnesian. See Ernest Cadman Colwell and H. R. Willoughby, *McCormick Apocalypse*, 2: 21.

24. Ernest Cadman Colwell and H. R. Willoughby, *McCormick Apocalypse*, 2: 23. Ernest Colwell correctly observes: "It was not a common or ordinary thing for a pious Greek to translate the New Testament" (2: 25).

25. Nomikos Michael Vaporis, "Last Phase," 227–29.

26. Ernest Cadman Colwell and H. R. Willoughby, *Elizabeth Day McCormick Apocalypse*, 2:120. "Maximos began his work with the intention of blending the best of Andreas and Arethas and increasing the scriptural element; that blending decreased as the work progressed, with the result that the dominant source for most of the commentary is that of Andreas." *McCormick Apocalypse*, 2:42. The same observations are made by Josef Schmid who discusses the content and manuscripts of Maximos in *Einleitung*, 97–98. The Maximos commentary survives in four manuscripts.

was still not universally regarded as entirely canonical in the seventeenth century since its translation was not disapproved.²⁷ However, it appears that Revelation had "turned the corner" by then.²⁸ Most of the controversy at that point in time centered on the question of the vernacular Greek translation of the Scriptures in general rather than on the acceptance of the Apocalypse.

The availability of the printed New Testament in a single volume which included the Apocalypse must have had some impact on popular perception regarding which books comprised the canon. Absent an acceptable and orthodox interpretation of the Apocalypse, the book would never have been accepted as canonical. Andrew of Caesarea provided that necessary explanation. It is very possible that Maximos produced the commentary to support his inclusion of Revelation within his translated New Testament, due to the uneven position of the Apocalypse in the history of the Orthodox Church.

In 1672, a council met in Jerusalem to investigate the Calvinistic "Confession of Faith" attributed to Patriarch of Constantinople, Cyril Loukaris. Loukaris had been killed some years earlier by the Ottoman Turks, one of many "neo-martyrs" from this period in Orthodox Church history.²⁹ Despite this, two previous councils had condemned him for Calvinistic statements which had been attributed to him. The synod meeting at Jerusalem went to great lengths to examine his "Confession," compared it to his known writings and concluded that in fact Loukaris was entirely Orthodox and could not have written the

27. Ernest Cadman Colwell and H. R. Willoughby, *McCormick Apocalypse*, 2:22.
28. Panagiotis I. Bratsiotis observes that by the seventeenth century, local synods seem to have accepted it. "Apocalypse," Θρησκευτικὴ καὶ Ἠθικὴ Ἐγκυκλοπαιδεία, ed. A. Martinos, 12 vols (Athens, 1962–68).
29. Some later Greek commentators identified the Antichrist as Mohammed, such as Apostolos Makrakis in 1882 (*Interpretation of the Book of Revelation by St. John the Divine*, trans. A. G. Alexander [Hellenic Christian Educational Society, 1948]), and an anonymous commentary earlier in the nineteenth century, possibly by Theodore of Ioannina. This commentary only saw a very small circulation because the Ecumenical Patriarchate suppressed it due to fear of Turkish reprisals. Panagiotis I. Bratsiotis, Ἡ Ἀποκάλυψις τοῦ Ἀποστόλου Ἰωάννου (Athens: Synodinos, 1950), 49.

"Confession" or agreed with its contents.[30] This synod also stated that the canon of the Orthodox Church was that of the Council of Laodicea, presumably the sixtieth canon, which, as we have seen, omitted Revelation.[31]

But the Jerusalem council also provided an explicit canonical list which *included* the Apocalypse of John, indicating that perhaps the participants were not aware that the Council of Laodicea had rejected the Apocalypse of John. Although the Synod of Jerusalem has often been cited as conclusively stating or officially determining the canon of Scripture for the Orthodox, this is not correct since a local synod does not speak with authority for the entire Church. However, the synod's acceptance of Revelation certainly confirms an advance. It is likely that the increased circulation and awareness of Andrew's commentary, such as its extensive appropriation by Maximos for his commentary, contributed to this positive development.[32] Interest in the Apocalypse remained alive. Although other commentaries were produced, none was as popular as Andrew of Caesarea's commentary, which continued to dominate Apocalypse interpretation for the Orthodox in the ensuing centuries.

The influence of Andrew's commentary on the acceptance of the Apocalypse into the canon of Orthodox Christianity is unmistakable. It had already directly influenced the reception of Revelation among the Orthodox who were not Greek. In fact, the status of Revelation and the New Testament canon was resolved among the non-Greek Orthodox long before it was for the Greeks. Here we see the impact of good vernacular translation as a significant factor to define and settle the entire New Testament canon for an ethnic group, and the impact of

30. J. N. W. B. Robertson, trans., *The Acts and Decrees of the Synod of Jerusalem* (London: Baker, 1899). The synod insisted that Calvinists falsified Cyril's views and forged his "Confession," stating that publicly and privately Cyril had always expressed beliefs contrary to Calvinism. The council supported its finding that Cyril was entirely Orthodox, and he had specifically repudiated Calvinism with an oath, by presenting numerous quotations from Cyril's sermons (16–60).

31. See chapter 2.

32. On the commentary by Maximos, see also chapter 16.

Andrew's commentary on the reception of the Apocalypse in particular. For example, Revelation was not accepted among the Armenians as Scripture until a famous Armenian Archbishop, Nerses of Lampron, Archbishop of Tarsus (d. 1198), spearheaded the translation of Andrew's commentary along with a new Armenian translation of Revelation.[33] Although John's Apocalypse was known among the Armenians and an Armenian translation of it already existed, Revelation was not listed in any New Testament canons before the time of Nerses, who pushed for its official acceptance at an Armenian synod held in Constantinople in the twelfth century. The synod approved Revelation on the basis of Andrew's commentary.[34]

Similarly, the Georgian Orthodox Church also received Revelation into the New Testament canon due to one individual's efforts, St. Euthymios (Ekwthime). The acceptance of Revelation, when it had previously been excluded from the Georgian canon, was again bolstered by the commentary of Andrew of Caesarea. Euthymios, a Greek monk from Mt. Athos, revised the old Georgian gospel text with good Greek manuscripts and also used a manuscript of the Andreas commentary as the basis for his translation of Revelation into Georgian. His superior translations helped to establish the Georgian New Testament text and canon in the late tenth century.[35] Andrew of Caesarea's commentary accompanied Revelation's introduction to the Georgian Orthodox Church in an abbreviated, paraphrased Georgian translation produced by Euthymios.[36] Again, a similar pattern can be seen with respect to the Russian Orthodox tradition when Andrew's commentary paved the way for the reception of the Apocalypse. The oldest extant

---

33. Robert W. Thomson, *Nerses of Lambron Commentary on the Revelation of Saint John*, Hebrew University Armenian Studies 9 (Leuven: Peeters, 2007), 3–4.

34. Robert W. Thomson, *Nerses of Lambron*, 4. See also Bruce Metzger, *Canon*, 224, and for the full story, see Josef Schmid, *Einleitung*, 99–113, or chapter 16.

35. D. M. Lang "Recent Work on the Georgian New Testament," *Bulletin of the School of Oriental and African Studies* 19, no. 1. (1957): 82–93, 86. Bruce Metzger, *Canon of the New Testament*, 224.

36. See J. Neville Birdsall, "'Revelation' by Euthymus the Athonite," *Beda Kartlisa* 41 (1983): 96–101, 99.

Slavic manuscript of Revelation contains a translation of Andrew's commentary in a condensed thirteenth century version, *The Nikol'skij Apocalypse Codex*.[37]

It is clear that the Apocalypse eventually met with ecclesiastical approval among the Greek Orthodox through the enduring work of Andrew of Caesarea, just as it had for other Orthodox in earlier centuries. The mere fact that a commentary existed was not decisive in the reception of the Apocalypse for the Orthodox but rather, it was the nature and quality of Andrew of Caesarea's commentary that allowed the Orthodox to accept Revelation. Andrew's commentary explained the book in a manner entirely in accordance with Church tradition, reflecting the attitude, thought, character, style, theology, and spirituality of the ancient East.

37. Thomas Hilary Oller, "The Nikol'skij Apocalypse Codex and Its Place in the Textual History of Medieval Slavic Apocalypse Manuscripts" (Ph.D. diss., Brown University, 1993).

4

DATING ANDREW OF CAESAREA AND OIKOUMENIOS

The person and work of Andrew of Caesarea are veiled in mystery. Virtually nothing is known about his life. Little remains of his exegetical work, except for his *Commentary on the Apocalypse* and a few small fragments consisting of questions and answers.[1] Although in the past scholars have placed Andrew's episcopal tenure as early as the fifth century and as late as the ninth century, today most locate him in the second half of the sixth century or early seventh.

The ancient city of Caesarea, Cappadocia, was located in eastern central Asia Minor, in the geographical center of modern-day Turkey, approximately 150 miles almost due north of that corner of the Mediterranean Sea which is just west of Antioch.[2] For centuries it was the civil and religious center of the Roman province, and later the Byzantine province, of Cappadocia. The episcopal see of Caesarea was among the

1. These fragments came from a work entitled Θεραπευτική and were published by Franz Diekamp, "Texte und Abhandlungen zur Griechischen Patristik," Orientalia christiana analecta 117 (Rome: Pontifical Institute of Oriental Studies, 1938), 161–72. Andrew produced at least one other commentary, *Commentary On Daniel*, which is attributed to him in a catalogue of the Patriarchal Library of Constantinople, printed at Strasbourg in 1578, but that commentary is otherwise entirely unknown as no manuscript of it has been found. *Bibliotheca Sive Antiquitates Urbis Constantinopolitanae* (Argentorati, 1578), 22. See *Clavis Patrum Graecorum*, 7478.

2. Present day "Kaysari."

most prominent of the Byzantine empire. Indeed, among the episcopal sees under the jurisdiction of the capital, the metropolis of Caesarea was second in importance only to Constantinople itself. The bishop of Caesarea held the titular rank of "Archbishop" and his see was designated as *protothronos*, giving the Archbishop of Caesarea a precedence which is consistently recorded as such in the *Notitiae episcopatuum*.[3]

Little can be said about Andrew with certainty except that he was the Archbishop of Caesarea in the late sixth or early seventh centuries. Apart from his ecclesiastical rank and see, and his authorship of a commentary on Revelation, we only know that Andrew wrote other commentaries, now lost, and responded to exegetical questions. Therefore, he must have been a well known and respected expert in Scripture interpretation. He confessed in the opening lines of his commentary that he was pressed by many people to undertake the job of writing a commentary on the Book of Revelation, a request which until then he had repeatedly declined.

It is not surprising that Andrew had previously declined to comment upon Revelation, despite his expertise in Scripture. Due to the very nature of the book, an interpretation of Revelation is challenging and difficult for anyone. In addition, almost no Greek exegetical tradition existed for the Apocalypse that Andrew could rely upon for assistance. But his statement that numerous persons appealed to him to assume this difficult task reveals that he was recognized as a proven exegete, technically and theologically well-qualified, and a respected hierarch.

Dating Andrew's Episcopal Reign

In recent years, scholarly opinion has finally reached a general consensus that Andrew flourished in the late sixth and early seventh centuries. However, arrival at this consensus has been extremely slow.

---

3. Daniel Stiernon, "Caesarea, Cappadocia," *Encyclopedia of the Early Church*, 2 vols. vol. 1, ed. Angelo Di Berardino, trans. Adrian Walford (Cambridge, England: James Clark & Co., 1992), citing Jean Darrouzes, *Notitiae epsicopatuum Ecclesiae Constantinopolitanae* (Paris, 1981).

Even very recently, scholars appear entirely unaware of the discoveries (now more than 100 years old) which have affirmatively and unquestionably established the parameters for dating Andrew and Oikoumenios, the author of the first Greek commentary on Revelation.[4] Andrew cites Pseudo-Dionysios who is generally dated in the late fifth or early sixth centuries, therefore Andrew could not have written prior to the sixth century. Andrew's episcopal reign is generally dated from 563 to 614 because we know the names of the archbishops of Caesarea from the year 500 through 563.[5] The best *terminus post quem* is 563, the year in which Theokritos, Archbishop of Caesarea, died. Andrew became Archbishop at some point thereafter. At the very end of Andrew's commentary is a paragraph consisting of an epilogue by a compiler or an editor who explains that he put the commentary together from rough drafts with the help of the author.[6] It seems that Andrew must have died shortly after the commentary was completed. This also helps to narrow the date of Andrew's episcopal reign. The *terminus ante quem* is the date of the destruction of Jerusalem by the Persians, an extremely significant event about which Andrew gives no hint of any knowledge in his commentary.

While the range of 563 to 614 is a useful approximation, it is highly unlikely that Andrew reigned for fifty-one years as a bishop, although

4. See, for example, Manlio Simonetti, *Biblical Interpretation in the Early Church*, trans. John Hughes (Edinburgh: T. & T. Clark, 1994), 112, who writes vaguely that Andrew and Oikoumenios "followed each other at an uncertain date in the sixth or seventh centuries." William Weinrich, situates Oikoumenios and Andrew in the early sixth century, *Revelation*, ed. and trans. William Weinrich, Ancient Christian Commentary 12, (Downers Grove, Ill.: InterVarsity Press, 2005), xxvii–xxviii. Frederick W. Norris, dates Andrew in the fifth century. "Andrew of Caesarea," *Encyclopedia of Early Christianity*, ed. Everett Ferguson (New York: Garland, 1990), 38. Georgios B. Mavromatis, Ἡ Ἀποκάλυψις τοῦ Ἰωάννου με Πατερική Ἀνάλυση (Athens: Apostolike Dianoia, 1994), also places Andrew in the fifth century and, even more surprisingly, places Oikoumenios around 600, well *after* Andrew (21). Panagiotis Chrestou correctly states that Andrew lived in the sixth and seventh centuries. Ἑλληνική Πατρολογία, 5 vols. (Thessalonika: Kyromanos, 1992), 5:514. Also see Panagiotis K. Chrestou in Πατέρες καὶ Θεολόγοι τοῦ Χριστιανισμοῦ, 2 vols. (Thessalonika: Tehnika Studio, 1971), 1:338.

5. See Franz Diekamp, *Texte und Abhandlungen zur Griechischen Patristik*, Orientalia christiana analecta 117 (Rome: Pontifical Institute of Oriental Studies, 1938), 162.

6. Andrew, Epilogue, *Comm.* 246.

it is not entirely impossible. It is more plausible that another bishop or bishops held the see during an intervening period of time, between the end of Theokritos's episcopacy in 563 and Andrew's ascent. Andrew could have occupied the see toward the end of the sixth century, but internal evidence in the commentary suggests that he most definitely served as the Archbishop of Caesarea during the critical first years of the seventh century.

Dating the Oikoumenios Commentary

For centuries, Andrew's commentary was believed to be the first Greek commentary on the Apocalypse. But in fact that distinction must go to Oikoumenios, a late sixth-century writer. We know for certain that while Andrew was writing his own commentary he had before him the earlier Oikoumenios commentary on Revelation, which had probably been authored only a few years prior. Oikoumenios's commentary was not known to have preceded Andrew's until the discovery of an Oikoumenios manuscript in 1901 at Messina by Franz Diekamp.[7]

Ascribing a reliable date for the life and work of Andrew is vitally and inextricably connected to the commentary of Oikoumenios. Oikoumenios provided us with a rough date for his own commentary when he remarked that he was writing more than five hundred years after John experienced his revelation.[8] This places Oikoumenios's work

---

7. Franz Diekamp, "Mittheilungen über den neuaufgefundenen Kommentar des Oekumenius zur Apokalypse," *Sitzungberichte der Königlichen Preussischen Akademie der Wissenschaften* 43 (1901): 1046–56. A commentary had circulated falsely under the name of Oikoumenios since 1532, when Donatus had edited a work wrongly attributed to him. The discovery of the Messina manuscript, now entitled San Salvatore 99, also revealed that the works previously attributed to Oikoumenios which were edited by Cramer in *Catenae Graecorum Patrum* VIII (Oxford: University Press, 1844), 497–582, proved to be nothing more than a conflation of the commentaries of Andrew and Arethas, a tenth century bishop of Caesarea, Cappadocia.

8. "But what does he mean by adding *what must soon take place* since those things which were going to happen have not yet been fulfilled, although a very long time, more than five hundred years has elapsed since this was said?" (Oik. 1.3.6) Oecumenius, *Commentary on the Apocalypse*, 22. Citations to Oikoumenios's commentary are hereinafter abbreviated as Oik. Translated statements of Oikoumenios are cited as FOTC 112 followed by the page number of

at the end of the sixth century and establishes the first parameter for dating Andrew's commentary. Since Andrew's commentary followed Oikoumenios, Andrew could not have written prior to the very end of the sixth or early part of the seventh century.

Discovery of the Oikoumenios commentary proved conclusively that his commentary preceded Andrew's. Andrew mentions Oikoumenios's opinions frequently, usually to refute them but sometimes to add to them. Prior to Diekamp's finding, it was impossible to attribute the references in Andrew's commentary to Oikoumenios, since Andrew never referred to Oikoumenios by name. Instead, Andrew prefaced references to Oikoumenios's opinions with vague statements that gave no clue as to authorship, such as "some say." Since we now possess Oikoumenios's complete commentary, we know that Andrew was in fact frequently referring to Oikoumenios.

Determining Oikoumenios's identity is extremely difficult, partly due to an absence of historical information, further complicated and muddled by a conflation of sources. Oikoumenios, author of the commentary, has been misidentified and confused with a tenth century bishop of Trikki by the same name and further confused with a sixth century Miaphysite count, rhetor, and philosopher of the same name.[9] Diekamp conflated all of these details and concluded that Oikoumenios lived in the first half of the sixth century, that he was a Miaphysite and follower of Severus who later became bishop of Trikki in Thessaly.[10] Diekamp's efforts to harmonize the traditions about Oikoumenios are obviously untenable.

But the errors and inconsistencies continue to be repeated. Some scholars make no attempt to resolve the issue, most recently Charles Kannengiesser.[11] In the entry under "Oecumenius," he describes Oikou-

---

the translation in the Fathers of the Church, vol. 112. Oikoumenios's identity and dating are discussed in greater detail below and in chapter 5.

9. Panagiotis K. Chrestou, Πατέρες καὶ Θεολόγοι 1: 338. Chrestou comments on the problem but does not confuse them.

10. Franz Diekamp, "Mittheilungen," 1046f.

11. Charles Kannengiesser, *Handbook of Patristic Exegesis*, 2 vols. (Brill: Leiden, 2004), 2: 937–38.

menios as "Count of Isauria," "philosopher and rhetor," and "a Monophysite in line with Severus of Antioch" who wrote the first Greek commentary on Revelation five hundred years after the Apocalypse.[12] In that entry Kannengiesser does not refer to Oikoumenios as a bishop and omits the fact that Count Oikoumenios was an actual correspondent with and friend of Severus (not simply "in line with"), which must place Count Oikoumenios in the first half of the century, a fact which renders his authorship of the commentary "five hundred years after" the Apocalypse extremely problematic. Compounding the confusion is Kannengiesser's entry for Andrew of Caesarea on the very next page in which Kannengiesser describes Oikoumenios as "the Thessalian bishop who, a few decades earlier, had written the very first Greek Commentary on the Apocalypse."[13] The second entry curiously contains no reference to Oikoumenios being a rhetor, Monophysite, Count of Isauria, or writing five hundred years after the Apocalypse.

Kannengiesser avoids confronting the discrepancies about Oikoumenios, which admittedly has challenged scholars for decades. Resolving the question of Oikoumenios's identity has been a difficult task and scholars are not in agreement. Perhaps there were two different Oikoumenioi, Count Oikoumenios and a later Commentary Oikoumenios, but they cannot both be credited as the author of the first Greek commentary on the Apocalypse.

Although a known exegete named Oikoumenios served as bishop of Trikki, he lived much later in the tenth century. The fact that he shared this unusual name and was an exegete has contributed to the confusion concerning the identity of the first Greek Apocalypse interpreter. Scholars now almost universally acknowledge that the Oikoumenios who authored the commentary was not the bishop of Trikki. Yet some still believe Oikoumenios, the author of the Apocalypse commentary, to be the sixth century Miaphysite count and rhetor. Scholars are currently divided on two issues: First, the date of the commentary,

---

12. Charles Kannengiesser, *Handbook*, 937.
13. Charles Kannengiesser, *Handbook*, 938.

and second, Oikoumenios's theological orientation, namely whether he was a "Monophysite" or not. The question becomes further complicated since the dating and theology are also interrelated. Oikoumenios appears influenced by Origen and he cites Evagrius Ponticus, both of whom were condemned at the Fifth Ecumenical Council in 553, leading some scholars to conclude that Oikoumenios must have written before then.

With respect to the date, some clues exist to establish an identity and date for Oikoumenios. However, one piece of information is the most crucial for the date of the commentary: Oikoumenios remarks that he is writing more than five hundred years after John witnessed the Apocalypse. This would place his work toward the very end of the sixth century, since Oikoumenios believed that John wrote the Apocalypse during the time of Domitian.[14]

Some scholars maintain that the Oikoumenios who authored the Apocalypse commentary was the sixth-century Miaphysite Oikoumenios, a non-Chalcedonian rhetor and friend of Severus of Antioch.[15] During the first half of the sixth century a certain well-educated Oikoumenios was the governor of Isauria, a province bordering Cappadocia to the south and west. This "Count" Oikoumenios received two letters from the Miaphysite Patriarch of Antioch, Severus, who died in 538.[16] Severus regards him as a friend, refers to his wife, and addresses him as a "Count." Thus, we know that Count Oikoumenios is

---

14. Oik., 1.21.1, 2.13.9 and 12. 20.6. FOTC 112:28, 47–48 and 203.

15. Those who belong to the "Oriental" Orthodox Churches sometimes object to the term "Monophysite," which they believe mischaracterizes their Christology since they accept that Christ is both fully human and fully divine. They identify the term "Monophysite" with the heresy of Eutyches, who held that the human nature of Christ was fused with and dissolved into the divine. They also consider the application of that term to their theology misleading and rather pejorative. "Monophysite" has been employed historically to describe those Christians who rejected Nestorianism but who also did not accept the Ecumenical Council at Chalcedon. Recently, an alternative term is gaining favor, "Miaphysite," which is preferable and more accurate to the extent that it is closer to the Greek terminology and describes the reason why Non-Chalcedonians were given the "Monophysite" designation: they insist on the terminology of "one nature" for Christ (μία φύσις) after the Incarnation of the Logos.

16. Panagiotis K. Chrestou, Ἑλληνική Πατρολογία, 5:512.

an imperial official, married, and engages in theological discussions with Severus. It is clear that this Oikoumenios was a mature man who therefore would have necessarily flourished in the *first* half of the sixth century.

But the Oikoumenios who wrote the commentary clearly indicates that he is writing at the *end* of the sixth century. Commenting on Revelation 1:1, "The Revelation of Jesus Christ which God gave him to show his servants what must take place soon," Oikoumenios writes, "But what does he mean by adding 'what must soon take place' since those things which were going to happen have not yet been fulfilled, although a very long time, more than five hundred years, has elapsed since this was said?"[17]

Numerous efforts have been made to resolve the problem of Oikoumenios's identity by challenging this statement that clearly places the Oikoumenian commentary at the end of the sixth century. Scholars such as Josef Schmid,[18] and more recently John Lamoreaux,[19] and William Weinrich,[20] insist that the author of the Oikoumenian commentary is the same Oikoumenios who was the Miaphysite correspondent of Severus of Antioch in the earlier part of the same century. Adele Monaci Castagno and Marc De Groote, on the other hand, place Oikoumenios at the end of the sixth century.[21] De Groote analyzed the Christological statements in the commentary and compares them with the Christological statements in the correspondence between Count Oikoumenios and Severus, and concluded that the theological interests

---

17. Oik. 1.3.6, FOTC 112: 22.

18. Josef Schmid, "Die griechischen Apokalypse-Kommentare," *Biblische Zeitschrift* 19 (1931): 228–54.

19. John Lamoreaux, "The Provenance of Ecumenios' Commentary on the Apocalypse," *Vigiliae christianae* 52, no. 1 (1998): 88–108.

20. William C. Weinrich, introduction to *Greek Commentaries on Revelation*, trans. William C. Weinrich, ed. Thomas C. Oden, Ancient Christian Texts (Downers Grove, Ill.: InterVarsity Press Academic, 2011), xxiii.

21. See Adele Monaci Castagno, "Il Problema della datazione dei commenti al' Apocalisse di Ecumenio e di Andrea di Cesarea," *Atti della Accademia delle scienze di Torino II, Classe de scienze morali, storiche e filologiche* 114 [1980]: 224–46, 227. Marc De Groote, "Die Quaestio Oecumeniana," *Sacris Eruditi* 36 (1996): 67–105, 97.

and terminology are somewhat different and militate against identifying the two men as the same individual.[22]

One of the most important factors for scholars who place Oikoumenios in the first part of the sixth century is a seventh century Syriac fragment of a catena which includes quotations from the Oikoumenios commentary. The fragment describes Oikoumenios as a correspondent of Severus who also wrote a commentary on the Apocalypse. This could be strong evidence for an earlier date and for identifying Count Oikoumenios with the commentary author, but the fragment is problematic. Scholars would be advised to seriously reconsider the reliability of the fragment. De Groote points to certain concerns with the Syriac fragment, including that the folio in question appears in a different color than the rest of the text, a portion is missing and it is clear that the Syriac fragment was not translated from Greek.[23] Weinrich, who relies to a significant extent on the fragment to identify the two Oikoumenioi as the same individual, notes that the fragment states that the quotation from Oikoumenios within the catena is found in the *sixth* discourse, when in fact it appears in the *eleventh*.[24] The fragment is wrong about the catena itself which it is describing! How reliable, then, is its second-hand information about Oikoumenios, who lived well before the fragment's creation and did not write in Syriac? The fragment *on its face* suggests unreliability. At the very least the fragment raises issues which caution against giving it too much weight, especially when the details it relates contradict evidence within the commentary itself.

As to the interrelationship between dating and theology, John Suggit seems to be persuaded by Lamoreaux's arguments and dates Oikoumenios to the first half of the sixth century, despite Oikoumenios's own statement that he is writing five hundred years after Revelation. Suggit points to Oikoumenios's many peculiar inconsistencies

---

22. Marc De Groote "Die Quaestio," 103
23. Marc De Groote, "Die Quaestio," 82.
24. William C. Weinrich, *Greek Commentaries*, xxi, n. 15.

and Oikoumenios's citation of Evagrius, who was condemned at the Fifth Ecumenical Council along with Origen.[25] Suggit and Lamoreaux conclude that Oikoumenios wrote prior to 553 because they believe he would not have cited Evagrius otherwise.[26] Suggit writes: "In view of Oikoumenios' insistence on his own orthodoxy ... it is unlikely that he would refer to Evagrius in such terms after 553."[27]

However, neither Suggit nor Lamoreaux appear to consider the reality that, as a Miaphysite, Oikoumenios would *not* have recognized *any* Ecumenical Council after Ephesus in 431. Thus, the decision by Chalcedonians to condemn Origen and Evagrius would not have impacted Oikoumenios's use of those sources. Likewise, Adele Monaci Castagno also interprets Oikoumenios from her own historical or religious perspective and ignores the perspective of Oikoumenios himself. She concludes that Oikoumenios was "not Monophysite" because he attempts to align himself with the theological position of "the Church."[28] She seemly never considers the fact that Miaphysites, and certainly Oikoumenios himself, considered themselves part of "the Church," even comprising the *only* Church. Those who did *not* conform to Miaphysite views—including Chalcedonian Christians—were the ones whom Oikoumenios would have considered to be "outside" the Church, certainly not himself! De Groote makes the same argument as Castagno regarding Oikoumenios's openness to the doctrine of *apokatastasis*.[29] Oikoumenios accepts this idea as a possibility but also wishes to align himself with "the dogma of the Church," which recognizes punishment as eternal.[30] De Groote discusses the extent to which

---

25. FOTC 112: 4–6.
26. John Lamoreaux, "Provenance," 101–8.
27. FOTC 112:5–6.
28. Adele Monaci Castagno, "I Commenti de Ecumenio e di Andrea di Cesarea: Due letture divergenti dell' Apocalisse," *Memorie della Accademia delle scienze di Torino II, Classe di scienze morali, storiche e filologiche* V, Fascicolo IV, (1981): 303–424, 324.
29. The "restoration" of all things, a belief identified with Origen that in the end, all would be saved. This was condemned as heresy by the Church at the Fifth Ecumenical Council at Constantinople in 553. See chapter 14.
30. Oik. 5.19.2.

Oikoumenios might be using the term "dogma" in an absolute sense, presumably since this suggests a particular theological orientation.[31] But again, the critical question is *whose* orthodoxy does Oikoumenios represent? Furthermore, and more significant, is not the question of how Oikoumenios understands "dogma" but which group constitutes "the Church" for him?

Because Oikoumenios wishes to align himself with "the Church," rather than proving that he was a Chalcedonian, or pointing to an earlier date for the commentary due to his citation of Evagrius and his Origenistic tendencies, these details work toward the opposite conclusion. They help to identify Oikoumenios as a Miaphysite, since non-Chalcedonians then, as now, do not recognize any Ecumenical Council after Ephesus in 431. De Groote appropriately notes that due to efforts during this period to find a theological compromise, Christological terminology developed which was common to both sides. This, coupled with the fact that the commentary bears no hint of antagonism toward the empire which had engaged in some persecution of Miaphysites, leads De Groote to the conclusion that Oikoumenios was a neo-Chalcedonian.[32] However, it is rather risky to draw conclusions based upon what we might expect to find in an author's work, rather than basing our opinions on what the author reveals about himself from his own words. Furthermore, the commentary might have been composed during the reign of Tiberius II (574–582), a period which De Groote himself acknowledges as free of imperial persecution of Miaphysites.[33]

Theological evidence of Oikoumenios's Miaphysite identity is discussed in detail below in chapter 6. However, it deserves to be mentioned here that one important source to examine the question Oikoumenios's dating and identity, a source which has not been heretofore considered by scholars, is Andrew of Caesarea's commentary and its relationship to the Oikoumenian commentary.

The fact that the Oikoumenios commentary barely survived antiqui-

---

31. Marc De Groote, Die *Quaestio*," 103.   32. Marc De Groote, Die *Quaestio*," 100–2.
33. Marc De Groote, Die *Quaestio*," 100.

ty seems to suggest a later dating particularly because of the apocalyptic atmosphere at the time. The commentary only exists in one complete copy and only in Greek. A date closer to that of Andrew's commentary might help explain why the Oikoumenios commentary was not more prodigiously copied. If more time elapsed between the appearance of the commentary of Oikoumenios and that of Andrew—several decades if Count Oikoumenios and Commentary Oikoumenios are the same individual—this would have given much more time for the Oikoumenios commentary to be copied and circulate to a far greater degree, which may have resulted in more copies surviving. As the first—and only Greek commentary on Revelation until Andrew's composition—Oikoumenios's commentary would have been in great demand especially during the apocalyptic climate of the mid to late sixth century. This is speculative, of course, but a late sixth century date may be one factor why Oikoumenios's commentary did not achieve more recognition before it was eclipsed by the work of Andrew, whose commentary proved considerably more popular.

As to Oikoumenios's theology, Andrew's consistent correction of Oikoumenios and, in particular, Andrew's statements which appear to be Chalcedonian responses to Oikoumenios, should be considered when arriving at conclusions about Oikoumenios's identity. We may be uncertain as to the precise identity of Oikoumenios, but Andrew was *not*. He knew who Oikoumenios was and he knew Oikoumenios's theology. Andrew's statements as an interlocutor of Oikoumenios should be seriously considered as clues to Oikoumenios's theological orientation.

One of Lamoreaux's primary arguments for identifying Count Oikoumenios and Commentary Oikoumenios as the same individual is that it is extremely unlikely that two highly educated men with the "unusual" name of Oikoumenios could have lived in the same century. This is an extremely weak argument, given the fact that local and chronological preferences exist for certain names, especially uncommon names. The name is not common today, but do we truly know how common it was at the time? Traditional preferences for names existed then, and still do in many parts in the world. Rather than opting for "unique" names as parents often do today, for centuries parents chose names which were meaningful and not unusual for their particular cultural group and locale.

Furthermore, Lamoreaux and other scholars do not seem to consider the possibility that the commentary could have been falsely attributed to the well-known earlier figure of Oikoumenios since the earliest manuscript of the Oikoumenios commentary does not bear his name.[34] It is not impossible that there were two learned men with the name Oikoumenios in the sixth century and that they were confused with one another, or, more likely, that the commentary was originally unsigned and at a later date was attributed to the earlier well-known Count and Miaphysite Oikoumenios and passed along with his name attached.

Dating the Oikoumenios commentary in the first half of the sixth century would neatly provide us with an important bishop named "Makarios" as a potential recipient of Andrew's commentary, since this appellation is an important clue as to the intended recipient of Andrew's commentary. However, in dating the Oikoumenios commentary we cannot circumvent, and certainly should not ignore, the explicit statement of the author himself. If the evidence is objectively analyzed, the conclusion that the commentary was composed by the earlier Oikoumenios, the Miaphysite rhetor and friend of Severus, must be rejected. A desire to neatly wrap up Oikoumenios's identity by dismissing Oikoumenios's *own* reference to the date as a mistake, as Schmid does, or straining to interpret the statement "five hundred years after" the Revelation as a reference to Christ's Incarnation, as Lamoreaux does, is unsupportable and lacks credibility. Such logic is weak, somewhat circuitous, and the reasoning is not persuasive. Lamoreaux's argument that what Oikoumenios actually *meant* is five hundred years since the

---

34. See Adele Monaci Castagno, "Il Problema," 227.

Incarnation, is a highly strained effort to place Oikoumenios in the early part of the sixth century.[35]

The greatest weight must be given to Oikoumenios's clear statement that he is writing more than five hundred years after the Revelation was received and related by John. Oikoumenios writes, "Five hundred years since this was *said,*" thus clearly and unequivocally pointing to five hundred years after John's *experience* not five hundred years after the Incarnation. To support his idea, Lamoreaux points to the sentence which follows. Oikoumenios remarks that a thousand years are like yesterday to God, like a watch in the night, in other words, a brief amount of time for God.[36] Lamoreaux uses this comment to introduce doubt regarding Oikoumenios's statement that he is writing five hundred years after the Revelation. But Oikoumenios makes the "thousand years" comment as an explanation for the fact that Revelation itself says that the prophesied events must take place "soon" (Rev. 1:1). The "thousand years" does not impact the date of Oikoumenios's composition, which he has already given as "five hundred years" after the prophecy announcing these events "was *said.*" The reference to "soon" is the reason Oikoumenios mentions that "a thousand years" is virtually no time for God. It does not operate to annul the date which Oikoumenios has created for his commentary, over five hundred years since the Revelation was given to John.

Oikoumenios's own clear statement about the times in which he lived deserves to be respected. Any scholar would have to counter the author's own statement with overwhelming evidence to convincingly argue that the Oikoumenios who was the correspondent of Severus at the beginning of the century and the Oikoumenios who wrote a commentary on the Apocalypse the end of the sixth century are the same individual. As satisfying as it might be to resolve the mystery of Oikoumenios's identity by connecting the two, Oikoumenios's unequivocal statement about the dating of his commentary makes this associa-

---

35. John Lamoreaux, "Provenance," 88–108.
36. Oik. 1.3.6, citing Ps. 89(88).4. See FOTC 112:22.

tion impossible. Despite concerted efforts to explain away, discount, or creatively reinterpret the plain meaning of the author's "more than five hundred years" statement in order to identify Oikoumenios the author of the commentary with Oikoumenios the friend of Severus of Antioch, the two cannot be reconciled. The identity of Oikoumenios the Commentator remains a mystery.

Dating Andrew of Caesarea's Apocalypse Commentary

Oikoumenios provides the initial parameter for dating Andrew's commentary: it could not have been composed prior to Oikoumenios's commentary in the late sixth century. What remains to be established is the other parameter for our chronology. The latest possible date for the composition of Andrew's commentary is the Persian conquest and destruction of Jerusalem in 614 because Andrew refers to the city as under the rule of "pious ones," that is, Christian Roman emperors.[37] Many scholars surmise that Andrew's commentary was composed not only prior to the sack of Jerusalem, but also prior to the Persian sack of Caesarea in 610 and that Andrew's episcopal reign had ceased by then. This conclusion is based on the opinion that Andrew made no reference to the sack of Caesarea in his commentary on the Apocalypse. However, the commentary contains three references to "barbarian" invasions as well as other clues that Andrew had in fact experienced the conquest of Caesarea. Twice Andrew refers to "bloodshed" by barbarian hands,[38] and later Andrew refers to "the unspeakable misfortunes encircling us by barbarian hands."[39]

An additional and easily overlooked clue can also be found in Andrew's comments about the swiftness of the fall of Babylon in Revelation 18:8. The biblical text reads: "So shall her plagues come in a single day, pestilence and mourning and famine, and she shall be burned

---

37. Andrew, Chap. 52, *Comm.* 179.
38. Andrew, Chap. 22, *Comm.* 115; Chap. 27 *Comm.* 125.
39. Andrew, Chap. 49, *Comm.* 172.

with fire; for mighty is the Lord God who judges her." Andrew mentions how quickly evils and deaths of various kinds can take place after "enemies" take the city. But there are no "enemies" in the scenario presented in the text of Revelation itself: *God* destroys Babylon. Andrew's comments betray his own recent experience:

> [It is] in the course of this [same] day in which these things prophesied will prevail over her. For after the enemies have taken control of the city, it suffices that in one day all of the evils are to be brought upon the defeated ones and various manners of death.[40]

Another reference also indirectly hints at important details which help to narrow the time frame and suggests that Andrew had witnessed disasters on a great scale. Andrew quotes from a section of Eusebius's *Ecclesiastical History*, which describes famine, plague, an Armenian revolt, and casualties so numerous that there were not enough people to bury the dead.[41] Andrew then remarks: "In our own generation we have known each of these happenings."[42] In the decades prior to the composition of Andrew's commentary, seven waves of bubonic plague had scourged the empire, beginning in 541 during the reign of Justinian and continuing through 610.[43] The loss of population due to the plague adversely affected planting and harvests triggering famines, which were further compounded by severe winters in the early seventh century, civil war in the empire and war with the Persians.[44] The Armenians had revolted against the Persian and the Roman Empires on numerous occasions but the revolt which occurred nearest the time of the composition of Andrew's commentary took place in 572.[45] Andrew's community had recently experienced famine, plague, and an Armenian revolt, just

---

40. Andrew, Chap. 55, *Comm.* 192.   41. Eusebius, *E.H.* 9.8.
42. Andrew, Chap. 16, *Comm.* 95.
43. Warren Treadgold, *A History of Byzantine State and Society* (Stanford: Stanford University Press, 1997), 276.
44. See chapter 5 for additional details on the historical milieu.
45. Warren Treadgold, *A History*, 222. When the Armenians had revolted against their Persian governor, the Roman emperor Justin II came to their aid, triggering a prolonged war with Persia. The Persians attacked regions in eastern parts of the empire, successfully cap-

as Eusebius had described. However, the most critical clue is Andrew's statement that they had experienced so many casualties that there were not enough among the living to bury the dead. Internal evidence thus strongly suggests that his commentary was written in the context of the traumatic events of the early seventh century, primarily the Persian invasion and sack of Caesarea.

The Persians had raided the eastern areas of the Roman empire for decades. The Euphrates River was located approximately 300 kilometers east of Caesarea, Cappadocia. The Euphrates did not mark the border with Persia, which actually lay another 200 kilometers further to the east. The area between the Euphrates River and the Persian border further east was subjected to countless Persian incursions over the centuries. Border cites which were situated on the immediate frontier, such as Dara and Nisibis, were often raided and changed hands often. They were frequently captured and held by the Persians until liberated by the Romans. This pattern occurred time and again. Andrew's commentary was not composed in the context of these earlier raids which occurred regularly prior to the seventh century. Raids and border skirmishes were smaller scale military conflicts and transpired too far away to have threatened Caesarea or other cities deeper within the empire. But a full scale Persian invasion did occur in the early seventh century which unquestionably frames the historical context and forms the final parameter necessary to date this commentary.

In the early seventh century, the Persians not only took and devastated border towns, but continued further into Roman territory to capture cities well within the Empire's borders but which were still located east of the Euphrates, such as Amida, Edessa, and Martyropolis. The

---

turing the Roman border city of Dara in 573 and sacking other border areas. In 590, during these on-going skirmishes with the Romans, a leading Persian general revolted against the Persian king. The heir to the Persian throne, Khosrov II, fled into Roman territory. When the Roman Emperor Maurice assisted Khosrov II to recapture his throne the following year, the Persians returned the captured territory to the Romans. Peace was temporarily established between the two empires and for a few years the two sides cooperated in quelling Armenian revolts. Treadgold, *A History*, 230–32.

two massive Persian armies then *crossed* the Euphrates River, which had historically served as a natural barrier protecting the empire from eastern invaders. The Euphrates had long been important as a geographic obstacle which inhibited Persian invasion. The ancient expectation, already centuries old, that the end-times would be signified by the appearance of invaders from the east who crossed the Euphrates, is reflected in the Apocalypse itself.[46] This belief was well known among Christians, even those who did not accept the Apocalypse as Scripture. For the Romans of Late Antiquity, this monumental crossing resulted in actual, physical devastation. But the psychological impact was also tremendous. The prophetic and religious significance of enemies traversing the Euphrates was unquestionably monumental and must have contributed to the appeals for Andrew to compose the commentary.

After crossing the Euphrates, the entire east lay open to the Persians, areas which had not experienced invasion in hundreds of years. The armies continued westward plundering and destroying, slaughtering the inhabitants of cities that resisted and taking as prisoners the occupants of cities which had surrendered. One force, led by the Persian general Shahrbaraz, moved southward, laying waste to massive territory and quickly taking many cities, including Hierapolis, Antioch, and Damascus. To the north, a second army led by the general Shahin, took cites such as Melitene, Sebaste, Satala, Comana, and Caesarea, Cappadocia. The scale of death and destruction to which Andrew clearly alludes, coupled by the highly significant crossing of the

46. See Rev. 9:13–16: "And the sixth angel blew the trumpet, and I heard a voice from the four horns of the golden altar before God, saying to the sixth angel who has the trumpet, 'Release the four angels who are bound up at the great river Euphrates.' And the four angels were released, who had been held ready for the hour, the day, the month, and the year, in order to kill a third of humankind. The number of the troops of cavalry was twice ten thousand times ten thousand. I heard their number." See also Rev. 16:12: "And the sixth angel began to pour out his bowl on the great river Euphrates. And the water was dried up, to prepare the way for the kings from the east." Regarding this second passage, Andrew writes: "Probably by divine permission the Euphrates is lessened to give passage to the kings of the nations for the purpose of them utterly destroying one another and the rest of humanity, which [kings] we think were set into motion out of parts of Scythia recalling Gog and Magog, according to that which is brought out later in the Apocalypse." Andrew, Chap. 51, *Comm.* 175.

Euphrates River, leaves no doubt that this commentary was composed in the context of these momentous events.

Unfortunately, the seventh century, especially the earliest years, is among the worst documented periods of history. Not only are sources very limited, but the few dates available among the sources frequently conflict, often by a year or more.[47] Confusion and disagreement persist among historians regarding precisely when Caesarea was captured by the Persians and for how long it remained occupied. Some sources suggest that the Persians remained in Caesarea for three years until they were forced out by the Romans in 613, but it is more likely that that they moved on to conquer other areas and later returned. Recently consensus seems to be gaining among scholars that Caesarea, Cappadocia, was actually taken by the Persians *twice* within two years, the first time in 609 or 610, and then again in 611.[48] The first capture occurred while the empire was engaged in a civil war between factions led by Phocas, a usurper to the throne, and Heraclius. The Persians took full advantage of the chaos to make an incursion westward toward Constantinople, which they never actually reached. In the meantime, Heraclius arrived in Constantinople in 610 and killed the tyrant, Phocas. Heraclius was crowned emperor, began to restore order, and immediately mounted a campaign to push the Persians back. The second capture of Caesarea occurred in 611 during the retreat of the Persian army on its way back to Persia. In that instance, they not only sacked the city but they occupied it for one year while the Roman army besieged them. They finally quit the city in 612 and as they withdrew, the Persians set fire to Caesarea and completely destroyed the city.[49]

---

47. See J. F. Haldon's prefatory chapter about the sources of the period, in *Byzantium in the Seventh Century* (Cambridge: Cambridge University Press, 1990, rev. ed. 1997), xxi–xxvii. Haldon writes, "For a historian of the seventh century, the interrelationship between evidence and hypothesis plays a more than usually central role" (xxviii). See also Warren Treadgold, *A History*, 905, on the problems with the sources of this period.

48. J. F. Haldon, *Byzantium in the Seventh Century*, 103. Warren Treadgold, *A History*, 288; Andreas Stratos, *Byzantium in the Seventh Century*, 5 vols., trans. by Marc Ogilvie-Grant (Amsterdam: Hakkert, 1968), 1:104–5.

49. Clive Foss dates the capture of Caesarea at 611 and states that the Persians occupied

While Andrew makes veiled references to these traumatic events, he does not suggest any knowledge of a far more momentous historical event: the Persian sack of Jerusalem by the army which had marched southward, led by General Shahrbaraz. This took place in 614 and also resulted in unspeakable carnage. As was the case for many other eastern cities, the Persian assault on Jerusalem was nothing less than catastrophic. Thousands of people were put to the sword and survivors were taken away into slavery. For the sheer scale of human suffering both the events at Caesarea and Jerusalem would have had an immense effect on Andrew. But in the case of Jerusalem, the trauma rocked the entire Christian world. Not only did Jerusalem experience bloodshed and destruction on a massive scale, as did Caesarea, but the Persians destroyed countless monasteries and churches on sacred sites associated with the life of Christ. The staggering losses included the Church of the Resurrection which contained both the site of Golgotha and the tomb of Christ. The Persians even captured "the True Cross."[50] Those who escaped the initial massacre[51] were made captives and taken back to Persia as slaves.[52] Among them was the Patriarch of Jerusalem, Zacharias.

---

the city for one year and burned it when they withdrew. Clive Foss, "The Persians in Asia Minor at the end of Antiquity," *The English Historical Review* 96 (1975): 721–43. Kaegi concurs. See W. E. Kaegi, Jr., "New Evidence on the Early Reign of Heraclius," *Byzantinische Zeitschrift* 66 [1973]: 308–30, 323. This was only the beginning of many such tragic occurrences for the city. In fact, Caesarea was sacked four times between 636 and 740 (J. F. Haldon, *Byzantium in the Seventh Century*, 107), most notably in 647 by the Syrians and in 726 by the Arabs. The city was later sacked again by various parties: in 1067 by the second sultan of the Seltsak, in 1243 by the Mongols and finally by the Ottoman Turks, also in the thirteenth century.

50. Perhaps the single most important relic of the Christian Roman empire, the True Cross was believed to be the actual cross of Christ, reportedly discovered by Helen, mother of Constantine the Great, during her fourth century pilgrimage to the Holy Land. She was responsible for constructing numerous churches on sites identified with events in the life of Christ which the Persians destroyed during this invasion.

51. The number of dead, arrived at by an actual count of the bodies, was 66,509 people. "Antiochus Strategos: The Capture of Jerusalem by the Persians in 614 AD," trans. F. C. Conybeare, *English Historical Review* 25 (1910): 502–17, 515–16. Details about the sack of Jerusalem, as well as what transpired for the captives who were taken back to Persia, were preserved in a very gripping and heartbreaking account composed by a monk, Antiochus Strategos, who was an eyewitness to the events and recorded them.

52. Approximately 35,000 captives were taken to Persia as slaves from Jerusalem. Sebeos

Drawing conclusions from silence is hazardous. The absence of reference does not necessarily mean an absence of knowledge. However, in the context of a commentary on the Book of Revelation, the absence of any express or implied reference to the sack of Jerusalem is far more significant than the absence of explicit references to the sack of Caesarea because of Jerusalem's special historical, spiritual, theological, and prophetic importance, especially in relation to Revelation. Andrew clearly refers to Jerusalem as a Christian-controlled city.[53] One might expect that the sack of one's own city would more likely warrant a specific reference than the sack of another city, even that of Jerusalem. But notice that the anonymous compiler of the *Chronicon Paschale*, writing in Constantinople not many years later, simply observes that numerous cities were destroyed by the Persians during this period without mentioning any of the cities by name, except for Jerusalem.[54]

It also seems unlikely that Andrew would have devoted time to writing a commentary immediately after either of the sacks which Caesarea had experienced, since he would probably have been leading efforts to provide relief for the populace, ransoming captives and organizing reconstruction efforts. By this period of history, bishops usually took the initiative to organize civic activities and relief efforts during a crisis. As the archbishop, Andrew would have shouldered a significant amount of responsibility for the city. In late antiquity, episcopal leadership in

---

24, *The Armenian History Attributed to Sebeos*, trans. R. W. Thomson and commentary by James Howard-Johnston, Translated Texts for Historians 31 (Liverpool: Liverpool University Press, 1999).

53. The city is ruled by "pious ones," i.e., Christian kings. Andrew, Chap. 52, *Comm.* 179.

54. The author of the *Chronicon Paschale* devotes a detailed paragraph to the sack of Jerusalem, which reads as follows: "In this year [614] about the month of June, we suffered a calamity which deserves unceasing lamentations. For, together with many cites of the east, Jerusalem too was captured by the Persians, and in it were slain many thousands of clerics, monks, and virgin nuns. The Lord's tomb was burnt and the far-famed temples of God, and, in short, all of the precious things were destroyed. The venerated wood of the Cross, together with the holy vessels that were beyond enumeration, was taken by the Persians, and the Patriarch Zacharias also became a prisoner." *Chronicon Paschale*, trans. Michael Whitby and Mary Whitby, Translated Texts for Historians 7 (Liverpool: Liverpool University Press, 1989), 156.

civic matters was the norm, not the exception.[55] One would expect at least a year to elapse before the worst effects of the sacks had subsided and some measure of stability and normalcy was restored in the city. If the first sack of Caesarea occurred in 609 or 610, we should allow for a reasonable intervening period of time in the aftermath to address the needs and problems of the population which would have demanded Andrew's time and leadership. It is reasonable to conclude, therefore, that he wrote the commentary in 610/611, after the first conquest, when the city had been taken yet not destroyed, but prior to the return of the Persians in 612 which began their year-long occupation that culminated in the complete destruction of Caesarea by fire.

An alternative possibility is that Andrew wrote the commentary subsequent to the second sack, after the occupation of the city had ended. In that instance, again, allowing time for his efforts helping the city rebuild and recover, the commentary might have been written in 613. However, since we know that upon their return the Persians occupied the city for an entire year and burnt it as they withdrew, considering the likely devastation to the populace and to the city's infrastructure,

55. Warren Treadgold notes: "With the decline of city councils, bishops were often the most powerful men in their cities, and were on a par with the provincial governors whom they helped to select. Bishops judged court cases and conducted civic business whenever those involved the Church, and sometimes when they did not. The clergy and monks, all subject to their local bishops, numbered in the tens of thousands, far surpassing the bureaucracy and approaching the army in size. The churches of Constantinople, Alexandria, and Antioch possessed a great many church buildings, monasteries, and charitable institutions, besides wholly secular properties with income that contributed to church salaries and charities. Lesser sees had smaller but still substantial buildings, endowments and incomes" *A History*, 259. "Few of the remaining decurions were still influential in their cities, where the leaders were men of higher rank, and increasingly the bishops. Beginning with the reign of Anastasius, bishops had a voice in choosing local officials, including provincial governors. Justinian gave bishops jurisdiction over many civil cases in their courts and in some cases precedence over governors." Warren Treadgold, *A History*, 257. Andreas Stratos also writes about the significant involvement of bishops in the administration of the empire. *Byzantium in the Seventh Century*, 1:8. See also A. H. M Jones, *The Greek City from Alexander to Justinian* (Oxford: Clarendon Press, 1940), 209, on episcopal involvement in electing city officials and 253–54, on episcopal responsibilities for providing not only charitable services, but also assisting with various public expenditures normally borne by the city, such as the construction of baths and aqueducts.

a date of 613 for the composition of the commentary seems unlikely. We do not know the exact circumstances within Caesarea following the second sack, but it is difficult to imagine that Andrew would have found time to compose the commentary after the second sack but prior to the shocking destruction of Jerusalem in 614. A year-long siege by the Roman army to liberate Caesarea would have depleted all the resources within the city and greatly ravaged the surrounding countryside as well. Agricultural production would have been disrupted, leading to food shortages within the city and its environs. These difficult conditions would have continued long after the Persians had withdrawn. This second, catastrophic sack involved the destruction of city walls and the destruction by fire of many homes, merchant establishments and other significant infrastructures needed for daily life. In addition, the second sack and the resulting fire would have meant the complete destruction of churches and the destruction or theft of many valuables, including liturgical items, and probably even the loss by fire of the episcopal library which Andrew would have needed for the composition of his commentary. Since the second sack resulted in the total destruction of the city, the commentary could not have been composed at Caesarea within the short period of time after the second sack and destruction of Caesarea in 613 but prior to the destruction of Jerusalem in 614.

The question must be asked whether Andrew would have had the resources available to write a commentary even after the first capture of Caesarea. The Persians were known for their devastating destruction of cities and the massacre of populations. Not long before the capture of Caesarea, the Persian king Khosrov had captured the border city of Dara in 604, approximately 400 kilometers from Caesarea, where he not only destroyed the walls and plundered the city but "put all [the inhabitants] to the sword."[56] When Khosrov returned to Persia from Dara and other expeditions he had conducted at that time, he or-

---

56. Sebeos 31, *Armenian History*, 58. This was the same king whom Maurice had helped to acquire his throne. See n. 45. When Maurice was assassinated by the army officer, Phocas, who seized the throne, this gave Khosrov an excuse to invade the Roman empire, supposedly to avenge his benefactor.

ganized the two armies to be led Shahin and Shahrbaraz for the full-scale invasion of Roman territory.[57] According to the historian Sebeos, "He gave them the following order: 'Receive in a friendly way those who will submit, and keep them in peace and prosperity. But put to the sword those who may offer resistance and make war.'"[58] Syrian cities which submitted, such as Edessa, were spared destruction.[59] Soon after this, Sebeos briefly chronicles the first capture of Caesarea when the Persian general Shahin "made an incursion, raiding the regions of the west and reaching Caesarea of Cappadocia. Then the Christian inhabitants of the city left the city and departed. But the Jews went out to meet him and submitted."[60] Since the Jewish citizens of Caesarea surrendered and opened the city gates, the city would have been spared destruction at that time and Andrew would still have his library available to him during the period following the first Persian conquest and occupation.[61]

Even if most of the Christians left the city, it is almost certain that Andrew would have remained in Caesarea. Not only would this be the most common course of action for a bishop, but his references to "barbarians," "bloodshed," and being "surrounded," strongly suggest that he in fact remained in Caesarea. It is impossible to account for these references, and especially the reference to the vast numbers of dead, if he had fled prior to the arrival of the Persians. Although some bishops departed when faced with foreign invasion,[62] most would not have

57. Andreas Stratos, *Byzantium in the Seventh Century*, 63–65.
58. Sebeos, 33. *Armenian History*, 62–63.   59. Sebeos, 33, *Armenian History*, 63.
60. Sebeos, 33, *Armenian History*, 64.
61. The inhabitants of Jerusalem also surrendered and the city was not initially destroyed. After the Persian army had continued on its way toward Alexandria, a few youths killed the Persian officers who had been left in charge at Jerusalem. When the Persians learned of the revolt, they returned and destroyed the city, killing approximately 66,000 people and leading the survivors back to Persia into slavery. Sebeos, 34.115–16, *Armenian History* 68–69. See n. 54.
62. If Andrew had fled the city he would have almost certainly gone to Constantinople because of his rank within the Church and the safety of its fortifications. When the Armenians rebelled against the Persians from 571 to 572 and revolution erupted, the Armenian Patriarch, Catholikos John, sought refuge in Constantinople. Andreas Stratos, *Byzantium in the Seventh*

abandoned their sees.⁶³ What is absolutely certain from the historical record is that when the Persians returned they occupied Caesarea for one year while the Romans besieged the city in an effort to push the Persians out, and that when the Persians finally left they set the city on fire.⁶⁴

A date for the commentary cannot be based on one or two historical events or details within the commentary. However, taking into consideration *all* of these factors in their *totality*, allows us to conclude with a significant degree of confidence that Andrew's commentary was written after the initial capture of Caesarea in 609/10, but prior to the sack of Jerusalem in 614. The most likely date for the composition of the commentary is 611, subsequent to the first capture of Caesarea and allowing for a period of time to recover from its effects, but prior to the second occupation in 612 and its catastrophic destruction in 613.

Century, 22. When the Persian general Shahrbaraz was marching toward Egypt in 616, John, the Patriarch of Alexandria, left for Constantinople (113). If Andrew *had* fled to Constantinople, he might have been urged to write the commentary during his stay there, since he would have had the patriarchal library at his disposal. But if he had indeed fled the city in advance of the Persian army it would be difficult to explain his comments, such as "the unspeakable misfortunes encircling us by barbarian hands." Andrew, Chap. 49, *Comm.* 172.

63. A memorable example is the Patriarch of Jerusalem, Zacharias, who could have fled but remained in the city when the Persians attacked. He was captured and taken to Persia as a slave. *Chronicon*, trans. Michael Whitby and Mary Whitby, 156.

64. Sebeos 34.113, *Armenian History*, 66.

5

ANDREW'S RECIPIENT

"Makarios" and the Historical Milieu

Understanding Oikoumenios's commentary is critical to the Andreas commentary. Not only does it provide a clue for dating Andrew, but the existence of the Oikoumenian commentary was likely a primary factor prompting a request for Andrew's commentary and motivating its composition. In the opening sentence of his commentary, Andrew refers to a number of unnamed persons who had appealed to him to write a commentary on the Book of Revelation. Apparently he resisted until he received a request from an individual whose exact identity is unclear. This person, whom Andrew addresses as "Blessed One" or "Makarios," apparently made a request that could not be denied, thus compelling the composition of the commentary.[1] The only concrete clue as to Makarios's identity, other than possibly the name itself, is found in the very first line: Andrew refers to Makarios as "my lord brother and co-celebrant."[2] This can only mean that Makarios was a clergyman. Had it not been for this detail, our search for the man who prompted this commentary could have included men of political or social prominence. With this detail, we can safely exclude them.[3]

---

1. Andrew, Prologue, *Comm.* 52.
2. συλλειτουργός. Andrew, Prologue, *Comm.* 51.
3. Had this detail not been included, one could argue that "Makarios" or "Blessed One"

Even though "co-celebrant" might include any clergyman, we can confidently exclude men holding only priestly rank and look instead for a fellow bishop, on account of the additional title "lord" and other clues regarding Andrew's relationship to Makarios. Most likely, Makarios was a hierarch of great importance in the church, probably ranking higher than Andrew. We can assume this for a number of reasons. First, Andrew is pressed to write a commentary on Revelation, which he would rather not write. Second, the commentary is in fact personally addressed to Makarios and to him alone. Third, despite the fact that "many people" had requested that Andrew write this commentary, he had declined these requests repeatedly. But when Makarios made the request, Andrew acquiesced. In addition, we should not assume that Andrew was insincere, feigning reluctance to assume this task or expressing false modesty. Of all the books of the Bible, Revelation is by far the most difficult to interpret. Many famous exegetes shrank from the task. If Makarios is indeed a superior hierarch, Andrew writes from a sense of obligation, out of obedience or, possibly, but less likely, out of great affection. More than once in the early lines of the commentary, Andrew mentions a sense of obligation to Makarios. Consequently, Makarios is a man to whom Andrew feels significantly obligated, perhaps as a close personal friend, but most likely as someone to whom Andrew must obediently acquiesce by reason of his superior rank.

Protestations of inadequacy or expressions of modesty with respect to one's abilities were common features in ancient prologues. However, Andrew addresses Makarios not with a tone of friendship, often seen in other prologues, but with a greater degree of deference than is typi-

---

might refer to any reader of the commentary, in the same manner that some have suggested that the recipient of the Gospel of Luke and Acts of the Apostles, Theophilus, (whose name means "One who loves God" or "Friend of God"), was not a real person but a literary device employed by the author of Luke-Acts to address the books to anyone who loves God. Absent the descriptive detail "co-liturgist," a persuasive argument could be have been made that Makarios represents the reader of the commentary, especially since Revelation contains seven beatitudes, all of which begin "Makarios" ("Blessed is the one who" in 1:3; 14:13; 16:15; 19:9; 20:6; 22:6; 22:14), some of which are directed specifically at the reader of Revelation.

cal. Emphasis on submission to the request and being designated this responsibility suggests that his statements do not simply reflect the ordinary literary convention of modesty or expressions of ecclesiastical protocol. Andrew writes the commentary only at the request of Makarios. He notes his "obedience"[4] to the request *three* times and states that he hopes to shortly complete the task which had been "assigned" to him.[5] A final consideration is Andrew's status as the highest ranking bishop in the region, second only to the Patriarch of Constantinople in his jurisdiction. If Makarios is not a close personal friend, someone to whom Andrew acquiesces out of affection, then Makarios would likely not have been an ordinary bishop. Since Andrew himself held such a high rank in the church, Makarios would have been a bishop of even higher rank, one whose request Andrew feels obligated or compelled to accommodate.

A review of the names of the bishops on the five patriarchal thrones during the late sixth and early seventh centuries reveals no one bearing the proper name "Makarios" who fits our time frame, a time frame for which we have significant confidence.[6] A certain Makarios II served as Patriarch of Jerusalem in 552, was deposed, and then restored to occupy the see again from 563 to 575. It might have been appropriate to consider him as a potential recipient of this commentary since his name was Makarios and a possible start for Andrew's episcopal reign has been given as early as 563. But we know that Andrew wrote *after* Oikoumenios. The date of our commentary depends upon the dating of Oikoumenios, which we have previously resolved by concluding that Oikoumenios wrote at the very end of the sixth century. Since Oikoumenios wrote at the end of the sixth century, Makarios II of Jerusalem cannot be the recipient of the commentary by Andrew.

Had we found a patriarch or other notable hierarch with the given name Makarios, we might conclude that we had found our man. Since we have found no hierarch ranking higher than Andrew who bears the

---

4. ὑπακοή. See Andrew, Prologue, *Comm.* 51, 52, and 53.
5. τὸ ἐπιταχθέν. Andrew, Prologue, *Comm.* 52.
6. See chapter 4.

actual name, "Makarios," we must consider another possibility. While Makarios is in fact a proper Greek name, it could have been used by Andrew as a title of address according to its literal meaning: "Blessed One." Andrew only addresses Makarios once, in the prologue of the commentary, and in that instance the name takes the form of a direct address, necessitating the use of the vocative case: "Μακάριε."[7] Because it appears in the vocative case, it is impossible to ascertain whether the word was being employed as a title of address or an actual name.

The actual given name of the addressee might in fact be "Makarios." But since it appears that someone of *higher* rank induced Andrew to write the commentary and we have no one on record by that name occupying any of the patriarchal sees within our established time frame, it appears more likely that "Μακάριε" is employed by Andrew as a deferential title, "Blessed One," or a form of address equal to "Your Beatitude." Precedent exists for this use of the word as a term of address for bishops by this time and also simply as a literary device to address the reader.[8] As a matter of fact, it is so used by three of the authors whom Andrew employed for his commentary: Methodios of Olympos, Pseudo-Dionysios, and Athanasius the Great.[9] In Andrew's case, we know it was not a phrase employed to address a general readership because the commentary addresses the reader as "my lord brother and co-celebrant."[10]

If "Μακάριε" functioned simply as a literary device addressing the reader of the commentary, then the recipient of the commentary could be any bishop, either one with the actual name "Makarios" or any individual bishop who stood in a unique relationship to Andrew, a relationship of great respect and affection, which would prompt deference

---

7. Translated as "O blessed one." Andrew, Prologue, *Comm.* 52.

8. See Emmanuel Konstantinides, "Μακάριος," Θρησκευτικὴ καὶ Ἠθικὴ Ἐγκυκλοπαιδεία, 12 vols., ed. A. Martinos (Athens, 1962–68).

9. It can be found in the prologue to Methodios's *Symposium*, *Proem.* 6.13 as a simple mode of address. It is specifically directed to the reader in Pseudo-Dionysios, *The Divine Names* 1.1 and in Athanasius, *Against the Gentiles* 1. See *A Greek Patristic Lexicon*, ed. G. W. H. Lampe (Oxford: Clarendon Press, 1961), 822.

10. Andrew, Prologue, *Comm.* 51.

and compliance to such a request. This could be Andrew's spiritual father or possibly even a very close friend. Could Makarios be a monk-priest or a monk-bishop who served as Andrew's father confessor? This is certainly conceivable, but the likelihood of Andrew accommodating the request of a peer or friend appears less plausible. Why this conclusion? First, it is very likely that Andrew was advanced in years and approaching the end of his episcopal reign. An epilogue at the very end of his commentary by an anonymous individual explains that the commentary was pieced together from Andrew's drafts, suggesting that he died shortly after the commentary was completed. Second, Andrew's own rank in the Church was extremely high. His title *protothronos* indicates the dominance of his episcopal see which was second only to the Archbishop of Constantinople, the Ecumenical Patriarch. Third, the many burdens of his office, especially during such turbulent times demanded that he shoulder a large number of civic duties, especially during the crisis of the Persian invasions, as discussed above. Finally, his reluctance to undertake this "task," indicated by multiple comments regarding his hesitation, and his repeated references to "obedience" to Makarios, suggest more than a conventional expression of piety and humility.

If we are correct that a bishop ranking higher than Andrew within his jurisdiction pressured a reluctant (or even a willing) Andrew to write this commentary, then the most likely person to have been the recipient of the commentary would be the Patriarch of Constantinople. If our dating of the commentary is correct, "Makarios" could be Sergius I, whose reign as Patriarch of Constantinople lasted from 610 to 638. This is an entirely plausible conclusion. Sergius I was Andrew's ecclesiastical superior and assigning such a task is completely compatible with other details that we know about Sergius's character and about the literary atmosphere in Constantinople during his tenure. In his introduction to his translation of *Chronicon Paschale*, Michael Whitby notes that during the time of Sergius's episcopacy "classicizing historiography was being revived" by Theophylact Simocatta and that Sergius was serving as his patron in this endeavor.[11] Sergius was the most likely individual to become a writer's patron and to commission literary works at this time.[12] Whitby furthermore believes that Sergius was the patron of the anonymous author of the *Chronicon Paschale*.[13] Whitby also remarks that Constantinople experienced a literary revival or an increase in literary activity during the 620s, a period which includes Sergius's reign. Moreover, Sergius was the dominant figure in Constantinople. The Emperor Heraclius was absent on military campaigns combating the Persian invasions of that era. The final detail which supports Sergius I as the recipient of this commentary is Sergius's leadership during the crises of the early seventh century, especially his commitment to motivate the populace, to combat fatalism and to rally the empire in a spirited fight for survival against the foreign invaders.

Motivation and Historical Milieu

For five hundred years the Greek-speaking half of the Church showed little interest in a commentary on Revelation. What would prompt need for one now? Why would Andrew be asked to write a commentary on a book which for half a millennium had been largely ignored by the Christian East, whether that request be from friend, ecclesiastical colleague, or even by the very Patriarch of Constantinople himself? The answer appears to be bound up in a series of calami-

---

11. *Chronicon Paschale*, trans. Michael Whitby and Mary Whitby, Translated Texts for Historians 7 (Liverpool: Liverpool University Press, 1989), xiii.

12. "While Heraclius was absent on his campaign against the Persians, Sergius was the dominant figure in the civil administration of Constantinople, a suitable patron for any aspiring writer, and the most likely person to commission an established author to produce a particular work." Michael Whitby, *The Emperor Maurice and His Historian: Theophylact Simocatta on Persian and Balkan Warfare* (Oxford: Clarendon Press, 1988), 33.

13. Michael Whitby, *Emperor Maurice*, 357; *Chronicon*, trans. Michael Whitby and Mary Whitby, 149, n. 419. Also operating within Sergius's circle during this period was the poet and deacon, George Pisidia. See George Ostrogorsky, *History of the Byzantine State*, trans. Joan Hussey (New Brunswick, N.J.: Rutgers University Press, 1957), 79.

ties that befell the Eastern empire. This sad and tragically pivotal era in the history of the Roman empire provides the context for how this important commentary came to be. Andrew himself alludes to these circumstances when he remarks that his congregation had experienced plague, famine, Armenian revolt, and an overwhelming number of casualties.[14] The events Andrew refers to were of epic proportion, transforming life and society.

This series of calamities, from roughly the middle of the sixth century through the beginning of the seventh, brought about the end of Late Antiquity in Asia Minor. The brilliant late Roman era resurgence, which had reached its apogee under Justinian, saw the empire victorious in war, reclaiming lost portions of the Western empire and achieving new sophistication in art, architecture, and Church expansion. But this was to be a last flowering and what followed has been identified as marking the end of the Roman empire and the beginning of Byzantium.[15]

The first blow was bubonic plague which broke out during the reign of Justinian in 541. The disease killed over one quarter of the inhabitants of the empire[16] with an estimated 230,000 deaths in Constantinople alone.[17] Six more outbreaks of the disease ravaged the empire between the initial outbreak in 541 and 610.[18] The effect was shattering. Over the course of two generations the empire lost one-third of its population.[19]

Every aspect of society and life was affected. The loss of life meant fields went fallow, and farms abandoned. This created enormous disruption in trade and agriculture leading to many outbreaks of famine.[20] Famine also resulted from a severe winter and from the civil war which

---

14. Andrew, Chap. 16, *Comm.* 95.
15. Clive Foss, "The Persians in Asia Minor at the End of Antiquity," *The English Historical Review* 96 (1975): 747. Ostrogorsky, *History of the Byzantine State*, 76.
16. Warren Treadgold, *A History of Byzantine State and Society* (Stanford: Stanford University Press, 1997), 276.
17. Warren Treadgold, *A History*, 196 and 279.
18. Warren Treadgold, *A History*, 276. 19. Warren Treadgold, *A History*, 278.
20. Warren Treadgold, *A History*, 276.

raged in the empire for several years, from 602 to 610.[21] Famine grew even worse as the cycle of planting and harvesting in many communities was broken. When the Persian invasions occurred, the masses of people that crowded into walled cities to escape invaders and the number of troops confined inside the cities with them compounded the effect, both concentrating disease and putting the food supply under even greater strain.[22]

Then, in 602, the emperor Maurice was murdered by a usurper, Phocas, an army officer who took the throne by force. The event was a great shock since it marked the first time that the throne of the Roman emperor had been forcibly seized since the founding of Constantinople.[23] Phocas's ascent inaugurated a period of horrific anarchy and upheaval,[24] not only in the capital but in cities throughout the empire.[25] The result was a civil war which raged throughout the Eastern empire for nearly a decade, furthering the cycle of famine and disease, as an

---

21. A severe winter in 601–2 and bad weather impeded the grain shipments (Andreas Stratos, *Byzantium in the Seventh Century*, trans. Marc Ogilvie-Grant, 5 vols. [Amsterdam: Hakkert, 1968], 41), and led to riots in Constantinople (Warren Treadgold, *A History*, 235). In 609 the winter was so severe that the sea even froze at Constantinople. *Theophanis Chronographia*, ed. Carl de Boor, 2 vols. (Leipzig: Teubner, 1883, 1885), 1:297. *Chronicle of Theophanes Confessor*, trans. Cyril Mango and Roger Scott (Oxford: Clarendon Press, 1997), 426. See also Warren Treadgold, *A History*, 240. Many people and animals died of hunger in 608 and 609. Andreas Stratos, *Byzantium in the Seventh Century*, 78.

22. Clive Foss, "The Persians in Asia Minor," 746.

23. Warren Treadgold, *A History*, 235.

24. "The capital was a perpetual scene of torturing and executions. Phocas had killed all [former Emperor] Maurice's relations, many leaders and senators. Many more had been exiled. Michael the Syrian says succinctly that while the Persians were capturing territory, Phocas was killing everybody so that nobody was left to fight them." Andreas Stratos, *Byzantium in the Seventh Century*, 79, citing Roman historian, Michael the Syrian 2.378.

25. This situation in Thessalonica has been vividly described: "The demes, not satisfied with shedding the blood of their fellow demesmen in the streets, have forced their way into each others' houses and mercilessly murdered those within, throwing down alive from the upper stories women and children, young and old, who were too weak to save themselves by flight; in barbarian fashion they have plundered their fellow-citizens, their acquaintances and relations, and have set fire to their houses." George Ostrogorsky, *History of the Byzantine State*, 77, n. 3, citing *Miracula S. Demetrii*, *Acta Sanctorum* IV, 132 (Antwerp, 1643). PG, 116, 1261F. Long before the seventh century, the deme factions had spread from Constantinople throughout the empire, bringing their enmity and rivalry.

increasingly urban populace dependent on imported grain was denied critical supplies.[26] Phocas was eventually opposed by Heraclius who mustered an army in Egypt and arrived in Constantinople, defeating and killing Phocas, and becoming the emperor in 610.

Meanwhile, in the west and north, numerous nations and tribes, such as the Huns, the Visigoths, Lombards, Avars, Bulgars, and Slavs had been invading and attacking various parts of the empire for decades. In the East, the years of civil war had left the empire especially vulnerable to attack by the Persians, historically the empire's most troublesome and feared enemy. The plague, famine, and the consequent loss revenue and manpower had diminished the strength of the empire. The Persians took full advantage of the upheaval caused by the civil war to invade. They besieged, conquered, occupied, and plundered many leading cities, including Caesarea, Cappadocia, often completely destroying them and taking their inhabitants back to Persia as slaves.[27] For the first time in three centuries the interior of Asia Minor, which had only known peace and prosperity since the time of Diocletian, experienced war and devastation.[28] In the midst of all of this, massive earthquakes in Antioch killed tens of thousands in 526 and 588 and other quakes in the empire wreaked havoc and took lives,[29] including large tremors in Constantinople in 554[30] and 611.[31]

These and other traumatic events of the age led people to wonder whether the prophecies of Revelation were indeed coming true: Had the end of the world arrived? Even before such dire developments as

---

26. Heraclius, who was in Egypt when Phocas seized the throne, prevented grain shipments from Egypt and Carthage to the capital as part of his strategy to remove Phocas from power. Almost all of Constantinople's grain supply came from Africa. Warren Treadgold, *A History*, 239. The remainder came from Asia Minor which had been severely impacted by the Persian invasions.

27. Although the Persians had invaded during the late sixth century, those incursions had the nature of raids which had no lasting effects on the empire. Clive Foss, "The Persians in Asia Minor," 722, n. 3.

28. Clive Foss, "The Persians in Asia Minor," 722.

29. Warren Treadgold, *A History*, 279.

30. *Chronicon*, trans. Michael Whitby and Mary Whitby, 196, Appendix 2.8.

31. *Chronicon*, trans. Michael Whitby and Mary Whitby, 153.

the civil war and Persian invasion, Gregory the Great, writing in 593, was convinced that the end was at hand. "The very plagues of the earth have now become like the page of our books."[32] Later that same year, he wrote to the emperor Maurice expressing the same apocalyptic sentiment: "There will be no delay" and described the imminent end in graphic detail.[33] Apocalyptic expectation was at its absolute height in the empire when Andrew composed his commentary. The situation was so dire that people living during the opening years of the seventh century could hardly have imagined that even worse disasters were yet to come.[34] "City life, as it had been known for centuries under the Greeks and Romans, almost entirely disappeared."[35] Clive Foss poignantly describes how people reacted during the first two decades of the seventh century. "Panic and desolation struck every province of the empire, and those who feared the end of the world were in a sense justified, for the society which they and thirty generations of their ancestors had known was never to be restored."[36] The consider-

---

32. Gregory the Great, *Ep.* 3.29.

33. Gregory the Great, *Ep.* 3.61. See Brian Daley, *Hope of the Early Church* (Cambridge: Cambridge University Press, 1991), 212.

34. Terrible destruction continued in the years immediately following the composition of Andrew's commentary. Foss notes the Persian capture of Ancyra, Rhodes, Cyprus, Alexandria, and Chalcedon, not to mention the destruction of Ephesus, Sardis, Pergamum, and Magnesia. Perhaps the most scarring event was the destruction of Jerusalem, the massacre of the Christian population and the wholesale destruction of churches and monasteries on holy sites. Although the occupation of Jerusalem lasted for a relatively short period (614–628), shock and distress of the empire over the destruction of Jerusalem was unsurpassed. To this day, the return of the "True Cross" to Jerusalem, which had been stolen by the Persians, is an significant feast day of the Orthodox Church but its commemoration is marked by a strict fast. The Persian invasion permanently altered the political and administrative stability of the region. The war with the Persians lasted until 628 when Heraclius finally triumphed. In the meanwhile, losses to the empire were equally dramatic to the west where the Avars and Slavs reached the Aegean and took all of Greece. (See George Ostrogorsky, *History of the Byzantine State*, 74–76 and 84–85). Only Thessalonica was spared. *Chronicon*, trans. Michael Whitby and Mary Whitby, xii.

35. Clive Foss, "The Persians in Asia Minor," 747.

36. Clive Foss, "The Persians in Asia Minor," 746. For more details on the apocalyptic mood in the empire during the late sixth and early seventh centuries, see Paul Magdalino's article, "The History of the Future and its Uses: Prophecy, Policy and Propaganda," in *The Making of Byzantine History*, ed. Roderick Beaton and Charlotte Roueché (London: Variorum,

able and serious vicissitudes of plague, famine, civil war, incursions by barbarian invaders, and the general weakening of the empire, led to a renewed interest in apocalyptic writings, and prompted requests for a commentary on Revelation.

Even though Oikoumenios's commentary already existed, it will be demonstrated that Oikoumenios's commentary was mostly unacceptable with regard to both its style and its conclusions.[37] But was it only dissatisfaction with Oikoumenios's work that motivated Andrew and "Makarios"? Perhaps the Oikoumenian commentary was *gaining* influence and readership, if simply for no other reason than the lack of an alternative Greek commentary. This, just as easily, could have provided at least some motivation for Sergius or the anonymous "Makarios" to pressure Andrew to write his commentary, particularly since Oikoumenios had composed his commentary only recently. Considering the content and tone of Andrew's commentary, it is evident that Andrew wrote to provide an acceptable, sanctioned, orthodox guide to the Apocalypse, so that Greek-speaking Christians would not be forced to resort to Oikoumenios's commentary. Andrew's refutation of specific points made in the Oikoumenian commentary indicate that Andrew's commentary was intended, at least in part, as a response to Oikoumenios and an alternative to usurp any growing influence the earlier commentary might have achieved. Andrew and "Makarios" simply could not allow Oikoumenios's interpretation to stand without a re-

---

1993), 3–34. Magdalino mistakenly believes, however, that Andrew of Caesarea was also swept up into this apocalyptic fervor and that in his interpretation of Revelation Andrew "tries systematically to relate its prophecies to the Roman Empire." *Making of Byzantine History*, 11. Magdalino badly misreads Andrew. If Andrew wished to relate the events of the Apocalypse to current events he easily could have done so, but he does not. Instead, he made very clear his position that the end times have *not* arrived for numerous reasons. He does believe that the Antichrist will come as the King of the Romans because of the traditional patristic interpretation of the succession of kingdoms and because Andrew could not imagine a kingdom after the Roman empire, uniformly believed to be the final kingdom in the sequence. At some future point, the Antichrist will come as King of the Romans but Andrew does not believe that that time has arrived. For Andrew's view of history and eschatology see chapters 11 and 13.

37. See chapter 6.

sponse from an intelligent and educated ecclesiastical representative of Chalcedonian Christianity.[38]

In addition to a theological response to Oikoumenios, the commentary could have served as a tool for Sergius who, together with the emperor Heraclius, was the empire's greatest leader during this period and developed into its most exceptional and critical morale booster during the war with Persia. Andrew did not believe that the end of the world was near, despite the desperate state of the empire. But many in the empire were not so convinced. A well-reasoned and entirely orthodox commentary which explained why the end was *not* near might be exactly what the people needed to maintain their fighting spirit. Rather than allow them to sink into despair or hopelessness, Andrew's commentary would bolster their spirits, help to maintain Christian hope and to encourage them with confidence for a future. This would be balanced with the appropriate spirit of vigilance which is expected of all Christians, even in the best of times, so that spiritual laziness and indifference would not result in exclusion from the kingdom of heaven. It is very possible that Andrew's attitude in this area, which shines through in the commentary, was also a motivating factor for "Makarios" to request the commentary, especially if Patriarch Sergius was the "Makarios" who had prompted its composition.

The fighting spirit and optimism exemplified by the Patriarch of Constantinople, Sergius I, in the face of overwhelming difficulties during the empire's darkest moments have been well-documented. Not only does Sergius's known-patronage of authors suggest him as the recipient of the commentary, but also his assertive leadership during those troubled times. Sergius's personal determination and his partnership with Emperor Heraclius literally saved the empire during the harrowing period of the early seventh century. Sergius never showed any belief that the end was near. When the emperor and most of the

---

38. Andrew's orthodox Chalcedonian theology and interpretive skill, in contrast to Oikoumenios's apparent Miaphysite background, Origenism, and problematic interpretations, are discussed in chapters 6, 8, 10, and 14.

84 ANDREW'S RECIPIENT

army were fighting the Persians in the eastern regions, the Avars and Slavs took advantage of the army's absence to surround and besiege the capital city.[39] Sergius effectively rallied the demoralized populace to courageously resist the invaders. He led religious processions on the walls of Constantinople, singing hymns and carrying the icon of the Theotokos and her relics.[40] Sergius's courage and resolve not only motivated the people of Constantinople but his conviction and enthusiasm spread throughout the empire. This has been well expressed by Dimitri Obolensky who described the crucial role played by Sergius while Heraclius was absent on military campaigns against the Persians and the capital was surrounded by the Avars:

> In the absence of Heraclius, the citizens of Constantinople were inspired during the siege with civic and religious fervor by the Patriarch Sergius, the head of the Byzantine Church. He, no less than his sovereign, instilled a fresh spirit of resistance into the people of Byzantium, and provided this resistance with a new spiritual and moral foundation. The belief that the empire was divinely protected, and that its victories were those of the Christian religion, was not new in Byzantium; but it acquired a more compelling force in the reign of Heraclius, whose victories over the Persians, the Avars and the Slavs were hailed as the triumph of Christ and his Church over the forces of pagan barbarism. This conviction ... sustained the citizens of Thessalonica and Constantinople during the sieges of their cities by the Avaro-Slav hordes in the early seventh century; and it led them to ascribe the salvation of their cities to the personal intervention of their supernatural defenders, St. Demetrius, the patron saint of Thessalonica, and the Mother of God, the heavenly protectress of Constantinople. Nowhere is this belief in the heavenly protection vouchsafed to the empire more eloquently expressed than in the words of the *Akathist Hymn* still in current use in the liturgy of the Orthodox Church, which was probably composed by the Patriarch Sergius after the Avars and the Slavs retreated from Constantinople in 626.[41]

---

39. See *Chronicon*, trans. Michael Whitby and Mary Whitby, 173, n. 462, citing Theodore Syncellus 305.13–28, *Theodore Syncellus*, ed. L. Sternback, *Analecta Avarica* (Cracow, 1900).

40. *Chronicon*, trans. Michael Whitby and Mary Whitby, 180, n. 476, citing Theodore Syncellus 301.17–35.

41. Dimitri Obolensky, *The Byzantine Commonwealth: Eastern Europe, 500–1453* (New York: Praeger, 1971), 54.

Andreas Stratos agrees that the role played by Sergius was unequaled and monumental, not only in raising the morale of the people but also helping the emperor Heraclius on a personal basis psychologically and financially:

> From the beginning he ranged himself on Heraclius' side and helped him in a variety of ways. He was constantly with him. He exercised an immense influence over him and succeeded in encouraging him in his moments of despair and raising his morale.... He was not concerned with religious duties alone, but tried to turn the situation in favor both of Christianity and the Empire. When he saw the danger threatening Byzantium he did not hesitate to place the Church treasure at Heraclios's disposal, with which the latter was able to confront the situation. This act alone is sufficient to show his courage and high quality. During the emperor's absence he acted as Regent and was the real inspiration of the people during the siege of Constantinople in 626.[42]

We can never know whether Sergius was already convinced that the end-times were not at hand prior to reading Andrew's commentary, or whether Andrew's conclusions influenced Sergius or inspired him to this spirited resistance. Certainly, Andrew's commentary itself played a role in lessening apocalyptic expectations. In light of all of the tragic events that befell the empire, and the quest for insight and understanding for which people hungered during those troubled times, Andrew's commentary offered a traditional, spiritual, well-thought, and rather reassuring analysis of Revelation. The effectiveness of Andrew's commentary, which also succeeded in shaping Eastern Christian eschatological attitudes to the present day, is confirmed by the numerous manuscripts which preserved the commentary, the fact that his commentary has never been superseded by any other ancient interpretation of the Book of Revelation, and by the eventual acceptance of Revelation as canonical by the Orthodox Church.

42. Andreas Stratos, *Byzantium in the Seventh Century*, 96.

6

WHY THE OIKOUMENIOS COMMENTARY FAILED

Andrew of Caesarea's Assessment

If Oikoumenios's commentary was available to Andrew for his use, it follows that it was available to others as well. Since it has been established that Oikoumenios's commentary is the first complete Greek commentary on the Book of Revelation, it is a curious phenomenon that this commentary has been scarcely utilized by the Christian East. After five hundred years without a Greek Apocalypse commentary, one would expect Oikoumenios's work to be eagerly embraced and enthusiastically employed by Greek-speaking Christians in the centuries that followed. But it was not. It can fairly be said that the Oikoumenios commentary failed since it had virtually no impact on the interpretation of the Apocalypse in the Christian East. In fact, Andrew's commentary, although subsequent in time to that of Oikoumenios, was so well received that it eclipsed the prior commentary to the extent that Oikoumenios's work was almost entirely lost to history. Ignored and apparently rejected by the Church at large, the Oikoumenian commentary must have been viewed as unacceptable or unsuitable.

Does any objective evidence exist that the Oikoumenios commentary was considered unacceptable or unsatisfactory? Yes, on several counts. First, had Oikoumenios's commentary been acceptable according to the prevailing ecclesiastical standards of the time, it hardly seems likely that Andrew would have felt compelled to undertake such a difficult task as to explain the Apocalypse, by far the most difficult book of the Bible to interpret. Indeed, as we have seen, Andrew openly expresses his reluctance to attempt this difficult task which "Makarios" assigned to him. If Oikoumenios's commentary had been satisfactory, Andrew could have referred people to it and would have used it himself.

Secondly, few copies of the Oikoumenios commentary survive. The manuscript witness is perhaps the most compelling evidence that the commentary did not receive widespread endorsement over the centuries following. The meager number of existing Oikoumenios manuscripts is strong proof that the commentary was unacceptable. Only one complete copy of the commentary exists along with only a few partial manuscripts.[1] Andreas manuscripts, on the other hand, number eighty-three complete copies, thirteen abbreviated versions, fifteen manuscripts with scholia and numerous other manuscripts with notes from the commentary. In addition, Andrew's translated commentary exists in numerous additional manuscripts in the Georgian, Armenian, Latin, and Slavonic languages. Had Andrew's commentary *preceded* Oikoumenios, the scant number of Oikoumenios manuscripts might have been more easily explainable: one could surmise that Andrew's commentary was copied more frequently because it was the first, and for that reason Oikoumenios was overlooked or perceived as less necessary. But strangely, the reverse is true: although the Oikoumenios commentary came first, it was Andrew's which quickly became predominant.

Andrew's commentary was earnestly translated, prodigiously cop-

---

1. Marc De Groote discusses the status of Oikoumenios manuscripts and describes in detail the complete manuscript, the partial manuscripts, as well as existing fragments and scholia. *Oecumenii Commentarius in Apocalypsin*, Traditio Exegetica Graeca 8 (Louvain: Peeters, 1999), 9–21.

ied, and became the standard and authoritative Eastern Christian commentary on Revelation. In contrast, Oikoumenios's commentary was almost entirely lost to posterity. But why was the Oikoumenios exposition not well received or widely accepted? This question is fundamental since it bears on Andrew's purpose and motivation for composing his own commentary, and possibly has a bearing upon other underlying premises, presumptions, objectives of his interpretation and conclusions in the commentary.

Andrew himself personally must have found the Oikoumenian commentary unacceptable overall. We reach this conclusion for several reasons. First, when Andrew was pressed to write a commentary on Revelation, he could simply have referred people to Oikoumenios's commentary, which he did not. Second, Andrew could have borrowed heavily from Oikoumenios without citing him to produce his own commentary, but he did not.[2] Third, Andrew never names Oikoumenios, although this in itself is not surprising or unusual.[3] However, if Oikoumenios *were* a respected ecclesiastical figure and commentator, Andrew *might* have referred to him, not as a patristic authority, but in some favorable fashion as a contemporary expert, authority, teacher or source.[4] Instead, Andrew usually mentions Oikoumenios's views to refute him, disagree with him, to distinguish himself from Oikoumenios, or to supplement Oikoumenios's opinions.

We cannot presume that Oikoumenios's commentary was unac-

---

2. Ambrose of Milan, in his composition, *On the Six Days of Creation*, borrowed heavily from Basil the Great's work of the same name without crediting him. This was considered acceptable by ancient standards.

3. Chrysostom, for example, never referred to other exegetes by name when citing the opinions of others.

4. An example of this type of citation can be seen in the correspondence between Augustine and Jerome, each of whom cites ecclesiastical writers to support his particular interpretation. See, for example, Jerome's letter to Augustine in which Jerome refers to numerous ecclesiastical authorities, past and contemporary, in his famous exegetical dispute with Augustine. Augustine's *Ep.* 75 in *Augustine: Letters*, trans. Wilfred Parsons, 5 vols., FOTC 12, 18, 20, 30 and 32 (Washington, D.C: The Catholic University of America Press, 1951–56), 12:345–48, 364. See also, Augustine's *Ep.* 148 to Fortunatianus, in which Augustine cites Ambrose, Jerome, Athanasius the Great, and Gregory Nazianzen as authorities. FOTC 20: 228, 229, 231 and 232, respectively.

ceptable solely because Oikoumenios was a heretic or schismatic, if indeed he was one. If in all other respects Oikoumenios's work was acceptable, Andrew could have borrowed heavily from Oikoumenios and still produced his own orthodox commentary. This pattern has been seen in the case of Tyconius, the Donatist commentator on the Apocalypse, whose work was extremely influential in the West. Latin writers from Jerome and Augustine all the way down to Bede borrowed heavily from Tyconius, usually without naming him.[5]

Although Andrew frequently mentions Oikoumenios's opinions, he does not "depend upon" Oikoumenios for his conclusions. Andrew's theological conclusions and interpretations, especially for key passages of Revelation, are dramatically different than those of Oikoumenios, seriously undermining arguments of Andrew's "dependence." Although Andrew often reports Oikoumenios's opinions, just as he reports the opinions of other interpreters, he is fully capable of producing, and does in fact produce, a commentary which is independent from that of Oikoumenios because Andrew is consistently refining and correcting Oikoumenios throughout. Clearly, he did not find Oikoumenios's exposition acceptable overall and easily arrived at numerous independent conclusions.

The argument that Andrew relies on Oikoumenios is based on the many instances in which Andrew expresses the same opinion as Oikoumenios or refers to his interpretation. De Groote lists 235 parallels.[6]

---

5. As noted in chapter 1, Tyconius was so popular that even though his original commentary is no longer extant, it can be recreated in its entirety from quotations and other references found in subsequent Latin authors who borrowed from him extensively, including Jerome (in his revision of Victorinus of Pettau's commentary), Caesarius of Arles (aka, Pseudo-Augustine), Cassiodorus (*Complexiones*), Pseudo-Jerome (*Commemoratorium*), the Venerable Bede, Ambrosius Autpertus, and Beatus of Liebana. See Kenneth B. Steinhauser, *Apocalypse Commentary of Tyconius: A History of Its Reception and Influence* (Peter Lang: Frankfurt am Main, 1986). Steinhauser provides examples of the work done by Jerome to excerpt the chiliastic portions and correct any theological weaknesses in Victorinus's work (Steinhauser, 32). He certainly would have done the same for any errors he saw in Tyconius. Jerome's revision of Victorinus also serves as an example of what Andrew might have done to the Oikoumenian commentary if he had believed that Oikoumenios's commentary was acceptable for the most part.

6. Marc De Groote, *Oecumenii commentarius*, 337–42.

However, the inventory of parallels alone should not be the sole basis for evaluating the independent quality of Andrew's thought and his own unique contribution to the interpretation of the text. First, Andrew often mentions Oikoumenios to disagree with him, but the mere reference is counted as a "parallel." Many of the parallels De Groote cites are simply Andrew reporting Oikoumenios's opinion, and at times correcting it or adding his own opinion, which again would militate against the assertion that Andrew truly relied upon Oikoumenios for his exegetical conclusions. Second, Andrew conveys Oikoumenios's opinions along with the conclusions of as many other interpreters as are known to him. Again, this undermines the argument that Andrew relies on Oikoumenios since Andrew acts as a reporter of a variety of views. Andrew certainly borrows ideas from Oikoumenios, frequently summarizing Oikoumenios's expositions, which tended to be wordy, and replacing them with a concise statement. This occurs to a greater degree in the early part of Andrew's commentary, especially in the letters to the seven churches. As Andrew progresses through Revelation, he occasionally "borrows" from Oikoumenios, but overwhelmingly he acts as a corrector and reporter of Oikoumenios since he departs from Oikoumenios's conclusions repeatedly and to a significant extent.

It is also important to note that certain parallels would naturally be unavoidable. Some identical conclusions would have been reached by Andrew regardless of the presence of Oikoumenios's commentary since both men were using the same Greek biblical text, both were Greek interpreters and both shared an Eastern Christian tradition. For example, referring to life in this world as a turbulent sea in which we are tossed about, with the Church representing a safe harbor, is a *very* common image in the patristic tradition. Oikoumenios interprets the "sea" as this life,[7] and Andrew also does frequently.[8] Although Andrew utilizes the same imagery this could be because of its prevalence in pa-

---

7. Oik. 5.11.3.
8. Andrew, Chap. 23, *Comm.* 116, Chap. 34, *Comm.* 145, Chap. 36, *Comm.* 147, Chap. 55, *Comm* 194, Chap. 65, *Comm.* 220.

tristic interpretation. It is technically a "parallel" but Andrew clearly does not rely on Oikoumenios for this point since Andrew has a superior theological education and training and could easily have come to this same interpretation himself. Furthermore, Andrew demonstrates that he does not rely on Oikoumenios's interpretation of "sea" as "this life" when he indicates that Oikoumenios's overall exposition is "incongruous" with the details in the text of Revelation.[9] He also rejects Oikoumenios's allegorical elaboration on the sea, for example that one third of the ships destroyed (Rev. 8:9) represents "human beings wriggling in their salty and bitter sins."[10]

Nonetheless, the existence of the Oikoumenios commentary certainly made Andrew's assigned task much easier and he used the Oikoumenios commentary freely, reporting Oikoumenios's opinions even when Andrew found them objectionable. A careful analysis of the exact nature of the literary relationship between Andrew and Oikoumenios remains to be done. Adele Monaci Castagno observes that Andrew uses the Oikoumenian commentary as a point of departure, a sort of "canvas" upon which Andrew begins, but that Andrew sees Oikoumenios's work as devoid of authority and requiring correction on decisive points.[11] Juan Hernández also summarized the relationship between the two commentaries well, noting that even when Andrew departs to express a different opinion, Oikoumenios has framed the discussion in advance.[12]

We have established that Oikoumenios's commentary was unacceptable to the Church at large, established by the fact that it was not copied, and it was unacceptable to Andrew personally, established by the fact that he wrote his own commentary. But the question remains, why? What specific characteristics of Oikoumenios's work rendered

---

9. Andrew, Chap. 23, *Comm.* 116.
10. Oik. 5.11.3, FOTC 112:85.
11. Adele Monaci Castagno, "Il Problema," 224–46, 246.
12. Juan Hernández, Jr.,"Andrew of Caesarea and His Reading of Revelation: Catechesis and Paranesis," *Die Johannesapokalypse: Kontexte und Konzepte*, ed. Jörg Frey, James A. Kelhoffer, and Franz Tóth (Tübingen: Mohr Siebeck, 2012), 766.

it unacceptable? If this question can be answered, it may reveal some insights into the purpose or aim of Andrew's commentary. In the end, the answer to this question must remain only speculation; however several possibilities may explain the absence of any enduring popular acceptance of Oikoumenios's commentary.

First, it is likely that Oikoumenios was not Chalcedonian. He probably was a Miaphysite and perhaps had Origenist leanings. Modern readers may be in the dark about Oikoumenios's identity and theological affiliation, but these details would have been well known to Andrew and other contemporary church leaders. Secondly, perhaps Oikoumenios himself was not objectionable, but his commentary was simply perceived as too influenced by Origenism, or possibly too Hellenistic, too philosophical, or too Miaphysite in tone. Third, Oikoumenios's commentary may not have been sufficiently orthodox in style and methodology. Long on imagination and short on traditional explanations, Oikoumenios often surprises the reader with extremely unusual conclusions which might easily have led someone to question the validity or soundness of his other opinions.[13] Modern commentators and writers on the history of exegesis often prefer Oikoumenios to Andrew. They treat Andrew as a lackluster compiler of "chains" and praise Oikoumenios for his innovation and originality.[14] However, theological "originality" would not have been considered an admirable trait in ecclesiastical circles in Andrew's time, or even now among Orthodox Christians. Another pos-

---

13. One example of Oikoumenios's imaginary propensity is his interpretation of the twenty-four elders (Rev. 4:4), whom interpreters almost universally consider to be representatives of the people of God, the Old and New Israel. But Oikoumenios believes these to be specific persons whom John saw in heaven, twenty-one personalities from the Old Testament and three from the New. Oikoumenios even names them. Another example is his interpretation of the four animals by the throne (Rev. 4:6), which are widely interpreted in the patristic tradition as representing the four evangelists. Oikoumenios believes they represent the four basic elements: earth, fire, water, and air. Oik. 3.9.3.

14. Among them, Adele Monaci Castagno, "I Commenti," 423. Castagno concludes that Oikoumenios is more original and more educated than Andrew (426). She finds Andrew's commentary rather disappointing and believes it is akin to a catena (423), but later she expresses some appreciation for Andrew's preservation of the Greek tradition of Apocalypse interpretation (426).

sibility is that Oikoumenios was not a clergyman, or perhaps he simply was not a bishop. Nearly all of the notable interpreters of the Bible in the early centuries of the Church were bishops, or at least presbyters.

Presentation: Philosophical and Learned, but Unskilled and Unorthodox

The presentation of Andrew's commentary stands in marked contrast to that of Oikoumenios and the whole exposition has an entirely different character. As we have seen, the peculiarities of Oikoumenios's commentary were factors which most likely prompted the composition of Andrew's commentary. Oikoumenios divides his commentary into twelve sections, but does not explain the reason for the division. The chapters are basically equal in length, and it appears that Oikoumenios ends the chapter when he thinks the chapter is long enough, rather than concluding the chapter at a logical point based on content, theme or sequence of thought. For example, Oikoumenios discusses six of the seven letters to the churches in his chapter 2, but leaves his explanation about the last letter for his chapter 3 and discusses it along with the vision of heaven. Oikoumenios makes a comment which confirms that his chapter divisions are determined by length rather than by anything else.[15] Also in contrast to Andrew, Oikoumenios typically quotes a fairly large section of text, several verses at a time before interpreting it. He refers back to the particular details he wishes to explain and simply ignores the rest. Not only is Oikoumenios less methodical in his approach, he tends to heap Scripture quotations and explanations to support his interpretation of the text. Oikoumenios has far more Scripture quotations than Andrew but they are not as well-considered and his exposition is not carefully crafted.

Oikoumenios's presentation may be yet another reason for his less-

---

15. See Oikoumenios's introductory comments to his chapter 6 (FOTC 112: 95) in which Oikoumenios explains that he did not finish the exposition about the seven churches in the previous chapter because the chapter was becoming too lengthy.

er popularity since the commentary is neither easy to read nor easy to use. Oikoumenios does not quote the text of Revelation and then comment upon it in an orderly fashion, as do most commentators. In the original Greek manuscripts Oikoumenios's commentary is extremely difficult to follow. The text of Revelation, other biblical quotations, and Oikoumenios's comments flow into and out of each other in a continuous stream with no easy differentiation between what is text and what is comment. It is often difficult to distinguish the text of Revelation from biblical allusions, citations, and from the comments of Oikoumenios himself.[16] Other than chapter divisions, the Oikoumenios commentary has little structure.

Hoskier (who first published the commentary and expressed great frustration with Oikoumenios's presentation) and De Groote, who published the critical text, expended great efforts to sift through the commentary in order to separate his own words from the Scripture quotations and create a readable and more organized exposition. Hoskier noted,

it is not always easy to differentiate between what is text and what is commentary. In the volume now before the reader this may not appear to be the case, but that is because we have been at considerable pains to make the matter clear. In the original document the commentary sweeps along without halting between the sections of text and is without the slightest mark to guide the reader as to what is text and what commentary.[17]

Oikoumenios believed that he stood within the tradition of the Church and proudly aligned himself with it.[18] Oikoumenios was certainly a Christian scholar, but not a cleric. His interpretation is more explanatory than ecclesiastical in tone. He makes references to the sacraments and to Scripture, but his commentary has a strong philosophical flavor. John Suggit noted that Oikoumenios frequently draws a distinction between that which can be perceived by the senses and

---

16. Herman Hoskier, *Complete Commentary of Oecumenius*, 4.
17. Herman Hoskier, *Complete Commentary of Oecumenius*, 4.
18. Oik. 1.1.4 and 5.19.2.

that which can be perceived by the intellect, the *nous*. Suggit concluded that this indicates Origen's influence on Oikoumenios.[19] In fact, most of the Fathers, including Andrew, made such distinctions which had been popularized by the Cappadocian Fathers. Such categories are often utilized in theological and spiritual writings, although rarely with frequency in a commentary as we see in Oikoumenios. Rather than indicating a dependence on Origen per se, Oikoumenios's use of such terms shows a philosophical rather than ecclesiastical inclination. Other hints of Origenism are indeed present in Oikoumenios, however, and are discussed below.

Oikoumenios gives many additional clues that his orientation is primarily philosophical rather than ecclesiastical. References to being "wise" and to "wisdom" in general are found four times in his introductory comments alone.[20] Most striking and highly unusual are the references to St. Paul as "wise,"[21] "most wise,"[22] and "very wise."[23] Only twice is Paul simply called "the Apostle,"[24] which is the usual Eastern Christian mode of reference for Paul. Methodios is "very wise."[25] Moses is also described as "very wise,"[26] and even the prophet Daniel is "the wisest Daniel."[27] Oikoumenios's effort to interpret Revelation seems to be an intellectual challenge to unlock the "mystical" message of the book.[28] Andrew, on the other hand, while recognizing that Revelation supplies training for the mind, sees its benefits as almost exclusively spiritual.

Oikoumenios interprets the four living beings by the throne of God (Rev. 4) as representing the four elements of creation, a common

---

19. But not to the extent of subordinating the Son to the Father. FOTC 112:10.
20. Oik. 1.1.1, 1.1.3 (twice) and 1.1.6.   21. Oik. 3.3.3, 6.11.3, 10.9.5, 11.3.3, 12.7.4.
22. Oik. 1.3.1, 3.3.15, 10.9.3. Also 2.11.2, which Suggit translates as, "Paul, in his great wisdom." FOTC 112:44.
23. Oik. 8.21.2, 12.13.10.   24. Oik. 11.12.12, 11.14.4.
25. Oik. 1.1.5.   26. Oik. 2.7.3.
27. Oik. 12.7.11.
28. There are two references to the general "mystical" character of the book (1.1.2 and 6.11.5). Later, the one hundred forty-four cubit measurement of the city is described as a "mystical" number, but Oikoumenios does not explain it (12.1.5), and the garb of the high priest is said to convey "mystical" symbolism (12.1.10).

Greek philosophical concept.²⁹ Oikoumenios argues in favor of the reality of the resurrected body against philosophers who maintained that decomposed bodies could not be resurrected because of the separation of the four elements within the body.³⁰ Andrew entirely ignores this and is not the least interested in defending the resurrection against philosophers. Oikoumenios feels comfortable with Christian philosophers such as Clement of Alexandria, and he cites Clement.³¹ He cites the *Shepherd of Hermas* as well, also very unusual for the late sixth century.³² It is unlikely that *Shepherd* would be considered Scripture by anyone at such a late date, and even if Oikoumenios does not consider it Scripture, its citation represents a lack of discrimination among sources on the part of Oikoumenios, which also may not speak well of his training. Oikoumenios alludes to Homer, Hesiod, and the Greek belief that prophecy contained three levels.³³ By this time in the patristic tradition, an appeal to Greek learning would have been rather unthinkable, certainly for one who holds ecclesiastical authority, which is an indication that Oikoumenios is not a member of the clergy. Also surprising is his citation of the "all-knowledgeable Evagrius," a known Origenist.³⁴

29. Oik. 3.9.3.

30. Oik. 11.10.1–9. Castagno believes that Oikoumenios is echoing the objections to the concept of the resurrection raised by two of the Origenist interlocutors found in Methodios's *Symposium*. "I Commenti," 351.

31. Oik. 3.7.5. This is also rather unusual. Clement of Alexandria is not regarded as a Church Father in the East.

32. Oik. 2.11.2. He refers to "Scripture" and then cites Paul and *Shepherd of Hermas*. It is not clear whether Oikoumenios considered *Shepherd* to be Scripture along with Paul's epistles. He does not introduce either quotation with any formulaic statement, such as "It is written," which might have provided us with a clue as to Oikoumenios's opinion about the canon of Scripture.

33. Oik. 1.1.2.

34. Oik. 6.3.12. As noted in chapter 4, some have used the presence of this detail to support an earlier date of the commentary, arguing that Oikoumenios would not have cited Evagrius, who was condemned at the Fifth Ecumenical Council in 553 (also known as the Second Council of Constantinople), if he wrote the commentary after that date. But this is not persuasive since Oikoumenios was a non-Chalcedonian, and he would not have recognized that Council or any Ecumenical Council after Ephesus in 431. Even if Oikoumenios were Chalcedonian, given the rather eclectic nature of his commentary and unorthodox style

Oikoumenios refers to the suffering befalling sinners who refuse to repent, and he speaks occasionally about the love of God for humanity, but there is no hint within his commentary that he bears responsibility for souls. He was most certainly neither a presbyter nor a bishop. He refers to sacraments, and sometimes finds sacramental overtones in Revelation imagery, but even by these observations he reveals his lack of exegetical training and makes surprising departures in his conclusions. When interpreting obvious symbols for which one would expect a sacramental connection to be drawn, Oikoumenios does not, but then he finds sacramental allusions where they are inappropriate due to the context.[35] Many of his points are not well considered while other observations are not well placed. For example, rather than resolving authorship or canonical issues as a preliminary matter, Oikoumenios's defense of the inspiration and apostolic authorship of Revelation can be found both at the beginning[36] and at the very end of the commentary[37] and its placement at the end makes for a rather awkward conclusion.

Oikoumenios also becomes easily distracted in his exposition and deviates from the interpretation to comment on other matters unrelated to the text of Revelation. For example, because of the phrase "the beginning of creation" (Rev. 3:14) in the description of Christ, he digresses to refute Arianism.[38] Even if this could arguably be related to the interpretation of the text, another digression occurs a little later when he stops to comment on "an error among the Jews" and why this results in a certain statement found in Isaiah.[39] Oikoumenios also expends a significant amount of effort attacking Greek pagan ideas about their gods, for example how Greeks defended their belief in many gods by comparing it to the Christian belief in angels.[40]

---

and conclusions, it can hardly be argued that Oikoumenios would have felt bound to conform to such conventions.

35. For example, he interprets Rev. 7:14 in which the saints "washed their robes in the blood of the lamb" as a Eucharistic symbol, rather than explaining that this meant that they had died as martyrs. Oik. 5.3.7.

36. Oik. 1.2.4–6.
37. Oik. 12.20.1–6.
38. Oik. 3.3.2–4.
39. Oik. 3.9.2, FOTC 112:57.
40. Oik. 10.11.3–6.

98 THE OIKOUMENIOS COMMENTARY

Oikoumenios makes lengthy statements about Christian doctrine which are distracting, unnecessary, and not directly related to the exposition of the text.[41] One is forced to ponder whether they serve more as a recitation of his theological prowess, a defense of his orthodoxy, or simply reflect a lack discipline or training. His exposition of Revelation 1:1, for example, includes a Christological statement which does not seem to be offered for the purpose of illuminating the meaning of the text. After noting that John's presentation of Christ in the Fourth Gospel is more focused on his divinity, whereas the Apocalypse is more appropriate to Christ's humanity, Oikoumenios makes a lengthy digression.[42] This type of aside is not uncommon when a "commentary" was actually a series of sermons, but it is not expected when the comments were never extemporaneously delivered.[43]

Oikoumenios's commentary contains many inconsistencies, such as his interpretation of Babylon. When the image first appears (Rev. 14:8), he gives both a figurative and a literal interpretation of Babylon. Oikoumenios concludes that Babylon is either the "confusion of the pres-

---

41. Castagno believes that Oikoumenios is primarily reading Revelation in light of the theological issues of his day and uses the text to support his theological views. "I Commenti," 319. Biblical interpretation certainly reflects the interpreter's theological opinions, but the commentary is not primarily theologically oriented. Perhaps Castagno reaches this conclusion because Oikoumenios promulgates theological statements which are unrelated to the exegesis. She later writes that for Oikoumenios, Revelation serves as a kind of *Summa Theologica* (392). This is a tremendous exaggeration and entirely unsupportable. In that case, Oikoumenios's purpose would not have been to interpret the text but to use it as a springboard or a platform to discuss theology. However, the commentary has only a few discussions of doctrine, certainly not enough to indicate that it was intended to be anything other than a commentary, or that Revelation was anything other than history or prophecy.

42. Oik. 1.3.2–3, FOTC 112:21.

43. Castagno believes that Oikoumenios was driven to find the internal logic of the Book of Revelation. "I Commenti," 304. Hence, what appear to be inconsistencies are not, and his return to previous themes already discussed are efforts to find coherence in the text. *Ibid*, 330. But Castagno gives Oikoumenios far too much credit and she does not succeed in demonstrating this internal coherence which she says Oikoumenios sought and presumably found, if this was as important to his exposition as she claims. Furthermore, Castagno does not even explain how she arrived at the opinion that Oikoumenios was pursuing this internal coherence by pointing to details in the commentary to support her conclusion. In fact, Oikoumenios ignores logical sequence and even dismisses it, such as by saying that John "is often shown the first things last and contrariwise the last first." Oik. 9.5.3, FOTC 112:142.

ent life" or the actual Persian city.[44] But later, Oikoumenios believes that a second reference to Babylon (Rev. 17) refers to a *different* city, Rome, and he interprets the text to mean the absolute destruction of Rome.[45] Andrew, however, concludes that Babylon is probably not Rome because the text describes a city with worldwide domination, and long ago Rome lost that type of dominance.[46]

A simple, but greatly illustrative example of Oikoumenios's lack of exegetical training and the general uneven quality of his exposition is seen in his interpretation of the seven churches. Throughout his exposition, Oikoumenios almost without exception interprets the number "seven" as a symbol of perfection.[47] But in the opening vision in which John is instructed to write to the seven churches, an image which easily lends itself to an interpretation of fullness or perfection, Oikoumenios blandly explains that John wrote to these seven because those were the cities converted by him.[48] By the late sixth century, the seven churches of Asia and the seven churches to which Paul had written had been interpreted for hundreds of years as symbolic of the entire Church. It is difficult to imagine how Oikoumenios either would not know this tradition or would not have arrived at such a conclusion on his own, considering the abundant references to "seven" in Revelation and his typical interpretation of seven as a symbol of perfection.

Theology: Non-Chalcedonian

The precise reason why Oikoumenios's commentary was not more widely embraced in the Christian East may never be known with certainty. However, it is without question that the commentary would have been unacceptable or unsatisfactory in Chalcedonian circles. The small number of extant manuscripts is the best evidence of that fact. Oikoumenios's commentary contains many fanciful interpretations and unusual conclusions. A careful reading of his commentary reveals

44. Oik. 8.11.1, FOTC 112:128.
45. Oik. 9.15.1.
46. Andrew, Chap. 53, *Comm.* 181.
47. Oik. 5.3.5.
48. Oik. 1.25.

clear indications that Oikoumenios was a non-Chalcedonian. We do not reach this conclusion because the Miaphysite bishop Severus of Antioch had a friend named Oikoumenios. We have already concluded that Severus's friend could not have been the author of this commentary. The author of the Oikoumenios commentary can be classified as non-Chalcedonian based on the terminology of his commentary alone. Two lengthy Christological statements can be found in the commentary, one near the beginning and one near the end. The first reads:

It is a sign of genuine theology to believe that God the Word has been begotten from God and the Father before all eternity and temporal interval, being co-eternal and consubstantial with the Father and the Spirit, and joint-ruler of the ages and of all spiritual and perceptible creation, according to the saying of the most-wise Paul.[49] ... But it is also a sign of genuine theology to believe that in the last days he has become for us and for our salvation a human being, not by divesting himself of his divinity, but by assuming human flesh, animated by a mind. (ἀλλὰ προσλήψει σαρκὸς ἀνθρωπίνης, ἐμψυχωμένης νοερῶς). In this way, he who is Emmanuel is understood to have been made one from two natures (ἐκ δύο φύσεων), divinity and humanity, each being complete according to the indwelling Word and according to the different specific characteristics of each nature (κατὰ ποιότητα φυσικὴν ἰδιότητα), without being confused or altered by their combination into a unity, and without being kept separate after the inexpressible and authentic union.[50]

It has been said, based on this passage, that Oikoumenios was Chalcedonian orthodox because of his acceptance of the phrase "from two natures." But the key word here is "from," which signals the belief in one person *(hypostatsis)*, a term which was sometimes used interchangeably with "nature" *(physis)*. "One nature," or "one *from* two natures *after* the union," was the Miaphysite position as opposed to the Chalcedonian terminology, "one person *in* two natures" (ἐν δύο φύσεων). Miaphysites believed that the Chalcedonian definition which maintained the distinction of "two natures" after their "union" in the person of Christ created a Nestorian-type of division between the natures which amounted to two Christs. Oikoumenios frequently em-

---

49. Citing Colossians 1:18 and 16.   50. Oik. 1.3.3, FOTC 112:21.

phasizes the union of the divine and the human in Christ[51] and specifically refers to the quality of the "hypostatic union."[52] He also uses other common Miaphysite phrases, such as the Lord's body "animated by a mind"[53] or "animated by the soul,"[54] as well as terms which refer to the specific properties or qualities of each nature preserved as they were prior to the union.[55] Also noteworthy is Oikoumenios's use of "Emmanuel," which was a favorite title of Miaphysites for Christ,[56] as well as his citation of Fathers who were especially favored by non-Chalcedonian theologians.[57]

The use of similar terms by Chalcedonians and Miaphysites led Adele Monaci Castagno to say that Oikoumenios could be either "Monophysite" or a "neo-Chalcedonian." She remarks that after Justinian's failure to achieve union in the Church, subsequent emperors persecuted the Miaphysites, especially toward the end of the sixth century. She assumes that Oikoumenios would show hostility toward the empire if he were Miaphysite. Castagno concluded that Oikoumenios leans more toward the Chalcedonian camp primarily because his theology is not

---

51. Oik. 1.3.3, 1.11.1, 2.13.13, 10.13.20, 12.3.20.

52. Including καθ' ὑπόστασιν ἑνωθῆναι (Oik. 2.13.13), καθ' ὑπόστασιν ἑνωθεὶς (Oik. 10.13.20), and καθ' ὑπόστασιν ὁ Λόγος ἥνωται (Oik. 12.3.20).

53. ἐμψυχωμένης νοερῶς (Oik. 1.3.3, FOTC 112:21), and νοερῶς ἐμψυχωμένου σώματος (Oik. 3.3.3, FOTC 112:50).

54. ἐμψυχωμένος νοερῶς (Oik. 12.3.20, FOTC 112:193).

55. κατὰ ποιότητα φυσικὴν ἰδιότητα "specific characteristic of each nature," (Oik. 1.3.3 FOTC 112:21), and ἡ κατὰ ποιότητα φυσικὴν ἰδιότης "peculiar quality of each nature" (Oik. 12.13.6, FOTC 112:200). For a concise discussion of the use and meanings of all of these terminologies as classic Monophysite expressions, see Jaroslav Pelikan, *The Christian Tradition: A History of the Development of Doctrine*, vol. 2, *The Spirit of Eastern Christendom* (Chicago: University of Chicago Press, 1974), 48–65. See also J. N. D. Kelly, *Early Christian Doctrines*, 2nd ed. (London: Adam and Charles Black, 1960), 310–43; John Meyendorff, *Byzantine Theology* (New York: Fordham University Press, 1974), 32–38; John Meyendorff, *Christ in Eastern Christian Thought* (Washington, D.C.: Corpus Books, 1969), 3–31; and John Meyendorff, *Imperial Unity and Christian Divisions* (Crestwood, N.Y.: St. Vladimir's Seminary Press, 1989), 177–78 and 216–30.

56. Jaroslav Pelikan, *Spirit of Eastern Christendom*, 58–59.

57. Jaroslav Pelikan, *Spirit of Eastern Christendom*, 51. Athanasius, Basil the Great, Gregory the Theologian of Nazianzus, Gregory of Nyssa, and Cyril of Alexandria, each of whom is used by Oikoumenios. They are also mentioned in his introduction (Oik.1.1.5), except for Gregory of Nyssa.

easily defined, he does not rely on the Cyrillian formula "one nature of the incarnate Logos," and his commentary does not reflect any tensions with the figure of the emperor.[58]

Oikoumenios's emphasis on the union of the human and the divine in Christ is not contrary to Chalcedon. In fact, the union of the two natures in the one Christ was the entire point of the decision at Chalcedon against Nestorianism. On the other hand, emphasizing the unity of Christ does not make Oikoumenios a Chalcedonian Christian since non-Chalcedonians also emphasized the unity. Miaphysites rejected Chalcedon because they were convinced that Chalcedon had in fact maintained a Nestorian separation of the humanity and divinity in Christ by choosing the terminology "one person in two natures." For this reason, the emphasis in Oikoumenios on one person *from* the *unity* of the natures is not only anti-Nestorian, it is anti-Chalcedonian.[59] Other shorter Christological comments are sprinkled throughout the commentary, but the second lengthy statement made by Oikoumenios is also very telling.

> He is Emmanuel in his divinity and in his humanity, each of the two natures being complete according to their respective qualities, without confusion (ἀσυγχύτως), without change (ἀτρέπτως), immutable (ἀναλοιώτως), unimaginable (ἀφαντασιάστως). We believe that after the inexpressible union there is one person, one hypostasis, and one activity (ἓν πρόσωπον καὶ μίαν ὑπόστασιν καὶ μίαν ἐνέργειαν), "even if the difference of the natures, from which we say that the ineffable union has been effected, may not be overlooked," as well as the peculiar quality of each nature (ἡ κατὰ ποιότητα φυσικὴν ἰδιότης), according to the words of our blessed father Cyril.[60]

Again, the similarity to the formula of Chalcedon has led some to conclude that Oikoumenios was not Miaphysite.[61] A Chalcedonian would have been more likely to repeat the exact words of the Chalcedonian definition but in the excerpt above only two of the key words

58. Adele Monaci Castagno, "Il Problema," 227.
59. Adele Monaci Castagno would disagree. "I Commenti," 324–26.
60. Oik. 12.13.6, FOTC 112:200. Oikoumenios is quoting Cyril of Alexandria, *Epistle to John of Antioch* 8.
61. Adele Monaci Castagno, "I Commenti," 318–24.

are the same.⁶² Regardless of the terminology Oikoumenios employed, two important facts remain: the emphasis on the union of the person of Christ and that the union has been affected *from* the natures. Another detail in the quotation above provides additional proof: Oikoumenios's reference to "one activity," to further accentuate the unity of the person of Christ. This eventually led to the doctrine of Monoenergism and later Monotheletism, both of which were efforts to resolve the schism between the Chalcedonians and the Miaphysites. Both terms were later rejected by the Chalcedonian Orthodox. The combination of Oikoumenios's theological expressions confirms that he was non-Chalcedonian. Miaphysites would not distinguish between nature and hypostasis. Only one nature or hypostasis could exist after the union. "Energy" reflected the hypostasis, person, agent or actor.⁶³ To accept two "activities" or two "energies" meant to have two Christs.

Another significant clue that Oikoumenios was non-Chalcedonian can be found in his pointed assertion that the hymn of the Seraphim was sung to Christ. Oikoumenios alludes to the Trisagion Hymn, which had become a focal point for dogmatic debates between Miaphysites and Chalcedonians.⁶⁴ This detail in Oikoumenios's exposition and Andrew's emphatic Chalcedonian reply has not been cited by previous scholars, yet it unmistakably identifies Oikoumenios as non-Chalcedonian.⁶⁵ Andrew of Caesarea would step forward to respond to Oikoumenios and provide a Revelation commentary to satisfy Chalcedonian Christians.

62. ἐν δύο φύσεσιν ἀσυγχύτως, ἀτρέπτως, ἀδιαιρέτως, ἀχωρίστως, "Jesus Christ ... must be confessed to be in two natures without confusion, change, division or separation."

63. John Meyendorff, *Byzantine Theology*, 38.

64. Oik. 2.13.1. On the use of the Trisagion hymn during this controversy, see John Meyendorff, *Imperial Unity*, 200 and 224; John Meyendorff, *Byzantine Theology*, 36–38; and Jaroslav Pelikan, *Spirit of Eastern Christendom*, 59–60. Castagno does not notice this detail. She focuses on the similarity of terms used by Monophysites and neo-Chalcedonians, and Oikoumenios's lack of animosity toward the empire to conclude that he was not Monophysite. Adele Monaci Castagno, "I Commenti," 323–24.

65. See chapter 10.

7

ANDREW'S COMMENTARY

Purpose and Motivation

Expressed Purpose and Motivation

As we have seen, Andrew began his commentary by expressing his reluctance to undertake the job of interpreting the Apocalypse, the most challenging of all scriptural texts. He noted that he had repeatedly demurred to previous requests and accepted the task only after being pressured to do so by "Makarios," whose motivation and possible identity as Sergius I, Patriarch of Constantinople, have been addressed in chapter 5. Andrew's initial incentive is simply "obedience." He perceives himself as "deprived of the prophetic spirit"[1] but resolves to complete the task which had been "assigned" to him, placing his trust on the hope that God "will enlighten" him.[2] These remarks, even though they reflect literary conventions to some degree, nonetheless can provide important insight into Andrew's character and motivation, especially since it confirms the personality of Andrew as it is revealed throughout the commentary as a whole. It would be a mistake to either dismiss Andrew's comment that he undertakes the task out of "obedience" as insignificant, or merely a conventional expression of modesty.

Obedience, especially in an ecclesiastical context or in the monas-

---

1. Andrew, Prologue, *Comm.* 5.   2. Andrew, Prologue, *Comm.* 52.

tic life, is an extremely important virtue. Connected to faith and humility, it is regarded as more important than the performance of ascetic exercises or one's episcopal or sacerdotal duties in this instance. In explaining that he intends to be obedient to the request by "Makarios," Andrew quotes 1 Samuel, that "obedience is better than sacrifice."[3] However, it is not obedience alone which motivates Andrew, but love. Andrew refers twice to his love for "Makarios," suggesting great respect and esteem for the "man of God"[4] whose soul Andrew describes as "God-like."[5] The initial impression we receive of Andrew is of an individual with a strong spiritual orientation. Again, this opinion is only further confirmed by the disposition he reveals throughout the entire content of his exposition and by the tenor of his commentary. Andrew consoles himself about the impossibility of his assigned task to explain the Apocalypse by remarking that even the prophets of old, whose writings have been interpreted by so many, remain a mystery whose full understanding will not occur until the end.[6] He expresses the hope that he will receive rewards for his obedience, but such rewards are spiritual: "Compensate our labor with your prayers."[7] He perceives another spiritual benefit resulting from this task. Focusing on the Apocalypse will serve as "a form of contempt for the present things, since they are transitory, and [for the purpose of] coveting the future things, since these remain."[8] This spiritual benefit extends to the reader and Andrew refers to it on more than one occasion. Studying the Apocalypse contributes "not a little to compunction."[9] It teaches that "death must be despised."[10] "The book is also worthy for reading by the faithful.... It guides those who read it to true life."[11] It "is holy and God-inspired, guiding those who read it to a blessed end."[12]

---

3. Andrew, Prologue, *Comm.* 51.
4. Andrew, Prologue, *Comm.* 54. This is a conventional expression.
5. Andrew, Prologue, *Comm.* 52. This is also a conventional expression.
6. Andrew, Prologue, *Comm.* 51.   7. Andrew, Prologue, *Comm.* 54.
8. Andrew, Prologue, *Comm.* 53.   9. Andrew, Prologue, *Comm.* 54.
10. Andrew, Chap. 4, *Comm.* 67.   11. Andrew, Chap. 71, *Comm.* 238–39.
12. Andrew, Chap. 72, *Comm.* 242.

Having acknowledged the spiritual benefit derived from studying the Apocalypse and having resigned himself to the challenging task, Andrew finds one additional benefit from his work: it is good mental exercise and will serve as "training for the quick-wittedness of the mind."[13] This benefit also extends to the reader. The interpretation of the names of the twelve tribes is given "for the exercise of the mind by those who are quick-witted."[14] After offering numerous possible interpretations of the symbolism of the twenty four elders, he states: "Let the reader be tested."[15] Explaining the precious stones which describe the heavenly Jerusalem, he remarks that such symbols "serve as training for those pondering enigmas of truth."[16] We see that Andrew expects the reader to also be actively engaged in discovering the meaning of the text, and not simply read passively.

Unexpressed Purpose and Motivation

There were unexpressed purposes which also motivated Andrew. The most important purpose, entirely unstated but extremely obvious, is his response to the Oikoumenios commentary. Andrew would not have made such a concerted effort to reply to Oikoumenios if his only intended reader was "Makarios." It is within the context of this tacit objective that we recognize that Andrew anticipated a wider readership even if the commentary was formally addressed to "Makarios," the man who had ultimately compelled Andrew to write it. Prior to the request made by "Makarios," Andrew tells us that he had been asked "many times by many people ... to elucidate the Apocalypse of John."[17] We also know from comments in an epilogue, probably composed by an editor or compiler, that Andrew gave at least parts of the commentary to others to read in draft form.[18]

Two additional clues of a wider audience are evident. First, the el-

---

13. Andrew, Prologue, *Comm.* 53.
14. Andrew, Chap. 19, *Comm.* 109.
15. Andrew, Chap. 10, *Comm.* 82.
16. Andrew, Chap. 67, *Comm.* 230.
17. Andrew, Prologue, *Comm.* 51.
18. Andrew, Epilogue, *Comm.* 246.

ementary explanation of the three parts of Scripture,[19] which "Makarios" would not have required because that concept was very basic and well-known to the clergy, and secondly, the expressed purpose of the commentary: for the benefit of the faithful, since it "contributes not a little to compunction through remembrance of both the rewards that will be bestowed on the righteous and the retribution of the wicked and sinful."[20]

Oikoumenios's commentary may have initially been well-received, or at the very least it had kindled a significant amount of attention and interest since it was the only commentary on the Apocalypse available in the Greek language. To Andrew, Oikoumenios's exposition of Revelation was unacceptable, deficient, and misleading. It could not be allowed to stand unanswered. Andrew's purpose in relation to the Oikoumenian commentary has been previously discussed in chapter 5. From a solely pastoral perspective, Andrew may have also been interested in promoting a balanced attitude toward the end times, an outlook which Oikoumenios's commentary had distorted since it presented Revelation primarily as a book of past events, as history which had already occurred. Interpreting Revelation primarily as a symbolic retelling of the life of Christ, Oikoumenios robbed the book of its prophetic power. Reducing many symbols to allegories of the life of Christ, Oikoumenios marginalized the visions and their prophetic quality. According to that interpretation, reading Revelation would not cultivate the appropriate attitude of watchfulness and preparation for the end times, or for one's own end. If indeed Revelation is a vision of completed history, and if most of the destruction it describes is not literal but a metaphor, then why should anyone be concerned? Andrew might have perceived Oikoumenios's commentary as presenting a spiritual danger, which as a pastoral matter Andrew would have wanted to correct.

At the other extreme, Andrew must have been concerned about the many individuals living in the early seventh century who were firmly

---

19. Andrew, Prologue, *Comm.* 52.
20. Andrew, Prologue, *Comm.* 54.

convinced that the end of the world was at hand. After the eastern Roman empire had enjoyed centuries of relative peace and stability, the early 600s brought not only revolt, plague, famine, and earthquakes, but also civil war, societal chaos, and barbarian invasions with accompanying slaughter on a massive scale, including the wholesale destruction of many cities. The resulting pessimism of the population could have taken two forms: (1) hedonism, in consequence of the philosophy "eat, drink and be merry, for tomorrow we die," or (2) fatalism, leading to defeatism and hopelessness, and which would hinder the vigorous defense of the empire from loss of morale.

Part of Andrew's purpose must have been to eradicate the conviction that the end of the world was near. Despite tremendous catastrophes, the combination of which had never been seen before in the Roman empire, amazingly Andrew himself does not believe that the end is near. "How could anyone who is deprived of the prophetic spirit, not appear bold by attempting [to explain] these things whose end is not in sight?"[21] Andrew is remarkably stoic and almost dispassionate about the calamities which his generation has witnessed. He is convinced—based on his reading of Revelation—that far worse disasters will accompany the end times, even worse than those which they had recently experienced and were still facing even while he was composing his commentary. The afflictions which will come with the arrival of the Antichrist will be "of which sort as we have never known."[22]

Andrew also does not apply Revelation to the events of his day for two primary reasons: (1) it is useless and spiritually harmful to speculate about the time of the end, and, (2) various statements made by Christ and the apostles instruct us that the end time cannot be known by us.[23] Andrew believes that reading the events of one's own times into the prophecy of Revelation is irresponsible and unorthodox. While it may be acceptable to interpret the plagues described in Rev-

---

21. Andrew, Prologue, *Comm.* 51.   22. Andrew, Chap. 18, *Comm.* 98.
23. "The hour" will not be known (Matt. 24:42, 44, 24:50). It will come like a "thief in the night" (Matt. 24:43, 1 Thess. 5:2, 2 Pet. 3:10).

elation as specific events to occur at the end,[24] the actual time of the end is not even known by the angels[25] and it is even something which one is "forbidden to seek."[26] Adele Monaci Castagno entirely misreads Andrew. She maintains that Oikoumenios considered Revelation a book about events which already occurred because he believed that the end was far in the future. But she mistakenly concludes that Andrew's interpretation shows he believed the end was very near (because of his references to barbarians) and that he saw the world as rushing toward destruction. Castagno also believes that differences between the commentaries of Andrew and Oikoumenios regarding the time of the end are largely due to their views of history and eschatology. She is correct that they differ on such matters, however not because Andrew believes that the end is near while Oikoumenios does not. They differ because differences in their theological education, exegetical skill, interpretive techniques, and training, have led them to divergent conclusions about the meaning of the biblical text. Castagno claims that Andrew saw Revelation primarily as a prophecy of the end times and as a key to decipher the tragic and painful events of the present.[27] Andrew did believe that Revelation operated as future prophecy. Castagno is entirely incorrect, however, in her assessment that Andrew applied the images in the Apocalypse to his own times and believed the end to be near.

A true understanding of Andrew's interpretation requires a more careful reading.

24. Andrew, Chap. 45, *Comm.* 167.
25. Andrew, Chap. 21, *Comm.* 112.
26. Andrew, Prologue, *Comm.* 53. This is in reference to certain statements by Christ, such as, "It is not for you to know" (Acts 1:7) and "But of that day and hour no one knows, not even the angels of heaven, nor the Son, but the Father only" (Matt. 24:36). Andrew's stance is in keeping with the ancient tradition. Commenting on the last verse, Chrysostom informed his congregation that Christ instructed the disciples that "they should not seek to learn what these angels know not and ... forbids them not only to learn, but even to inquire." *Hom. on Matthew* 77.1, in *Chrysostom: Homilies on Matthew*, trans. George Prevost, ed. Philip Schaff, NPNF[1] 10: 445.
27. Adele Monaci Castagno, "I Commenti de Ecumenio e di Andrea di Cesarea: Due letture divergenti dell' Apocalisse," *Memorie della Accademia delle scienze di Torino II, Classe di scienze, morali, storiche e filologiche* V, Fascicolo IV (1981): 426.

It is difficult to comprehend how Castagno arrives at the conclusion that Andrew sees Revelation as a key to deciphering his own tumultuous times since Andrew makes no references to the recent outbreaks of plague, the civil war or earthquakes, and only hints at famine and barbarian invasions. It is inconceivable that he would be silent on such matters if in fact he were indeed attempting to interpret the events of his own times and apply them to Revelation. Rather, Andrew is interpreting the text of Revelation, not his own times. He does not apply the events of his day to the text, although a less skilled interpreter probably would have. In light of the upheaval of his era, including the Persian invasion of his own city, it is truly remarkable that Andrew does not read current events into Revelation, even though he ascribes to a literal interpretation of most of the destruction described in the visions. This is a great testament to Andrew's exegetical skill and his theological education but also speaks to his spiritual maturity and depth.

Calming fears among the populace that the end was approaching may also have been a motivating factor for "Makarios," as discussed above. Andrew is certainly sincere in his belief that "the end is not in sight," but what is his motivation in publicizing this view? It would have been easy for him—and one might argue even spiritually beneficial for the faithful—to encourage a belief that the end is near. He could have justified such a stance in his own mind. After all, Andrew himself wrote that the Apocalypse prompts compunction.[28] Wouldn't the Apocalypse have greater impact—greater repentance, more baptisms, church attendance, almsgiving, etc.—if people believed that the end was at hand? He could have at least left a window partly open to the *possibility* that the end *might* be near. But he does not. This also is a very strong indicator of his integrity and the fact that he respects the text and does not manipulate it by distorting or exaggerating the message.

Instead of engaging in fear mongering or fanning the flames of anxiety, Andrew appropriately uses Revelation for a spiritual purpose: as a message of encouragement and hope. This may appear paradoxi-

---

28. Andrew, Prologue, *Comm.* 54.

cal in the context of the common perception of the Apocalypse and the related adjective "apocalyptic," but in fact, Revelation's original message and purpose *(skopos)* was one of hope and perseverance through tribulation.[29] Andrew's commentary promotes and preserves the original purpose of Revelation: to encourage the reader to persevere and remain faithful, and hopefully to live a spiritually improved life. Revelation offers no promise of deliverance from tribulation, but hope always remains because of Christ and the promise of eternal life.

A very telling detail illuminates Andrew's unexpressed purpose in this respect. Christ's message to the church of Smyrna in Revelation 2:10 warns them that "the devil is about to put some of you into prison." Christ encourages the Smyrnaeans to be faithful until death because the tribulation will only last "for ten days." Andrew uses this instruction to encourage his readers, and his paraphrase of Christ's words is very revealing: "Do not fear the tribulation from the enemies of God through afflictions and trials, for [it will last only] ten days and not [be] long-lived." Andrew's paraphrase does *not* reflect what the *Smyrnaeans* faced. The Apocalypse text speaks of the *devil* putting the Smyrnaeans into *prison*. Andrew's language reflects what *his* community faced: "afflictions and trials" caused by the "enemies of God." He encourages them to persevere, since these hardships will not last long: "For this reason, death must be despised, since in a little while it grants the 'unfading crown of life.'"[30]

Andrew's exposition offered a balanced view of the Book of Revelation. It countered the fear that the end had arrived, but also combated the threat to the other extreme, that of indifference, a hazard bolstered by Oikoumenios's interpretation. Andrew's unexpressed purposes were to encourage spiritual vigilance, to temper apocalyptic expectations and calm fears. The commentary neither promoted indifference nor fueled hysteria, but struck an appropriately balanced note in its attitude toward the end times, a note which continues to resonate today in Eastern Christianity.

29. See chapter 10.   30. Andrew, Chap. 4. *Comm.* 67.

8

ORIENTATION, STRUCTURE, AND CHARACTERISTICS

A Pastoral Orientation

A notable quality of Andrew's commentary is his pastoral disposition. His expectation that reading Revelation will result in spiritual benefit by prompting compunction may be the most noteworthy characteristic of Andrew's orientation and is closely connected to his purpose.[1] The Apocalypse teaches that "death must be despised"[2] and it guides the reader "to true life"[3] and "to a blessed end."[4] The purpose of Revelation and the commentary are to lead the reader "to compunction," remembering the rewards promised to the righteous and punishment that awaits the wicked.[5] He hoped the commentary would produce "contempt" for present and transitory facets of life, and focus attention on a desire for the abiding "future things."[6]

In his orientation we see tremendous contrast between the two commentaries. Andrew's purpose and tone are consistently pastoral, whereas Oikoumenios's tone could be described as "scholarly," or "philosophical." Andrew's role as a devoted shepherd of souls shines through in the style and content of the commentary. His tone is never one of

---

1. See chapter 7.
2. Andrew, Chap. 4, *Comm.* 67.
3. Andrew, Chap. 71, *Comm.* 239.
4. Andrew, Chap. 72, *Comm.* 242.
5. Andrew, Prologue, *Comm.* 54.
6. Andrew, Prologue, *Comm.* 53.

"hell-fire and brimstone," not even of admonition, warning, threats, or scolding. There is no elaboration on the description of sufferings, only a discussion of what the text of Revelation itself already contains. He does not resort to manipulative or inflammatory language to motivate people with warnings that the end is near, he does not dwell on the suffering or destruction described in Revelation to frighten his readers into action. Instead, Andrew emphasizes the love of God for all people, their freedom to choose between right and wrong, and God's desire that "all be saved and come to knowledge of the truth."[7] His comments are consistently and remarkably positive and affirming. This is the mark of a true pastor and shepherd, not to mention the mark of an experienced, genuine and gentle spiritual father.

This pastoral orientation is evident in the difference between Andrew and Oikoumenios on the matter of unrepentant sinners. Oikoumenios might remark about the punishment of sinners and note their lack of repentance, a detail which is found in the text of Revelation itself. But when Andrew mentions the punishment of sinners, he repeatedly and actively encourages the repentance and reformation of all, including himself, and emphasizes that it is within the power of all to choose to be saved. "For to be born or not to be born is not up to us, but to struggle and to be victorious [against] evil demons and to gain the eternal blessings is for us."[8]

The commentary has a gentle tone which is even reflected in the way that Andrew responds to Oikoumenios, who is never named. Andrew has nothing negative to say about any opponents, not even the Persians.[9] Compare this to Oikoumenios's description of the "Greeks" (meaning pagans) as "accursed and God-forsaken."[10] Nestorius and

---

7. Andrew, Chap. 59, *Comm.* 203. 1 Tim. 2:4.   8. Andrew, Chap. 50, *Comm.* 174.

9. Andrew does refer to the Persians as "barbarians," however this was not a pejorative term in the Greek language, but was the generic term to refer to anyone who did not know Greek. It came to be identified with people who were not cultured because the Greeks closely identified the Greek language with culture. The Greek use of the term "barbarians" is comparable to the catch-all term "gentiles" or "the nations" that biblical authors used to refer to all those who were not Jewish.

10. Oik. 10.11.1, FOTC 112:160.

Eutyches are described by Oikoumenios as "abominable."[11] Nestorius is "accursed" and Eutyches is "hated by God."[12] The Manicheans are "accursed and disgusting,[13] and Nicolaus, considered to be the founder of the Nicolaitan sect, is a "blasphemous and disgusting heresiarch."[14]

In dramatic contrast, Andrew does not use the commentary as an opportunity to attack pagans or heretics. The only hint of any use of the commentary other than as a purely pastoral message directed at the flock might be found in one instance in which Andrew is promoting doctrinal orthodoxy, probably in response to Oikoumenios, a Miaphysite.[15] Although at times he expresses puzzlement about Oikoumenios's conclusions, there is never any antagonism toward Oikoumenios or toward anyone with whom Andrew disagrees. Even when Andrew contradicts Oikoumenios, he is not very harsh in his criticism. In Andrew's strongest rejection of Oikoumenios's opinion, he simply describes Oikoumenios's conclusion as "incongruous" with the context.[16] But he rarely rejects Oikoumenios's interpretation entirely except where he believes it is baseless, spiritually unprofitable, harmful, or misleading. With great generosity of spirit, and in a gentle and self-assured manner, he offers the interpretation of Oikoumenios first, usually allowing it to stand, but then provides his own opinion afterwards in addition to other possible interpretations.

A Liturgical Orientation

A second feature of Andrew's orientation is its liturgical character. The commentary contains many liturgical references and allusions which are not immediately obvious. Andrew does not quote Scripture only to support his conclusion, but to evoke a familiar prayer or a hymn in the mind of the reader which happens to contain that bit of Scrip-

---

11. Oik. 1.3.3, FOTC 112:21.
12. Oik. 2.13.2, FOTC 112:46.
13. Oik. 2.13.2, FOTC 112:46.
14. Oik. 2.3.9, FOTC 112:37.
15. In response to Oikoumenios's comment that the Trisagion hymn ("Holy God, Holy Mighty, Holy Immortal, have mercy on us") refers to Christ (Oik. 2.13.1), Andrew explained how it refers to all three members of the Trinity. Andrew, Chap. 1, *Comm.* 58.
16. Andrew, Chap. 23, *Comm.* 116.

ture. Often it is not a direct quotation but an allusion to a passage as it is used and known in the life of the Church. Examples can be found in the many references to prayer rising up as incense to God, which would remind the reader of an extremely well-known vesper hymn based on Psalm 141:2: "Let my prayer arise in your sight as incense." Andrew's reference to "leaving one's father's house"[17] would instantly remind the reader of a well-known *prokeimenon* (a responsorial refrain) as well as its meaning in the spiritual life.[18] Commenting on Revelation 7:16 "They will no longer hunger nor thirst," Andrew remarks, "Naturally. For they will have the 'heavenly bread' and the 'water of life.'"[19] "Heavenly bread" is an expression from a hymn in the Liturgy of the Pre-sanctified Gifts, which we know was in use in Andrew's time.[20] The reference to those words would evoke in the reader the entire hymn, especially the phrase "heavenly bread and cup of life, taste and see that the Lord is good."

Such allusions are very subtle and would easily pass unrecognized by those who are not active in the liturgical and sacramental life of the Eastern Orthodox tradition. Of course, Revelation inherently contains many liturgical references: hymnody, incense, altar, prayers, and worship. But we know that Andrew's interpretation of these details was influenced by his liturgical orientation because the comments he makes and the conclusions he reaches are not obvious from the Apocalypse text itself but clearly arise out of his liturgical life. Andrew's exegesis is influenced by the prayers and hymns of the Church. For example, he remarks that the hymn of the Cherubim, "holy, holy, holy," can be applied to each member of the Trinity separately. In support of this, he cites two passages from Scripture, one in which the hymn is applied to the Son and the other to the Holy Spirit, but he supports his exegetical conclusion about the Father by citing a prayer of the Divine Liturgy.[21] His assumes that the biblical text can never be properly understood

---

17. Andrew, Chap. 19, *Comm.* 108. "Hear, O daughter, and consider and incline your ear; forget your people and your father's house, and the king will desire your beauty" (Ps. 45:10).

18. The verse was interpreted by the Fathers as an allegorical call to the soul (a feminine noun in Greek), to make herself attractive to her king, God.

19. Andrew, Chap. 20, *Comm.* 111.   20. ἄρτον οὐράνιον.

21. Andrew, Chap. 1, *Comm.* 58.

apart from an ecclesiastical context. Just as the biblical text shapes the Church—its doctrines, prayers, hymns, sacraments, etc.—the Church, through the entirety of its life and expression, provides the context for understanding the biblical text.

One of the interesting historical details in Revelation is the mention of an early martyr from Pergamum, Antipas (Rev. 2:13). Andrew would have certainly commemorated the martyrdom of Antipas during the course of the liturgical year[22] and he tells us that he has read the account of Antipas's martyrdom.[23] Oikoumenios does not even mention Antipas but passes over the detail of a named martyr in the Bible without any comment.[24] This also indicates an entirely different orientation for the two men.

One of the most consistent liturgical themes in the commentary, besides the many references to incense and hymnody, involves the activity and participation of the angels in prayer and petitions. Angels offer prayers up as incense[25] and even coliturgize with people.[26] During the "small entrance" (a procession with the Gospels during the divine liturgy of St. John Chrysostom), the priest prays: "cause that with our entrance there may be an entrance of holy angels serving with us." In his many comments about the angels in Revelation, Andrew reflects the entire Eastern liturgical tradition with its many references to angelic participation in worship, references to angels in hymns and prayers, and the artistic representation of angels on liturgical objects and in iconography on church walls.

But perhaps the most striking, and yet also the most subtle liturgical allusion, is Andrew's interpretation of the throne, the dominant image of God in Revelation, as a place of "repose" rather than as a place of power, rule, authority or judgment. Andrew consistently describes the throne as "repose."[27] The altar in an Orthodox Church is

---

22. His feast day is April 11 on the Orthodox Christian calendar.
23. Andrew, Chap. 5, *Comm.* 67.   24. Oik. 2.7.
25. Andrew, Chap. 21, *Comm.* 112.   26. Andrew, Chap. 20, *Comm.* 110.
27. Andrew, Chap. 9, *Comm.* 79; Andrew, Chap. 10, *Comm.* 81; Andrew, Chap. 10, *Comm.* 83; Andrew, Chap. 20, *Comm.* 109; Andrew, Chap. 64, *Comm.* 216; Andrew, Chap. 68, *Comm.* 235.

called the "throne of God," yet the symbol does not usually evoke the image of a judgment seat but a place of rest. His consistent reference to the throne as "repose" reveals Andrew's liturgical perspective and may have been inspired by two of the most important prayers which a priest recites in the Divine Liturgy of St. John Chrysostom. During the Trisagion hymn the priest stands before the altar and reads the prayer that begins, "Holy God, who *rests* in thy holy place."[28] And during the Cherubic hymn, the people recall the presence of the angels and represent them in their chanting as the priest prays to God, "Borne on the throne of the Cherubim and Lord of the Seraphim and King of Israel, who alone art holy and *rests* in the Holy Place."[29]

A Sacramental Orientation

Andrew's commentary also evinces a strong sacramental orientation. For example, his use of the phrase "garment of incorruption" to describe the white robes of the Christians of Sardis (3:4) is an allusion to the baptismal service in which this phrase is used multiple times.[30] The expression "garment of incorruption" also occurs in a prayer during the Divine Liturgy said for the catechumens preparing for baptism. Revelation 7:11 states that the twenty-four elders, the four animals, the angels, and the saints stood around the throne of God, but Andrew makes the startling comment that they *dance* around the throne.[31] It is difficult to imagine how such an idea could have come to his mind except possibly in connection with the circular ceremonial "dances" which take place at the Orthodox sacraments of baptism and marriage.[32] Andrew's allu-

---

28. "Holy God, Holy Mighty, Holy Immortal, have mercy on us."
29. "We who mystically represent the cherubim and sing the thrice-holy hymn to the life-giving Trinity, let us lay aside all earthly care, that we may receive the King of all, invisibly upborne by angelic hosts."
30. Andrew, Chap. 7, *Comm.* 74.   31. Andrew, Chap. 20, *Comm.* 109.
32. At a baptism, the participants process three times around the baptismal font. At a wedding they walk three times around the table in front of which the couple was married. The "dance" in both sacraments is more akin to a ceremonial walk, but it is accompanied by joyful chanting. The hymns sung during these "dances" include images found in Revela-

sion to a choral dance taking place around the throne is a very striking detail because there is no reference to dancing in the Apocalypse and in the scene depicted by Revelation 7 the individuals are described in the kingdom of heaven as standing around the throne.

When Christ promises the "hidden manna" in the letters to the churches (Rev. 2:17), Andrew associates this promise with Eucharist. "The 'Bread of Life' is the 'hidden manna,' the One who descended from heaven for us and has become edible."[33] Andrew connects manna to the Eucharist through the Bread of Life statements in John 6 which is strongly Eucharistic (John 6:35, 48). Compare this to Oikoumenios who blandly concludes that the hidden manna represents "spiritual and future blessings."[34] Another example of Andrew's sacramental orientation is that he consistently connects water images with the Holy Spirit. When the opening vision describes Christ's voice "like the sound of many waters" (Rev. 1:15b), Oikoumenios simply remarks that it was a loud sound. But Andrew sees a connection to baptism and the "rivers of living water" promised by Christ (John 7:38). In another instance, commenting upon Revelation 7:17 ("For the Lamb in the midst of the throne will shepherd them, and he will guide them to springs of waters of life"), Andrew again interprets the water as the Spirit.[35] Oikoumenios does not even mention the water reference, let alone connect it to the Spirit. Likewise, in Revelation 22:1, the "river of the water of life, bright as crystal, flowing from the throne of God and of the Lamb" is the Holy Spirit for Andrew and it "hints at a baptism of regeneration being activated through the Spirit."[36] But Oikoumenios makes no sacramental association, saying that the river is "the rich

---

tion. The word "dance" here can also refer to forming a chorus in a circle, but singing in a circle was usually accompanied by dancing. Many images from Revelation itself and themes in Andrew's commentary are closely paralleled in the hymns sung during these ceremonial, sacramental "dances." The sacraments of baptism and marriage both begin with an invocation of the kingdom of heaven ("Blessed be the Kingdom of the Father, and of the Son and of the Holy Spirit, now and ever and unto the ages of ages"), which is also the setting for the scene in Revelation 7.

33. Andrew, Chap. 5, *Comm.* 69.
35. Andrew, Chap. 20, *Comm.* 111.
34. Oik. 2.7.5, FOTC 112:41.
36. Andrew, Chap. 68, *Comm.* 232.

and abundant graces of Christ."[37] Still another example of a baptismal interpretation is the woman wrapped in the sun with the moon under her feet (Rev.12). Baptismal references dominate Andrew's interpretation of that section of Revelation.[38] For Andrew, the moon represents baptism, a classic patristic interpretation of moon imagery because of its association with tides, hence with water. It is under her feet because baptism is the foundation of the Church. Again, the contrast with Oikoumenios's orientation is striking: for Oikoumenios the moon is the Law of Moses, which is waning.[39]

Another very striking and surprising difference between Andrew and Oikoumenios, which again highlights their differing orientations, is the interpretation of the faithful who have a "seal" on their foreheads (Rev. 7:3). Andrew makes an immediate and obvious connection between the seal on the forehead and the sacrament of Holy Chrismation ("confirmation" in the West).[40] Oikoumenios makes no connection at that point between the seal and Chrismation. Later, in Revelation 9:1–4, when the locusts are instructed not to harm those who are sealed on the forehead, Andrew again connects this to Chrismation and writes that the people who are harmed are those "who had not been sealed with the divine seal on their foreheads and [who do not] shine round about with the enlightenment of the life-giving cross through the Holy Spirit."[41] Commenting on the verse, in that particular instance Oikoumenios connects the seal with baptism, but his conclusion is extremely peculiar and creates theological problems.[42]

Like Andrew, Oikoumenios is also an Eastern Christian and occasionally associates Revelation's imagery with the sacraments and the liturgy. However, such connections are not as consistent, as frequent, or

---

37. Oik. 12.7.3, FOTC 112:195.
38. Andrew, Chap. 33, *Comm.* 136–40.
39. Oik. 6.19.3.
40. In the sacrament of Chrismation, the individual who has just been baptized is dedicated to Christ by being anointed with the oil of Chrism, made in the form of a cross on the forehead and elsewhere on the body. Chrismation conveys the "gifts of the Holy Spirit" and is referred to as "the seal of the gift of the Holy Spirit."
41. Andrew, Chap. 26, *Comm.* 121.
42. Oik. 5.17.7–9. See chapter 14.

as specifically liturgical as those found in Andrew's commentary. A very good example is the formulation of the concluding doxologies found in each commentary. Both Andrew and Oikoumenios close each chapter with a doxology. Oikoumenios's commentary contains twelve chapters. Ten doxologies are directed to Christ, one is directed to "God"[43] and only one is directed to all three members of the Holy Trinity.[44] Oikoumenios's formula is very simple, typically: "to him [Christ] be the glory forever, amen."[45] Andrew's doxologies, however, are more elaborate and specifically liturgical in style and tone. Andrew's commentary has twenty four doxologies and each of them references all three members of the Trinity, as doxologies in the Orthodox Church always do. The doxologies mention Christ first, with the description of Christ varying depending upon the theme of the preceding exposition, followed by a reference to the Father, (usually "together with the Father"), continuing with a reference to the "Holy" or "All-holy" or "Life-giving" Spirit, and ending in a classic liturgical style, "now and ever and unto the ages of ages. Amen."[46]

The Structure of the Commentary

Andrew informs the reader in his prologue that he will divide his commentary into twenty-four "sections" (λόγους) and further into seventy two "chapters" (κεφάλαια). The twenty four sections stand for the twenty-four elders who symbolize all "those who have pleased God from the beginning to the end of times."[47] The further division of each section into three parts or "chapters" stands for the three part existence of each elder: body, soul, and spirit.[48] The seventy-two chapters are numbered sequentially from one through seventy-two and each chapter has a heading which informs the reader of the subject matter of that chapter. The choice to create the twenty four large sections which overarch

---

43. Oik. 7.15.4. See FOTC 112: 122. 44. Oik. 5.25.4. See FOTC 112: 94.
45. ᾧ ἡ δόξα εἰς τοὺς αἰῶνας, ἀμήν.
46. νῦν καὶ ἀεὶ καὶ εἰς τοὺς αἰῶνας τῶν αἰώνων. ἀμήν.
47. Andrew, Prologue, *Comm.* 53.
48. Andrew has already identified humans as possessing these three components. Prologue, *Comm.* 53.

the seventy-two smaller chapters creates an artificial structure which is not based on the intrinsic structure of the Apocalypse itself. This is actually unnecessary and somewhat awkward since events in the Apocalypse often occur in groups of seven, a number not divisible by three. Events which occur in groups of seven cannot be contained in two sections since each section only contains three chapters. But because the chapters are much smaller and are numbered consecutively from one through seventy two, the larger section divisions are basically irrelevant to the structure and the reading of the commentary. The chapter divisions are the most important element of the commentary's structure. Each chapter discusses a small, specific episode in the Apocalypse and the length of each chapter varies depending upon the subject matter. The larger section divisions would be entirely unnoticeable except that each section ends with a doxology at the end of the third chapter in that section, which to some extent affects the flow of the commentary.

The presentation of the commentary is extremely orderly and easy to follow. Andrew usually quotes one or two verses from the text of Revelation and then comments upon the text, although frequently he does not even quote an entire verse but only a small portion before explaining it. Occasionally he quotes larger sections of Revelation text, up to four or five verses, but this is unusual. In this respect, except for the division into seventy-two chapters, the presentation of his analysis is very similar to what a modern commentator would do. It is clear that he is handling the text according to what is required for an effective exposition. After he has concluded his explanation of all the chapters, Andrew offers a summary of the interpretation as an overall review of the entire commentary.[49]

Style and Characteristics of the Commentary

Andrew's writing style is concise. At times he is so brief that the exposition would have benefited from more elaboration. But his style has

---

49. Andrew, Chap. 72, *Comm.* 242–45.

certain advantages over that of Oikoumenios. He presents his ideas in a careful, thoughtful, straightforward, and uncluttered manner. Andrew is very confident and comfortable with the text and he is very consistent in his interpretation. He lacks egoism and does not feel the need to make displays of knowledge. He stays on task and is not distracted from his purpose, neither straying to make doctrinal proclamations, nor to denounce heretics, nor to make unrelated historical observations. He will make a comment on Christology or other doctrine when such a comment is called for by the text under consideration. Stylistically and methodologically, Andrew stands firmly within the patristic tradition.

Andrew cites other Fathers and quotes from them on a number of occasions, but his commentary is not in any respect a catena. Too little exegetical tradition existed in the East for Andrew to be able to rely entirely on preexisting interpretations. He is not reluctant to embrace more than one interpretive option for a given detail or passage. This does not indicate weakness or indecisiveness on his part. Rather, it indicates Andrew's recognition of the richness in the text which allows for more than one level of meaning. When a verse is controversial or has a number of possible interpretations, Andrew reports the various possibilities and the opinions of others. Since his view is not always immediately evident, one must usually read to the end of the discussion to know which view is Andrew's opinion, if indeed he prefers one over another.

Andrew is remarkably flexible and inclusive in reporting the interpretations of others and usually does not reject alternative ideas outright. For example, he gives five possible interpretations of the symbolism of the four living beings of Revelation 4,[50] four possibilities for the image of the sky rolled up like a scroll (Rev. 6:14),[51] and five options for the symbolism of the feet in the vision of Christ in Revelation 1:15.[52] Andrew often signals optional interpretations with, "It is either this,

---

50. Andrew, Chap. 10, *Comm.* 83–84. 51. Andrew, Chap. 18, *Comm.* 99.
52. Andrew, Chap. 2, *Comm.* 61–62.

or ...." He respects the reader's intelligence and is confident enough in his own opinions to report various alternatives. He allows other interpretations to stand if he finds nothing especially objectionable in them. If he reports a variety of opinions, Andrew's opinion is usually last. He signals his disapproval of a foregoing opinion and introduces his own with a variety of expressions such as, "This may be understood differently,"[53] "either this or perhaps,"[54] "more suitably,"[55] "more correctly,"[56] or "much more,"[57] and then continues by very matter-of-factly supporting his interpretation and leading the reader to realize why his view is to be preferred and the other is less acceptable.

We find many of the same characteristics displayed by Andrew in the expositions of an earlier era, the "golden age" of the Fathers. Chrysostom, for example, also quoted the text one or two verses at a time and commented upon them before moving on to the next verse. Chrysostom also occasionally referred to the opinions of others without naming them, using the same type of expression which we see in Andrew: "some say." Augustine did likewise. Augustine and Chrysostom also often gave more than one meaning of a difficult passage.

Andrew's generous reporting of a variety of opinions can create misconceptions, however. Considerable caution is advised when seeking Andrew's interpretation of almost any given passage. In order to determine which opinion is actually that of Andrew, it is advisable to carefully read the entire discussion of the pericope under consideration. A hasty or sloppy reading of Andrew will result in reporting of someone else's views by mistake, often the opinion of Oikoumenios with whom Andrew frequently disagrees. For example, Andrew is typically reported as interpreting Revelation 1:4 ("Grace to you and peace from the One who is, and who was, and who is to come, and from the seven spirits which are before his throne") as referring to the Holy Trinity. This mistake is found in two books which had published ex-

---

53. Andrew, Chap. 1, *Comm.* 59.
54. Andrew, Chap. 10, *Comm.* 82.
55. Andrew, Chap. 10, *Comm.* 82.
56. Andrew, Chap. 19, *Comm.* 106.
57. Andrew, Chap. 19, *Comm.* 102.

cerpts in English from Andrew's commentary.⁵⁸ In fact, in that statement Andrew is reporting the opinion of *Oikoumenios*, with whom Andrew *disagrees*. It is tempting to identify the Trinity in the statement "who is, was and is to come," as Oikoumenios did, but Andrew's exegetical skill leads him to easily recognize the flaw in Oikoumenios's interpretation: it does not fit the immediate context of the passage.⁵⁹ Andrew believes that particular statement *theologically* can be applied to each member of the Trinity individually, but specifically the statement in Revelation 1:4 is made with respect to the Father alone because the verse states that the revelation is "from the One who is, was and is to come, *and* from Jesus Christ." The Son cannot be the "one who was," as Oikoumenios claims, since the Son is about to be introduced by the words "and from Jesus Christ."⁶⁰

Another example of how one could easily mistake Oikoumenios's opinion for that of Andrew can be seen in Andrew's explanation of the locusts of Revelation 9. He begins in a typical manner, "Some said ... the star is a divine angel," a reference to Oikoumenios.⁶¹ Andrew then proceeds to present several details of Oikoumenios's interpretation with no hint that Andrew will shortly disagree with almost everything he has just reported from Oikoumenios's commentary. Furthermore, no language suggests that the initial "some said" includes several of

---

58. *Revelation*, ed. and trans. William Weinrich, Ancient Christian Commentary on Scripture 12 (Downers Grove, Ill.: InterVarsity Press, 2005), 3; Archbishop Averky Taushev, *Apocalypse*, trans. Seraphim Rose (Platina, Calif.: Valaam Society of America, 1985), 44.

59. Oik. 1.7.1–3, FOTC 112: 23.

60. Andrew continues his argument against Oikoumenios's interpretation by explaining how "is, was, and is to come" can refer to all three members of the Trinity, even if the phrase does not refer to all three in this particular instance. Even though Andrew has rejected the interpretation of Oikoumenios, by the examples which follow he explains how this expression is properly applied to all three persons together and can also apply to each member of the Trinity individually because they share the same nature and because of the unity of the divine will and purpose. What follows is a very good example of patristic exegetical technique. Because the phrase can be *theologically* applied to all three, he allows Oikoumenios's interpretation to stand. Andrew does not reject it outright and signals that Oikoumenios's interpretation is allowable by prefacing Oikoumenios's interpretation of the seven spirits as angels rather than as the Holy Spirit, with the words "it is possible." Andrew, Chap. 1, *Comm.* 57.

61. Andrew, Chap. 26, *Comm.*120.

Oikoumenios's ideas which follow afterwards not just the statement about the angel. The reporting of Oikoumenios's opinion is straightforward and matter-of-fact, devoid of any negative or critical tone: the pit is Gehenna, the locusts are worms, the smoke, the five months, etc. If one were to simply peruse the initial comments for that passage looking for Andrew's interpretation, it would be extremely easy to mistake Oikoumenios's statements for Andrew's opinions. His inclusive style can create a misimpression on the part of a careless reader.

9

ANDREW'S EXEGETICAL EDUCATION AND SKILL

Andrew admits that he is incapable of fully understanding Revelation, certainly not on its highest level. "We ourselves do not understand the entire depth of the hidden spirit within it."[1] But also not even on its most basic level. "We neither dare to understand everything according to the letter."[2] These are typical expressions of modesty in a prologue of this kind. In spite of assertions of inadequacy, Andrew proceeds with his exposition, stating that he will attempt to explain it "since it has been ordered by God to be proclaimed to those who are more perfect in knowledge"[3] He asserts that he will not offer conjecture,[4] which may be a comment directed at Oikoumenios who engages in a significant amount of imaginative interpretation and even admits to "guessing" at the identity of the twenty-four elders on the thrones.[5]

---

1. Andrew, Prologue, *Comm* 53.
2. Andrew, Prologue, *Comm.* 53.
3. Andrew, Prologue, *Comm.* 53. Probably a reference to Rev. 22:10 "Do not seal up the words of prophecy in this book."
4. τῶν ἐστοχασμένων. Andrew, Prologue, *Comm.* 53.
5. "My guess is that they were Abel, Enoch, and Noah, Abraham, Isaac and Jacob, Melchisedek and Job, Moses and Aaron, Joshua the son of Nun, and Samuel, David, Elijah and Elisha, the twelve minor prophets combined together as one, Isaiah and Jeremiah, Ezekiel, Daniel, Zechariah, and John, James the son of Joseph and Stephen the martyrs of the New Testament." Oik. 3.7.1, FOTC 112: 55.

Andrew may not resort to guessing and conjecture, but his task is difficult since he has little interpretive tradition about Revelation to draw upon. He turns for help instead to the techniques of interpretation in which he was trained.[6]

Andrew preserves a rich tradition of Eastern Christian Apocalypse interpretation. He consistently gives various possible interpretations, sometimes referring to "teachers," "Fathers," or otherwise hinting at unnamed sources. Oikoumenios only seems to refer to unnamed sources on three occasions.[7] Andrew uses exegetical terms of art, and even when he does not use the terminology, one can see the application of the technique. He has a good familiarity with the Scripture, which will be discussed below, and he knows how to apply it appropriately. Andrew's exegetical training can be seen in his initial reference to basic concepts and methodology. He begins his exposition by expressing the classic patristic understanding of Scripture as having three levels.[8] Oikoumenios, on the other hand refers to three levels of prophecy—past, present and future—something with which Andrew strongly disagrees and which is not part of the mainstream patristic tradition.

Juan Hernández has observed that Andrew does not apply his tripartite hermeneutical principle for Scripture interpretation "with rigor and consistency" but rather we consistently see "Andrew's arbitrary appeal to various modes of reading, as necessary."[9] This is hardly surprising. In fact, this is the norm in patristic Scripture interpretation. Methodological rigidity, consistency, or even discipline was not expected. The interpreter was neither expected nor required to identify three levels of

---

6. Faced with the same problem, Oikoumenios, on the other hand, turns to other arenas, such as philosophy, medicine and physics. Adele Monaci Castagno draws the same conclusion. "I Commenti de Ecumenio e di Andrea di Cesarea: Due letture divergenti dell' Apocalisse," *Memorie della Accademia delle scienze di Torino II, Classe di scienze, morali, storiche e filologiche* V, Fascicolo IV (1981): 327.

7. Castagno observes that Oikoumenios, whom she admires for his originality and theological richness, almost entirely ignores the Eastern patristic tradition which Andrew's commentary recovered and preserved. "I Commenti," 426.

8. Andrew, Prologue, *Comm.* 52.

9. Juan Hernández, Jr., "The Relevance of Andrew of Caesarea for New Testament Textual Criticism," *Journal of Biblical Literature*, 130, no. 1 (2011): 183–96, 187.

scripture for every passage. The statement about three levels of Scripture merely acknowledged that multiple levels of meaning were always present. This allowed the interpreter to employ whatever was useful for the exposition of that passage, particularly when the expositor was a pastor, as in this case. Andrew was not writing to produce a scholarly commentary, but trying to draw out the meaning of the passage for the spiritual edification of a congregation or a reader.[10] Andrew's lack of methodological consistency would not have engendered criticism. Origen himself, who initially articulated the idea of three levels of Scripture, did not apply it consistently but usually gave some small amount of attention to the literal sense and then quickly moved on to the allegorical interpretation which dominated his expositions. The same can be said of Augustine and other interpreters, especially those who preferred allegory. Patristic commentaries did not present a consistent and balanced exposition of a passage according to all three (and sometimes four) identified levels.

Knowledge of Manuscript Variations

Oikoumenios does not comment on any manuscript variations in Revelation, although he is at least aware of differing versions of the Old Testament.[11] By contrast, Andrew is aware of well-known manuscript variations and comments upon them, something to be expected of a skilled and educated interpreter. For example, Andrew is aware that Revelation 3:7, "These things says the Holy One, the True One, who has the key of David," has a common variant, "key of Hades." He interprets the passage according to what he believes to be the better reading, "key of David," but then offers an alternative interpretation

---

10. Gregory of Nyssa, in the Prologue to his *Homilies on Song of Songs* declined to engage in "quibbles" over interpretive terminology. The important thing was finding what was "useful" (χρήσιμον) in the text. His only apparent mandate was to rise above the literal interpretation to discover the spiritual meaning.

11. He references the Greek translation of the Old Testament by Aquila (Oik. 8.17.2, FOTC 112:131), which was an alternative to the Septuagint.

in case this is not the original reading: "Since in some manuscripts instead of 'David,' 'Hades' is written, [this would mean that] through the key of Hades, the authority over life and death has been confirmed in Christ."[12] Elsewhere he comments on another well-known variation in Revelation 15:6 which describes the angels dressed in pure "linen," but some manuscripts read "stone." "From out of this temple the angels will come dressed in clean 'linen' or 'stone,' as some copies have, on account of the purity of their nature and their closeness to the Cornerstone."[13] Again, Andrew is following the typical practice of patristic interpreters to report known manuscript variations and interpret both, occasionally expressing an opinion regarding the accuracy of one reading over another. They typically did not engage in extensive analysis or a discussion on the merits of a textual variation since their task was not a scholarly endeavor but a spiritual one.[14]

Hernández expresses some surprise that Andrew seems so unconcerned about textual variations and did not "restore the wording of the Apocalypse when he had the chance." Hernández correctly observes that "Andrew's text-critical practices indicate, however, that what fascinates us may not be what held the attention of the ancients."[15] This is correct. Since all books were hand-copied, manuscript variations were a fact of life and did not warrant alarm, outrage or tremendous interest. Perhaps Andrew does not condemn scribes for such variations because he attributes these two variations to unintentional human error. However, he indeed had harsh words for those who intentionally changed Scripture, and he expresses his distain in remarks found in the final chapter of his commentary. The context is Revelation 22:18–19: "I bear witness to everyone who hears the words of the prophecy of this book: if anyone adds to them, God will add to him the seven

---

12. Andrew, Chap. 8, *Comm.* 75.
13. Andrew, Chap. 45, *Comm.* 163.
14. Hernández has analyzed Andrew's awareness of textual variations and his lack of reaction to the variants, and compares them to his dramatic condemnation of scribes who "atticize" the text. "The Relevance of Andrew of Caesarea," 189–91.
15. Juan Hernández, "The Relevance of Andrew of Caesarea," 195.

plagues which have been written in this book. And if anyone takes away from the words of the book of this prophecy, God will take away his share from the tree of life and from the holy city, which have been written in this book." Andrew writes,

Fearful is the curse against those who falsify the Holy Scripture, since their rashness and boldness is able to alienate the stubborn from the good things of the future age. Indeed, in order that we not suffer, it warns us who hear to neither add anything nor subtract, but to consider the written peculiarities [of the Apocalypse] as more trustworthy and dignified than the Attic syntax and dialectic syllogisms, since also when someone discovers many things in those [writings] that do not measure up according to the rules, he is guided by the trustworthiness of the poets and authors in them. As far as [finding] a mid-point in matters of opinion between us and them, [it is] even impossible to grasp in the mind. I think there is more [difference] than the difference between light and darkness.[16]

This is may have been a comment directed toward those scribes who intentionally attempted to "correct" the biblical text, a problem which especially afflicted the Book of Revelation because of the peculiar and frequent Hebraisms of its Greek. It may also be a comment directed at those who rejected the Apocalypse entirely because of its very poor Greek.[17] Andrew may be offering an additional defense of the book against its detractors, echoing patristic authorities of the past who rose to the defense of apostolic writings against pagan and Jewish critics who ridiculed Christian Scriptures for their low level of Greek and lack of sophistication. Even though Andrew is living in a period in which Greek paganism has largely disappeared, the sting of such

---

16. See Andrew, Chap. 72, *Comm.* 241–42.

17. Dionysios, Bishop of Alexandria, concluded that the Apocalypse could not have been written by John the Apostle because the language of the Gospel was beautiful and grammatically correct, but not that of Revelation. Dionysios commented about the author of the Apocalypse: "I perceive, however, that his dialect and language are not accurate Greek, but that he uses barbarous idioms, and, in some places, solecisms" (Eusebius, *E.H.* 7.26, NPNF² 1:311). As we have seen in chapter 2, the differences in literary style between the Apocalypse and the Gospel of John was the primary reason Dionysios gave for rejecting the apostolic authorship of the Apocalypse.

criticisms remained and Andrew would have been very familiar with patristic apologies which defended the Scriptures from pagan critics who had attacked the Bible as crude and unrefined. Andrew may have been inspired to take a stance for the simplicity and truthfulness of "the fishermen" against the slick but empty sophistry of pagan philosophers, just as his ecclesiastical predecessors of earlier eras had done.[18]

Knowledge of the Canonical Status of Revelation

In his prologue Andrew dismisses any objection to the status of Revelation as scripture by stating: "Concerning the divine inspiration of the book [τοῦ θεοπνεύστου τῆς βίβλου] we believe it superfluous to lengthen the discussion."[19] "Makarios" certainly accepts Revelation as Scripture otherwise he would not have asked Andrew to write the commentary. Andrew does not discuss the authorship or inspiration of Revelation, nonetheless, he feels the need to defend its canonical status, a matter which must be addressed before he can proceed further. Oikoumenios also faces the same concern and takes up the issue twice, both at the beginning and at the end of his commentary.[20] Oikoumenios provides an interesting detail and affirms our assessment of Revelation's canonical status in the East at that time. He notes that the *majority* believes that Revelation was written by "some other John," not the apostle.[21]

Knowledge of Other Traditional Scripture Interpretations

Despite his self-confessed limitations and professions of inadequacy, Andrew nonetheless proves himself fully capable and well-qualified for the task. His modesty reflects the literary conventions of

---

18. See, for example, John Chrysostom *Homilies on Matthew* 1.9–12.
19. Andrew, Prologue, *Comm.* 53.   20. Oik.1.1.4–6 and 12.20.
21. Oik.12.20.4.

the age, but in this case his remarks may honestly hint at the daunting job of interpreting Revelation. But Andrew prevails over all his concerns. He demonstrates knowledge of traditional explanations from earlier eras, employs well-known techniques of patristic interpretation, and skillfully handles the text. Clues that he had exegetical training abound. For example, Andrew knows the traditional interpretation that the seven churches addressed in Revelation 2 and 3 signify all churches everywhere.[22] Oikoumenios, who stated that John only wrote to seven churches because those were the cities converted by him,[23] probably did not know of the tradition that seven represented all, an interpretation which had long been applied to Paul's epistles as well.[24] Andrew is also aware of traditional explanations that resolve problems found in the gospels regarding the two differing genealogies of Christ in Matthew and Luke. Andrew's comments hint that he knows how the problem was resolved in the interpretative tradition.[25] He is also aware of a well-known problem raised by John 7:38 and shows that he knows the traditional resolution of that problem as well, which is based on the correct punctuation of the text.[26] Andrew is aware of the etymology

---

22. Andrew, Chap. 1, *Comm.* 56.   23. Oik. 1.25, FOTC 112: 28.

24. This is a very common patristic interpretation of this verse. The number seven was said to symbolize perfection and completeness, hence early interpreters understood the number of churches addressed by John and Paul as signifying the universality of the message. This interpretation is found in the Muratorian Canon, in Augustine (*Ep.* 49), Victorinus, *Commentary on the Apocalypse* 1.7, Cyprian *Exhortation for Martyrdom* 11, Tertullian, *Against Marcion* 5.17, and Gregory the Great, *Morals on the Book of Job*, 17.29(43) and 35.9(18).

25. Andrew, Chap.10, *Comm.* 84. Matthew gives the genealogy of Jesus as descending down from Abraham to David through Solomon to *Jacob*, the father of Joseph. But Luke traces the lineage backwards, stating that the father of Joseph was *Heli*, and then goes back through Nathan, the son of David. The problem was tackled by Julius Africanus (died c. 240) in his famous *Epistle to Aristides*. He concluded that both men were the father of Joseph due to a levirate marriage. (See Deut. 25:5.) Joseph's mother had first married Heli, but when he died childless she married his brother Jacob. Hence, Heli is the "legal" father of Joseph, as Andrew states, because he is Joseph's father through the Mosaic Law of levirate marriage. However, the biological father of Joseph is Jacob, or his father "by nature, not by law" according to Andrew. Julius's solution to the genealogical conflict was well known and widely followed. See Eusebius of Caesarea (*E. H.* 1.7.1–17), Jerome (*Comm. on Matthew* 1.16), Augustine (*Retractions* 2.7 and *Serm.* 1.27 [*Serm.* 51] Benedictine Edition, and Photios (cod. 34.22).

26. See Andrew, Chap. 20, *Comm.* 111.

of certain Hebrew words, such as "Satan," meaning "adversary,"[27] and "amen," meaning "let it be so."[28] Oikoumenios's exposition lacks many of these details, and while he shows some knowledge of other traditional etymologies, it is not to the extent shown by Andrew.

Andrew also knows what is expected of him as an interpreter and what is important for him to comment upon. Two general characteristics distinguish Andrew's exposition from Oikoumenios's very unique commentary and demonstrate that Andrew does not rely on Oikoumenios for his exegesis. The first is that Oikoumenios states peculiar and surprising conclusions which Andrew consistently refutes. The second, and equally surprising feature, is the large number of interpretations which go *unmentioned* by Oikoumenios. It is through a comparison of these particular features in the Oikoumenios commentary that Andrew's training and skill are most evident.

For example, Andrew explains the meanings of people and place names (such as the names of the twelve tribes), information acquired either from written compilations *(Onomastica)* or from an oral exegetical tradition. Oikoumenios does not even *write down* the names of the tribes as he copies those verses in the text of Revelation itself into his commentary, let alone explain them.[29] This would have been a very surprising omission at the time, signaling a lack of exegetical training. Another example of a traditional explanation missing from Oikoumenios is the interpretation of the twelve types of precious stones which decorate the New Jerusalem in Revelation 20. Oikoumenios ignores any symbolic meaning behind the different gems, simply remarking that the precious stones represent virtue. A spiritual explanation of the stone symbolism would have been of great interest to early readers and would have been expected from any interpreter. Most surprisingly, Oikoumenios does not even mention the opinion that the four living beings of chapter 4 represent the four evangelists, probably the most famous and enduring patristic interpretation about Revelation.

---

27. Andrew, Chap. 34, *Comm.* 143.   28. Andrew, Chap.1, *Comm.* 59.
29. Oik. 5.2–3, FOTC 112: 79–81.

Oikoumenios also does not interpret the various animal components of the beast of the sea (Rev. 13:1–2) as representing successive kingdoms, a renowned and venerable interpretation in Christian history. Instead Oikoumenios gives a rather naturalistic interpretation, entirely inconsistent with patristic tradition, assigning specific qualities to the beast based on the physical characteristics of those four animals.[30]

Oikoumenios concludes that the twenty-four elders of Revelation 4 are specific individuals whom John "saw" in his heavenly vision, and—compounding his error—Oikoumenios actually *names* them, after first admitting that he is guessing as to who they might be. Oikoumenios does not associate the white hair of Christ in the opening vision with the Ancient of Days (Dan. 7:9), but explains it as the "age-old intention of God."[31] He does not even associate the Lamb, the dominant image of Christ in Revelation, with sacrifice but offers a very weak explanation that the lamb is a symbol of "guilelessness and ability to provide," such as providing wool.[32] It is impossible to explain the glaring omissions from Oikoumenios's commentary without concluding that he lacked specific exegetical skills and an extensive knowledge of the interpretive tradition. He does show awareness of some traditional interpretations, such as the belief that the two witnesses of Revelation 11:3 are Enoch and Elijah.[33] He also has some knowledge of traditional Hebrew etymologies and traditions about the meaning of 666 given by Irenaeus, although he does not cite him,[34] which may indicate that he is not aware that this interpretation came from Irenaeus. And so it continues.

Andrew provides all of the classic patristic explanations of famous passages, as well as many other traditional interpretations, demonstrating a competence and theological education absent in the Oikoumenios commentary. The "successive kingdoms" explanation is relied upon heavily by Andrew, who also cites the Fathers before him. He also gives the interpretation of the four living beings as the four evan-

---

30. Oik. 7.11.8–9.
32. Oik. 3.13.11, FOTC 112: 62.
34. Oik. 12.20.5.
31. Oik. 1.27.9, FOTC 112: 30.
33. Oik. 6.11.3.

gelists and the twenty four elders as representing all those who have pleased God in the old and the new covenants, an obvious and well-known reference to the twelve tribes and twelve apostles in the Bible. Many other examples could be brought forward, and some will be discussed below, but it is clear that Oikoumenios was not as technically trained nor as steeped in the interpretive tradition as was Andrew. Oikoumenios's silence about these interpretations is so surprising that it strongly suggests that he either did not know them, or he did not deem them important—probably the former. The striking differences in their commentaries reflect Andrew's exegetical training and skill, and dramatically demonstrate that Andrew was not dependent upon Oikoumenios's interpretation.

Andrew's Limitations

Andrew is reluctant to undertake an exposition of Revelation, a task which "befits a great mind and [one] enlightened by the Divine Spirit."[35] He knew that "the exact knowledge of these matters" lies within the sphere of God, who alone "knows the times in which these prophesized things will come to pass, which is forbidden to seek."[36] Furthermore, on a personal level, he is well aware of his limitations and sees himself as spiritually unqualified since he is "deprived of the prophetic spirit"[37] and inadequate "to explain the things which are secretly and mysteriously seen by the saints."[38] As we have seen in chapter 7, such statements were common features in ancient literary works, but when faced with the difficulty of interpreting of Revelation, such a statement should not be dismissed as merely a conventional expression of modesty. Nonetheless, Andrew is not only fully qualified for the task, he demonstrates that the confidence which "Makarios" placed in him was justified. In sharp contrast with Oikoumenios, Andrew refuses to engage in "conjecture," so there will be no flights of untethered imagi-

---

35. Andrew, Prologue, *Comm.* 51.
36. Andrew, Prologue, *Comm.* 52.
37. Andrew, Prologue, *Comm.* 51.
38. Andrew, Prologue, *Comm.* 51.

nation with Andrew.[39] Thus, with little existing patristic guidance for Revelation, Andrew must have drawn from his theological education. The result is clear and compelling: the commentary demonstrates that Andrew was well-trained in patristic methodology and the existing techniques of biblical interpretation. Modest though he may have been when he begins the enterprise, by remarking that "many people" had asked him to undertake this effort, we are to understand that Andrew must have been a recognized expert in the Scriptures.

The Three Levels of Scripture Interpretation

It is a sign of a good interpreter to begin his commentary by explaining his methodology, which is exactly what Andrew does, even though he expresses what he knows to be obvious to "Makarios": "as you yourself well know, since there are three parts to a human being," (body, soul and spirit) "all divinely inspired Scripture has been endowed with three parts by divine grace."[40] He continues to explain how each level of meaning corresponds to the spiritual state of the reader.

The body is somewhat like the letter and history established according to sense perception. In like manner, the soul is the figurative sense, guiding the reader from that which can be perceived by the senses to that which can be perceived by the intellect. Likewise, the spirit has appeared to be the anagogical sense and the contemplation of the future and higher things.[41]

This statement reveals a fundamental belief about Andrew's view of Scripture and its interpretation: at least three layers of meaning are already present. It is for the reader to discover them and his/her ability to do so is entirely dependent upon the individual's level of spirituality, reflected by that part of the individual acting as the dominant operative. This is why Andrew has no difficulty accepting many possible meanings for the text, and commonly offers three and four possible interpretations. Although Origen popularized the idea that Scripture contained

---

39. Andrew, Prologue, *Comm.* 53.
40. Andrew, Prologue, *Comm.* 52.
41. Andrew, Prologue, *Comm.* 52.

three parts, by the time of Andrew this perspective was widely accepted and so deeply in-grained in ecclesiastical tradition that it was no longer identified with Origen and was not considered "Origenistic." By contrast, Oikoumenios refers to the literal narrative only on one occasion, and he never seems aware of the "three levels" of Scripture, never explains his basic interpretive approach or the reason for the division of his commentary.[42] As we shall see, Oikoumenios's terminology does not suggest technical exegetical expertise.

The Literal Sense: *Historia*

The first and lowest level of meaning, "the letter and history," is represented by the body. This is *historia* (ἱστορία), the historical or literal narrative. It can be the actual historical event as described by the text or simply refer to the plain meaning or literal meaning of the text, what Andrew refers to as "the letter" (τὸ γράμμα). This first level is "like the letter and like history established according to sense perception."[43] *Historia* is the level of understanding that one might expect from those "guided by the Law," that is, those who would observe the mere letter of biblical injunctions or who limit their interpretation to the historical meaning of a pericope.[44] Although Christian identification of this level of interpretation originally arose in the polemical debates with Judaism, the reference here by Andrew to "the Law" is certainly not suggesting a Jewish interpretation of Revelation. It is a comment about those who do not see a level of meaning in Scripture beyond the literal or the historical event because of their low level of spirituality.

Andrew hints that he is well-aware that Revelation had a historical context and an original audience when he states in the opening line of the commentary that he has been asked to "adapt the prophecies to the time after this vision."[45] He recognizes that certain events already took place in fulfillment of the prophecy during John's time and dur-

---

42. τὸ γράμμα τῆς ἱστορίας Oik. 7.11.2.
44. Andrew, Prologue, *Comm.* 52.
43. Andrew, Prologue, *Comm.* 52.
45. Andrew, Prologue, *Comm.* 51.

ing the intervening centuries between John's era and Andrew's, and that which remains will be fulfilled in the future. He explains that the first verse "The Apocalypse of Jesus Christ, which God gave to him, to show to his servants that which must come to pass soon" (Rev. 1:1) indicates that "some of the predictions concerning them are to come to pass immediately thereafter."[46]

However, the literal sense alone is inadequate since it is a bare recitation of history, even if it is a foretelling of future events. More important are the moral and spiritual lessons to be derived from these prophecies. But Andrew does not denigrate the literal sense. In fact, he often insists upon the reality of the literal sense against Oikoumenios's allegorization. Andrew realizes that the literal sense is important for the prophecy to be true. If the purpose of the punishments is to bring about the repentance and salvation of sinners, events such as the plagues must be understood literally.[47] The literal sense is also important if Revelation is to function as prophecy, particularly since Oikoumenios allegorized many images as past events. Andrew is very aware of those passages which ought to be interpreted literally, such as the letters to the churches (Rev. 2–3) and the destruction occurring after the seven trumpets (Rev. 8:7–9:21). He is equally aware what ought to be understood spiritually and metaphorically, such as the opening vision (Rev. 1), the vision of heaven with the twenty four elders (Rev. 4), and the woman wrapped in the sun (Rev. 12).

In contrast, a great weakness of Oikoumenios's interpretation is that he allegorizes what ought to be understood literally, such as the plagues and devastation caused by the four horsemen[48] and the seven trumpets.[49] For example upon the blowing of the first trumpet, a third of the earth and one third of the vegetation are burnt up (Rev. 8:7). Oikoumenios states: "If one takes this quite literally, he will not find the

---

46. Andrew, Chap.1, *Comm.* 55.

47. Rev. 9:20–21. "The rest of mankind who were not killed by these plagues, did not repent of the works of their hands, nor give up worshiping demons and idols of gold and silver and bronze and stone and wood, which cannot either see or hear or walk; nor did they repent of their murders or their sorceries or their immorality or their thefts."

48. Oik. 4.7.1–17.10.   49. Oik. 5.9.1–5.23.12.

true meaning."⁵⁰ Oikoumenios then entirely allegorizes the destruction: "When the text says trees and grass were burnt up, it refers allegorically (ὁ λόγος τροπολογεῖ) to sinners because of their folly and the insensibility of their soul, their woodenness all ready for burning."⁵¹

Elsewhere, Oikoumenios surprises by giving a literal interpretation of something that is clearly symbolic, such as the twenty-four elders around the throne of God⁵² or the escape of the woman to the desert.⁵³ The 1,260 days during which the woman wrapped in the sun remained in the desert is interpreted by Oikoumenios literally as the amount of time the Virgin Mary hid in Egypt with the Christ child.⁵⁴ This sudden shift to a literal explanation is extremely surprising since twice before Oikoumenios explained that forty-two months is a "figurative" amount of time.⁵⁵ One wonders whether he realized that forty-two months amounts to 1,260 days. When the woman wrapped in the sun cries out with birth pains, the pains are *not* interpreted literally by Oikoumenios, but her cries *are* taken literally.⁵⁶ Oikoumenios's surprising conclusion, that her cries were literal but the labor pain was not, is for theological reasons: Mary could not have experienced pain in childbirth because Christ was born entirely free from sin and labor pains are punishment for the sin of Eve. Oikoumenios explains Mary's cries are literal, although not from labor pains but because Joseph initially believed that she had been unfaithful to him. However, Revelation 12:2 specifically describes the pain of the woman as labor pains. Oikoumenios does not take this literally, but he should have if he were at least to be consistent with his interpretation that the woman of chapter 12 is Mary.

The literal sense can refer to past history where appropriate, such as in the letters to the churches, or to future events, or to both at once. For example, concerning the verse, "Because you have kept the word of my patience, I will keep you from the hour of trial which is coming on the whole world" (Rev. 3:10–11), Andrew remarks that this was said,

50. Oik. 5.9.3, FOTC 112: 84.
51. Oik. 5.9.4, FOTC 112: 84.
52. Oik. 3.7.1.
53. Oik. 7.9.2–3.
54. Oik. 7.3.10.
55. Oik. 6.9.8 and 6.11.5.
56. Oik. 6.19.7–8.

either [regarding] the persecution by the impious kings of Rome against the Christians which will come immediately at that particular time, from which he promises she [the church] is to be delivered; or [regarding] the world-wide movement at the end of the age against those who believe in the Antichrist, from which he promises to free her zealous ones.[57]

Typology

In the patristic tradition, typology functioned to unite the Old and New Testaments.[58] Historical events in the Bible were not considered "mere" history, but often were seen as a "foreshadowing (τύπος) that anticipates the truth."[59] By this comment, Andrew shows that he must have used typology in his interpretation of the Old Testament. Yet because he mentions it in connection with *historia* we know that he understands typology as firmly connected to the historical event, and not a purely allegorical elaboration. For example, he refers to the tabernacle of the Hebrews in the wilderness as a type of the heavenly altar, of which "the foreshadowing was shown to Moses on the mountain together with the tabernacle."[60] The persecution of the Jews under Antiochus IV "Epiphanes" was also seen by Andrew as historical typology: "Daniel prophesied about Antiochus as being a type of the coming of the Antichrist."[61] In one instance three levels of typology are expressed when the heavenly Jerusalem comes down and a voice proclaims to John, "Behold, the dwelling of God is with men" (Rev. 21:3). Andrew explains that "the type" of this "dwelling" or "tabernacle" (ἡ σκηνή), which will be revealed later in its fullness, is the Church today, and furthermore, the tabernacle which Moses saw (Exod. 25:9) was the prefiguration of the type.[62] Typology was an exegetical technique

---

57. Andrew, Chap.8, *Comm.* 76.
58. Bradley Nassif, "Antiochene Θεωρία in John Chrysostom's Exegesis," *Exegesis and Hermeneutics in the Churches of the East*, ed. Vahan Hovanessian (New York: Peter Lang, 2009), 51–65, 56.
59. Andrew, *Prologue, Comm.* 52.   60. Andrew, Chap. 21, *Comm.* 113.
61. Andrew, Chap. 33, *Comm.* 140.
62. Andrew, Chap. 65, *Comm.* 220, προτύπωσις.

greatly favored in the patristic tradition, however we see little application of typology in this commentary since typology usually would have been applied in an analysis of the Old Testament.

The Moral Sense: *Tropologia*

The second level, *tropologia* (τροπολογία), known as the "figurative" or "moral" sense, corresponds to the soul of the human person, "guiding the reader from that which can be perceived by the senses to that which can be perceived by the intellect."[63] This level of interpretation is the moral lesson to be derived from the text. Andrew explains that this interpretation is applied to Scriptures which contain "proverbial advice and other such pedagogical uses."[64] This level is appropriate for those who have risen from the basic level of understanding, the literal sense as mere story, represented by the body and the Law of Moses, and are able to extract the moral message from the passage. This level of understanding occurs when one is "governed by grace," presumably those who are active in the life of the Church.[65] Such people can perceive two levels of understanding, the moral lesson of the Scripture as well as its historical meaning. This is an important level for Andrew who consistently expresses the moral lesson in Revelation as basic pedagogy about the Christian way of life, such as the importance of performing good deeds, despising death, pursuing virtue, etc. Andrew accurately understands *tropos* and *tropologia* as related to proverbs as figures of speech, but not because a proverb has *symbolic* meaning, but because the proverb expresses a *moral* lesson and relates to morals and proper behavior.

The term *tropologia* engenders some confusion due to the inconsistent use of this term in the patristic tradition. *Tropologia* may indicate either the "figurative sense" or the "moral sense." The problem arises because *tropos* means "behavior," hence the "moral" sense of the Scripture,

63. Andrew, Prologue, *Comm.* 52.
64. Andrew, Prologue, *Comm.* 52.
65. Andrew, Prologue, *Comm.* 52.

meaning that which relates to one's manner of life. But *tropos* also means "a figure of speech," hence Andrew's application of *tropologia* to understanding proverbs as figures of speech. Because of its relationship to figurative speech in proverbial sayings, the word *tropos* was often employed when an interpretation was purely metaphorical and in a manner practically synonymous with allegory. Compounding the confusion, *tropologia, allegoria* (ἀλληγορία) and even *anagoge* (ἀναγωγή, discussed below) have all been generally referred to as the "figurative sense" in patristic writings. Oikoumenios frequently takes note of "figurative" language in Revelation, but no more so than anyone else who is familiar with basic literary analysis. On one occasion Oikoumenios used the term "allegorically" (ἀλληγορικῶς),[66] but it is identical to his use of "figurative" (τροπικῶς) or "metaphor" (μεταφορά) and it is used to describe figurative language, rather than as an exegetical technique or term of art.

When the literal sense was difficult to accept, or it conflicted with a predetermined conclusion or previously made observations, it was not uncommon for the literal sense to be discounted or disregarded by an interpreter stating that the words have a "figurative" meaning. Thus, a difficult text was basically allegorized and the interpreter simply used his imagination to arrive at a meaning. We consistently see Andrew fighting against this practice, which is typified in Oikoumenios who frequently allegorizes by referring to the text's "figurative" meaning. Oikoumenios is willing to concede that the tribulations of the bowls (Rev. 16:2–7) *might* occur literally or physically (αἰσθητῶς) and allows that they might also be describing events allegorically (ἀλληγορικῶς).[67] But in fact, Oikoumenios's exposition of the bowls is *entirely* allegorical. For example, referring to the fourth and fifth bowls poured out, resulting in a scorching hot sun and darkness, Oikoumenios states: "It is not difficult to explain all this by means of the rules of metaphor."[68] He continues to explain that the scorching sun is simply drought[69] and the darkness poured out on the throne of the beast means that when

---

66. Oik. 8.25.1.
67. Oik. 8.25.1.
68. τοὺς τῆς τροπῆς λόγους. Oik. 9.1.3, FOTC 112: 140.
69. Oik. 9.1.3.

the tyranny of the Antichrist comes to an end "those who are under his command ... will experience darkness in their reasoning."[70]

Usually the word employed by Oikoumenios to indicate a figurative interpretation is τροπικῶς,[71] but he also uses a variety of related expressions, such as τροπολογία,[72] τροπικότερον,[73] τροπή,[74] τροπικόν,[75] and ὁ λόγος τροπολογεῖ.[76] He also uses the term "metaphor" (μεταφορά) to signify allegory[77] as well as other terms to indicate a symbolic meaning, including αἰνίττεται,[78] αἰνιττομενοι[79] and ἀναγωγή.[80] Oikoumenios appears to use these words interchangeably and without precision. Andrew never uses the word "metaphor" and rarely uses *tropos* to indicate a figurative meaning. Oikoumenios's frequent use of these terms demonstrates the highly allegorical nature of his commentary and that his background and training were probably literary and philosophical rather than theological and exegetical.

The Spiritual Sense: *Theoria* and *Anagoge*

The highest level of meaning corresponds to the third part of the human person, the spirit, and relates to "the future and higher things."[81] Although Andrew does not expressly bifurcate this level, it is clear that he perceives the spiritual level as encompassing two parts: *theoria* (θεωρία) or "the higher things," and *anagoge* (ἀναγωγή), which relates to "the future things." The spiritual level is the most difficult level of interpretation to attain and insights at this level are acquired by few, only those who live a life "in which the Spirit governs, having subordinated to It all carnal thoughts and motions."[82]

70. Oik. 9.1.3, FOTC 112:141.
71. Oik. 1.15.2, 3.13.1, 4.17.9, 5.9.3 (twice), 5.13.2, 7.11.2, 11.10.15, 11.12.12.
72. Oik. 5.13.3.   73. Oik. 11.10.10.
74. Oik. 5.11.3; 9.3.1.   75. Oik. 8.19.8.
76. Oik. 5.9.4.
77. See, for example, Oik. 8.13.2, 8.19.4, and 8.23.1.
78. Oik. 4.17.4, 8.21.4.   79. Oik. 8.19.6.
80. Oik. 5.11.3.   81. Andrew, Prologue, *Comm.* 52.
82. τῇ μακαρίᾳ λήξει, ἐν ᾗ τὸ πνεῦμα βασιλεύει. Andrew, Prologue, *Comm.* 52.

Andrew recognizes the wealth of meaning to be found in Revelation on this third level because God ordered Revelation to be proclaimed "to those who are more perfect in knowledge."[83] Having compared Revelation to "other prophets," meaning the Old Testament, he concluded that the content and interpretation of those prophets primarily consisted of the first two levels.

> The third part, that is to say, the spiritual part, [is] found to be especially abundant in the Apocalypse of the Theological Man; on the one hand, lavishly seen with historical form and figurative speech in the other prophets, whereas, on the other hand here [in the Apocalypse], [the spiritual part] is especially seen in abundance.[84]

We can surmise from this comment that Andrew sees Revelation as a prophetic book, future-oriented, and above all, as a book which primarily conveys a spiritual message. This drives his interpretation. To what extent is Andrew's own personal spiritual insight at work behind what is expressly stated in the commentary? It is impossible to know. The commentary is clearly oriented toward a spiritual interpretation but Andrew confesses that his understanding is limited. "Even though we ourselves do not understand the entire depth of the hidden spirit within it, we too will elucidate what was seen by the blessed one."[85] Furthermore, "the exact knowledge of these matters" must be relegated "to divine wisdom."[86]

Since the spiritual level is found abundantly in the Apocalypse, the purpose of Revelation as a whole, and the purpose of Andrew's exposition, is to lead the reader and interpreter to spiritual insight. Even though he does "not understand the entire depth of the hidden spirit within" the book, nor its literal sense in its entirety, and declines to employ "conjecture," he takes up the challenge and finds value in the challenge itself. The very difficulties posed by the book and faced by the interpreter operate to "exercise" the reader, "as if supplying train-

---

83. Andrew, Prologue, Comm. 53.
84. Andrew, Prologue, *Comm.* 53.
85. Andrew, Prologue, *Comm.* 53.
86. Andrew, Prologue, *Comm.* 53.

ing for the quick-wittedness of the mind."[87] "Conjecture" is to be rejected but genuine insights can be achieved according to one's spiritual level. The result is deeper apprehension and spiritual progress.

Andrew is conscious of the fact that he is dependent upon assistance from God in order to draw the spiritual meaning out of the text. This awareness is revealed occasionally in his comments in the course of his exposition, including several times in the prologue, as we have just mentioned. After professing his personal inadequacy, Andrew accepts his task with the help of "God who will enlighten me."[88] Elsewhere in the commentary his awareness of the operation of *theoria* is evident. For example, he interprets the sky being rolled up like a scroll (Rev. 6:14) in four different ways "as it has been given to us from God."[89]

In some Christian circles, especially Alexandria, allegory had been employed to arrive at a spiritual interpretation. Origen had identified the spiritual understanding as the highest level, and used the term (ἀλληγορία) when reaching conclusions on this highest level. One famous Cappadocian, Gregory of Nyssa, greatly enjoyed and promoted allegory. However, our Cappadocian bishop appears to follow the example of his celebrated predecessor on the episcopal throne of Caesarea, Basil the Great, who rejected allegory as an attempt "by false arguments and allegorical interpretations to bestow on the Scriptures a dignity of their own imagining.... [T]heirs is the attitude of one who considers himself wiser than the revelations of the Spirit and introduces his own ideas in pretense of an explanation. Therefore, let it be understood as it has been written."[90]

Andrew's reluctance to engage in allegory can be seen not only in his avoidance of the term itself, but also in the absence of comments characteristic of interpreters who preferred allegory. For example, he avoids the excessive allegorization of numbers and shows no interest

---

87. Andrew, Prologue, *Comm*. 53.
88. Andrew, Prologue, *Comm*. 52.
89. Andrew, Chap. 18, *Comm*. 99.
90. *On the Six Days of Creation, Hom*. 9.1, in *Basil: Exegetical Homilies*, trans. Agnes Clare Way, FOTC 46 (Washington, D.C.: The Catholic University of America Press, 1963), 135–36.

in the interpretative analysis of numbers. He explains numbers which are clearly symbolic, such as 666, 7 or 24, but he neither dissects them nor engages in explanations of their properties or their components, such as what makes 10 a perfect number, or other such discussions which we find among Fathers who delighted in allegory.[91]

One passage in the Andreas commentary may border on an allegorical interpretation, although Andrew would undoubtedly consider it to be *theoria*: his interpretation of the twelve precious stones which adorn the heavenly Jerusalem (Rev. 21:19–20). Andrew carefully identifies each of the gems mentioned with a specific apostle according to the color of the stone and Church traditions about the life and ministry of each apostle.[92] He defends his interpretation against any charge that such an exposition is "forced." Perhaps he anticipates some criticism that this type of exposition is too allegorical in nature. However he supports the interpretation as in accordance with patristic tradition, citing a similar interpretation by Epiphanios who identified each of the twelve stones on the high priest's breastplate with a specific tribe in his work, *de Gemmis*. He also comments that such exercises "serve as training for those pondering enigmas of truth, although the precise understanding of which is known only to the one who has revealed [it]."[93]

We can conclude that Andrew is more closely aligned with the Antiochean style of interpretation,[94] which is not surprising since Antioch was in relatively close proximity geographically to Caesarea, approximately 240 kilometers. Andrew understands and interprets symbols, but does not engage in pure allegory, and in fact never uses the word

---

91. Such as Augustine. See his discussion of the allegorical meaning of the 153 fish caught by the disciples in John 21:11. Question 57. *Augustine Eighty Three Different Questions*, trans. David Mosher, ed. Hermigild Dressler, FOTC 70 (Washington, D.C.: The Catholic University of America Press, 1977), 99–103.

92. Andrew, Chap. 67, *Comm.* 227–30.

93. Andrew, Chap. 67, *Comm.* 230.

94. See Paul Ternant, "La θεωρία d'Antioche dans le cadre des sens de l'Écriture," *Biblica* 34 (1953): 135–58, 354–83, and 456–86.

"allegory," preferring *theoria* and *anagoge* to describe the spiritual level of interpretation. This is characteristic of the Antiochean School, which disfavored the use of *allegoria* and allowed for allegory only when it was specifically called for by the symbolic nature of the text (such as in the interpretation of parables). The imaginative allegorical interpretation engaged in by Oikoumenios is clearly disapproved by Andrew.

As Andrew explains in his prologue, the spiritual level consists of both "the future things," *anagoge*, and "the higher things," *theoria*. At times *anagoge* also suffers from misunderstanding, as *tropologia* does. *Anagoge* literally means "to raise up," hence it is sometimes treated as synonymous with *theoria* and *allegoria* because of the misperception that, since it raises the mind upward, *anagoge* applies to spiritual interpretation in general. Many Fathers often used *anagoge* in various forms in its ordinary sense, meaning to lead upwards, to elucidate a passage or give a spiritual interpretation as opposed to a literal one. The diverse usage of this word has contributed to the confusion. It should also be noted that exegetical terms were also not employed consistently among all of the Fathers and a given patristic authority might be operating on any one of these three levels without explicitly using the terminology.

Anagoge had a specific meaning known and applied by trained exegetes as a term of art. It is clear that Andrew is aware of this meaning and he uses it in his prologue with precision: *anagoge* refers to the "future things," that is, the afterlife or life in the kingdom of God, which includes existence and activities in the kingdom at the present time as well. Andrew's precise application of these terms shows that he had a good education and training in interpretation. He had the expertise to know the difference between *theoria* and *anagoge*, just as he did not confuse a symbolic or metaphorical meaning with *tropos* as a technical exegetical term.

The application of *anagoge* is frequent in the commentary, without the use of the term, since much of Revelation describes activity taking place in the kingdom, future life in the kingdom, the description of the New Jerusalem, etc. Interpretation and specific application of the term can be seen in a couple of instances. For example, regarding the "talking altar" of Revelation 16:7 ("And I heard the altar saying, 'Yes, Lord God the Almighty, your judgments are true and just'"), Andrew writes that the altar "at some times signifies Christ as in him and through him we offer to the Father our 'rational' whole burnt offerings and 'living sacrifices' as we have been taught by the Apostle."[95] This observation would be *theoria*: it is a Christological statement about the role of Christ as mediator between humans and the Father. Andrew continues with the *anagoge* portion of his spiritual interpretation: "And at other times it symbolizes the angelic powers, because they carry up our prayers and spiritual whole burnt offerings which, we have heard, 'are sent for service for the sake of those [who are] to inherit salvation.'"[96] This is *anagoge* because it refers to the activity of the angels in the kingdom of heaven. Andrew concludes his exposition of this passage with *tropologia*, which takes the form of didactic instruction and moral application when he comments about the role of angels in our lives. Each of us has a guardian angel who silently "instructs us in the things we must do." Andrew tells a story about a guardian angel and encourages the readers to live in such a manner that "our way of life" may become "the cause of dejection in the demons and gladness for the angels."[97]

Theoria, which can be translated as "contemplation" or "spiritual insight," is the other component of the spiritual level. *Theoria* has accurately been described by Bradley Nassif as "spiritual illumination into the deeper meaning of divine revelation as it relates to salvation history."[98] *Theoria* can be found in and through historical events, places, names, prophecies, figures of speech, and other aspects of the biblical text. But the deeper, spiritual meaning of such details is not self-evident. "The enlightening power needed to discern those realities is

---

95. Andrew, Chap. 48, *Comm.* 170, referring to Romans 12:1.
96. Andrew, Chap. 48, *Comm.* 170, citing Heb. 1:14.
97. Andrew, Chap. 48, *Comm.* 171.
98. Bradley Nassif, "Antiochene Theoria," 54.

given by the Holy Spirit to the biblical author and/or a later apostolic or post-apostolic exegete."[99] Andrew would concur. It should be noted that although *theoria* is at times characterized by scholars as a "method," it cannot truly be considered a form of methodology because it cannot be taught. The insights one achieves through *theoria* are dependent upon one's spiritual state and illumination by the Holy Spirit. *Theoria* is the spiritual interpretation which the interpreter brings to the text, as well as insight into the meaning of events which the original biblical author has perceived and conveyed to the reader.

Andrew also recognizes the Seer's *theoria*. Such visions as the Apocalypse of John are not easily comprehensible by others. The interpretation of "things which are secretly and mysteriously seen by the saints ... befits a great mind and one enlightened by the Divine Spirit." Andrew fears he will "appear bold" by "attempting [to explain] these things."[100] The vision takes place in the mind of the Seer and is not "visible" regardless of the fact that it is "described" as though it had indeed been "seen." "Even if the things seen by the saints take form in matter and colors ... yet they happen to be invisible and mental."[101] Andrew uses the word *theoria* in the heading for his chapter 12: "Concerning the Vision (θεωρία) in the Middle of the Throne and the Four Living Beings." After John was taken up through the open door of heaven (4:1), Andrew correctly identifies John's experience as spiritual illumination, not as something which John "saw."

In his explanation of the harlot of chapter 17, we see Andrew's recognition of his own *theoria* as well as that of John. Andrew applies his own spiritual insight to the vision while also being aware of how the vision was experienced by John and understood by him. Commenting on the verse, "And he carried me away in the Spirit into a wilderness, and I saw a woman sitting on a scarlet beast full of blasphemous names, having seven heads and ten horns" (Rev. 17:2b–3). Andrew writes,

99. Bradley Nassif, "Antiochene Theoria," 54.
100. Andrew, Prologue, *Comm.* 51.
101. Andrew, Chap. 21, *Comm.* 112.

And regarding this, in what follows, if God grants, let us express [ourselves] accurately. It is necessary to remark what the wilderness must mean into which one is carried off in the Spirit. 'Wilderness' we regard, therefore, as the spiritual deserts in every city, or a great throng which is drunk in the soul both by the fornication against God and being charged with other such recklessness. And alternatively one must realize that the Apostle perceives, as a mental vision in the Spirit, the desolation of the aforementioned "harlot" whom he saw as womanish because of the luxuriant indulgence toward sin and being without a husband.[102]

Even when the explanation of an image is provided in the text of Revelation, usually by an angel, God's help is still sought and needed for proper understanding. As the exposition of this passage continues, Andrew writes: "About 'the seven heads and ten horns' with [the help] of God we will learn from the divine angel in what follows."[103]

Theoria also leads to theological or Christological interpretations of details which otherwise remain on the literal level or that would appear to merely tend toward a metaphorical interpretation. For example, Oikoumenios interprets the feet of Christ like "glowing brass," (χαλκολιβάνῳ) in Revelation 1:15, as the foundation of the preaching of the gospel.[104] Andrew gives several interpretations of this image, one of which is clearly in the realm of *theoria*. The word typically translated as "glowing brass" is composed of two Greek words, "brass" and "incense" and seems to recall a specific type of incense, which was also called "masculine incense." Oikoumenios mentions this type of incense as well.[105] Both Andrew and Oikoumenios offer several interpretations of that image, but Andrew goes higher than Oikoumenios to the level of *theoria*, and expresses a theological truth hidden in the symbol. The dual composition of the feet shows the "unconfused union" (τὸ ἀσύγχυτον τῆς ἑνώσεως) of the two natures of Christ, the χαλκός or brass, signifying the human nature—and λίβανος the incense, signifying the divine nature.[106]

---

102. Andrew, Chap. 53, *Comm.* 181–82.
104. Oik. 1.27.12–13.
106. Andrew, Chap. 2, *Comm.* 61–62.

103. Andrew, Chap. 53, *Comm.* 182.
105. Oik. 1.27.12.

In the case of Apocalypse interpretation, it can be rather difficult to identify the operation of *theoria* because the Apocalypse is heavily symbolic. The book often calls for a spiritual interpretation as opposed to a literal one. When Andrew draws out the meaning of the symbols, at times it is clear that he is employing exegetical techniques, such as those discussed in chapter 10: sequence, context, the author's purpose, etc. For example, word association is often employed by Andrew to shed light on the meaning of a symbol, such as an earthquake. He recognizes that "earthquake" is an expression found in the Old Testament for a shift or a change in the course of events.[107] This is clearly a result of his exegetical training, since he does not interpret the earthquake as primarily a literal event (or perhaps not at all as a literal event) nor does he arrive at an interpretation pulled from his own imagination. The interpretation of any given symbol could be a literary interpretation of its metaphorical meaning according to its use elsewhere in the Bible, or it might be genuine spiritual insight, *theoria*. Even when the symbol is identified as a metaphor, it can it have a spiritual interpretation.

107. Andrew, Chap. 18, *Comm.* 97, Chap. 31, *Comm.* 134, Chap. 33, *Comm.* 136, Chap. 52, *Comm.* 178, Chap. 72, *Comm.* 243.

10

ANDREW'S TECHNIQUE AND SOURCES

As we have seen, Andrew is familiar with levels of interpretation and techniques of *historia*, typology, *anagoge*, *theoria*, and *tropologia*. Oikoumenios is not. Although he allegorizes, Oikoumenios does not seem to apply allegory in a systematic or technical manner. Furthermore, he is unskilled or untrained in basic premises such as awareness of a biblical author's purpose *(skopos)*, the sequence of thought or expression *(akolouthia)*, or how to use context *(ta symphrazomena)* to arrive at exegetical conclusions. In fact, such terminology is entirely absent from Oikoumenios. Although occasionally one of those words may be used it by Oikoumenios, is not applied in a technical manner.

Purpose—*Skopos*

Skopos (σκοπός) is the goal, purpose or aim of the biblical writer. Every book of the Bible has a *skopos* and this is the first observation an interpreter is expected to make. We see this practiced by Chrysostom, for example, who consistently begins his exposition of a given book with an explanation of the biblical author's purpose for writing, the author's *skopos*.[1] Although *skopos* is an ordinary Greek word mean-

---

1. See, for example, Chrysostom's introductory argument to Paul's Epistle to the Romans, or his discussion of Paul's reasoning in 1 Cor. 15. *Hom. on 1 Cor.* 39.8. He also analyzes the sequence of the argument.

ing "goal" or "end," it is also an exegetical term of art. The awareness of *skopos* and consideration of a biblical author's *skopos* when making exegetical decisions was regarded as fundamental and basic. *Skopos* is extremely important for understanding the overall message of the book as well as the meaning of individual pericopes. The interpreter is expected to constantly bear in mind the purpose of the book as a general guide for the evaluation of a passage. Exegetical conclusions which conflict with the author's purpose must be reconsidered and are probably incorrect. Individual passages or details within a pericope also have a *skopos* and were expected to prompt the interpreter to ask why the biblical author included that detail. Andrew's faithfulness to the *skopos* of Revelation is evident in his exposition. He mentions a spiritual purpose at the end of the commentary:

> Starting from these things by the vision and the enjoyment we might, by ardent yearning through keeping the divine commandments, acquire these in long suffering and meekness and humility and purity of heart. From which [heart] unsullied prayer is born free of distraction and offers to God, the Overseer of all hidden things, a mind devoid of every material thought uncorrupted by demonic deception and attacks.[2]

The original historical purpose of Revelation was to encourage hope and perseverance through tribulation, and this *skopos* was not lost on Andrew. His awareness of John's *skopos* for Revelation directs his interpretation on many unexpressed levels and brings Andrew into direct conflict with Oikoumenios. Andrew sees the purpose of the book as spiritual: to encourage repentance, vigilance, and perseverance. If the *skopos* is perseverance through tribulations or admonishment by the warning of future punishments, then the disasters described by the bowls or the trumpets must be interpreted literally and should not be allegorized, which is what Oikoumenios does. Furthermore, Andrew sees the *skopos* of Revelation as prophecy, therefore it must relate primarily to the future. Events such as those launched by opening the seven seals cannot be an allegory of the life of Christ, as Oikoumenios believed.

2. *Summary* following Andrew, Chap. 72, *Comm.* 244.

Context—*Ta symphrazomena*

The first example of Andrew's application of context as an interpretive technique is seen early in the commentary, in his treatment of "the one who is, was, and is to come" (Rev. 1:4). Oikoumenios believes the phrase represents the Trinity: the one "who is" being the Father (who said "I am" to Moses),[3] the one "who was" is the Son, (the Logos "who was in the beginning" in John 1:1) and the one "who is to come" refers to the Paraclete. But Andrew concludes that this phrase in this *specific* context can *only* be referring to the Father since the very next verse mentions "Jesus Christ." Therefore, the Son *cannot* be included as the one "who was."

> For here the addition of "and from Jesus Christ" appears to confirm the understanding we have presented. For it would be unnecessary if he were talking about the only Logos of God and the person of the Son to immediately add "and from Jesus Christ" in order to show him [as distinct] from the other one.[4]

Andrew points out that *later* in Revelation "the one who is, was and is to come" is also said of Christ alone (Rev. 1:8), and that the same words could also be said of the Spirit alone, because all three persons of the Trinity share the same divine essence. But specifically there, in Rev. 1:4, Andrew corrects Oikoumenios and insists that the phrase can only refer to the Father. Andrew does not employ the words for "context" (συμφράζω or τά συμφραζόμενα) but the force of his argument is entirely contextual. Oikoumenios also notices that Christ is referenced in the next verse, but rather than considering the context and conforming his interpretation to reflect it, Oikoumenios adheres to his Trinitarian interpretation of the verse "is, was and is to come," and decides that this second reference "and from Jesus Christ" must be made

---

3. This small detail is yet another clue that Oikoumenios's formal theological education was limited, in spite of his Christological quotations. In Eastern Christianity and consistently in the understanding of the early Church, the person of the Trinity who spoke to Moses in the burning bush was not the Father but the Son. Manifestations of God in the Old Testament were invariably considered to be the Logos.

4. Andrew, Chap. 1, *Comm.* 58.

with regard to his "human nature." This creates yet another problem because such a statement appears Nestorian, since Oikoumenios could be accused of separating Christ's divinity from his humanity. But again, rather than reconsidering his interpretation, realizing that his initial opinion was incorrect due to the context, Oikoumenios simply pushes forward. He dismissively defends himself against any suspicion of Nestorianism and quickly moves on.[5]

Another example of Andrew's attention to context is the differing interpretations he gives for the "white garment" imagery found throughout Revelation. Oikoumenios usually interprets the white garment as a symbol of purity, regardless of the context. But Andrew's interpretation of the white garment always depends on the context. For example, the white robes of the twenty four elders in Rev. 4:4 represent purity for Oikoumenios, as usual. But Andrew, thinking probably of banquet parables of the kingdom,[6] concludes that "the white clothes are symbols of the brilliant life and the unending feast and gladness"[7] because the scene describes the elders in heaven. The white robes worn by the crowd of Revelation 7:9 are again a symbol of purity for Oikoumenios, but are robes of martyrdom for Andrew because a few verses later the text states that they have come out of "great tribulation" and "washed their robes in the blood of the lamb" (7:14). Oikoumenios notices the detail of the "blood of the lamb" but he yet again maintains that the white robes represent purity, as though he is applying a stock explanation rather than doing actual exegesis.[8] He dismisses the "blood of the lamb" detail as a reference to their participation in Eucharist.[9]

Sequence—*Akolouthia*

Early patristic interpreters were also conscious of sequence in the biblical text (ἀκολουθία) and considered it when reaching exegetical

---

5. "He [John] does not separate him [Christ] into two." Oik. 1.11.1, FOTC 112:24.
6. Matt. 22:1–10; 25:1–13.   7. Andrew, Chap. 10, *Comm.* 82.
8. Oik. 5.3.2.   9. Oik. 5.3.7.

conclusions. Sequence as an interpretive technique was applied by noting the logical progression of historical events, a biblical author's line of reasoning or the order in which statements were made. Sequence by its nature is closely related to context.[10] Sequence was very important to Andrew and is one of Oikoumenios's greatest problems. In the Book of Revelation, the sequence of events can be especially problematic. Andrew effectively manages the text by engaging in basically a straight chronological progression through the book.

Andrew believes that because Revelation is prophecy, it refers only to the present (meaning the present time when the Revelation was received by John, which would be the past for us), or the future, (that which was in the future for John, but which could be past, present or future for us).[11] Andrew perceives a definite shift in Revelation into the eschatological future, which he believes has not arrived yet. This shift happens during the "seven seals" section and is represented by the earthquake which occurs with the opening of the sixth seal.[12] Everything prior to that moment either has or may have take place between the time when John received the Revelation and the beginning of the eschaton. Most of the descriptions were of persecutions endured by Christians under the Romans, but the images may also have included other later historical occurrences. Once the shift occurs with the opening of the sixth seal, an eschatological scenario is being described. After that, one cannot interpret a *subsequent* passage by relating it to the times *before* the end which began with the opening of the sixth seal and the earthquake.

The sequence of events described by Revelation has long puzzled interpreters. Some, such as Tyconius and Victorinus, solved the problem by applying the theory of "recapitulation," namely that the same events were described using differing imagery. (The seven bowls were

---

10. See Chrysostom's *Hom. on Rom.* 6 for an analysis of Rom. 3:1–7, with many references to context and sequence.
11. See chapter 11, View of Prophecy.
12. Andrew, Chap. 18, *Comm.* 97.

the same occurrences as the seven trumpets, etc.) Oikoumenios has tremendous difficulty with sequence. He does not exactly practice "recapitulation" because he does not engage in an orderly retelling of events and he does not see an inherent structure in the book, something which recapitulation presumes. Instead, whenever Oikoumenios's interpretation does not fit the context because his explanation conflicts with the sequence, he concludes that the image is referring back to prior events, in what today we would call a "flashback." The scene which follows that passage might very well require him to "flash forward," which he does, only to immediately "flash back," according to whatever is expedient for his interpretation. Oikoumenios's exposition is extremely difficult to follow as he jumps back and forth in time. This creates a logical and sequential inconsistency in Oikoumenios and even theological problems.[13]

Sequence, context and *skopos* are interrelated. In the seven seals section (Rev. 6), Oikoumenios understands the seals to represent events in the life of Christ.[14] When the fifth seal is opened "the souls of people who had been slain on account of the word of God and for the witness which they had borne" cried out for vengeance (Rev. 6:9). They were told to be patient until the completion of the number of martyrs in the future. Considering the historical context of Revelation—its original *skopos* being to support and encourage Christians during the persecution of Domitian—the souls under the altar would *have* to be under-

---

13. Castagno concluded that Oikoumenios intended to demonstrate the continuity and internal coherence of the text of Revelation rather than interpreting it as an unrelated series of images. "I Commenti," 330. If indeed that was his intention, he either did not accomplish his goal or did not articulate a coherent understanding of Revelation. Andrew would object that Oikoumenios strains the text in order to arrive at his interpretations. Castagno recognizes that Oikoumenios's interpretation does not see Revelation as progressing in a linear fashion, but she believes that Oikoumenios understands Revelation as the story of salvation in code form, frequently returning to themes already treated. "I Commenti," 334–36. Oikoumenios himself, however, does not seem to indicate that this is his approach or understanding.

14. The first seal is his birth (Oik. 4.7.3), the second is his temptation (4.8.2), the third is his teaching and miracles (4.10.1–3), the fourth is the blows and wounds suffered before Pilate (4.11.2), the fifth is the reaction of the "souls under the altar" to the abuse of the Lord (4.13.3), and the sixth is the cross, death, resurrection and ascension (4.15.2).

stood as Christian martyrs, not to mention because of the customary Christian association of altars with the relics of martyrs.[15]

But Oikoumenios had wedded himself to an exposition of the seven seals as the life of Christ. The death of Christ does not even occur until the sixth seal in his interpretation, and Christian martyrdoms certainly could not occur before the death of Christ *himself*. Therefore, Oikoumenios is forced to conclude that the souls crying out for vengeance after the fifth seal are martyrs of the *Old* Testament who object to the treatment of the Christ during his Passion. Oikoumenios's mistake here, interpreting Christian martyrs as Jewish departed, is particularly egregious since his manuscript contained a peculiar variation. Instead of reading that the souls were people slain on account of the witness (μαρτυρία), his manuscript read that they were "slain on account of the *Church*" (ἐκκλησία). Oikoumenios ignored this detail which should have signaled a problem with his interpretation, and he dismissed it by saying that "church" meant "synagogue." Every detail in the text pointed to a different interpretation than what Oikoumenios decided, yet he neither reconsidered nor modified his exposition to reflect the logical sequence of events.[16]

Andrew points out that Oikoumenios's sequence is illogical and therefore his conclusions are strained and violate the plain meaning of the text. Referring to Oikoumenios's interpretation, Andrew remarks,

If anyone forces the loosening of the four seals to apply to the foregoing acts of dispensation by Christ, he will naturally adapt this to the previously fulfilled prophets and the remaining saints who cry out loud because of the divine forbearance, after whom He [Christ] endured unto the cross, being insulted by the Jews.[17]

Andrew argues that it makes more sense (it "is fitting") to understand the souls as Christian martyrs and the seals as referring to persecu-

---

15. This detail was well-known, even by Oikoumenios who thrice refers to the Apocalypse having been composed during the reign of Domitian. Oik. 1.21.1, 2.13.9 and 12.20.6.
16. Oik. 4.13.3–5. See FOTC 112: 71, n. 31.
17. Andrew, Chap. 17, *Comm.* 96.

tions still to take place in the future (the future from the historical perspective of John), and he states that this is the ecclesiastical tradition: "And if any take these things to mean a foretelling of future events according to the teachers of the Church, he will suppose that such a thing is fitting, that those who were killed for Christ will cry out against their persecutors."[18]

Oikoumenios struggles with the problem of sequence throughout his exposition. For example, Oikoumenios faces problems explaining the two witnesses of chapter 11. When the first of seven trumpets is blown (Rev. 8:7) Oikoumenios interprets this image as the return of Christ at the end of the world, because he associates the word "trumpet" with the Second Coming of Christ as described by Paul (1 Thess. 4:16). But the stated purpose of the two witnesses is to help people oppose the deception of the beast (Rev. 11:3–10) *before* the second coming of Christ. If the first trumpet in chapter 8 announces the second coming of Christ, Oikoumenios has difficulty explaining why the two witnesses appear in the Apocalypse in chapter 11, *after* the Second Coming. Oikoumenios concludes that the account of the two witnesses was something which John had "set aside" and has now gone back to explain. But immediately afterwards, according to Oikoumenios, John returns to his description of the future reward of the saints in the very next scene (Rev. 11:15ff).[19]

The problem with sequence grows even worse in his analysis of the following chapter, Revelation 12. Oikoumenios returns to his practice of interpreting Revelation as events in the life of Christ. First he interprets the woman wrapped in the sun (12:1–2) as the Theotokos (the Virgin Mary).[20] The immediate appearance of the dragon requires the explanation of Satan's fall from heaven (12:3–4a), which occurred long before the birth of Christ, even before recorded time, so chronologically we must go far back into the past. Then, according to Oikoumenios, the birth of Christ is described (12:4b–6), returning us to the first century,

18. Andrew, Chap. 17, *Comm.* 96. 19. Oik. 6.17.1.
20. Oik. 6.19.2.

but quickly his explanation reverts back to a period before recorded time, to the war in heaven between Michael and Satan (12:7–9). This is followed by the dragon's pursuit of the woman (12:13–17), which Oikoumenios believes represents the holy family's flight to Egypt, returning us again to the first century and to his "life of Christ" exposition.[21]

We see Oikoumenios struggling with the problem of sequence elsewhere. The coming of Christ by the first trumpet destroys the Antichrist, and Oikoumenios also interpreted the fifth bowl poured out, putting the kingdom of the beast into darkness (Rev. 16:10), as describing the destruction of the Antichrist and his kingdom. But moments later, the devil, false prophet or the Antichrist appear again when the frogs come out of the mouth of the false prophet (Rev. 16:13). Oikoumenios's explanation for why the Antichrist appears in the text again, after he had already been destroyed, is very weak.

If he really means the Antichrist, do not be surprised that you meet him again after he had been earlier described as having been destroyed by the Spirit of the Lord, and is now described as still alive, spewing forth demons through his mouth. For all that the evangelist sees are a vision, and he is often shown the first things last and contrariwise the last first.[22]

He makes similar comments and similar departures from logical sequence elsewhere, always attributing the reversals to the author of the Apocalypse. "After many digressions and after reverting from these starting points to previous beginnings, he came to the serious business. This was to explain to us the facts about the impious and abominable Antichrist."[23]

Oikoumenios creates many confusing reversals in the course of his commentary. The final destruction of the devil and the Antichrist in the lake of fire (Rev. 19:20) is a scenario for the future eschaton. Oikoumenios says it is the devil and the Antichrist, but the text actually says it is the beast and the false prophet.[24] Commenting on the very next verse (Rev. 20:2–3a), *after* the final destruction of the devil has already been

---

21. Oik. 7.3.10.
23. Oik. 8.1. FOTC 112:123.
22. Oik. 9.5.3, FOTC 112:142.
24. Oik. 10.15.7.

described, Oikoumenios immediately jumps back to the past when he interprets the binding of the devil for a thousand years as the Incarnation. Oikoumenios then returns to the future with the loosening of the devil "for a little while" which represents the age between the ascension of Christ and his second coming.[25] Then in the next sentence (a continuation of the very same verse, 20:3) he interprets the passage again as from the earthly life of Christ. At this point, even Oikoumenios realizes the problematic nature of his exposition and he implores the reader to try to continue to follow his exposition: "Keep a grasp on this sequence."[26] The word which Suggit has translated as "sequence" (συνέχειαν) is more properly translated as "continuation" or "progression." It is not the technical term that would be used by an exegete, *akoloutheia*. Oikoumenios does not show an awareness of how to apply sequence to his exposition or he does not seem to know the word as an exegetical term.

The loosening of the devil represents the present age, but with the next vision ("I saw thrones … and judgment" [Rev. 20:4–5]), remarkably Oikoumenios goes back to the earthly life of Christ when Satan was "bound." His dominant interpretation of Revelation as the life of Christ continues to be tremendously problematic. For Oikoumenios the judgment thrones of Rev. 20 cannot refer to the last judgment because the previous image—the binding of Satan—represents Christ's earthly ministry in which Satan's activities are restricted. So the thrones are the authority promised to the apostles, and were already given to them during Christ's Incarnation.[27] The judgment scene in Revelation 20 explicitly describes "the souls of those who had been beheaded for their testimony *to Jesus*." But Oikoumenios is tied to his earthly-life-of-Christ interpretation, so those beheaded for Jesus cannot mean *Christian* martyrs who *actually* lost their heads, since Christ himself has not yet died according to Oikoumenios's scenario because the binding of Satan represents the ministry of Christ during his In-

---

25. Oik. 10.17.10.
26. FOTC 112: 168. Oik. 10.15.7. τὴν συνέχειαν ὥσπερ φυλάττων τοῦ λόγου.
27. Oik. 11.3.2.

carnation. This requires Oikoumenios to entirely allegorize and minimize martyrdom by beheading as merely the abuse suffered by those who believed in Christ during his lifetime when they were expelled from the synagogue and lost their possessions.[28] This significantly dilutes the prophetic power of the text, diminishes its emotional and inspirational impact, and entirely ignores its *skopos*.

Excusing or ignoring the sequence allows Oikoumenios to do with the text whatever he wishes. Rather than reevaluating the soundness of his previous interpretation, Oikoumenios simply interprets the images as he finds them and makes no attempt to discover coherence in John's presentation. Oikoumenios's disregard for sequence and context wreaks havoc on his interpretation and illustrates his lack of exegetical skill.

Word Association

Both Andrew and Oikoumenios commonly use Scripture to interpret Scripture. That is, they use one passage of Scripture to explain another, especially by the use of word association. The technique of scriptural "word association" was probably the most common method of patristic exegesis. When interpreting a passage of Revelation, both Andrew and Oikoumenios identify a word or idea in the passage and then look for the same word or concept elsewhere in the Bible. The meaning or understanding of the word in the other location is employed to explain its meaning in Revelation. This is acceptable if done correctly and this is also practiced by modern interpreters, especially to determine the use or meaning of a word by examining how it is used in another passage or book by the same author. Andrew's application of word association is evident throughout the commentary, including his awareness of traditional biblical apocalyptic imagery, such as earthquakes, the sky being "rolled," the sun becoming dark and the

---

28. Oik. 11.3.3. "They came to life and ruled with Christ for a thousand years" refers to their faith in Christ during his earthly ministry.

moon turning to blood (Rev. 6:12–13). Even though Andrew does not label this imagery as "apocalyptic," Andrew is aware of the symbolic use of such language and interprets it according to the context and according to how such images were used in other apocalyptic passages found in the Old Testament.[29]

A very interesting and careful use of word association by Andrew can be seen in the discussion concerning the identity of "the one who is, was and is to come" where he uses the word association technique to support a theological point. He has explained that the description "is, was and is to come" in Revelation 1:4 can only refer to the Father because of the context. However, *theologically* the same statement can be made of all three members of the Trinity because they share the same properties of divinity. He continues by giving an example of another characteristic which applies to all three members of the Trinity—holiness—and cites a point of contention between the Chalcedonians and the Miaphysites: the Trisagion Hymn ("Holy God, Holy Mighty, Holy Immortal, have mercy on us.") The hymn had long been considered Trinitarian, emphasizing the equality of all three Persons, and was based on the hymn of the Seraphim in Isaiah 6:3: "Holy, holy, holy is the Lord Almighty."

To affirm the real union of the divinity and humanity in Christ, the Miaphysites stressed that the Logos suffered in the flesh. Severus of Antioch inserted a phrase into the Trisagion Hymn which altered the hymn to apply it to Christ alone: "Holy God, Holy Mighty, Holy Immortal, who was crucified for us, have mercy on us." The Miaphysite theology of Oikoumenios is apparent in his reference to the holiness of Christ proven through the hymn of the Seraphim. While commenting on Revelation 3:7 ("And to the angel of the church in Philadelphia write: "These things says the Holy One, the True One"), Oikoumenios cannot pass up the description of Christ as the "Holy One" without supporting the Miaphysite position on the Trisagion Hymn: "The holy one is the Son of God, so also he receives witness from the Seraphim,

---

29. Andrew, Chap. 18, *Comm.* 98–99.

who combine the three acclamations of holy in the one lordship."[30] This is an obvious reference to the Trisagion hymn.

Andrew is no doubt responding to Oikoumenios's challenge and supports the Chalcedonian position that the hymn is Trinitarian by a skillful use of word association alone. Andrew maintains that the hymn of the Seraphim, "Holy, Holy, Holy," is applied to all three Divine Persons. First, he remarks that "we learn that in the Gospel" the hymn of the Seraphim "is said about the Son."[31] Such a statement is surprising to modern readers because the angelic hymn is not found in the gospels. This conclusion is only possible through word association. Andrew states that "holy, holy, holy" was said about the Son because after the hymn of the Seraphim, in which Isaiah receives his commission (Isa. 6:9–10), the Lord tells Isaiah, "Go and say to these people, 'Keep listening but do not comprehend, keep looking but do not understand. Make the mind of this people dull and stop their ears and shut their eyes so that they may not look with their eyes, and listen with their ears and comprehend with their minds, and turn and be healed.'" Andrew connects that passage with its quotation by Christ in Matthew and Mark.[32] The Isaiah reference "associates" the hymn with its original setting in Isaiah, allowing Andrew to bring into the gospel setting and write that the hymn is found "in the Gospel."

Andrew then finds that the hymn of the Seraphim was also said "about the Spirit" in another similar tour de force by linking the Isaiah passage to the words of Paul at the close of Acts of the Apostles when Paul quotes the same passage in connection with the Spirit.[33] Finally, Andrew establishes that "holy, holy, holy" was also said about the Father alone, although this time not through biblical word association, but through a prayer of the Divine Liturgy. While the congregation

---

30. Oik. 2.13.1, FOTC 112:46.   31. Andrew, Chap. 1, *Comm.* 58.
32. Matt. 13:13–15, Mark 4:12.
33. Andrew, Chap. 1, *Comm.* 58. "So, as they disagreed among themselves, they departed, after Paul had made one statement: 'The Holy Spirit was right in saying to your fathers through Isaiah the prophet, "Go to this people and say, You shall indeed hear but never understand, and you shall indeed see but never perceive"'" (Acts 28:24–25).

sings yet another hymn inspired by the words of the Seraphim, "Holy, holy, holy Lord of Sabaoth," the priest quietly recites a prayer to the Father which begins, "With these blessed powers, we also, O Master who loves mankind, say: Holy art Thou and all-holy, thou and thy only-begotten Son and thy All-Holy Spirit, holy art Thou and all-holy and magnificent is Thy glory." Therefore, Andrew can conclude that the Thrice-Holy hymn is also addressed to the Father alone, even though in this instance it is not the Trisagion hymn but the "holy, holy, holy." Word association for Andrew, therefore, is not limited to words in the Bible, but encompasses the entire experience of the Church, including liturgical prayers and hymns. This reflects the patristic view that one can fully understand the Bible only within the life of the Church.

Word association is Oikoumenios's primary technique and, as a matter of fact, it is the only type of methodology which he expressly articulates. "We must examine whether any such description occurs in another text, so that one might be able to form a judgment by comparing similar terms."[34] But word association can be applied poorly, resulting in a distortion of meaning rather than a clarification, especially when a word is interpreted without regard for its use in the context or the sequence of the passage being interpreted. This is exactly what happens in Oikoumenios's commentary on numerous occasions. For example, in the case of earthquakes, which are mentioned several times in the Apocalypse, Oikoumenios is likely to look for a corresponding historical earthquake rather than understand the term "earthquake" as having representative meaning. Andrew consistently understands the descriptions of earthquakes in Revelation as pointing to a shift in events.[35] The earthquake and cosmological signs accompanying the opening of the sixth seal (Rev. 6:12–13) are interpreted by Oikoumenios as having historically occurred at the crucifixion of Christ, despite the accompanying descriptions in Revelation of the moon becoming like blood or the stars falling from the sky, which did

---

34. Oik. 3.9.2, FOTC 112:50.
35. Andrew, Chap. 18, *Comm.* 97.

not occur during the crucifixion of Christ. Andrew, on the other hand, takes note of the cosmic signs, finds where they occur in the prophetic books of the Old Testament, notes what they mean in that context, and applies the Old Testament meaning to interpreting the text of Revelation.[36]

The application of word association is evident in Oikoumenios's exposition of the judgment scene of Revelation 20. Oikoumenios had primarily applied this section to the life of Christ, as we have seen, therefore those dead who were described as "beheaded for Jesus" could not be interpreted as those physically martyred for Christ because Christian martyrdom did not happen in Christ's lifetime. When the next verse (20:4) states that *"the rest* of the dead did not come to life" Oikoumenios ignores the reference to "the rest," thus ignoring the context of the statement. He then uses word association—the word "dead"—to interpret the meaning of "dead" in Rev. 20:4. Oikoumenios finds the word "dead" in Christ's statement, "Leave the dead to bury their own dead" (Matt. 8:22), which leads him to interpret the dead in Rev. 20:4 as those who did not accept the preaching of Christ during the time of his Incarnation.[37] But the text of Revelation refers to "the *rest* of the dead." That means there was a prior reference to "dead" by which we must interpret the meaning of "the *rest of* the dead." The first reference to "dead" was to those dead "who had been beheaded for their testimony to Jesus" (Rev. 20:4). These are distinguished from "the rest of the dead" (Rev. 20:5). The beheaded dead had actually died, contrary to Oikoumenios's allegorical explanation. The "rest of the dead" must also have experienced physical death, otherwise if they truly represent those who did not accept Christ, then how were the aforementioned dead those who had been beheaded for Jesus? His interpretation of "dead" contradicts the use of "dead" in Revelation, since the "dead" of Christ's words were those who had *not* accepted Christ, but the "beheaded" dead in Revelation 20:4 are martyrs, who clearly had

---

36. Andrew, Chap. 18, *Comm.* 98–99.
37. Oik. 11.3.6.

affirmed Christ to the greatest degree. Oikoumenios's use of word association here distorts the plain meaning of the text, not to mention violating the sequence.

Another misapplication of word association which creates significant problems for Oikoumenios occurs when he interprets the first trumpet (Rev. 8:7) as the second coming of Christ because of the association of the word "trumpet." Rather than understanding the trumpet as a symbol, he notes that the word "trumpet," as we have seen, is also found in Paul's description of the Parousia in 1 Thess. 4:16, in which the Second Coming of Christ is heralded by the blowing of a trumpet. His conclusion that the blowing of the first trumpet in Revelation symbolizes the Second Coming of Christ creates tremendous difficulty for Oikoumenios to explain the appearance of the two witnesses later. But far worse are the problems Oikoumenios faces and his strained interpretative conclusions when he attempts to explain the events brought by the blowing of subsequent trumpets. In the text of Revelation afflictions brought upon the sinners by the later trumpets are efforts to prompt them to repentance (Rev. 9:20–21). Since Christ has *already* come with the blowing of the first trumpet, Oikoumenios is forced to allegorize all of the afflictions poured out upon the earth and conclude that they represent the sufferings of the sinners in hell.[38] This becomes an insurmountable exegetical problem, and even a theological one, when the locusts are described as torturing people for "only five months" (Rev. 9:5) and, according to Oikoumenios, the locusts which bring the tortures upon the sinners in hell symbolize angels. Oikoumenios's creative "solution" and his theological error will be described in chapter 14.

Word association, sequence and context require a coordinated and thoughtful application. An effective use of word association can be seen in Andrew's analysis of the reward promised to the Church of Thyatira, "And I will give him the morning star" (Rev. 2:28). Oikoumenios relies on word association and a stock interpretation of Isa-

---

38. Oik. 5.9.1–2, 5.13.1–2.

iah 14:12, which refers to the "morning star" which fell from heaven. Church tradition had routinely identified the fallen star in Isaiah with Satan. Andrew reports this as a possibility, (most likely because Oikoumenios is expressing a traditional interpretation), but Andrew arrives at a different explanation which he prefers and which better fits the context: *Christ* is the morning star.[39] We know that Andrew prefers this interpretation because while he simply reports Oikoumenios's explanation, he offers support for his own opinion. That Christ is the morning star is a more appropriate explanation than Satan because it is based on the context. In the letters to the churches, the rewards consistently promised at the end of each letter are Christ himself, so the reward for the Church of Thyatira would not be Satan. Furthermore Christ is described as the "bright morning star" elsewhere in Revelation (Rev. 22:16).

Andrew's Use of Scripture

Andrew was very well versed in the Bible and he used the Scripture effectively in both his analysis and in support of his conclusions. He quotes from the Old Testament approximately 180 times and from the New Testament approximately 325 times.[40] Quotations in Andrew's commentary are carefully chosen and are never part of a string of quotations in the form of a proof text. Besides actual quotations, Andrew refers to many additional scriptural persons, events and concepts in the form of countless allusions without actually quoting directly from the Bible. Andrew has no understanding of Hebrew, apart from a limited knowledge of the etymology of certain Hebrew words, such as "Amen."[41] The Old Testament he knows and employs is the Septuagint.

---

39. Andrew, Chap. 6, *Comm.* 00.

40. This is a conservative number. It is difficult to decide what constitutes a true "quotation," since frequently Andrew only quotes a word or two, while making an obvious allusion to a specific scriptural text. Such references and allusions have not been counted as quotations.

41. Andrew, Chap. 1, *Comm.* 59.

Andrew's Use of Sources

Oikoumenios ◈ As we have seen, Andrew does not depend on Oikoumenios for his interpretations, although he certainly utilizes Oikoumenios and reports his opinions, especially in the earlier portions of Revelation, when Oikoumenios's explanations are more sound and less quirky. As will be seen below, Andrew cannot fairly be said to rely on Oikoumenios since he consistently demonstrates superior exegetical skill and since he departs from Oikoumenios on so many critical points, usually offering more suitable alternatives and conclusions which better fit the context. If Andrew truly "relied" in Oikoumenios he would not have the capability to consistently offer alternative explanations, often even multiple alternatives, nor would he be able to articulate his rationale for preferable alternatives. Furthermore, agreement between the two authors does not always indicate that Andrew borrowed from Oikoumenios. He would have arrived at many of their shared conclusions without ever having read Oikoumenios since they also shared a common Bible, a common language and a common Eastern tradition. Both men derived many of the interpretations by searching for the same word elsewhere in the Bible and they would unavoidably arrive at some of the same conclusions independently of each other.[42]

When Andrew presents the opinion of Oikoumenios it is usually offered first. The opinion is usually allowed as a possible explanation followed by an alternative, indicated by words such as "it is either this or …"[43] He takes the same approach with other exegetical opinions. If Andrew dislikes Oikoumenios's interpretation or believes another is better, he signals his dissatisfaction with statements of mild dis-

---

42. See chapter 6.
43. Numerous examples of Andrew's "either … or" are found throughout the commentary, such as in Chap. 5, *Comm.* 67; Chap. 7, *Comm.* 73; Chap. 8, *Comm.* 76; Chap. 10, *Comm.* 82, 83; Chap. 11, *Comm.* 85, Chap. 14, *Comm.* 92; Chap. 19, *Comm.* 102, 106, 107; Chap. 24, *Comm.* 117; Chap. 26, *Comm.* 121, 122; Chap. 27, *Comm.* 124, 125; Chap. 30, *Comm.* 132, 133, 136; Chap. 33, *Comm.* 137, 139; Chap. 48, *Comm.* 169; Chap. 59, *Comm.* 203; Chap. 64, *Comm.* 218.

approval, such as "this may be understood differently,"[44] "more suitably,"[45] "more correctly,"[46] or "much more."[47]

Unnamed Sources and Oral Traditions ~ Andrew refers to certain "teachers" without naming them, and occasionally offers a traditional interpretation which would have been otherwise unknown to us. He stands firmly within the patristic tradition and draws from a depository of traditional interpretations with which he is very familiar. One difficulty in identifying Andrew's influences is the fact that a great many books were lost in the destruction accompanying the Persian and Arab conquests during the years immediately following the composition of this commentary.[48]

Eighteen unnamed teachers or unknown sources of interpretive tradition are mentioned or can be discerned in the commentary.

1. About the warning made to the Church of Ephesus, that their lampstand would be removed, Andrew comments: "Some understood the removal of the lampstand [to refer to] the throne of the archpriest of Ephesus, because it was moved to the seat of the King."[49] This is not mentioned by any other known interpreter.

2. Andrew cites an interpretation of the four living beings of Revelation 4:6 as representing the mastery over things in heaven and on earth and in the sea.[50]

3. He also mentions an interpretation of the four living beings as the "four virtues," represented by the four gospels. Earlier interpreters had identified the gospels with animals based on characteristics of the gospels, not with virtues. But Andrew combines them. This interpreta-

---

44. Andrew, Chap. 1, *Comm.* 57.
45. Andrew, Chap. 10, *Comm.* 82.
46. Andrew, Chap. 19, *Comm.* 106.
47. Andrew, Chap. 25, *Comm.* 119.
48. Far more books were "in circulation from the fifth to sixth centuries AD than survived into the ninth, and of the latter group a good portion has since been lost." Cyril Mango, "The Revival of Learning," *The Oxford History of Byzantium*, ed. Cyril Mango (Oxford: Oxford University Press, 2002), 219.
49. Andrew, Chap. 3, *Comm.* 64.
50. Andrew, Chap. 10, *Comm.* 83.

tion, or at least the number four representing a particular set of virtues, must have been well-known to his readers at the time.[51]

4. Andrew reports that the four living beings represent the four gospels according to Irenaeus, but adds that this has "been well-stated by others."[52] The reference to "others" here cannot mean Irenaeus only but that many interpreters subsequent to Irenaeus held the same opinion and that this interpretation was well-known in exegetical circles. This is confirmed by Augustine, who was also aware that this opinion was widely held.[53]

5. After reporting the opinion of Irenaeus that the four living beings represent the four evangelists, Andrew lastly mentions a purely Christological interpretation, which probably came from an unnamed earlier source or tradition.[54] Andrew may have arrived at this interpretation himself, since he does not specifically refer to this as a tradition. But it is more likely that he was reporting an existing tradition, since other purely Christological interpretations of the four living beings were also reported by Augustine,[55] Ambrose,[56] and Gregory the Great.[57]

---

51. Andrew, Chap. 10, *Comm.* 83. The idea of four primary virtues was popular from Stoic philosophy, but not everyone agreed upon which virtues they were. Andrew presumes that the reader knows the "four virtues," possibly four principle virtues in Stoic philosophy: courage, justice, self-control and intellectual discernment. It is unlikely that Andrew or the interpreters who held this view were referencing philosophy directly. Rather, many Greek philosophical concepts had permeated the general culture to the extent that they were no longer identified with philosophy per se, but were simply widely accepted societal notions. Sometimes other virtues were listed as the four. Gerhard Podskalsky, "Virtue," *Oxford Dictionary of Byzantium*, 3 vols. (Oxford: Oxford University Press, 1991), 3:2178.

52. Andrew, Chap. 10, *Comm.* 83–84.

53. "Very many [of those] who have commented on the mysteries of the holy Scriptures before us have understood the four evangelists in this animal, or rather in these animals." *Tractates on the Gospel of John* 36.5.2 (Augustine, *Tractates on the Gospel of John*, 4 vols., trans. John W. Suggit, FOTC 78, 79, 88 and 90 [Washington, D.C.: The Catholic University of America Press, 1988–94], 88:86.).

54. Andrew, Chap. 10, *Comm.* 84.

55. Augustine, *Sermon* 210.4, "For the Lenten Season," *Augustine, Sermons on the Liturgical Seasons*, trans. Mary Sarah Muldowney, Fathers of the Church 38 (New York: Fathers of the Church, 195), 101–2.

56. Ambrose, *Homily on Luke*, Prologue 8, *Exposition of Luke*, 5.

57. Gregory the Great, *Morals on the Book of Job* 31.47(94), LF 18, 21, 23, and 31, (Oxford: John Henry Parker, 1844–50), 31: 495–96.

This interpretation most likely predates the fourth century and could have come from a common early tradition which has been lost.

6. Concerning the opening of the fifth seal (in which the souls under the altar who have been slain for their witness cry out for justice in Rev. 6:9–10), Andrew points out the distorted nature of Oikoumenios's interpretation that the seven seals refer to past history and events in the life of Christ.[58] Oikoumenios's interpretation continues to strain the text because he was then forced to interpret the souls under the altar as martyrs of the Old Testament protesting the abuse and crucifixion of Christ.[59] Drawing a contrast between Oikoumenios and himself, Andrew argues for a more natural interpretation appropriate to the historical sequence and hints that *he* is in line with the earlier established ecclesiastical tradition: "And if any take these things to mean a foretelling of future events according to the teachers of the Church, he will suppose that such a thing is fitting, that those who were killed for Christ will cry out against their persecutors."[60] This comment not only shows that Andrew sees himself as standing with "the teachers of the Church," but that he is following a line of tradition which had interpreted this sequence of events (the seven seals) and that the visions refer to events in the future for John.

7. He reports that "some of the teachers" said that the great mountain of Rev. 8:8 represents the devil.[61]

8. Commenting on the instruction given to John, "You must again prophesy" (Rev. 10:11), Andrew remarks that it might mean "that he has not yet tasted death but he will come in the end to hinder the acceptance of the Antichrist's deception."[62] In this instance, Andrew is not only referring to the legend that John would not die, but to a *second* legend, also known in the West, that John would return in the end times with the two witnesses to hinder the Antichrist's effectiveness and to prevent people from being led astray.[63]

---

58. Andrew, Chap. 17, *Comm.* 96.
59. Oik. 4.13.3–5.
60. Andrew, Chap. 17, *Comm.* 96.
61. Andrew, Chap. 23, *Comm.* 116.
62. Andrew, Chap. 29, *Comm.* 130.
63. Andrew refers to a legend that the apostle John would never die (hinted at in John

9. About the identity of the two witnesses (Rev. 11:3–4), Andrew remarked: "Many of the teachers understood these [to be] Enoch and Elias."[64] We know that this interpretation was found in Irenaeus and Hippolytus, but Andrew does not cite them as authorities, which indicates that he is referring to a long line of tradition which includes them and may even predate them, but which certainly encompasses a number of other interpreters as well.

10. Regarding the beast of the earth (Rev. 13:11), Andrew reports that some interpreters believed its two horns represent the Antichrist and the false prophet.[65] This opinion is found in Hippolytus, but Andrew does not appear to limit it to Hippolytus and Andrew does not cite him as the source.

11. Andrew relates a story he had read taken "from narratives profitable to the soul" about the joy of a guardian angel over a man who had repented.[66]

12. An otherwise unknown interpretation of the millennium is mentioned. "Some" explain the one thousand years as the "three and a half years from the baptism of Christ until his ascension into heaven." Although it is possible that Andrew was misreading Oikoumenios, who believed that the millennium represented the entire earthly life of Christ, it is unlikely that Andrew is thinking of Oikoumenios here, since more than once Oikoumenios says that the millennium is the Incarnation and he does not mention Christ's baptism.[67] It is more probable that Andrew is relating yet another ancient interpretation which had explained the millennium as the years of Christ's ministry.[68]

13. On the destruction of Babylon in Revelation 18:21, Andrew comments that to identify this Babylon with ancient Rome, (as Oikoumenios does) "seems to be somehow contrary to the interpretation con-

---

21:23) and that he would return at the end times. This legend must have been quite ancient and clearly was known in both the East and the West. It is discussed extensively by Augustine in *Tractates on the Gospel of John* 124.2–3.

64. Andrew, Chap. 30, *Comm.* 131.
65. Andrew, Chap. 37, *Comm.* 151. Hippolytus, *On Christ and Antichrist*, 49.
66. Andrew, Chap. 48, *Comm.* 170–71. 67. Oik. 10.17. 4, 6 and 7.
68. Andrew, Chap. 63, *Comm.* 211.

cerning this by the ancient teachers of the Church, who spoke against making an analogy of Babylon with the Romans by these things being prophesied on account of the ten horns that had been seen on the fourth beast."[69] Andrew seems to be indicating that the consensus in the Christian tradition was that the Babylon described in Rev. 18 is not the city of Rome.

14. On Revelation 19:6, "Then I heard what seemed to be the voice of a great multitude, like the sound of many waters," Andrew states that "some perceived" the waters "to be those waters above the heavens, with which both the entire assembly of the righteous and the fullness [of creation] glorifies the Creator."[70]

15. Concerning Revelation 19:20, in which the beast and the false prophet would be thrown into the lake of fire, Andrew comments that "it is to be found in a saying of a certain one of the teachers that some are to be living after the destruction of the Antichrist."[71]

16. After noting that the birds gorged on flesh (Rev. 19:21), Andrew allegorizes this to mean the end of "fleshy things." He supports his interpretation with the following statement: "In addition to this, as some say God says through Isaiah, 'You have become loathsome to me'" (Isa. 1:14), so also "to the saints every fleshy activity is disgusting, grievous and loathsome."[72] He appears to be referring to a specific prior or traditional interpretation of that verse in Isaiah.

17. Regarding the identity of Gog and Magog (Rev. 20:7–8), Andrew reports three interpretations which attribute Gog and Magog to completed historical events that occurred in the history of Israel and Judah, which "some of the interpreters took [to mean] the fall of the Assyrians with Sennacherib, having occurred many years previously at the time of Hezekiah [during] the prophecy of Ezekiel (Ezek. 39:9) but on the other hand, some [interpret it as] the destruction of the nations, at-

---

69. Andrew, Chap. 55, *Comm.* 195–96, referring to Dan. 7:7, 20. The "ancient teachers" are more than simply Irenaeus (*Heres.* 5.26), who associated the visions of Daniel with Revelation. This opinion was widely held.

70. Andrew, Chap. 56, *Comm.* 197.   71. Andrew, Chap. 59, *Comm.* 204.

72. Andrew, Chap. 59, *Comm.* 205.

tacking those who undertook to rebuild Jerusalem after her capture by the Babylonians, first Cyrus the Persian, and after him Darius having commanded so to the governors of Syria. And some [see] it as meaning the forces of Antiochus that were defeated by the Maccabees." However, Andrew relies on other texts to conclude that the figures of Gog and Magog will come at the end time.[73]

18. Regarding the measurements of the heavenly city amounting to a cube with sides measuring 12,000 stadia (Rev. 21:14), Andrew seems to report that the 12,000 stadia were converted into miles and includes a traditional interpretation of the number of miles: "For the aforementioned thousands of stadia constitute signs, the so-called one thousand seven hundred and fourteen miles, the one thousand signifying the perfection of the endless life, the seven hundred being the perfection in [eternal] rest, and the fourteen being the double Sabbath of soul and body, for two sevens are fourteen."[74]

References to Noncanonical Sources ～ Andrew was not averse to using noncanonical sources of information to help elucidate the meaning of the Apocalypse text. Eusebius and Josephus were used for historical reference by both Andrew and Oikoumenios, although not for theology or exegesis by either man. Eusebius is only expressly cited by Andrew once when Andrew compared the massive number of deaths during his times to an earlier period during the reign of Maximin which had been described by Eusebius in *Ecclesiastical History*.[75] However Eusebius's writings may have influenced some of Andrew's other statements, such as Andrew's defense of the Greek of the Apocalypse against those who would try to "atticize" it, possibly a response

---

73. Andrew, Chap. 63, *Comm.* 212–13.
74. Andrew, Chap. 67, *Comm.* 226.
75. Andrew, Chap. 16, *Comm.* 94–95. "[D]uring the reign of Maximin the Roman Emperor, innumerable crowds were killed by the coming of famine and plague among them, along with other calamities; and such that [the living] were not able to bury them, and yet, the Christians then generously busied themselves with the burial [of the dead] and many of those who had been deceived, were led to the knowledge of the truth by the philanthropy of the Christians." Eusebius, *E.H.* 9.8.

to Dionysios of Alexandria's criticism of the Greek of the Apocalypse which, as we have seen, had been extensively reported by Eusebius.[76]

When discussing Revelation 13:14–17, which describes the image of the beast being given breath, appearing to speak, and leading people to worship the image, Andrew comments about what had been "historically learned, both from Apollonius and others" that the ancients were able to cause statues to speak by means of sorcery.[77] This particular Apollonius was a first century philosopher and magician whose life was described by Hierocles, a contemporary of Eusebius. Hierocles compared Apollonius to Christ and argued that Christ was nothing more than a magician. Andrew probably derived his knowledge about Apollonius from the *Reply to Hierocles*, a defense of Christ which had been composed by Eusebius.[78]

In connection with that same passage of Revelation, Andrew also refers to a story found in the *Acts of Peter*. Just as sorcerers were able to make demons speak through statues, the demons could speak "even through dead bodies just as Simon Magus showed to the Romans a dead person moving in the presence of Peter, even though the apostle refuted the deception to himself show, through those whom he [Peter] raised, how the dead were raised."[79] Another event reflected in the *Acts of Peter* is mentioned earlier in the commentary by Andrew in reference to the miraculous recovery of the beast from a mortal head wound, which leads people to worship it (Rev. 13:3). There also Andrew refers to a story found in *Acts of Peter* to illustrate that sorcery can be used to make someone who has died appear to rise.[80] Andrew does not cite this apocryphal work, but only references the stories it contains,

---

76. Andrew, Chap. 72, *Comm.* 241. See 26–27 in this volume.

77. Andrew, Chap. 37, *Comm.* 153.

78. Eusebius, *Reply to Hierocles* 1.1 Philostratus: *The Life of Apollonius of Tyana*, trans. Christopher P. Jones, 3 vols. LCL 16, 17, and 458 (Cambridge, Mass.: Harvard University Press, 2005–6), 3:157. Volume 458 contains the letters of Apollonius, ancient testimonia and Eusebius's treatise, *The reply of Eusebius, pupil of Pamphilus, to the work of Philostratus on Apollonius, concerning the comparison between him and Christ handed down by Hierocles.*

79. Andrew, Chap. 37, *Comm.* 153. *Acts of Peter* 28. Peter revealed the trickery.

80. See also Andrew, Chap. 36, *Comm.* 148, *Acts of Peter* 25.

indicating that he does not accept this apocryphal work as Scripture, but simply as a source which preserved certain traditions from the life of the apostle Peter.

Another noncanonical and nonpatristic source mentioned by Andrew is an account of the martyrdom of Antipas,[81] the martyr from Pergamum mentioned in Revelation 2:13. Exactly which martyrdom Andrew had read is unclear. It could have been a complete hagiography, but possibly only the account of the martyrdom as recounted in one of the ecclesiastical volumes which contain collected descriptions of the lives or martyrdoms of saints commemorated by the Church on each day of the year.[82]

Andrew refers to Flavius Josephus when he explains that the apocalyptic signs which occur upon the opening of the sixth seal (Rev. 6:12–17) are not referring to events which took place during the first century Jewish War when the Romans besieged Jerusalem from 67 to 70 C.E. That was Oikoumenios's interpretation. Andrew, however, believed that the sixth seal describes events in the future which will take place just prior to the end. He observed that the same imagery found in Rev. 6 was used by Jesus to predict the fall and destruction of Jerusalem, which was later narrated by Josephus.[83] Andrew cited Josephus only once, but Oikoumenios refers to Josephus several times, which is not surprising since he interpreted Revelation mostly as events from the life of Christ. Andrew is familiar with other historical sources and

---

81. Andrew, Chap. 5, *Comm.* 67.
82. One such volume could be the *Great Horologion* which states that Antipas was put into a hollow bronze "bull," which was a Roman torture device. The individual to be executed was placed inside and the device was heated over a fire until red-hot and the person inside roasted to death. See *Bibliotheca Hagiographica Graeca*, 3 vols. in 1, 3rd ed., ed. François Halkin (Brussels: Société des Bollandistes, 1957), 1:48. St. Antipas (whose feast day in the Orthodox Church is listed as April 11 in the *Acta Sanctorum* and the Greek *Menaion*), is said to have been a disciple of John the Theologian and the bishop of Pergamum. The description of Antipas's death might also have been found in the *Menaion*, a collection of twelve books, one for each month of the year, which lists the saints of each specific day and provides a brief description of that saint's life and/or martyrdom.
83. Andrew, Chap. 18, *Comm.* 100. Josephus's book was entitled, *The Jewish War*. For Christ's language, see Matt. 24:2ff, Mark 13:4ff, Luke 21:7ff.

alludes to them when he mentions the persecution of Christians under Diocletian and Julian the Apostate, the persecution of Christians in Persia and the persecution of the orthodox by the Arians.[84]

Recognized Fathers ❧ Another strong indicator of his exegetical training is how Andrew uses and cites earlier patristic sources. With respect to recognized Fathers, Andrew shows that he writes in an era when it had become especially important to align oneself with earlier authorities. Although Fathers in prior ages also felt strongly motivated to align themselves with apostolic tradition, by the time of Andrew, appeal to apostolic tradition was accomplished through citations of the Fathers. Andrew cites Gregory the Theologian, Cyril of Alexandria, Papias, Irenaeus, Methodios, and Hippolytus in his prologue as witness of the trustworthiness (τὸ ἀξιόπιστον) of the Apocalypse,[85] to authenticate its apostolic authorship. Andrew also cites these and other patristic authorities in the course of his interpretation: Gregory the Theologian (five additional times after initially citing him for the "trustworthiness" of the Apocalypse), Cyril of Alexandria and Papias (once more each after the citation for "trustworthiness"), Irenaeus (eleven additional citations), Methodios (eight additional times), Hippolytus (four more times), Epiphanios (four times), Pseudo-Dionysios (whom he calls Dionysios "the Great," four times), Basil the Great (twice), Justin Martyr (twice), and Antipater of Bostra (once). Andrew remarked that he has taken "many starting points from them,"[86] but he was fully aware that he cannot rely on them since very little Greek interpretive tradition for Revelation preceded him. "Starting points" were all that they could offer: only a beginning. Where there was no established patristic tradition, Andrew relied on his exegetical training and techniques, as discussed above.

Andrew cites the opinions of Fathers over thirty times, and often quotes from them, sometimes at length. This has led some scholars

84. Andrew, Chap. 54, *Comm.* 183–84.
85. Andrew, Prologue, *Comm.* 53.
86. Andrew, Prologue, *Comm.* 54.

to dismiss Andrew's commentary as a "catena."[87] Other references are very brief, as in the case of his sole quotation from Papias. The brief Papias quote preserved in Andrew's commentary is one of the scant fragments that has survived from the works of Papias.[88] Andrew also preserves a quotation from Justin Martyr from a work now lost, although that quotation was also preserved elsewhere.[89] Andrew cites one work by Epiphanios, *On the Twelve Stones*, to interpret the description of the twelve precious stones which adorned the walls of the heavenly Jerusalem in Revelation 21, and the description of the One who sat on the throne "who appeared like the stone jasper and carnelian" in Revelation 4:3.[90] The explanations about the qualities of gems which are taken from that particular work reflect the popular science of the day. Andrew writes that the green color of the jasper indicates life and the Father as the life-giver and also it indicates that the Father is "fearsome to opponents—for they say that jasper is fearsome to wild beasts and phantoms."[91] Again, citing Epiphanios, Andrew explains that the carnelian indicates "the therapeutic spiritual healing of those who receive [the Father]. For the great Epiphanios says that when placed upon [someone] this stone heals illnesses and wounds made by iron."[92]

However, most patristic quotations are directly exegetical. This striking difference distinguishes Andrew's use of patristic sources from Oikoumenios: Andrew cites the Fathers to support his *exegesis* in almost

87. Such as Adele Monaci Castagno, "I Commenti," 426.
88. Regarding the fall of the demons from heaven, "And Papias says in these words: "To some of them, that is, the divine angels of old, he gave [authority] to rule over the earth and commanded [them] to rule well." And then he says the following: 'And it happened that their arrangement came to nothing.'" Andrew, Chap. 34, *Comm.* 142–43.
89. "[A]fter the coming of Christ and the decree against him [to send him] to Gehenna, the devil is to become a greater blasphemer even [to the extent that] he had never before so shamelessly blasphemed God." Andrew, Chap. 34, *Comm.* 143–44. This statement was also preserved in Irenaeus and Eusebius.
90. *De duodecim gemmis*, PG 43, 293–366.
91. Andrew, Chap. 10, *Comm.* 82. Epiphanios, περὶ τῶν δώδεκα λίθων, *de Gemmis*, PG 43 297 D. τοῦτόν φασιν οἱ μυθυποιοὶ τοὺς θῆρας τοὺς ἐν ἀγρῷ φοβεῖσθαι καὶ τὰ φάσματα.
92. Andrew, Chap. 10, *Comm.* 82. Epiphanios, ibid. See also Plinius, *Nat. Hist.* 37.18 and Dioscurides, *De mat. med.* 5.142.

every instance. Oikoumenios, by contrast, almost exclusively cites the Fathers to support theological arguments he makes within the course of his commentary. Andrew very effectively demonstrates, and at times explicitly points out, that his interpretation is more consistent with the patristic tradition because he aligns himself with the Fathers in his interpretation of the *text*. Having proven that the "One who is, was and is to come" is the Father in Revelation 1:4, and that the Trisagion hymn refers to the Trinity, he states "[We say] these things to show that our own understanding does not contradict the patristic voices."[93] Later, to prove that Oikoumenios's interpretation of the seven seals as events in the life of Christ was neither logical nor a traditional understanding of prophecy, he wrote: "But we have agreed with Methodios ... 'John is speaking with authority concerning the present and future things.'"[94] Later, he draws attention to Oikoumenios's departure from the most accepted patristic interpretation of the woman wrapped in the sun (Rev. 12:1). Andrew observes that "some say," referring to Oikoumenios, she is the Theotokos, "But the great Methodios took [it] to be [referring to] the holy Church."[95]

Oikoumenios does not indicate that he is aware of other exegetical traditions. He rarely mentions the opinions of others who came before him on interpretive points and rarely gives alternative explanations. Oikoumenios also appeals to pagan learning,[96] which Andrew never does. All of these factors indicate that Oikoumenios primarily offered his own individual interpretation of Revelation and largely stood outside the stream of exegetical opinion, rather than continuing in a course of existing tradition. It was left for Andrew to conclusively establish that tradition.

93. Andrew, Chap. 1, *Comm.* 58.
95. Andrew, Chap. 33, *Comm.* 136.
94. Andrew, Chap. 13, *Comm.* 90–91.
96. Oik. 1.1.2.

11

ANDREW'S DOGMATIC THEOLOGY

Doctrine

Andrew was Chalcedonian orthodox in doctrine and Oikoumenios non-Chalcedonian. Both Andrew and Oikoumenios sprinkle their commentaries with occasional hints of their particular theological positions. In two places[1] Oikoumenios makes rather lengthy Christological statements which clearly indicate that he is Miaphysite, but the statements have the character of extraneous creedal proclamations rather than theological comments prompted by his exegesis.[2] Andrew does not engage in a dogmatic duel to directly refute Oikoumenios theologically, with one exception: his comments on the Trisagion hymn, which had become a symbol of the disagreement between Chalcedonians and non-Chalcedonians. The words of the ancient and well-known hymn are: "Holy God, Holy Mighty, Holy Immortal, have mercy on us." Miaphysites inserted the phrase "who was crucified for us" to emphasize that the Logos, which they insisted was "one nature after the union," had suffered in the flesh.

Oikoumenios had lobbed the first volley toward the Chalcedonian camp when expounding on "These things says the Holy One, the True One" (Rev. 3:7). Inspired by the description of Christ as "The Holy One," he immediately expresses the Miaphysite stance on the contro-

---

1. Oik. 1.3.3 and 12.13.6.
2. See chapter 6.

versy: "The holy one is the Son of God, so also he receives witness from the Seraphim, who combine the three acclamations of holy in the one lordship."[3] No reference to the "Seraphim" or to "three acclamations" is to be found in the Apocalypse text under consideration, which is the letter to the Church of Philadelphia. Oikoumenios's allusion to the Trisagion hymn here has not been considered in the many scholarly conversations and debates which have occurred since the discovery at Messina of the only complete Oikoumenios manuscript. The discussions regarding Oikoumenios's theological orientation have centered primarily on whether Oikoumenios's Christological terminology is Severan, Cyrillian, Miaphysite/Monophysite, or Neo-Chalcedonian. However this detail, and Andrew's obvious Chalcedonian retort, unquestionably places Oikoumenios within the Miaphysite party. Just as Oikoumenios wasted little time raising the debate and defending the Miaphysite position as soon as Christ was described as "holy," Andrew responds at his very first opportunity when he asserts that it is the Father alone who is described as "the one who was, is and is to come" (Rev. 1:4).[4] The verse under consideration would not immediately bring the Trisagion debate to mind, since there is no reference to angels praising God nor does the word "holy" appear. But Oikoumenios had interpreted "was, is and is to come" as a reference to the Trinity, opening the door for Andrew to engage in a very lengthy defense of the Chalcedonian position and bringing in the Trisagion hymn.

The Trisagion had been primarily regarded as Trinitarian in Chalcedonian circles. Even though the exact words of the Trisagion are not found in the Apocalypse, Church Fathers considered it "located" there in Rev. 4:8 (as well as in Isaiah 6:3), because of the repetition of the word "holy" in the angelic hymn: "Holy, holy, holy is the Lord Almighty." As we have seen, in chapter 10, Andrew expends much effort justifying the Chalcedonian view that the Trisagion hymn is Trinitarian, proving that "holy, holy, holy" is properly said of all three members

---

3. Oik. 2.13.1, FOTC 112:46.
4. See Andrew, Chap. 1, *Comm.* 57–58.

of the Trinity by finding scriptural links between each person of the Trinity and the Trisagion hymn through word association.[5]

It is particularly noteworthy that Andrew does not wait until Revelation chapter 4 where the words "holy, holy, holy" actually appear to make his defense of the Chalcedonian opinion. The phrase being interpreted is "the one who is, was and is to come" (Rev. 1:4) and even though his exegetical conclusion is that this phrase refers to the Father alone, his analysis consists almost entirely of an explanation of *why* the statement is properly *Trinitarian*, which at first glance seems to be Oikoumenios's point. It is very peculiar that Andrew's discussion explains why the statement is theologically Trinitarian when he has just disagreed with Oikoumenios and concluded that it is *not* Trinitarian in Revelation 1:4, but refers to the Father alone. What motivates this perplexing apparent digression when Andrew is typically very linear and focused? The only explanation is that Andrew is raising and responding to a different dispute: the important and well-known point of contention between Chalcedonians and Miaphysites. Furthermore, Andrew concludes his excursus with the comment: "[We say] these things to show that our own understanding does not contradict the patristic voices."[6] The use of the plural here is no mere formality: it is an unequivocal and overt assertion that the Chalcedonian view of the Trisagion hymn is the ancient and patristic tradition of the Church.

It has been correctly noted that efforts to find terminology which would bridge the theological divide during this period resulted in very similar terms being used by both Miaphysites and Neo-Chalcedonians.[7] This has contributed to the difficulty in arriving at a precise identification of Oikoumenios's ecclesiastical affiliation. However, his association of the "three acclamations of holy" with Christ and Andrew's response that this in fact is an acclamation of the entire Trinity conclusively resolves the debate: Oikoumenios was a Miaphysite.

---

5. Andrew, Chap. 1, *Comm.* 58.
6. Andrew, Chap. 1, *Comm.* 58.
7. Marc De Groote, "Die *Quaestio Oecumeniana*," *Sacris Erudiri* 36 (1996): 67–105, 98–99.

Other details in the commentary indicate Andrew's theological perspective. Later, when Andrew actually arrives at the angelic hymn, "holy, holy, holy" in chapter 4, he repeats his earlier conclusion about "was, is and is to come," tying the two passages together. "These holy powers do not rest, never ceasing the divine hymnody and offering the three-fold blessing to the tri-hypostatic divinity. And the 'who is and who was and who is to come' we said means the Holy Trinity."[8] He affirms that the phrase properly belongs to all three persons of the Trinity since each share the attribute of holiness (and all divine attributes) even though in its initial appearance the phrase described the Father only.[9] Andrew had expertly disproven Oikoumenios's identification of "the one who was, is and is to come" with the Trinity in Revelation 1:4. But his repeated statements that the angelic hymn of Revelation 4 *is* sung to the Trinity are very significant: he is making a case for the Chalcedonian position of the Trisagion hymn in the Church.

Andrew's rationale that the hymn and statement "who is, was and is to come" can be properly said of all three members of the Trinity is based upon their possession of identical divine nature while retaining their distinction as persons. This disappointingly brief dogmatic statement only gives us the barest suggestion of Andrew's theological knowledge, but it is concise, correct, and he uses a technical theological term for "relationship" (σχέσις). The overall tone is one of relaxed familiarity with doctrinal matters.

[T]he expressions which befit God equally honor and are appropriate to each of the divine persons (ἐφαρμοζουσῶν ἑκάστῃ θεϊκῇ ὑποστάσει), and are common to the three, except for their distinctive properties, that is to say, the relationships (τῶν ἰδιοτήτων ἤγουν σχέσεων) [between them], as said by Gregory the Theologian, and except for the Incarnation of the Logos.[10]

The only other strongly doctrinal passage is inspired by the description of Christ in Revelation 19:12–13. Andrew presents an impres-

---

8. Andrew, Chap. 10, *Comm*. 84. He also refers to the Tri-hypostatic divinity in Chap. 56, *Comm*. 197.
9. Andrew, Chap. 1, *Comm*. 57.
10. Andrew, Chap. 1, *Comm*. 58.

sive list of scriptural and theological adjectives applied to Christ. Commenting on Revelation 19:12, "He has a name inscribed which no one knows but himself," Andrew writes:

> The unknown name refers to his incomprehensible essence (τὸ τῆ˜ς οὐσίας αὐτοῦ σημαίνει ἀκατάληπτον). For by many names is the divine condescension [known], as good (ἀγαθός), as shepherd (ποιμήν), as sun (ἥλιος), as light (φῶς), as life (ζωή), as righteousness (δικαιοσύνη), as sanctification (ἁγιασμός), as redemption (ἀπολύτρωσις). And likewise in the apophatic sense as incorruptible (ἄφθαρτος), invisible (ἀόρατος), immortal (ἀθάνατος), immutable (ἀναλλοίωτος), ineffable and incomprehensible in his essence (τῇ οὐσίᾳ ἀνώνυμος καὶ ἀνέφικτος) being known only to himself together with the Father and the Spirit.[11]

Regarding verse 13, "the name by which he is called is the 'Word of God,'" Andrew remarks,

> Through these things is confirmed that which had been expounded before. How is He who is inexpressible and in every sense unknowable here called 'Word'? Either to show the fillial hypostasis (τῆς ὑϊκῆς ὑποστάσεως) and impassible begottenness from the Father (τῆς ἀπαθοῦς ἐκ πατρὸς γεννήσεως) just as our word exists beforehand in the mind, or that he carries in himself the principles for all things in existence, or he is the Messenger (τὸ ἐξαγγελεὺς) of the Paternal wisdom and power.[12]

Many theological statements are far more subtle, yet manifest Andrew's theological education. A good example can be seen in his comments on the praise offered by the angels, the living beings, and the elders in the throne room scene of Revelation 5. "And I heard every creature that is in heaven and on earth and under the earth and on the sea and all the things which are in them, saying to the one who sits upon the throne and to the Lamb, 'Blessing and honor and glory and might forever and ever! Amen.'" Andrew remarks,

> For God, as the originator of all, is glorified by all things, those known by the intellect, those perceived by the sense, those which are living beings, and

---

11. Andrew, Chap. 58, *Comm.* 201.
12. Andrew, Chap. 58, *Comm.* 201.

those which simply exist by the laws of nature. And his Only-Begotten and Consubstantial Son [is glorified], as the one who graciously bestows renewal on humankind and to the creation brought into being by him, even though it has been written that he would receive authority as a man over those in heaven and on earth.[13]

A significant amount of theology is imbedded in this passage which at first glance appears deceptively simple, almost a poetic elaboration of the Father and the Son being glorified by all that exists. However, a comment such as "God as the originator of all" (ὡς πάντων γενεσιάρχης), expresses the "monarchy" of the Father and is a clear reference to the Eastern Christian theological position that the Father alone is the "source" of the Godhead. The Father alone is "unoriginate" and the source of all that exists, including the Son and the Spirit. The Son is specifically described as "Only Begotten" (μονογενὴς) and "Consubstantial" (ὁμοούσιος) clear statements of the Son's complete divinity and equality with the Father, against Arianism. The passage notes that through the Son creation was brought into existence, not through the Father, and it is the Son who brought "renewal to humankind," which can only be a reference to the Resurrection. We also see a clear reference to the Incarnation of the Son, his subsequent ascension and enthronement and glorification by the Father, "receiving authority as a man over those in heaven and on earth." The presentation unmistakably recalls the Christological "hymn" of Philippians 2. Without question, these last theological concepts underlie Andrew's remarks since the context is the scene in which God and the Lamb are presented as enthroned together, just as Philippians 2 expresses the glorification of the Son after the crucifixion and resurrection, "Therefore God has highly exalted him ... that at the name of Jesus every knee should bow" (Phil. 2:9–10).

Although Andrew does not engage in a great deal of theological reflection apart from his exegesis, from what we can determine his theological education and stance appear sound and entirely Chalcedonian orthodox. He never suggests any view which would place him outside

13. Chap. 12, *Comm.* 88.

the mainstream tradition of the Church in the slightest respect. Oikoumenios, despite his two lengthy Christological statements, occasionally reaches conclusions which are innovative and very questionable theologically, at least in the Eastern tradition, whether Chalcedonian or non-Chalcedonian.

View of Prophecy

Andrew's first articulated disagreement with Oikoumenios concerns their differing views of prophecy. In his opening comments, Oikoumenios explains that it "is the mark of consummate prophecy to encompass three periods," past, present and future.[14] He does not provide any support for that notion, other than citing pagan tradition: "For even those who are not Christians introduce their own seers who knew the events of the 'present, the future and the past.'"[15] Castagno, noting that Oikoumenios's threefold view of prophecy emphasizes the interpretation of Revelation in terms of past history, remarks that the effect is to dull the more colorful and fantastic elements of the book in favor of a more rational or logical presentation of the events.[16] Oikoumenios does not leave much room in his commentary for the element of wonder, or of the terrifying, Castagno notes. She is correct in this assessment. The plagues either refer to the distant past, the sufferings of sinners after the judgment or they are minimized by allegorization.[17]

Andrew never directly expresses a position on whether prophetic statements can ever be interpreted as an event which occurred before the seer received the prophecy. Some statements might refer to past events, but only in very obvious situations. In Andrew's commentary only two Apocalypse scenes refer to the past before John received the Revelation and can be said to be out of sequence with the progression in the remainder of the book. Both function to explain the destructive

---

14. Oik. 1.1.2.
15. Oik.1.1.2, citing Homer, Iliad I.70. See also Hesiod, *Theogony*, 38.
16. Adele Monaci Castagno, "I Commenti," 304.
17. Adele Monaci Castagno, "I Commenti," 350.

actions of the devil. The first scene is the expulsion of the devil from heaven described in Revelation 12, which is sandwiched between the description of the woman clothed with the sun who gives birth to the male child and the dragon's subsequent pursuit of her to destroy her offspring. This scene serves to explain why the devil attacks the Church and her members. The second instance is the chaining of the devil for one thousand years in chapter 20, after which he is to be loosened at the end time. There the passage explains his activity during the reign of the Antichrist and why the devil had not unleashed such destruction during the intervening one thousand years. Other than these two instances, the Revelation of John does not refer to events prior to the time that John himself received the Revelation. However, events of the eschaton can serve as a fulfillment of earlier typologies, including events in the life of Christ. For example, the scroll with the seven seals that only the Lamb is able to open (Rev. 5:1–5) can be interpreted to mean the prophecy of Isaiah (Isa. 61:1–2) "which Christ himself said in the Gospel according to Luke had been fulfilled, which things occurring thereafter are to be fulfilled in the last days."[18]

Andrew's opinion about the meaning of prophecy in general—and in Revelation in particular—is clear. Based upon his reading of the text itself, Revelation only refers to the present (which would be the visionary's present) and the future. Citing Revelation 1:2, he remarks: "And [this is] clear from what he says: 'those which are and those which will come to pass.' These are descriptions of both the present time and of the future."[19] Immediately we see that Andrew is more likely than Oikoumenios to arrive at the meaning of a passage through interpretation of the text itself and by established ecclesiastical tradition.[20] Andrew

18. Andrew, Chap. 11, *Comm.* 86, citing Lk. 4:21.
19. Andrew, Chap. 1, *Comm.* 56.
20. Castagno concluded that the differences between the commentaries of Oikoumenios and Andrew were largely due to their views of history and prophecy and that they aligned themselves with the exegetical principles and perspectives of key ecclesiastical figures. Andrew follows Methodios's view of prophecy and is in line with the interpretive tradition of Irenaeus and Hippolytus. Oikoumenios, however, was largely influenced by Eusebius's view

was very influenced by Methodios, a mid-third century Father who frequently addressed symbols from Revelation in his work, *The Symposium*. Methodios wrote: "Remember that the mystery of the incarnation of the Word was fulfilled long before the Apocalypse, whereas John's prophetic message has to do with the present and the future."[21] Andrew never deviates from this prophetic framework.

View of History

As we have seen, Andrew believed that the Apocalypse could only refer to the present and the future at the time when John received his prophecy. The opening vision of Christ (Rev. 1) and the letters to the seven churches (Rev. 2 and 3) are in the past for Andrew but were the present and future for John when he received the Revelation. Since Oikoumenios believes that prophecy can refer to the past as well, he interprets the seven seals as events in the life of Christ which have already occurred. Andrew specifically repudiates that opinion and cites Methodios for corroboration.[22] For Andrew, the opening of the first seal (Rev. 6:1–2), the white horse and horseman, is the era of apostolic preaching, which is the present for John. The next two seals occur in the future for John, but are in the past for Andrew. The second seal (Rev. 6:3–4) and the coming of the red horse is the period of martyrdom endured by those who succeeded the apostles during the pagan Roman empire. The black horse of the third seal (Rev. 6:5–6) signifies sin and death, from bodily weakness or cowardice, or those who denied Christ under torture.

---

of history and Origen's exegesis. "I Commenti," 304, 306. She believed that Oikoumenios's exegesis was even influenced by Eusebius's reluctance to confront issues of the end times (384) and his rejection of the eschatological interpretation of Scripture in favor of a historical one (388). Castagno points to Eusebius's historicized interpretation of Daniel's period of seventy weeks as an interpretation which inspired Oikoumenios's perspective (385–86).

21. *Symp.* 8.7. *The Symposium: A Treatise on Chastity*, trans. Herbert Musurillo, Ancient Christian Writers 27 (Westminster, Md.: The Newman Press, 1958), 112.

22. Andrew, Chap. 13, *Comm.* 91.

The fourth and fifth seals stand historically in both the past *and* the present for Andrew. His interpretation of the pale green horse and rider of the fourth seal (Rev. 6:7–8), bringing death by the sword and famine, is one of most intriguing passages in the entire commentary. Andrew first refers specifically to *Ecclesiastical History* in which Eusebius describes of a series of calamities which had taken place during the reign of Maximin in the early fourth century. Then Andrew solemnly remarks: "In our own generation we have known each of these happenings."[23] And finally, the fifth seal, the souls under the altar (Rev. 6:9–10), are the departed saints who cry out to God asking how much longer they must wait for God's judgment.

The sixth seal presents a historical line of demarcation for Andrew. He is certain that the sixth seal lies in the future. He first bases his opinion on the earthquake which occurs with the opening of the sixth seal (Rev. 6:12) since earthquakes in the Scriptures represent a "shift" in events. Second, and equally important, his conclusion rests upon the extremely dramatic and horrific nature of the destruction described in the subsequent chapters of the Apocalypse. He concludes that the opening of the sixth seal will mark the beginning of the eschaton, which has not arrived yet.[24]

Nonetheless, even though the end time has not materialized, Andrew believes he is living in the final era of history, the "seventh age." He reveals this orientation early in the commentary. After explaining that John wrote to seven churches (Rev. 1:4), "mystically meaning by this number the churches everywhere," he immediately adds that the number seven "also corresponds to the present day life, in which the seventh period of days is taking place."[25] He repeats this idea when the seven churches are mentioned again in Revelation 1:11, "the aforementioned number seven applying to the Sabbath period of the future

---

23. Andrew, Chap. 16, *Comm.* 94. This passage has been discussed in chapter 4 with respect to the dating of Andrew's commentary. Eusebius of Caesarea, *Ecclesiastical History* 9.8.

24. This is discussed in greater detail in chapter 13.

25. Andrew, Chap. 1, *Comm.* 56.

age."[26] This is Andrew's standard interpretation of the number seven and he believed that it was also John's symbolic theological meaning. "Often the number seven is taken by this saint as corresponding to this age and to the Sabbath rest and the repose of the saints. Therefore, here by the loosening of the seventh seal ... is meant the loosening of the earthly life."[27] The same rationale is later applied to the seven bowls poured out upon the earth: "Everywhere he refers to the number seven, showing those offenses undertaken in the seven days of the present age are to be restrained by means of the seven plagues and seven angels."[28]

Different conceptions of world history existed in the early Church. Many Fathers divided history into six "days." A highly popular notion in early Christianity was that the earth would exist for as many millennia as days in which God took to create it. The end of time would occur on the seventh day, the time of eternal repose, corresponding to the Sabbath on which God rested. This interpretation arose as early as the *Epistle of Barnabas* and was influenced by the scripture verse which states that a thousand years is like a day to God.[29] Early Christians reasoned that if a day is like a thousand years, then six days of creation meant the earth would last for six thousand years. Irenaeus and Hippolytus, both among Andrew's important sources, held this belief. "For in as many days as this world was made, in so many thousand years shall it be concluded ... in six days created things were completed; it is evident, therefore, that they will come to an end at the six thousandth year."[30] But, when the earth did not end in the six thousandth year, Church writers began to modify the model, keeping the concept of "six" but rather than representing literal one thousand year peri-

---

26. Andrew, Chap. 2, *Comm.* 60.   27. Andrew, Chap. 21, *Comm.* 112.

28. Andrew, Chap. 45, *Comm.* 164. For Oikoumenios, seven almost always represents perfection. For example, see Oik. 3.13.3, 3.13.13, and 5.3.5.

29. Ps. 90:4.

30. Irenaeus, *Heres.* 5.28.3. *The Apostolic Fathers with Justin Martyr and Irenaeus*, trans. and ed. Alexander Roberts and James Donaldson, *ANF* 1 (Grand Rapids, Mich.: Eerdmans, repr. 1989), 557.

ods, the "six" was identified with ages or historical epochs. Augustine seems to have adopted this view. He wrote that the day of judgment

will be the seventh day, just as if the first day in the whole era from the time of Adam to Noe; the second, from Noe to Abraham; the third, from Abraham to David, as the Gospel of Matthew divides it; the fourth, from David to the Transmigration into Babylon; the fifth, from the Transmigration to the coming of our Lord Jesus Christ. The sixth day, therefore, begins with the coming of the Lord, and we are living in that sixth day. Hence, just as in Genesis, [we read that] man was fashioned in the image of God on the sixth day, so in our time, as if on the sixth day of the entire era, we are born again in baptism so that we may receive the image of our Creator. But, when that sixth day will have passed, rest will come after the judgment, and the holy and just ones of God will celebrate their Sabbath.[31]

But others, Andrew included, believed that the present era is the seventh day. According to Jean Daniélou, the Jewish-inspired notion which associated the seventh day with repose seems to have been combined with the Hellenistic concept of the "cosmic week."

Thus a system is arrived at in which seven millennia constitute the total time of the world, a scheme quite foreign to Judaism, in which the duration of the world is *six* days, the seventh day representing eternal life.... So then there is a Jewish contribution, the repose of the seventh day, and a Hellenistic one, the seven millennia. In the passage in *Barnabas* a third element intervenes—the eighth day.... Christ rose on the day after the sabbath, and thenceforward the eighth day is the day of the Resurrection. *Barnabas* kept the Hellenist notion of the seven millennia as constituting the sum of history, the Jewish idea of the privileged character of the seventh day as a time of rest, and, from Christianity, the conception of the eighth day as eternal life.[32]

Why does Andrew adopt a "seventh day" concept of the present rather than maintaining a "sixth day" view with the seventh day be-

---

31. Augustine, *Serm.* 259.2. *Augustine Sermons on the Liturgical Season*, FOTC 70:105.
32. Jean Daniélou, *The Theology of Jewish Christianity*, trans. and ed. John A. Baker, vol. 1 of *The Development of Christian Doctrine Before the Council of Nicea* (Chicago: Regnery, 1964), 396–98. Andrew never mentions the "eighth day," but it is clear that he considers the future life in the kingdom to represent the eighth day since the present life on this earth is described as the seventh day.

ing the eschaton, as did Augustine and others? The key may lie in Andrew's interpretation of Revelation 17:10: "They are also seven kings, five of whom have fallen, one is, the other has not yet come, and when he comes he must remain only a little while."

Hippolytus believed that the kings represented thousand year periods, but Andrew believed that the kings represented a succession of kingdoms which had world-wide domination. At the time John wrote the Revelation, five "had fallen" and "one is," meaning that five worldwide kingdoms were past—the Assyrians, the Medes, the Babylonians, the Persians, and the Macedonians. The current reigning kingdom, the one which "is" at the time John received the Revelation, was the pagan Roman empire.[33] Andrew believed that the Christian Roman empire under Constantine and the New Rome was "the other" king, the seventh king which had "not yet come" at the time of John's vision but was in existence during the time of Andrew.

How can the seventh age represent both the present time *and* the future repose of the saints, as it does for Andrew? This seventh age consists of both the present and the future repose because the resurrection of Christ opened the kingdom of heaven which is partially realized already, to be enjoyed by all the faithful in its fullness upon Christ's return. The saints are *already* in repose and reigning with Christ during this thousand year period (Rev. 20:4) between the binding of the devil (Rev. 20:1–3) and the battle with Gog, Magog, and the forces of evil at the end of the thousand years (Rev. 20:7–8). This is explicitly shown to be Andrew's view when he remarks that the martyrs *already* rule with Christ because they are "venerated by pious kings and faithful rulers, and manifesting God-given power against every bodily ailment and demonic activity."[34] They 'will co-reign' with Christ "until his second coming, afterwards enjoying these divine promises to an even greater degree."[35]

---

33. Andrew, Chap. 54, *Comm.* 187.
34. Andrew, Chap. 61, *Comm.* 208.
35. Andrew, Chap. 61, *Comm.* 209.

Ecclesiology

Andrew's commentary presents the classic patristic conception of the Church as encompassing both the Church "Triumphant" and the Church "Militant." The Church Triumphant includes the departed faithful, represented by the twenty-four elders who are "the full number of those who have pleased God from the beginning to the end of times."[36] They wear golden 'crowns of victory' and white robes indicating their "brilliant life and the unending feast and gladness."[37] The worship of the Trinity is the primary activity taking place in the realm above. The worship is "spiritual," like that of the Church below, and includes an altar, hymns, prayers, incense, and the presence of the Father and the Lamb. It is "spiritual" because it is bloodless, "rational worship" (λογικὴν λατρείαν) "a living sacrifice to the Father" offered by humans who have been made into a "royal priesthood."[38] The faithful stand before God along with the angels, "participating in the hymnody of the heavenly powers"[39] in a "harmonious and beautiful-sounding divine doxology."[40]

Andrew is struck by the unity and harmony between the bodiless powers and humans in the Church Triumphant and the presentation in Revelation of the Church's constitution as both human and angelic. The Apocalypse text describes the angels and elders encircling the throne of God and falling down in worship, to which Andrew exclaims, "Behold, one church of angels and humans!"[41] The saving work of Christ has united the Church and now "angels and human beings have become 'one flock' and one church." Christ has "joined together the things which were divided and has destroyed 'the middle wall of separation.'"[42] The 'middle wall of separation' is an expression originally used in Ephesians 2:14 to describe the union of Jews and Gentiles in the one Church. Andrew employs it to refer to the removal of any bar-

---

36. Andrew, Prologue, *Comm.* 53.
37. Andrew, Chap. 10, *Comm.* 82.
38. Andrew, Chap. 1, *Comm.* 59.
39. Andrew, Chap. 10, *Comm.* 85.
40. Andrew, Chap. 12, *Comm.* 87.
41. Andrew, Chap. 20, *Comm.* 110.
42. Andrew, Chap. 12, *Comm.* 88.

rier formerly separating two orders of created beings: Angels and humans, now fully equal and integrated within the Church Triumphant.

The united angels and saints are partners in prayer and in the events which result in the final consummation. The humans in the Church Triumphant patiently wait and pray for the end. The angels serve God, act as mediators between heaven and earth, raising prayers upward, bringing plagues downward. The angel of Revelation 8:3 holds a golden censer "containing incense, holding the prayers of the saints," which the angel offers up "as incense to God."[43] The saints pray for the end of the world and after offering these prayers before the altar of God, the angel fills the censer with fire from the altar and throws it upon the earth (Rev. 8:5), leading to the seven trumpets and the plagues which follow. In this activity, angels mirror the duties of bishops in the Church below as "'mediators between God and men,' both raising up their entreaties and bringing down his propitiation, converting the sinners either by spoken word or strict discipline."[44] Both angels and humans rejoice when the judgment of God finally arrives.

The Church, human and angelic, is also united in its glorification of God, not merely through thrilling and magnificent hymns and prayers but in their virtuous manner of life and in their devotion to God. The bowls of incense held by the elders in Rev. 5:7 represent not merely prayers. They are "the sweet-smelling sacrifice of the faithful being offered through a life of purity," Andrew writes, "the fragrance of good works and pure prayer."[45]

But what of the Church Militant? Who comprises it and what is its relationship to the Church Triumphant? Although Andrew mentions baptism as the first "death" and "sealing," clearly a reference to the sacrament of holy Chrismation, a Christian is not one who holds merely superficial "membership" in the Church. Rather, those who are truly "sealed" are the ones sealed "with the life-giving Cross separating the

43. Andrew, Chap. 21, *Comm.* 112.
44. Andrew, Chap. 21, *Comm.* 113.
45. Andrew, Chap. 12, *Comm.* 87, citing St. Paul, "We are a sweet fragrance of Christ." 2 Cor. 2:15.

faithful from the unfaithful. They are those distinguished by the sealing who serve the truth."[46] When Revelation 14 describes the 144,000 standing on Mt. Zion with the Lamb and the sound of many waters and of harps playing, Andrew explains that this signifies "the thrilling aspect of the hymns of the saints and their melodious, well-sounding and harmonious song echoing all around the church."[47] Their song sounds forth which they achieved by "'mortifying the desires' of the body."[48] Again, in Revelation 15, those who stand on the sea of glass with harps shows the "'mortification of members' and the harmonious life in a symphony of virtues plucked by the plectrum of the divine Spirit."[49]

Andrew recognizes that some Christians are hypocritical and their lives are a sham. Many "'profess to know God,' but they 'deny him,' first 'through deeds'[50] and then by 'wearing the appearance of piety but denying its power.'"[51] Others "are enslaved by 'mammon,'[52] which the Apostle calls idolatry, saying, 'and the love of money which is idolatry.'"[53] The "great city" is "split into three parts" in Rev. 16:19, and Andrew believes this could refer to "Christians, Jews and Samaritans" in the city of Jerusalem, or "the steadfast believers, and those who pollute their baptism with filthy actions, and those Jews who never accepted the apostolic preaching."[54] As his remarks continue, Andrew states that just as Jews and Samaritans are in a similar grouping, likewise "genuine Christians find themselves mixed together with those possessing only the name [of Christian]." During the course of the plagues, the final lot of each group will be determined by their chosen lifestyle. "When the burning of these temptations will reproach them, then the division of these into three will happen: the impious, the pious and the sinners, joining those with the same habits and answering as is appropriate for their own fate."[55] Elsewhere in Revelation, one of the "calls" for the "endurance of the saints,"

---

46. Andrew, Chap. 19, *Comm.* 103.
47. Andrew, Chap. 39, *Comm.* 155.
48. Andrew, Chap. 39, *Comm.* 155, alluding to Col. 3:5.
49. Andrew, Chap. 45, *Comm.* 165, alluding to Col. 3:5.
50. 1 Tim. 1:16
51. 2 Tim. 3:5
52. Matt. 6:24, Luke 16:13
53. Andrew, Chap. 27, *Comm.* 125, Col. 3:5.
54. Andrew, Chap. 52, *Comm.* 178–79.
55. Andrew, Chap. 52, *Comm.* 179.

describes them as "those who keep the commandments of God and the faith of Jesus" (Rev. 14:12). Andrew reiterates that "the saints here display patient endurance in [which] ... they preserve inviolate the divine commandments and the faith in Christ."[56] Clearly, for Andrew the true Church does not include nominal members.

A dynamic relationship is apparent between the Church Militant and the Church Triumphant when the "pious" receive assistance as they suffer through the plagues. The angels are not necessarily aware of who the righteous are, since "the hidden virtue of the saints is unknown even to the angels."[57] The angels who stand at the four corners of the world holding back the four winds (Rev. 7:1) are instructed by a "superior holy power ... to do nothing to those who committed offenses before the knowledge of those distinguished by the sealing who serve the truth."[58] The righteous will receive help from the bodiless powers, but not in the form of escape or "rapture." The angels at the four corners of the world are to wait until the righteous are revealed, indicating to Andrew "the inescapability of the evils."[59] However, "before the bringing of trials, the virtuous will be strengthened through angelic assistance."[60] Since the tribulations of the end are inescapable, the saints are expected to manifest "faith and endurance" (Rev. 13:10). Andrew remarks that "we will be shown in fellowship" with the saints if we also are "walking bravely on the 'narrow way'"[61] None will be spared from trials, but "those who have pure faith and immovable patience in tribulations will not be blotted out of the book of life."[62]

The Apostles

The apostles fulfilled a special role in the life of the Church and they are mentioned with some frequency by Andrew. The twenty four

---

56. Andrew, Chap. 42, *Comm.* 159.
57. Andrew, Chap. 19, *Comm.* 103.
58. Andrew, Chap. 19, *Comm.* 103.
59. Andrew, Chap. 19, *Comm.* 102.
60. Andrew, Chap. 19, *Comm.* 103.
61. Andrew, Chap. 36, *Comm.* 150, referring to Matt. 7:14.
62. Andrew, Chap. 36, *Comm.* 150.

elders represent the totality of those saved, but the apostles are "pre-eminent" among them, "whom the Lord promised to seat on twelve thrones."[63] They occupy "the first appointed place."[64] The feet of Christ in the inaugural vision represent the apostles who carried the message of Christ through the world and "have been tested by fire in the furnace of trials in imitation of their Teacher."[65] The apostles are represented in the vision of the first seal, the white horse and rider with a bow, because they "bend the gospel message like a bow against the demons, leading them to be fatally wounded by the saving arrows of Christ."[66] The apostles "conquered the leader of deception on the hope of a second victory, confessing the name of the Master to the point of a violent death."[67]

The 144,000 saved from among the twelve tribes in chapter 7 shows "the multiplication of the apostolic seed."[68] "For they were the disciples of the Kernel which fell upon the earth out of love for humankind, and, bursting forth, bore much fruit of the universal salvation."[69] The same observation is made later in chapter 14 in the vision of the 144,000 who stand on Mt. Zion with the Lamb (Rev. 14:1). That multitude signifies "the fruitful abundance of the apostolic seed of grace."[70] The apostles are not merely remembered as those who preached the gospel but their work remains the adornment and foundation of the Church. The woman wrapped in the sun of Revelation 12, is the Church and the crown of twelve stars on her head is "the crown of the apostolic precepts and virtues."[71] The "divine apostles [were] "the matchmakers for the marriage of the Lamb" to the Church.[72]

Andrew's impression of the role the apostles played in the Church is most evident in the description of the heavenly Jerusalem. The city has "a great, high wall" with twelve gates inscribed with the name of

---

63. Andrew, Chap. 10, *Comm.* 82, citing Matt. 9:28 and Luke 22:30.
64. Andrew, Chap. 32, *Comm.* 136.   65. Andrew, Chap. 2, *Comm.* 62.
66. Andrew, Chap. 13, *Comm.* 91.   67. Andrew, Chap. 13, *Comm.* 91.
68. Andrew, Chap. 19, *Comm.* 106.
69. Andrew, Chap. 19, *Comm.*106, alluding to John 12:2.
70. Andrew, Chap. 39, *Comm.*155.   71. Andrew, Chap. 33, *Comm.* 138.
72. Andrew, Chap. 56, *Comm.* 197.

the tribes of Israel (Rev. 21:12). The twelve gates are the "founders of the Church and sowers of the word of the Gospel," the holy apostles "through 'which we have had access' and entry 'to the Father.'"[73] The three gates on each of the four sides of the city represent the "triple quadrupleness of the apostles who preached the Holy Trinity and the sending forth of the four gospels into the four corners of the earth."[74] The walls of the city also have twelve foundations, which are the twelve apostles (Rev. 21:14) "the blessed apostles, upon whom the church of Christ has been founded, whose names have been inscribed upon them, giving public notice."[75] The wall measurement of 144 cubits (Rev. 21:17) is "composed of twelve times twelve, showing that this number conveys the apostolic teaching."[76]

The only explicit identification of the apostles in the details illustrating the heavenly Jerusalem within the text of Apocalypse itself is that apostles are the "foundations of the walls" (Rev. 21:14). However, in his exposition of this passage Andrew gives apostolic meaning to nearly every description of the city. The precious stones adorning the foundations of the city's walls represent the apostles "shown to have been adorned with every virtue."[77] The list of stones and the similarity to the twelve precious stones adorning the breastplate of the Jewish high priest in Exodus, expresses "the harmony of the new with the old."[78] Andrew identifies each gem with a specific apostle through the color of the gem and early Church traditions regarding the lives and activities of the apostles.[79] Andrew defends his interpretation against any charge that such an exposition is "forced" or that by emphasizing their distinctive virtues he has "separated" the apostles "in their communion and solidarity." Instead, by pointing out their various virtues "through greater distinction of the individuality," he was in fact show-

---

73. Andrew, Chap. 67, *Comm.* 224, citing Eph. 2:18.
74. Andrew, Chap. 67, *Comm.* 225, in reference to Rev. 21:13.
75. Andrew, Chap. 67, *Comm.* 225.
76. Andrew, Chap. 67, *Comm.* 226.
77. Andrew, Chap. 67, *Comm.* 227, in reference to Rev. 21:19.
78. Andrew, Chap. 67, *Comm.* 227, (Exod. 39:8–14, LXX 36:15–21).
79. Andrew, Chap. 67, *Comm.* 227–30.

ing their resemblance to each other, being "eager to point out their complete identity of content, closely connected to one another like a chain."[80]

Likewise, the text of Revelation describes each of the twelve gates of the city as made from one single pearl. These also represent the apostles for Andrew. He writes: "The 'twelve gates,' clearly the twelve disciples of Christ, through whom we have come to know 'the door' and 'the way,' are 'twelve pearls,' acquiring radiance from one 'pearl of great price,' Christ."[81] The image fits his consistent description of the apostles as the ones who showed the way to Christ, who is himself the door or way to the Father. In the final beatitude of the Apocalypse, "Blessed are they who do his commandments, that they may have the right to the tree of life and that they may enter the city by the gates" (Rev. 22:14),[82] the gates once again are apostolic teaching which leads to "the Tree of Life, Christ our God.... and by the apostolic gates, that is, through their instruction, they will enter into the heavenly city through the True Door."[83] In short, every reference to the number twelve in the description of the heavenly Jerusalem represents the apostles, including the twelve different kinds of fruits which the Tree of Life yields, "the twelve fruits of the apostolic choral assembly are granted to us, the unfailing fruit of the knowledge of God through whom the 'acceptable year of the Lord' and 'the day of recompense' is proclaimed to us."[84]

---

80. Andrew, Chap. 67, *Comm.* 230.

81. Andrew, Chap. 67, *Comm.* 230, referring to Rev. 21:21, John 10:9, John 14:6 and Matt. 13:46 respectively.

82. This is a significant textual variation. This reading (ποιοῦντες τὰς ἐντολὰς αὐτοῦ) is found in the Majority Andreas text, as well as Sinaiticus and Alexandrinus. The preferred reading is "Blessed are they who wash their robes" (πλύνοντες τὰς στολὰς αὐτῶν), which is also the reading in Oikoumenios. Metzger believes the scribal variation occurred because of the similarity in sound and because elsewhere (Rev. 12:17 and 14:12) the author writes of keeping the commandments (τηροῦντες τὰς ἐντολάς). Bruce Metzger, *A Textual Commentary*, 765.

83. Andrew, Chap. 71, *Comm.* 239–40.

84. Andrew, Chap. 68, *Comm.* 233, commenting on Rev. 22:2, citing Is. 61:2.

Angelology

Andrew is highly impressed with the descriptions of angels in Revelation and frequently comments about their duties and comportment. Andrew notes the "purity of their nature,"[85] their piety,[86] their virtue,[87] and their "purity and honor and limitlessness in service."[88] They have a "flow of fiery divine love in them and pure wisdom and knowledge."[89] He also notes the "good order" (εὐταξία) in heaven.[90] Andrew's understanding of the role of angels in Revelation is either influenced or confirmed by one of his favorite sources, Pseudo-Dionysios, also known as Dionysios the Aereopagite (but whom Andrew calls "Dionysios the Great"), who composed *The Celestial Hierarchy*. Andrew observes that angels have ranks and a hierarchy and that they are always "receiving the knowledge of the works to be done in heaven, to be conveyed always from the first ones to the second ones, according to Dionysios the Great."[91]

Angels have responsibilities over creation. "From this we learn that the angelic powers have been assigned to created things, some to water, some to fire, and some to another part of creation. So we learn that this one was assigned to the punishment by fire."[92] Angels also function liturgically: "The angel stood at this [altar] and [held] the incense holder, that is, the censer containing incense, holding the prayers of the saints, offered them as incense to God."[93] This is a typical descrip-

---

85. Andrew, Chap. 45, *Comm.* 166.
86. Andrew, Chap. 21, *Comm.* 112; Chap. 70, *Comm.* 238.
87. Andrew, Chap. 10, *Comm.* 82; Chap. 28, *Comm.* 127.
88. Andrew, Chap. 45, *Comm.* 166.
89. Andrew, Chap. 21, *Comm.* 113.
90. Andrew, Chap. 13, *Comm.* 90; Chap. 21, *Comm.* 112. See Chap. 67, *Comm.* 225 for the good order of the heavenly Jerusalem and Chap. 19, *Comm.* 102, for the "good order" of creation.
91. Andrew, Chap. 45, *Comm.* 166. See *Celestial Hierarchy* 8.2; 9.2; 12.2. *Ecclesiastical Hierarchy* 1.2; 3.14. *Pseudo-Dionysius: The Complete Works*, trans. Colm Luibheid, Classics of Western Spirituality (New York: Paulist Press, 1987).
92. Andrew, Chap. 44, *Comm.* 162. Andrew was commenting on Rev. 14:18, "Then another angel came out from the altar, the angel who has power over fire."
93. Andrew, Chap. 21, *Comm.* 112.

tion and Andrew often mentions the angels' role as intermediaries between heaven and earth, serving not only God but humanity: "the angelic powers ... carry up our prayers and spiritual whole burnt offerings, which, we have heard, 'they are sent for service for the sake of those [who are] to inherit salvation.'"[94]

Angels are not only part of the Church but they are "co-celebrants with men"[95] in the divine services: "either—according to some of the saints—appearing to them in their own bodies through an immediate impression—or, according to others—as not having the three dimensions, length, width and depth, which is a characteristic of bodies—they do not appear in their own nature, but according to the opinion, being made as figures and forms by God."[96] Their presence around the throne of God, "standing in a circle around the cherubim and elders" shows "through the placement the magnitude of honor,"[97] which they enjoy from God.

As part of the Church, angels actively participate in the life of the Church, their ranks and orderliness mirroring specific ranks and duties within the Church. The angels perform specific functions and occupy roles assigned to them, just as people execute specific roles and functions according to a hierarchy in the Church. Although Andrew does not usually cite Pseudo-Dionysios for these ideas there is no question that the works of Dionysios, especially *Celestial Hierarchy* and *Ecclesiastical Hierarchy*, which emphasize the specific ranks and duties

---

94. Andrew, Chap. 48, *Comm.* 170, quoting Heb. 1:14.

95. συλλειτουργοὶ ἀνθρώποις γενήσονται. Among the hagiographies are many stories of angels liturgizing with saints. An example of this is an event in the life of St. Spyridon which was incorporated into his *apolytikion*, the primary hymn sung in honor of a saint or for a feast day. The *apolytikion* for St. Spyridon, a fourth century bishop of Cyprus whose feast day is celebrated on December 12th, describes an incident in which no one from the town had attended the divine liturgy that day. Spyridon proceeded with the service and the responses were literally sung by an angelic choir (ἀγγέλους ἔσχες συλλειτουργοῦντας σοι, ἱερώτατε, according to the apolytikion of St. Spyridon.) The glorious choir could even be heard outside the church and people reportedly entered to see who was responsible for the magnificent singing. The *apolytikion* uses the same expression that Andrew does here to describe the event, συλλειτουργοί.

96. Andrew, Chap. 20, *Comm.* 110.

97. Andrew, Chap. 20, *Comm.* 110.

within the Church and within the angelic hosts, greatly influenced Andrew. The angelic orders above not only mirror the life and function in the Church below, but angels act as mediators and representatives before God as do ecclesiastical hierarchs.[98]

Angels also offer great assistance to humans, even when they administer the plagues. Andrew sees the events of the seven trumpets as literal descriptions of the sufferings to befall sinners in the end times. The angels carry out the plagues hoping for the repentance and salvation of unrepentant people. Oikoumenios, having concluded that the Second Coming of Christ has already occurred with the description of the first trumpet,[99] is forced to interpret the plagues which follow as representing sufferings in Gehenna, not plagues on earth during the end times.[100] This means that the angels would be responsible for the punishment in hell. This is especially evident in Oikoumenios's interpretation of the sixth trumpet which releases the four angels bound at the Euphrates. He interprets them as heavenly powers and believes the images of the terrifying army—horses with lion's heads, sulfur and smoke—describe angels punishing sinners in hell.[101]

But Andrew cannot accept this interpretation. Angels will not be involved in the eternal punishment of sinners in Gehenna. At the time of judgment they will "perform the harvest of the exceedingly impious"[102] and inflict whatever chastisement sinners will experience at the time of "harvest." However, their function is not to perform eternal punishment. Instead, Andrew's conception of the angels is that they are characterized by God-like love and care. They assist people by strengthening them before the coming of trials,[103] and when angels bring chastisements against sinners it is because the sinners need affliction to bring about repentance for their salvation.[104] "Through these it is shown that not only the angels apply distressing wounds, but they

---

98. Andrew, Chap. 21, *Comm.* 113.   99. Rev. 8:7. Oik. 5.9.1–3.
100. Oik. 5.17.3, FOTC 112:89.
101. Rev. 9:13–19. Oik. 5.23. Andrew believes the four angels bound at the Euphrates are fallen angels, that is, demonic powers. Andrew, Chap. 27, *Comm.* 123.
102. Andrew, Chap. 44, *Comm.* 162.   103. Andrew, Chap. 19, *Comm.* 103.
104. Andrew, Chap. 21, *Comm.* 113.

are like doctors, on one occasion cutting and on another pouring on assuaging medicines."[105] Andrew also compares the angels to doctors elsewhere. "The angels serve these [people] as sympathetic doctors imitating Christ, healing those weak from the horrific sickness of sin by cauterization and surgery or the more moderate [sickness affecting] the lazy, lightening the future punishments in whatever manner they thankfully receive it."[106]

The angels care about human beings and twice Andrew uses *philanthropia*, "love of humanity," to describe their love. The "angelic powers feel pain over those who fall from the faith as if they will have some kind of twisting on account of sympathy and sorrow."[107] Just as God punishes sinners out of hope for their salvation, the three woes pronounced by the angel in Revelation 8:13 is not a warning but expresses "the sympathy and love for humankind of the divine angels imitating God, pitying those sinners being punished, but even much more those who do not see the afflictions for the purpose of returning [back to God]."[108]

Like God, the angels also hope for the reformation of sinners. The "spiritual powers rejoice and celebrate over those who return from repentance to salvation, but grieve over those who turn aside from the straight path."[109] In this context, Andrew mentions the guardian angel assigned to each individual, who "without saying any word, instructs us in the things we must do, as if a mind invisibly speaking to our own mind, rejoicing at those who listen to his counsels, but sorrowing in imitation of God over those who disobey."[110] Andrew briefly recounts a beautiful story of the joy of a guardian angel over the repentance of a sinner under his care.

Just as also we know from narratives profitable to the soul[111] about some man, blackened by many transgressions; and when he was entering the church, an

---

105. Andrew, Chap. 67, *Comm.* 223.
106. Andrew, Chap. 21, *Comm.* 113–14.
107. Andrew, Chap. 18, *Comm.* 99.
108. Andrew, Chap. 25, *Comm.* 119–20.
109. Andrew, Chap. 48, *Comm.* 170.
110. Andrew, Chap. 48, *Comm.* 170.
111. ψυχωφελῶν διηγημάτων, an expression for spiritual readings, especially lives of the saints.

angel followed him from afar with a sad countenance. When this man was moved to compunction, and he had declared from his soul to the "One Who Desires Mercy" a change for the better and a rejection of his prior life, when he was coming out from there the angel went before him radiant and rejoicing; but the evil demon, distressed, followed from afar.[112]

Sin and Salvation

Synergy ❦ Contrary to Oikoumenios's exposition, Andrew's end-time scenario does not include any possibility for the restoration of sinners after the judgment, but instead he consistently affirms that *this* life is the time for repentance and for striving to attain salvation. Toward this end, Andrew affirms the classic Orthodox idea of "synergy," frequently misunderstood and maligned in the West as the heresy of "semi-Pelagianism."[113] Synergy is merely the *cooperation* of a person with God to achieve that individual's salvation. The concept is found throughout the New Testament and the term was used specifically by Paul in 1 Corinthians 3:9.[114] Andrew even uses the word early in his exposition when he encourages the reader to assist fallen brethren. "Becoming 'co-workers [synergists] with God,' we will delight forever in his blessings, by the grace and love for humankind of our Lord, Jesus Christ."[115] Humans also cooperate with the angels to do the work of God, just as the guardian angels of the twelve apostles were co-workers with them in spreading the gospel.[116]

Synergy is the affirmation of human free will and the recognition of God's respect for human freedom. God did not only do what was minimally necessary for our salvation, but in fact, he exerted the maximum effort for our salvation and did not neglect anything for our sakes.

---

112. Andrew, Chap. 48, *Comm.* 170–71, citing Mic. 7:18. Andrew also mentions guardian angels in Chap. 67, *Comm.* 224.
113. Suggit also misunderstands the Eastern understanding of free will and synergy. "Oecumenius's understanding of human free will at times seems to approximate to that of Pelagius." FOTC 112:7.
114. "We are God's fellow workers." θεοῦ γάρ ἐσμεν συνεργοί.
115. Andrew, Chap. 15, *Comm.* 93.
116. Andrew, Chap. 67, *Comm.* 224.

However, although we have been saved by the work already done by God, we are not deprived of our free-will. Synergy presumes a dynamic relationship between God and the human partner. God respects our choice to have a relationship with him or not, to receive the gift of salvation or to reject it. Synergy embraces what appear to be two opposites: First, the belief that God alone is entirely responsible for our salvation and that salvation can in no way be earned. Second is the equally firm belief that we maintain our free will completely, that we determine our final end and that we are entirely answerable for our response to God.

Embracing the paradox and tension between these two beliefs has never been a problem for the Eastern mind. Since Eastern spirituality and theology are not based upon philosophy, scholasticism, or deductive reasoning, the Eastern mentality does not require "either-or" paradigms. All of this is evident in Andrew's remarks and synergy is not a contradiction for him, and it is certainly not semi-Pelagianism. He affirms that God alone is Savior of all humankind, with the complete absence of predestination, while simultaneously holding that each human is entirely responsible for his or her individual salvation, with the complete absence of any concept of "merit." We are saved only because of the mercy of God. "He will reckon us among those who are saved on account of his goodness, not looking at the multitude of our sins, but in his compassion."[117]

Salvation is a gift, but one must choose to accept it and prove worthy of it. Commenting on Revelation 22:17b, "And let him who is thirsty come, let him who desires take the water of life without price," Andrew writes:

For thirst is necessary for the drink of life, for the firm possession of the one who has acquired it, especially because it is also granted as a gift, not to those who did not toil at all, but to those who offered not things worthy of the greatness of the gift, but only a genuine and fiery resolve instead of gold and silver and pains of the body.[118]

---

117. Andrew, Chap. 39, *Comm.* 156.   118. Andrew, Chap. 72, *Comm.* 241.

Andrew emphasizes the degree of Christ's saving action. "He did not refuse even to go through the Passion for our sakes, so that he neither destroyed the free exercise of our own power [of choice] nor did he appear to overlook the cure and correction for our sakes."[119] Christ did his part, not only with his death, but by preserving our free will that we might respond to him. Furthermore, he continues to give us his grace with the expectation of a response: "Therefore, let us not 'receive the grace of God in vain' but let us make his benefits productive through showing repentance and good deeds, that we might attain the promised blessings in Christ himself our God."[120]

In the doctrine of synergy, God takes the initiative but humans must respond if they are to enjoy a relationship with God. Andrew's comments on Revelation 3:20 reflect this presumption that synergy is operating in the relationship between Christ and the soul: "Behold, I stand at the door and I knock; if one will hear my voice and will open the door, I will come in to him and I will dine with him, and he with me." Andrew interprets the verse by restating it as though Christ was explaining why he knocks rather than simply entering uninvited: "'My presence is not forced,' he says. 'I knock at the door of the heart and rejoice with those who open for their salvation.'"[121]

Not only does synergy operate for one's ultimate salvation or damnation, but it operates to determine the depth of our individual spiritual gifts, insights, and relationship with God, while still remaining entirely a gift of God and not a matter of acquisition apart from the grace of God. Commenting on the mysterious "new song" that no one knew except the elders and living beings (Rev. 14:3), Andrew writes: "And this, it says, no one else is able to learn except them. Wherefore, to each one, knowledge is given abundantly by the measure of the way of life, just as the manifestation of the mysteries of the Lord is given to the servants of men proportionately according to his favor."[122]

---

119. Andrew, Chap. 66, *Comm.* 222.
120. Chap. 66, *Comm.* 222, quoting 2 Cor. 6:1.
121. Andrew, Chap. 9, *Comm.* 79.
122. Andrew, Chap. 39, *Comm.* 155–56.

His prayerful conclusion to his own chapter 63 displays the dynamic nature of synergy in the interplay between God and the human partner as Andrew gives instructions to the reader and expresses his pastoral wishes. His comments place equal emphasis on the responsibility of the individual in his/her relationship with God coupled with the necessity for help from God.

> Having been taught by the Savior Christ to pray that we not be "led into temptation," let us earnestly do this, knowing well our own weakness, to deliver [ourselves] from the prophesied trials, to see neither the coming of the false Christ, nor the movement of the aforementioned nations, nor the fatal danger assaulting us to give up the saving faith, but guarding unwounded, if possible, "the witness of conscience" and manifesting through good deeds the fiery ardor of love toward Christ who purchased us by his "precious blood," let us hope to enjoy the blessings of eternity, being strengthened for this by the rich mercies of God.[123]

The Savior Christ's actions are not only required for the successful enjoyment of "the blessings of eternity," they are greater actions since he is the dominant, more powerful partner. More importantly, his action is required, even after the Cross and Resurrection, since he initiates the relationship. Furthermore, Christ's acts precede the acts expected of the believer and work in concert with the believer's activity. In the excerpt above, Christ gave the prayer, delivers from trials, sacrificed himself, shed his precious blood, and strengthens through the great mercies of God. But we also see in the passage numerous tasks required by the human partner: obedience to Christ by praying, the instruction to pray that specific prayer, maintaining awareness of one's own weakness, keeping the faith, guarding of the conscience, doing good deeds, and having fiery love toward Christ.

God's Will Absolutely fundamental to Eastern theology, and frequently stated or presumed in Andrew's comments, is the will of God

---

123. Andrew, Chap. 63, *Comm.* 215, quoting Matt. 6:13, 2 Cor. 1:12, 1 Pet.1:19.

that all people be saved. The interplay between the roles of the human and divine partners for the salvation of the individual (synergy) is expressed by Andrew in countless passages. For example,

> On the one hand, the aforementioned will of God, which is called both "well-pleasing" and greatly desired "supper," is that "people be saved and come to knowledge of the truth" and that they "return and live," and on the other hand secondly [the will of God] is the punishment of those who pursue their own punishment.[124]

The biblical verse "God wills that all be saved and come to the knowledge of the truth,"[125] is a favorite in the Orthodox Church and can be found in many prayers. God does not simply desire our salvation; he "thirsts for our salvation."[126] Despite the ardent desire of God for our salvation, he honors human free will. No room exists for predestination. The responsibility for one's salvation falls squarely on the human being since God has done his part. The faithful will receive "angelic assistance" and help "through the seal of the Spirit," but help is "given to us and manifesting our own power according to the amount of work we have put into it. The rest will remain without help, for by their own will they will not be helped."[127]

Free Will

The entire purpose of life in this world is to acquire eternal life. "For to be born or not to be born is not up to us, but to struggle and to be victorious [against] evil demons and to gain the eternal blessings is for us."[128] Therefore, it is the will of God that all be saved, but those who chose to be punished by rejecting salvation, will be punished since that was their unhindered choice. Andrew accepts the idea of a fire of renewal to cleanse all of creation, but he does not believe that everyone

---

124. Andrew, Chap. 59, *Comm.* 203, quoting Matt. 11:26, Rev. 19:17, 1 Tim. 2:4 and Ezek. 18:23, 32.

125. 1 Tim. 2:4.
126. Andrew, Chap. 66, *Comm.* 222.
127. Andrew, Chap. 19, *Comm.* 103.
128. Andrew, Chap. 50, *Comm.* 174.

will endure a cleansing fire for the removal of sin. He rejects the analogy which some people made to gold, including Oikoumenios, and the belief that "purification" by fire was necessary for all. Andrew responds that in the case of gold "the filth is included by its nature, but it [the filth] was intentionally united [to the soul] by the reason-endowed [human beings] rather than having been born within them."[129]

The emphasis on free will also reflects the typical Eastern Christian anthropology which affirms the essential goodness of the human being. Sin is not in our nature. Gold, on the other hand, has contaminants as part of its nature and requires purification. But no purification by fire is necessary for human beings, and no excuse exists for human beings since they have intentionally chosen to sully their souls. Whatever filth humans add to their souls can and should be removed by them. No fire is necessary. Andrew's comment reveals not only human responsibility for salvation but also displays a fundamentally positive regard for human nature, typical of the Eastern view. Even after the Fall, human beings are not sinful by *nature*, only by *choice*. God respects that choice and "each one ... is to receive the wages befitting the labors done."[130] The "wages of sin are rendered to the deserving ones and to those who reached a decision chosen by them."[131]

Andrew often expressed the belief that the punishments of sinners will reflect the nature of their sin. "Whoever sins through them is also punished through them."[132] When the blood flowing from the winepress is described as reaching as high as the horses' bridles (Rev. 14:20), Andrew remarks: "Since the lawbreakers have become [like] horses, mad for women, devoted to pleasure, they will be seized by torments up to the height of the bridles, for they knew no bridle in their pleasures."[133] Andrew's repeated emphasis on the *voluntary* nature of the punishment in hell is striking: each "human being receiving through

---

129. Andrew, Chap. 50, *Comm.* 174.
130. Andrew, Chap. 36, *Comm.* 149.
131. Andrew, Chap. 45, *Comm.* 167.
132. Andrew, Chap. 42, *Comm.* 159, alluding to Wisdom of Sol. 11:16.
133. Andrew, Chap. 44, *Comm.* 163.

his deeds that which he desired, either the kingdom or punishment."[134] Even the text of Revelation itself acknowledges that individuals will ultimately do as they please without coercion on the part of God: "Let the evildoer still do evil, and the filthy still be filthy, and the righteous still do right, and the holy still be holy" (Rev. 22:11). Andrew comments,

> It is not as though urging wrong doing and filth that he said these things presented—may it not be so!—but as [expressing] the non-compulsion, of keeping one's own will, as though he said, "Each one may do as he likes. I do not compel free choice," showing for each pursuit the corresponding end to follow "when I come to render to each the wages of the things he has done."[135]

Synergy provides one rationale underlying Andrew's rejection of *apokatastasis*, the Origenistic expectation that God will ultimately save everyone.[136] Andrew believes in eternal punishment because it is the result of one's own free choice. It is an entirely voluntary decision which God does not inhibit.

> I surmise that in no way would he either threaten or strike those worthy of endless condemnation those deserving it if the condemned ones had already repented and hated the evil which they freely chose to commit. For it is not through necessity, but voluntarily that they are punished.[137]

The purpose of this life is to acquire the kingdom of heaven, which requires great effort. In describing the exertion necessary for salvation and the rewards which await those who persist and prevail, Andrew typically uses the imagery of work ("wages," "labor," etc.), warfare ("weapons," "enemies," "drafted," etc.), and athletic metaphors ("crowns," "contest," "arena," etc.). Perhaps the most common image Andrew utilizes for this life is the comparison to an athletic contest taking place in the arena, a very popular metaphor in the patristic writings. "[T]he stadium is open to all for the contest. For what the stadium is indeed for the contestants, such is the passage to this life for all."[138] The opponents are the

---

134. Andrew, Chap. 59, *Comm.* 203.
135. Andrew, Chap. 71, *Comm.* 239.
136. See chapter 14.
137. Andrew, Chap. 50, *Comm.* 173–74.
138. Andrew, Chap. 50, *Comm.* 174.

spiritual powers of darkness, "the evil demons who have been prepared for the war against us."[139] But the official presiding over the contest is God, who observes all that we do.

The Great Official, "who does not allow anyone to be tested beyond his strength," will deliver us from this, granting us steadfast disposition and manly strength in the assaults against us, so that "legitimately contending" "against the principalities and powers of darkness" we might be adorned with the "crown of righteousness" and receive the rewards of victory.[140]

Even though Andrew believes the sufferings at the end-times will be real and physical, the images of Revelation have a present meaning and message. Warfare is required, even for those who are living before the era of the Antichrist, but it is a spiritual warfare. Physical martyrdom is not required since the contest is entirely spiritual. In fact, the contest is taking place *now* for all of us. Andrew affirms the statement of Revelation 14:13, "Blessed are the dead who die in the Lord henceforth." Not *all* of the dead are blessed, he says, but only "those who die in the Lord, having been put to death in the world ... the prizes for those winning the contests by a wide margin of victory, [the prizes] which the contestants of Christ our God achieved against the invisible powers."[141]

There is no escape from the spiritual warfare of this life. When the Church tries to flee because of the attacks of the devil (Rev. 12:13–16), "behind her will come a river of water, that is, ungodly men or evil demons or a multitude of various temptations against her that he might enslave her."[142] But the earth assists her, by the length of the journey and the dryness of the desert "preventing impulses of evils, and swallowing up the river of the temptations.[143] Some will flee to "the desert" (the monastic life), and the Antichrist will turn instead to

---

139. Andrew, Chap. 26, *Comm.* 122. This is how Andrew interprets the locusts of Rev. 9:7, whom Oikoumenios believes are angels bringing eternal punishment.
140. Andrew, Chap. 33, *Comm.* 141, quoting 1 Cor. 10:13, 2 Tim. 2:5, Eph. 6:12 and 2 Tim. 4:2.
141. Andrew, Chap. 42, *Comm.* 160.   142. Andrew, Chap. 35, *Comm.* 146.
143. Andrew, Chap. 35, *Comm.* 146.

attack those "drafted in Christ in the world … finding them vulnerable in the occupations of life."[144] Yet, the members of the Church can be victorious in many ways, through contending "with the greatest bravery,"[145] "constancy and steadfastness in doing good,"[146] humble-mindedness,[147] virtue,[148] by the genuine love of Christ,[149] and by having a heavenly orientation.

Andrew frequently contrasts an earthly mindset with a heavenly mentality. Those who think in an earthly manner "breathe dirt" instead of Christ, who is "the Myrrh which was emptied out for us."[150] Those who have "hearts dwelling entirely on the earth" will be deceived by the Antichrist.[151]

"Woe to those" who dwell on the "earth" that is, to those who do not have "[dwelling] in heaven," but have their citizenship on earth. For many of them on the earth are victorious over the enemy and will be victorious.… Wherefore, it is necessary to deplore those who have their "minds on earthly things" and who are tossed by the waves in the sea of life here.[152]

Difficulties in this earthly life are nothing but opportunities for those with a heavenly mindset. "For those who have 'citizenship in heaven' difficulties become the starting point of unfading crowns and trophies."[153] We must be vigilant and prepared for the end.

[W]herefore, we are commanded "to be watchful and gird our loins and to have burning lamps" in the way of life according to God, and give "light" to our neighbors, let us unceasingly supplicate God with a contrite heart to "rescue us from all who persecute us," lest they defeat and take possession of our souls, and seize them unprepared as if there were "none redeemed and none saved," lest the soul of each be entangled by chains of base and earthen affairs.[154]

---

144. Andrew, Chap. 35, *Comm.* 146.
145. Andrew, Chap. 20, *Comm.* 109.
146. Andrew, Chap. 50, *Comm.* 175.
147. Andrew, Chap. 35, *Comm.* 146.
148. Andrew, Chap. 45, *Comm.* 177.
149. Andrew, Chap. 35, *Comm.* 146.
150. Andrew, Chap. 25, *Comm.* 120.
151. Andrew, Chap. 37, *Comm.* 152.
152. Andrew, Chap. 34, *Comm.* 145, quoting Rev. 12:12, Phil. 3:20 and Phil. 3:19.
153. Andrew, Chap. 25, *Comm.* 37, quoting Phil. 3:20.
154. Andrew, Chap. 68, *Comm.* 236–37, quoting Luke 12:35, Matt. 5:16, Ps. 7:1, and Ps. 7:2.

Salvation remains, therefore, nothing other than a matter of individual choice, with each human making his or her choice and God also choosing to do as he promised. "Just as the power of God saves those well-pleasing to him, in the same manner [it] also punishes those unrepentantly sinning against Him."[155]

155. Andrew, Chap. 55, *Comm.* 192.

12

AFFLICTIONS AND THE LOVE OF GOD

The Purpose of the Afflictions

Afflictions play a positive role for sinners as well as those who are actively struggling to be saved. This view accords with synergy and the purpose of this life according to Andrew. When the temple is described as "filled with smoke" just before the pouring out of the seven bowls (Rev. 15:8), Andrew recognizes it as a symbol of the wrath of God which is brought to bear against those who engaged in apostasy.

Through "the smoke" we learn the frightfulness, awesomeness, and chastisement of divine wrath, with which the temple is filled, and in the time of judgment it is to issue out against those deserving of this, and before this [time it issues out] against those who complied with the Antichrist and those practicing the deeds of apostasy.[1]

Many people will suffer as a result of the afflictions. When one-third of humanity is killed by the fire and sulfur emanating from the horses in chapter 9, the text notes that in spite of the massive deaths, the survivors did not repent of their idolatry, "nor of their murders nor of their sorceries nor of their fornication nor of their thefts" (Rev. 9:20–21). This passage prompts Andrew to list those types of people "who were deemed worthy to be spared" but nevertheless, "not having been

---

1. Andrew, Chap. 45, *Comm.*166–67.

convinced by these things, have remained unrepentant."[2] Chastisements will be directed in particular toward those hypocrites who outwardly present themselves as Christians. Because they refuse to repent for their sins "wrath will be brought down on a global scale, not only upon idolaters and those who worship creation instead of the Creator but, above all," upon nominal and hypocritical "Christians." Andrew describes them as "those who profess to know God, but deny him, first 'through deeds' and then by 'wearing the appearance of piety but denying its power,' and those who are enslaved by 'mammon,' which the Apostle calls idolatry, saying, 'and the love of money which is idolatry.'"[3] For sinners, the plagues do not serve as purposeless punishment, the consequence of sin, or even as an expression of God's "wrath." Andrew's conclusion, that the function of these afflictions is the reform of sinners, is based on the Apocalypse text itself. For example, after the fourth bowl is poured out and people are scorched by the sun, Revelation 16:9 states that they "cursed God and did not repent to give him glory." Later in verse 11, when the fifth angel pours out his bowl and the kingdom is darkened, yet again they "did not repent of their deeds." The purpose of plagues, he concludes, is to "restrain" sinners. When seven angels come forward with seven plagues in Revelation 15:1, Andrew continues his usual interpretation of seven as referring to the "present age" and connects this to the purpose of the afflictions: "Everywhere he refers to the number seven, showing those offenses undertaken in the seven days of the present age are to be restrained by means of the seven plagues and seven angels."[4]

Although the afflictions punish sinful behavior, they are motivated by the love of God. Since God loves humanity and respects human free will, he employs afflictions to prompt repentance. Just as a bit and bridle give a horse direction, "God who loves humanity, compels the

---

2. Andrew, Chap. 27, *Comm.* 125.

3. Andrew, Chap. 27, *Comm.* 125, quoting Titus 1:16, and 1 Tim. 3:5, Matt. 6:24/Luke 16:13, and Col. 3:5, respectively.

4. Andrew, Chap. 45, *Comm.*164.

jaws of those who do not approach him in order that they might know repentance."[5] The fearsome description of "sounds, and thunders and lightning, and an earthquake" when an angel fills the censer with fire and throws it upon the earth (Rev. 8:5–6) are "describing the horrors preceding the end of the world ... amazing all and leading the most prudent toward conversion."[6] Painful sores appear on those who bear the mark of the beast and worship its image when the first bowl of plagues is poured out (Rev. 16:2). The purpose is to alert people to the deceit of the Antichrist and the false prophet. Since their false signs and wonders are achieved by means of sorcery, they cannot alleviate the suffering of their misguided followers. "Those being afflicted by the plagues sent by God will gain not one cure by the Antichrist whom they have deified."[7] The suffering will become extreme to such an extent that people will seek death but it will elude them, because of the "divine judgments." Andrew distinguishes this from simple retribution. "It is judged advantageous to them, by the bitterness of pains being brought upon them to make sin hateful to the people, since sin is the mother and cause of these [pains]."[8]

Andrew frequently notes that in spite of God's efforts to "encourage" the return of sinners by chastisements, usually afflicted sinners do not repent, "just as even now it is possible to see many unwilling [to repent], blaming the Divine Goodness for the unspeakable misfortunes encircling us by barbarian hands."[9] Rather than repent, often the sinners curse God instead. "Those being afflicted by this do not proceed towards repentance, but to blasphemy."[10] When the sun is allowed to scorch people with fire (Rev. 16:8–9), the sinners curse God. "Those who fall into the depth of evil deeds do not turn toward repentance but turn away toward blasphemy and will be carried away by the wickedness of mind."[11] God desires that "by painful afflictions they will

---

5. Andrew, Chap. 49, *Comm.* 172. An allusion to Ps. 32:9.
6. Andrew, Chap. 21, *Comm.* 113.
7. Andrew, Chap. 46, *Comm.* 168.
8. Andrew, Chap. 26, *Comm.* 122.
9. Andrew, Chap. 49, *Comm.* 172.
10. Andrew, Chap. 50, *Comm.* 180.
11. Andrew, Chap. 49, *Comm.* 172.

hate sin, the mother of these [attacks]. But the fools, instead of being conscious of their own errors, will 'sharpen the tongue' against God."[12]

Again they cursed God when hail as heavy as a hundred-weight talent rained down from heaven upon people (Rev. 16:21). "Those being afflicted by this do not proceed toward repentance but to blasphemy, proving the hardness and obstinacy of their hearts."[13] Andrew compares such individuals to Pharaoh in Exodus, and in fact he concludes that these sinners are worse than Pharaoh, but "these will be even more stubborn than he was. When the plagues were sent by God at least he was more pliant, confessing his own impiety, and they blaspheme even during punishment."[14]

Andrew ponders what purpose the afflictions serve since the sinners whom God seeks to reform remain unrepentant. He concludes that perhaps suffering on earth for their sins might result in the diminution of their eternal punishment: "Perhaps they who are enslaved to [sin] will meet with a milder punishment in the future because they are being afflicted in part here."[15] The same language is used elsewhere: "But those who are like chaff, the impious and the exceedingly great sinners and the unrepentant are to be punished justly here, receiving a milder sentence at the judgment."[16] For this reason the saints are motivated to offer prayers for the onset of chastisements (Rev. 8:3) "punishing [the] affliction of the impious and lawless, to lessen the future suffering."[17] Andrew explains that this is also why the saints rejoice at the destruction of Babylon, "not as those rejoicing in misfortunes of others, but as those who have a fiery desire concerning the cutting-off of sin."[18]

The Nature of the Afflictions

Unlike Oikoumenios, Andrew does not allegorize the punishments. This is one of the most important distinctions between Andrew and

---

12. Andrew, Chap. 49, *Comm.* 172, quoting Ps. 64(63):3, 140(139):3.
13. Andrew, Chap. 52, *Comm.* 180.
14. Andrew, Chap. 52, *Comm.* 180, referring to Ex. 9:27–28.
15. Andrew, Chap. 55, *Comm.* 195.
16. Andrew, Chap. 27, *Comm.* 124.
17. Andrew, Chap. 21, *Comm.* 112.
18. Andrew, Chap. 55, *Comm.* 195.

Oikoumenios, who deprives Revelation of its salutary purpose and prophetic character by denying the reality of the afflictions of the end times. When one-third of the sea is destroyed, along with the fish in it and the ships upon it (Rev. 8:8–9), Andrew alludes to Oikoumenios's allegorical interpretation of the burning of the sea: "According to the opinion of some, we should think that through these things is meant ... the cleansing fire burning after the resurrection." But this cannot be correct, Andrew maintains, "since the mention of a third is shown to us to be incongruous to that. For those being punished are more than the saved, as was said."[19] Andrew's point is sound and well-reasoned. Andrew believes that one-third of the sea, ships and sea creatures will actually be destroyed. These events cannot be allegorical descriptions of the suffering of the damned partly because the detail of "one third" conflicts with the gospels. The one-third cannot represent the damned, as Oikoumenios asserts, because such an interpretation would mean that two-thirds of humanity were saved and only one-third would be damned. This is contrary to many statements made by Christ indicating that more people would be lost than saved.[20]

When the third trumpet is blown and one-third of the fresh water becomes bitter Oikoumenios again allegorizes the punishments and once more Andrew pointedly disagrees: "Some say that 'Wormwood' implies the bitter grief shown happening to the sinners being punished in Gehenna."[21] Andrew refutes the interpretation, basing his opinion on the context of the passage, which describes punishments on earth during the eschaton, not punishments of sinners after death. "We think that the grievous pains are what are signified through these things, according to the time being described."[22]

The afflictions described in Revelation as corporeal punishments might not manifest themselves physically, but nonetheless they are very real and cannot be allegorized to refer to suffering in hell. Afflic-

---

19. Andrew, Chap. 23, *Comm.* 116, referring to Oik. 5.11.2, FOTC 112: 85.
20. See Matt. 7:14, 13:18–23, 20:16, 22:14, Mark 4:14–20, Luke. 8:5–15.
21. Andrew, Chap. 24, *Comm.* 117.
22. Andrew, Chap. 24, *Comm.* 117.

tions at the end times will be both physical and spiritual for the reprimand and improvement of the soul.[23] The individual who refuses to repent will be punished later eternally in hell, in the body and in the soul, since both aspects of the person actively participated in the sin: "sinners and transgressors are very much tormented both here and in the future, or on account of the soul and body from which the deed [done] was common to both of them and against which the punishments will be."[24]

The torment described in Revelation, therefore, can even be experienced in the conscience of the sinner.[25] When the plague of the first bowl is poured out upon the earth and sores appear on those who worship the beast and bear his image, Andrew writes that the sores indicate both a physical ailment as well as the psychological distress when the apostates realize that the Antichrist cannot help them. The afflictions imply

> the throbbing distressful penalty of a discharge in a heart, which occurs in the hearts of the apostates when those being afflicted by the plague sent by God will gain not one cure by the Antichrist whom they deified. Probably, their bodies are to be physically wounded for the reprimand of their soul, ulcerated by the diabolical darts of error by the Deceiver.[26]

When horses breathing fire and sulfur kill one-third of humankind, Andrew interprets this image as both spiritual and physical realities, rather than Oikoumenios's symbolic descriptions of angels:

> "Fire, smoke and sulfur coming out of their mouths" by which a third are threatened with killing, either implies sins inflaming the fruit of the heart by poisonous strikes and instigations, or the setting fire to cities led by barbarian hands and the shedding of blood by divine permission, through which, as we see, not less than one-third of people have been destroyed.[27]

---

23. Andrew, Chap. 46, *Comm.* 168.
25. Andrew, Chap. 55, *Comm.* 192.
27. Andrew, Chap. 27, *Comm.* 124–25.

24. Andrew, Chap. 55, *Comm.* 191.
26. Andrew, Chap. 46, *Comm.* 168.

The Extent of the Afflictions

Andrew refuses to allegorize widespread destruction in the eschaton as the suffering of sinners in hell primarily due to the sequence of events in the Apocalypse and the frequent "fractional" description of the plagues that afflict one-third or one-fourth of sinners and various elements of the created order. As already noted, Andrew also relies on the words of Christ that few people would be saved, not the majority as Oikoumenios has stated.[28] "For those being punished are more than the saved."[29] The destruction and affliction will be widespread and actual, such that "people will seek death and will not find it; and they will long to die, and death will flee from them" (Rev. 9:6). Andrew remarks that this indicates the enormity of the affliction: "By these is signified the extreme extent of the sufferings."[30] Nonetheless, "God does not bring unmitigated suffering. In his mercy, he will shorten the time of the afflictions."[31]

The counterpoint to God's chastisements is his mercy, shown by the restriction of afflicted humanity to a fraction, rather than the plagues affecting all of humanity. God's mercy is also evident in the limitation placed on the duration of suffering, such as "five months" (Rev. 9:5) or "three and a half years" (Rev. 11:2 and 3, 12:6, 13:5, etc.). Andrew bases his opinion not on general sentiment about the mercy of God but on the statements of Christ in the gospels that days of tribulation will be shortened for the sake of the people of God.[32] The "five months" of torture unleashed by the locusts in Revelation 9

we believe to mean either the shortness of time, "if those days were not shortened, no flesh would have been saved," according to the statement of the Lord,

---

28. "Many are called, but few are chosen" (Matt. 20:16, 22:14). "For the gate is narrow and the way is hard, that leads to life, and those who find it are few" (Matt. 7:14). In the parable of the sower, the majority of seeds do not bear fruit (Matt. 13:18–23, Mark 4:14–20, Luke 8:5–15).

29. Andrew, Chap. 23, *Comm.* 116.   30. Andrew, Chap. 26, *Comm.* 121.

31. Andrew, Chap. 24, *Comm.* 119.

32. "And unless the Lord had shortened those days, no flesh would be saved; but for the elect's sake, whom He chose, He shortened the days." Matt. 24:20, Mark 13:20 (NKJV).

or [it means] some five-fold [period of] time on account of the five senses, through which [senses] sin goes into people, or it means a defined [period of] time known only to God.[33]

Likewise, the darkening of the heavenly bodies by one-third in Revelation 8:12 shows

an interval [of time], so that we might know that, even then, God does not bring unmitigated suffering, but allowing those who have been wounded to suffer the one-third interval of time, [he] imperceptibly encourages the greater portion which remains [to repent]. For who will be able to bear the cup of the divine wrath unmixed?[34]

Afflictions will also arrive at the time of judgment, indicated in the Apocalypse as the "harvest" of grapes. The angel casts his sickle on the earth, reaping and gathering the vintage which is then "thrown into the great wine press of the wrath of God" (Rev. 14:18–20). This particular passage of the commentary reveals numerous features of Andrew's thought which we have already discussed. First is the view that most people will not be saved. The wine press is described as "great," he explains, "because of the multitude of those tormented in it. 'For the road to destruction is wide and spacious.'"[35] Second, the punishment is real and extensive. "And their blood 'reached as high as the bridles of horses'... probably means the magnitude of the punishments... 'to the bridles' means the lamentations of those being tormented."[36] Finally, people will be punished according to the manner of their sins: "Since the lawbreakers have become [like] horses, mad for women, devoted to pleasure, they will be seized by torments up to the height of the bridles, for they knew no bridle in their pleasures."[37]

Andrew is convinced that the punishment will "fit the crime." He interprets Rev. 13:10, "If anyone is to go into captivity, he goes; if anyone slays by the sword, by the sword he must be slain" not as an ex-

33. Andrew, Chap. 26, *Comm.* 121.
34. Andrew, Chap. 25, *Comm.* 119.
35. Andrew, Chap. 44, *Comm.*, 163, citing Matt. 7:13.
36. Andrew, Chap. 44, *Comm.* 163.
37. Andrew, Chap. 44, *Comm.* 163.

pression of the inescapability of punishment, but of the appropriate nature of the punishment awaiting each individual.

Each one, it says, is to receive the wages befitting the labors done. Those who are prepared to do evil to their neighbor will be imprisoned by the devil and will succumb to spiritual death by the satanic dagger, and in those deeds in which "they were defeated, they are to be enslaved" to him.[38]

The Suffering of the Saints

Repeatedly the text of the Apocalypse calls upon the faithful to patiently endure trials. For example, "Here is a call for the endurance of the saints. Here are those who keep the commandments of God and the faith of Jesus" (Rev. 14:12). Andrew repeatedly notes the fleeting nature of the trials, the necessity of the saints to endure them, and to pursue and preserve virtue: "The impious, it says, will be tortured throughout the age to come, and so the saints here display patient endurance in [which], time quickly slipping away, they preserve inviolate the divine commandments and the faith in Christ."[39]

Andrew believes that the true members of the Church are not always evident, even to the angels.[40] When the Antichrist appears, all will face the afflictions of the end times. Christians will be tested and the true faithful will be revealed through their patient endurance of trials and their unwavering devotion to Christ. The afflictions are spiritually beneficial for all, even if all do not recognize it. What distinguishes "saint" from "sinner" is the individual's response to these trying circumstances. Sinners who avoid sufferings "will delight at escaping from the afflictions which are brought for reform," not recognizing that God has sent them for their improvement, "so that even by necessity, they might return to the straight road, from which, being deceived, they had strayed."[41]

The devil will attack the Church through the persecution of the An-

---

38. Andrew, Chap. 37, *Comm.* 149–50, citing 2 Peter 2:19.
39. Andrew, Chap. 42, *Comm.* 159.   40. See chapter 11.
41. Andrew, Chap. 30, *Comm.* 133.

tichrist. But the righteous can be victorious, just as Christians in the past, by "suffering for Christ."[42] "For many of them on the earth are victorious over the enemy and will be victorious."[43] The faithful will be tested also during the "forty-two months" when "the holy city" will be trampled by the nations (Rev. 11:2). "I think this means that the faithful and the ones being tested will be trampled upon and persecuted in the three and a half year appearance of the Antichrist."[44] As the woman who represents the Church "fled into the wilderness" (Rev. 12:6), likewise many Christians seeking to escape the persecutions of those days will seek refuge in the wilderness, as Christians had done during the Roman persecution.[45] At the time of tribulation, some will be "tormented on account of sin, others enduring these difficulties patiently in a test of virtue, not only in those difficulties will they be tormented by the Antichrist for the sake of Christ, but also in flights and in the miseries in mountains and in caves which, in order to preserve piety, they will prefer to the way of life in the city."[46] Those who are blameless will acquire "endurance in sufferings."[47]

The child born to the woman who represents the Church "was caught up to God and to his throne" (Rev. 12:5), which seems to suggest that Christians will be spared afflictions. However, Andrew interprets it to mean that they will be taken up to heaven by God through death "so that they not be overwhelmed by troubles beyond their power."[48] Andrew reasons that God "does not allow anyone to be tested beyond his strength" (1 Cor. 10:13), therefore trials at the end times might be shortened for some of the righteous by their deaths. He supports his view with the statement in the letter to the Church of Philadelphia: "Because you have kept the word of my patience, I will keep you from the hour of trial which is coming on the whole world" (Rev. 3:10). Andrew interprets this to mean either deliverance of the Church from the Roman persecution at the time, or a reference to the eschaton, in "the

---

42. Andrew, Chap. 34, *Comm.* 144–45.
43. Andrew, Chap. 34 *Comm.* 145.
44. Andrew, Chap. 29, *Comm.* 131.
45. Andrew, Chap. 35, *Comm.* 141, 146.
46. Andrew, Chap. 52, *Comm.* 180.
47. Andrew, Chap. 55, *Comm.* 191.
48. Andrew, Chap. 33, *Comm.* 141.

world-wide movement at the end of the age against those who believe in the Antichrist, from which he [God] promises to free her zealous ones who were arrested beforehand, through departure at that time, so that 'they will not be tested beyond their strength.'"[49] The "departure" they will be granted is death.

At times, Andrew seems to suggest that the righteous will not suffer the punishing plagues. Three times he quotes the verse, "The Lord will not allow the rod of the sinners to be upon them."[50] But a careful reading reveals that he is not suggesting that the righteous will be spared the suffering of the end times, certainly not by anything akin to a modern notion of "rapture." Rather, he repeatedly affirms that the responsibility of Christians is to suffer for Christ, even to the point of martyrdom, "for they did not love their lives even unto death" (Rev. 12:11).

The righteous will be spared certain chastisements, however, namely those which will occur in the course of the "harvest" (Rev. 14:18ff) that will take place upon the arrival of Christ in judgment. Andrew reaches this conclusion because when the harvest occurs, the wine press is "trodden outside the city" (Rev. 14:20). "The 'wine press' will be trampled on 'outside the city' of the righteous. For in no way is 'the rod of these sinners to be near the inheritance,' according to the prophetic saying. For their habitation will be unmingled [with the righteous], just as their way of life has become."[51]

Andrew contrasts the disposition of unreformed sinners with the attitude expected of the faithful who ought to recognize sufferings as spiritually beneficial.

> But we must pray to the Lord, saying: "It is good for me that you humbled me that I might learn your statutes".... For we are judged by you, the Master who loves mankind. "We are chastened in order that we may not be condemned along with the world" but with a few afflictions we might escape eternal punishment.[52]

---

49. Andrew, Chap. 8, *Comm.* 76.
50. Ps. 125:3. Andrew, Chap. 44, *Comm.* 164; Chap. 50, *Comm.* 175; Chap. 58, *Comm.* 202.
51. Andrew, Chap. 44, *Comm.* 164, citing Ps. 125:3.
52. Andrew, Chap. 30, *Comm.* 133, citing Ps. 119:71 and 1 Cor. 11:32.

His perception of the purpose of afflictions leads Andrew to offer pastoral advice about suffering in general. The four angels bound at the Euphrates are loosed to "rouse the nations," but also

> so that those tested might be revealed as the faithful ones and shown worthy of greater rewards and of the heavenly mansions or rather [worthy of] barns, like ripe wheat. But those who are like chaff, the impious and the exceedingly great sinners and the unrepentant are justly punished here, by these [punishments here] receiving a milder sentence at the judgment."[53]

He advises his readers to judge themselves and to recognize that afflictions in this life are for their benefit, and thereby, if properly understood, afflictions might hinder the judgment of God.

> Therefore, if we do not wish to be judged we must examine ourselves, according to the divine Apostle—"for if we judge ourselves, we will not be judged"—judging ourselves, corrected by the Lord, thankfully receiving the pains which are brought [upon us], just as we see the grateful ones among the sick in body bearing with patience the surgery and cauterization by the doctors because of their willingness to be healed.[54]

The Love of God: *Philanthropia*

God loves humanity and does not desire that humans suffer eternally. Therefore, he sends the plagues to encourage repentance. If sinners will not reform, at least their future punishment will be moderated. But even these measures do not suffice for God who actively employs additional means to accomplish the salvation of humanity. The two witnesses, whom Andrew believes to be Enoch and Elijah, are given powers to perform miracles. Andrew is impressed by the wisdom and goodness of God, not only sending the witnesses to preach with words, but equipping them with genuine powers to counteract the Antichrist's false display, that the witnesses might directly and completely refute the deception of the Antichrist.

---

53. Andrew, Chap. 27, *Comm.* 123–24, alluding to Jn. 14:2 and Matt. 13:30.
54. Andrew, Chap. 24, *Comm.* 117, citing 1 Cor. 11:31.

Oh, the great goodness of God! For he brings healing equivalent to the wound. For since the pseudo-Christ will be manifested in the "many signs and false wonders"... so God will equip these saints by the power of true signs and wonders, so that by the placing of truth and light they will refute falsehood and darkness; those who had been deceived will return.[55]

Andrew mentions various measures adopted by God out of love for humankind. In addition to the plagues and sending the two witnesses (Rev. 11), the dramatic changes in the natural world and the advent of wars should prompt repentance or at least will serve to diminish eternal suffering.

For God, being one who loves humanity, for the diminishment of endless punishments in the future, in the present life will consent to bring on punishing afflictions to those worthy to be burdened, by both the prophets Enoch and Elijah, and by the innovations of the elements and by the painful casualties of war, towards a moderation, at any rate, of the payment in full by those who had sinned themselves.[56]

All of God's actions toward human beings, from the beginning of time, are done out of his love for humanity, especially the Incarnation. Andrew refers frequently to Christ, "who became man for our sake."[57] "He became flesh for our sake [remaining] unchanged [in his divinity]."[58] Human beings "had been tempted by sin before His coming which was out of love for humanity."[59] Although the wicked will be punished eternally, this outcome is entirely preventable since God does not desire the death and punishment of sinners. If sinners repent, "God who loves mankind redeems us" from these afflictions and torments, "making us partakers of the eternal blessings which He has prepared for his saints."[60]

When the Seer falls down dead upon experiencing the inaugural vision of Christ (Rev. 1:17), Andrew paraphrases Christ's words as he revives John: "'Do not fear, for I have not come near to kill you, since I

---

55. Andrew, Chap. 30, *Comm.* 132.
56. Andrew, Chap. 45, *Comm.* 167.
57. Andrew, Chap. 1, *Comm.* 57, and Chap. 26, *Comm.* 121.
58. Andrew, Chap. 8, *Comm.* 77.
59. Andrew, Chap. 18, *Comm.* 100.
60. Andrew, Chap. 18, *Comm.* 101.

am beginningless and endless, having become dead for your sakes.'"[61] The Son is God by nature and yet he became incarnate for the benefit of humanity. "For if this were not the case, he would not have been able to share [the kingdom] with others ... he has imparted this to all the saints from his own fullness."[62] Through the Incarnation, Christ "imparts" his life and his "fullness" to us, particularly his kingdom, the Spirit, and a relationship with the Father. "Since he became human for our sake, being God and King before the ages, he had partaken of everything that is our own except sin, and imparted all that is his to those victorious over the devil."[63]

Furthermore, if we are saved, it is only due to the goodness of God, not our own virtue. "He will reckon us among those who are saved on account of his goodness, not looking at the multitude of our sins, but in his compassion, because of which he had come to earth and poured out his precious blood for us, in order to wash clean our defilements and stains, to bring us to the Father."[64]

Although the faithful are also afflicted in the course of the plagues, they are expected to endure such afflictions, and in their endurance they have Christ as a model for imitation who accepted his own affliction for our benefit.

[H]e exhorts us to such [good actions] not only through words, but also bringing about sufferings. For it does not suffice for him only to use good and evil for encouragement or discouragement and after this either to punish or to honor those deserving glory or punishment. He did not refuse even to go through the Passion for our sakes, so that he neither destroyed the free exercise of our own power [of choice] nor did he appear to overlook the cure and correction for our sakes.[65]

The existence of the Church is also confirmation of the love of God since "the helpful providential care of the Crucified One has been given to her for our sake."[66] When an angel shows John a vision of the Church as the Bride of Christ (Rev. 21:9), Andrew remarks,

61. Andrew, Chap. 2, *Comm.* 62.
62. Andrew, Chap. 9, *Comm.* 79.
63. Andrew, Chap. 9, *Comm.* 79.
64. Andrew, Chap. 39, *Comm.* 156.
65. Andrew, Chap. 66, *Comm.* 222.
66. Andrew, Chap. 35, *Comm.* 145.

[The angel] now shows to the saint the great blessedness of the Church. Correctly it says "the bride of the Lamb" is "wife," for when Christ was sacrificed as a lamb, he gave himself in marriage by his own blood. For just as the woman was formed out of the sleeping Adam, by [her] removal from [his] side, thus also, Christ having voluntarily slept by death on the cross, the Church, constituted by the pouring out of blood from his side, is given in marriage having been united to the One suffering for us.[67]

Philanthropia ~ In spite of the numerous and varied afflictions found in the Apocalypse, Andrew does not dwell on the punishment. His overriding message in the commentary is about the love of God. The frequency with which he refers to the love of God for humanity is a striking characteristic of his exposition and gives the commentary a positive tone overall and a quality of hope and encouragement. He refers to the love of God in many ways, as described above. In no fewer than seventeen instances he specifically uses the word *philanthropia*, "love for humanity," to describe the attitude of the Triune God and Christ the Logos toward humankind.[68] This word is very common in the prayers of the Eastern Christian tradition. The passage below is typical of the affirmative tone of the commentary, expressive of the love of God for humanity and God's respect for human self-determination.

In every way, God, who thirsts for our salvation, exhorts us for the inheritance of his blessings through both goodness and misfortunes, by leading us to see the splendor of the heavenly Jerusalem and the dark and grievous gloom of the Gehenna of fire, so that either by yearning for eternal glory or by fear of endless shame, since there is [still] time, we will work to effect the good, along with renouncing all the rest.... Therefore let us not "receive the grace of God in vain" but let us make his benefits productive through repentance and

---

67. Andrew, Chap. 67, *Comm.* 223, alluding to Gen. 2:21.
68. φιλανθρωπία, literally, "the love for humankind," is found either as a noun or as an adjective describing God's disposition toward humans in Andrew, Chap. 2, *Comm.* 61; Chap. 3, *Comm.* 65; Chap. 5, *Comm.* 68; Chap. 9, *Comm.* 78; Chap. 9, *Comm.* 80; Chap. 15, *Comm.* 93 (twice); Chap. 18, *Comm.* 100 and 101; Chap. 19, *Comm.* 106; Chap. 21, *Comm.* 114; Chap. 30, *Comm.* 133; Chap. 45, *Comm.* 167; Chap. 49, *Comm.* 172; Chap. 54, *Comm.* 189; Chap. 55, *Comm.* 192; Chap. 66, *Comm.* 221. Twice Andrew uses φιλανθρωπία to describe the love of angels for human beings in Chap. 25, *Comm.* 119 and Chap. 72, *Comm.* 243.

showing good deeds that we might attain the promised blessings in Christ himself.[69]

God's love for humankind is also revealed by the manner in which God restrains his anger. In the description of Christ in the opening vision, Andrew interprets the belt, which is placed around the chest of the One like the Son of Man, as symbolizing divine restraint because of his *philanthropia*.

A golden belt was wrapped around him, not on the hip as [worn by] other men as in the era of hedonisms—the divine flesh is inaccessible to these [hedonisms]—but on the chest by the breasts [to show] also how the boundless and righteous divine anger is restrained by love for mankind.[70]

In the letter to the Laodiceans, the community is warned to repent. "If I love someone, I reproach and correct [him]; Therefore, be zealous and repent" (Rev. 3:19). Andrew does not interpret this as a threat but as a marvelous expression of the love of God: "Oh, the love for humanity! How much goodness the reproach holds!"[71] Not only does God await our repentance but also our actions, especially good deeds. Because of his love for humankind, Christ gives eternal life and his blessings freely, Andrew explains. Commenting on Revelation 21:6b, "To the thirsty I will give from the fountain of the water of life freely," Andrew writes, "'Freely' because this [grace] is not acquired by money but acquired by good deeds and the love for humankind of the one who will give it."[72]

The punishments in this life, including the plagues and disasters described in Revelation, are sent by God out of love, to spare human beings from eternal punishment. "For God, being one who loves humanity, for the diminishment of endless punishments in the future, in the present life will consent to bring on punishing afflictions to those worthy to be burdened."[73] Because he is "the God who loves humanity," God attempts to direct humans toward salutary repentance and away from disaster, just as a rider uses the bit and bridle to steer a horse.

69. Andrew, Chap. 66, *Comm.* 222, citing 2 Cor. 6:1.
70. Andrew, Chap. 2, *Comm.* 61.
71. Andrew, Chap. 9, *Comm.* 78.
72. Andrew, Chap. 66, *Comm.* 221.
73. Andrew, Chap. 45, *Comm.* 167.

"With bit and bridle," God, who loves humanity, compels "the jaws of those who do not approach him" in order that they might know repentance, even though those who fall into the depth of evil deeds do not turn toward repentance but turn away toward blasphemy and will be carried away by the wickedness of mind.[74]

We are also called to imitate God's *philanthropia* and show love and mercy to our neighbors, following the example of the Good Samaritan:

Therefore, for the disease of our souls, so that we too will gain the Physician-God who loves mankind (φιλάνθρωπον ἰατρὸν τὸν θεόν) let us hurry to be such for our fallen brothers, by offering to them the oil of sympathy mingled with the wine of exhortation, "in order that the maimed parts not worsen but be healed," according to the divine Apostle, so that becoming "co-workers with God," we will delight forever in his blessings, by the grace and love for humankind of our Lord, Jesus Christ.[75]

Andrew frequently affirms the rewards which God has prepared because of his love.

God, who loves humanity, redeems us [to take us] to the heavenly capital, the Jerusalem above, in which he will enroll [us], in which "he will be all things in all" according to the divine Apostle, "when he will destroy every rule"—rebellious, that is—"and authority and power" and to those who have served him here faithfully and wisely "he gives rest" and "will serve them," that is to say, he will appoint for them every enjoyment of the eternal blessings that have been "prepared from the foundation of the world."[76]

---

74. Andrew, Chap. 49, *Comm.* 172, citing Ps. 32:9.
75. Andrew, Chap. 15, *Comm.* 93, citing Heb. 12:13 and 1 Cor. 3:9.
76. Andrew, Chap. 54, *Comm.* 189, quoting 1 Cor. 15:28, 1 Cor. 15:24, Matt. 11:28, Luke 12:37, and Matt. 25:34 respectively.

13

ANDREW'S ESCHATOLOGY

The End Is Not Near

Andrew believes he is living in the seventh age, however, he does not believe that the end of the world is near. In fact, despite the calamities which had befallen the empire in recent years he states that the end is "not in sight" since these catastrophes did not begin to approach the scale of destruction described by Revelation.[1] The opening of the sixth seal (Rev. 6:12) will inaugurate the end times and the afflictions that will occur at that point are "of which sort as we have never known."[2] Discussing "Wormwood" (Rev. 8:11), which caused one third of humanity to die because the water became bitter, he comments that "bitter things will happen to those who find themselves [living] before the end," clearly distinguishing his times from those of the end.[3] An objective evaluation of the various features of the end times as described in the Apocalypse confirms for Andrew that the signs of the end are absent. Andrew never presents an actual list of end-times signposts which are missing, but an analysis of his remarks in the commentary supplies three major eschaton indicators which are lacking during Andrew's era and lead him to the conclusion that the end is not

---

1. Andrew, Prologue, *Comm.* 51.
2. Andrew, Chap. 18, *Comm.* 98. See chapter 10 under "Sequence."
3. Andrew, Chap. 24, *Comm.* 117.

near: First, the most dramatic and obvious missing factor is the lack of widespread destruction on the level described in Revelation. Second is the absence of an Antichrist figure. Lastly, no city existed fitting the description of "Babylon," a corrupt metropolis which wields worldwide power. Andrew's sober assessment and refusal to associate his times with the end is truly impressive and admirable, especially since he lived in an era which was truly catastrophic in countless ways.[4] His restraint and moderation not only bear witness to his intelligence and scholarly judgment, but certainly contributed to the enduring appeal and value of the commentary.

Nonetheless, most scholars have concluded that Andrew believed the end was near. Manlio Simonetti writes that Andrew opposes Oikoumenios's "more generous chronological reference with his own more rigid version which refers the text to the last times, which for him are very near."[5] Simonetti could not be more mistaken on this point. As previously mentioned, Adele Monaci Castagno also erroneously arrives at the same conclusion.[6] Reading only limited portions of the commentary or a hasty reading of the commentary can lead to such mistaken conclusions regarding Andrew of Caesarea's views.[7] Perhaps this mistake is due to Andrew's repeated emphasis on virtues, constancy, and general spiritual progress, which one might presume indicated a belief in an imminent end. Scholars may have also misread Andrew because of his comments that—from a *spiritual* perspective—the end times are *always* near. This orientation was central to Andrew's interpretation of Revelation and the purpose of his commentary. Interpreting Christ's warning in Rev. 1.3, "the time is near," Andrew explains that it means

---

4. See chapter 5.

5. Manlio Simonetti, *Biblical Interpretation in the Early Church*, trans. John Hughes (Edinburgh: T. & T. Clark, 1994), 112.

6. Adele Monaci Castagno, "I Commenti de Ecumenio e di Andrea di Cesarea: Due letture divergenti dell' Apocalisse," *Memorie della Accademia delle scienze di Torino II, Classe di scienze, morali, storiche e filologiche* V, Fascicolo IV (1981): 426. As already noted, the same mistake has been made by others. See chapter 5, n. 36.

7. See chapter 7 for Andrew's purpose and motivation in relation to his views about the end.

"the time of the distribution of prizes, on account of the brevity of the present life in comparison to the future."[8] He repeats the same idea near the end of the commentary: "The 'I am coming soon' (Rev. 22:7) either meaning the shortness of the present time compared to the future or the sudden and quick end of each [person's life]. For to each human being the departure from here is his end."[9]

Andrew presents classic patristic eschatology, refraining from engaging in predictions regarding the time of the end and emphasizing instead the time of one's own death.[10] This is a typical Eastern Christian stance and was held by Oikoumenios as well. For each of us "the end is near," since our interval on this earth is very short compared to eternity. Andrew quotes Christ in this context, "Work while it is day" (John 9:4), meaning do what is necessary to acquire a place in the kingdom of heaven while you have the opportunity.[11] This intersects with another of Andrew's frequent themes: the need for continual effort and strenuous exertion in the spiritual life in order to acquire heavenly rewards.

The Millennium

By Andrew's time, millennialism, also known as chiliasm, had long been discredited in Church circles, and the archbishop of Caesarea expressed the typical ecclesiastical view, which rejected the idea of a literal earthly kingdom. One reason for the rejection of millennialism was that it presumes two resurrections: one for the saints, who will reign with Christ on earth, and a second, common resurrection for all

---

8. Andrew, Chap. 1, *Comm.* 56.

9. Andrew, Chap. 69, *Comm.* 236. Statements such as this may have led Simonetti, Castagno and others to hastily conclude that Andrew believed the end of the world was near. This misinterpretation highlights that fact that a careful reading of Andrew is necessary to determine his true opinions.

10. Castagno correctly noted that Oikoumenios did not find imminent signs of the end in Revelation for his times, but for some reason she was mistaken about Andrew. Adele Monaci Castagno, "I Commenti," 339.

11. Andrew, Chap. 1, *Comm.* 56.

the rest of humanity. Andrew reports the classic justification historically given for chiliasm: that the saints should have as their reward the enjoyment of this earth on which they had suffered.

Others said that after the completion of the six thousand years, the first resurrection of the dead is granted only to the saints, so that in this earth, in which they displayed endurance, they will enjoy delight and honor for one thousand years, and after that the universal resurrection will occur, not of the just only but also of the sinners.[12]

Andrew reported an otherwise unknown interpretation of the millennium: "Some, I don't know how, explain the aforementioned time of one thousand years as the three and a half years from the baptism of Christ until his ascension into heaven, after which they conjectured that the devil is to be loosed."[13] Andrew does not dwell on millennialism or expend any effort refuting its rationale. The one thousand years is neither the period of Christ's earthly ministry, nor will there be a literal kingdom on earth and two resurrections. He rejects the various explanations tersely: "It is unnecessary to note that the Church has accepted none of these."[14] Andrew indicates that his interpretation of the thousand year reign is the accepted ecclesiastical view, not simply his personal preference. In support of the Church's view, Andrew remarks that "We [are] listening to the Lord," who said "to the Sadducees that the righteous will be like 'angels of God in heaven' and the Apostle who said 'The kingdom of God is not food and drink' thus we took 'the one thousand years' to be the time of the preaching of the Gospel."[15] The millennium began with the Incarnation of Christ and it will end with the appearance of the Antichrist at which time the devil will be un-

---

12. Andrew, Chap. 63, *Comm.* 211.
13. Andrew, Chap. 63, *Comm.* 211. This precise opinion, not found in any previous author, is also not the opinion of Oikoumenios (10.17.5–7). Oikoumenios, in accordance with his method interpreting in the Apocalypse as events in the life of Christ, believes that the millennium is the entire earthly life of Christ, from his *birth* until his ascension. Andrew appears to be reporting another unknown, ancient tradition.
14. Andrew, Chap. 63, *Comm.* 211.
15. Andrew, Chap. 63, *Comm.* 211, quoting Matt. 22:30/Mark 12:25/Luke 20:36, Rom. 14:17.

chained. Andrew interprets the binding of the devil for one thousand years as "the restraint of his evil activity," but the number is symbolic and not necessarily a literal period of years.[16]

> By the number "one thousand years," by no means is it reasonable to understand so many [years]. For neither ... are we able to count out these things as ten times one hundred, rather [they are to mean] many [generations]. Here also, we infer the number one thousand to indicate either a great many or perfection. For these things require many years for the purpose of preaching the gospel everywhere in the entire world and the seeds of piety to take root in it.... The one thousand years, therefore, is the time from the year of the Incarnation of the Lord until the coming of the Antichrist.[17]

As proof that the devil has been bound since the crucifixion of Christ, Andrew points to the "disappearance of idolatry, the destruction of the temples of idols and the disappearance of the defilement[18] upon the altars and the universal knowledge of the divine will."[19] The limitation on the devil's powers is indicated by the angel placing him in the "abyss" and the description of his restraint as a "chain" (Rev. 20:1–3).[20] The devil is very weak since the Incarnation. "An angel administers such a sentence, it says, in order to show that [the devil] is both weaker than these ministering powers in terms of power and that from the beginning it was in vain that he boldly ruled over all."[21]

In addition to the binding of Satan, perhaps the most important detail in the millennial scenario is that the saints will come to life and reign with Christ for a thousand years (Rev. 20:4). Andrew cites this detail to support his interpretation against millennialism. In what

---

16. Andrew, Chap. 60, *Comm.* 206.
17. Andrew, Chap. 60, *Comm.* 206–7.
18. λύθρον, meaning literally filth or "defilement," also "gore." This word was used to indicate blood sacrifices of the type that were performed for pagan gods. Such sacrifices were inherently defiling because they were idolatrous.
19. Andrew, Chap. 60, *Comm.* 206. The "divine will," is an expression found frequently in prayers and patristic writings, expressing a well-known and deeply held theological principle and presumption in the Eastern tradition: God "desires that all people be saved and come to the knowledge of the truth" (1 Tim. 2:4).
20. Andrew, Chap. 60, *Comm.* 206.
21. Andrew, Chap. 60, *Comm.* 206.

manner will the saints rule with Christ for one thousand years if not on a physical earth? Andrew asserts that they are already ruling now, during the period since the Incarnation when Satan was bound. They will judge the demons in the future but they already rule and manifest their authority now, "being venerated by pious kings and faithful rulers, and manifesting God-given power against every bodily ailment and demonic activity."[22] Those who suffered for Christ "will co-reign until his second coming, afterwards enjoying these divine promises to an even greater degree."[23] Yet another reference to the one thousand years two verses later confirms Andrew's opinion. The Apocalypse text reads: "Blessed and holy is he who has a share in the first resurrection! Over such ones the second death has no power, but they will be priests of God and of Christ, and they will reign with him a thousand years" (Rev. 20:6). Andrew explains that those reigning with Christ during the millennium are those who are baptized having been "buried and raised with Christ." The "dead" are those "remaining in [a state of] death by sins."[24] According to Andrew's ecclesiology, mere baptism would not suffice to consider someone a member of the Church.[25] "Those praiseworthy ones" are those "who in Christ 'mortify the activities of the body,' who are crucified with Christ and are dead to the world."[26]

Andrew returns to the question of the millennium a few verses later when addressing the identity of Gog and Magog, who appear on the scene "when the thousand years ends" (Rev. 20:7). He reiterates that it is not necessary to consider the one thousand years as a literal number and then repeats his opinion: "We took the one thousand years to be the time of the preaching of the Gospel."[27] Andrew supports his interpretation with an example from the Song of Songs, in which the number one thousand represents "the great quantity and the perfection in harvest, just as here also the harvest of the faith in perfection

---

22. Andrew, Chap. 61, *Comm.* 208. 23. Andrew, Chap. 61, *Comm.* 209.
24. Andrew, Chap. 61, *Comm.* 210. 25. See chapter 11.
26. Andrew, Chap. 62, *Comm.* 209, quoting Rom. 6:4, Rom. 8:13, Col. 3:5.
27. Andrew, Chap. 63, *Comm.* 211.

[is implied] after which 'the son of perdition, the man of lawlessness,' will come."[28]

The millennium is the period allocated by God for the dissemination of the Gospel, which must be preached throughout the world before the end arrives, but how much time this will require is unknown. Andrew acknowledged that some interpreted the millennium literally as "ten times one hundred years."[29] When Andrew composed his commentary fewer than six hundred years had elapsed since the time of Christ. Since it is a symbolic number, Andrew conceded that the "millennium" might even be fewer than one thousand years. However, "it is [left] to God alone, who knows to what extent his forbearance is expedient for us, and in this way he determined the duration of life. After which [one thousand years] the Antichrist will disturb the entire world."[30]

Babylon and the Successive Kingdoms

Andrew did not interpret Revelation to apply to specific events or occurrences in his own time, nor did he predict the time of the end. However, he believed that the language of the Apocalypse may truly describe actual events. "If anyone attaches each of the plagues to things to be found at the end time, he will not entirely miss what is suitable."[31] Andrew also considered it a possibility that the end might not be too far off in the future because the seventh king, which he understands to represent the present age or era, is described as remaining "a little while" (Rev. 17:10). Earlier kingdoms had lasted for hundreds of years. At the time Andrew wrote this commentary about three hundred years had elapsed since the rise of Constantine the Great, who established the Christian Roman empire.

Consistent with his understanding of the present era as the seventh

---

28. Andrew, Chap. 63, *Comm.* 211. "A man will lay down one thousand pieces of silver for its fruit" ... "one thousand to Solomon and two hundred to those who keep his fruit." Song of Sol. 8:11–12. The expectation of a "man of lawlessness" is found in 2 Thess. 2:3.

29. Andrew, Chap. 60, *Comm.* 206. 30. Andrew, Chap. 60, *Comm.* 207.

31. Andrew, Chap. 45, *Comm.* 167.

age and his empire as New Rome, Andrew believed that the Antichrist would come as "king of the Romans."³² The "New" Roman empire was almost universally regarded in the patristic tradition as the "seventh kingdom," in a series of kingdoms that dominated the world. The "seventh kingdom" will probably not last as long as the earlier kingdoms, he surmised, since, according to the Apocalypse, it is to remain only "a little while." On the other hand, the seventh age/kingdom might last just as long as the others and "a little while" might only indicate the brevity of this life in comparison to the duration of eternal life.

> The Blessed Hippolytus understood these to mean ages, of which five have passed by, the sixth still stands, during which the apostle saw these things and the seventh, which is after the 6,000 years, "has not yet come," but coming it "must remain a little while" ... the statement about the world-wide Babylon would well be accomplished in the capital city until the Antichrist, reigning for a little while, as compared to the previous [kingdoms], some of which ruled more than five hundred years, and others more than one thousand. After all, every chronological number is short compared to the future everlasting kingdom of the saints.³³

He does not believe that the beast on which the harlot sits in Revelation 17:1–3 represents the city of Rome, despite the description of "seven hills" in the text of Revelation. John perceives the harlot "as a mental vision in the Spirit." Babylon takes the form of a woman because of her

> luxuriant indulgence toward sin. And she was seated on a scarlet beast, because of her resting upon the murderous and blood-delighting devil through her evil deeds through which she becomes a coworker with the apostate [devil] in the blasphemy against God. For both the beast and the scarlet color mark his savage cruelty, great ferocity and murderous intention.³⁴

Andrew identifies the beast upon which the harlot Babylon rides as the devil.³⁵ The beast is red and the woman is drunk with the blood

---

32. Andrew, Chap. 54, *Comm.* 187.
33. Andrew, Chap. 54, *Comm.* 187.
34. Andrew, Chap. 53, *Comm.* 182.
35. Andrew, Chap. 53, *Comm.* 182.

of the saints (Rev.17:6.), so Babylon must represent a ruling city which had persecuted the saints. Andrew does not believe the city to be ancient Rome, although he explores that along with various other possibilities,

> either that one chooses to understand it as the one ruling in the time of the Persians, or the old Rome or the New, or taken generally as the kingdom in one unit, as it is said. For in each of these [cities] various sins had been born and blood of the saints poured out, some more, some less, we have learned. And the blood the martyrs shed [in the former Rome] under Diocletian or the torments of those in Persia—who could enumerate them? These things were endured under Julian secretly and the things they dared to do in the time of the Arians against the orthodox in the New Rome, the histories present to those who read.[36]

Since Babylon persecutes the saints, any candidate which might be identified as Babylon must have persecuted the Church, whether the ancient Persian city, Old Rome or New Rome. The actual Persian Babylon was identified with sorcery and many saints had actually been martyred there, but Andrew concluded that "Babylon" cannot represent the actual Persian city because the Babylon of Revelation is the fourth in a succession of kingdoms and has ten kings under its subjugation, symbolized by the ten horns. This interpretation had been rejected long ago by most of the "teachers." This conviction on Andrew's part, in line with a traditional patristic interpretation of Daniel that the ten horns represent ten kingdoms under the domination of the worldwide Babylon, ruled out any existing city since during Andrew's time none possessed that level of worldly power.

But it seems to be somehow contrary to the interpretation concerning this by the ancient teachers of the Church, who spoke against making an analogy of Babylon with the Romans by these things being prophesied on account of the ten horns that had been seen on the fourth beast, that is, in the rule of the Romans, and from her the one sprouted uprooting the three and subjugating the rest, and to come as a king of the Romans, on the one hand coming on the

---

36. Andrew, Chap. 54, *Comm.* 183–84.

pretext of fostering and organizing their rule, and on the other hand in reality [coming] to work toward its complete dissolution.³⁷

Andrew joins earlier Fathers and does not identify Babylon with the city of Rome either, explaining the classic description of "seven hills" or mountains represents seven ruling kingdoms, "seven places standing out from the rest in worldly prominence and power, these upon which we know were established in due season the [ruling] kingdom of the world."³⁸ This comports with his view of history as seven ages. The seven mountains stand for seven heads or seven kings, which periphrastically represent the entire period of supremacy of that particular kingdom. "Nino of the Assyrians, Arbaces of the Medians, Nebuchadnezzar of the Babylonians, Cyrus of the Persians, Alexander of the Macedonians, Romulus of ancient Rome, and Constantine of the New [Rome]."³⁹ The hills upon which Babylon sits do not represent an actual place, but instead probably signify "ranks of glory."

So therefore, through "seven heads" femininely showing cities, and through the "seven mountains" in neuter [showing] seven heights surpassing the rest of the body of the earth in due season, this is not a specific place among the nations but relates to ranks of glory. And "kings" we have understood, so to speak, as either the places which have been honored with royal administration, or those who first reigned in each of the aforementioned, periphrastically defining the entire reign of each.⁴⁰

Andrew also decides against identifying the city of ancient Rome with Babylon, despite the detail of seven hills, because the Babylon of Revelation is described as a city which has worldwide dominion and "ancient Rome from long ago lost the power of its kingdom ... for the Apocalypse says, 'The woman which you see is the great city having dominion over the kings of the earth.'"⁴¹ However, Babylon might represent Rome to the extent that New Rome, the seventh kingdom, is a his-

---

37. Andrew, Chap. 55, *Comm.* 195–96.
38. Andrew, Chap. 54, *Comm.* 185.
39. Andrew, Chap. 54, *Comm.* 186.
40. Andrew, Chap. 54, *Comm.* 186.
41. Andrew, Chap. 53, *Comm.* 181, referring to Rev. 17:18.

torical continuation of the former Roman Empire, which he describes as the kingdom "in one unit."

> Wherefore, as it is said, someone who would truly take this to mean this [Roman] kingdom originally in one unit that has ruled until now, that poured out the blood of the apostles and prophets and martyrs, would not be led astray from what is appropriate. For just as also this is said about one chorus and one army and one city even if they exchange each of those [individuals] constituting them, likewise in the same way the kingdom is one, even though in many times and places it is divided.[42]

He does not identify it with the current Roman capital of Constantinople either, although it is doubtful that he would completely rule that out as a possibility if Constantinople were to acquire worldwide dominion and were also to become morally depraved. "How did the present Babylon 'water the nations with the wine of her own fornication?' By becoming altogether the leader in all these transgressions and by her sending to the cities subject to her, through gifts, rulers who were the enemies of truth and righteousness."[43] The city "has given itself over to fornication."[44] But Andrew gives no hint that he considers Constantinople to be in such a degenerate spiritual state. It is also clear that neither the capital nor any city then possessed that level of world domination. Therefore, he locates the eschaton at some point in the future.

In his comments on the identity of Babylon, Andrew reveals how much his interpretation of this passage in Revelation and his eschatological scenario is influenced by ecclesiastical tradition which goes back to Hippolytus's interpretation of Daniel 7 and the four beasts which come out of the sea. "Daniel also previously saw these 'ten horns' of the Antichrist. After the accursed one has uprooted three, he will make the rest subject to him."[45] The "successive kingdoms" interpretation was widespread among the Fathers of both the East and the West. The same conclusions are expressed by Jerome in his commentary on

---

42. Andrew, Chap. 55, *Comm.* 196.
43. Andrew, Chap. 55, *Comm.* 190–91.
44. Andrew, Chap. 54, *Comm.* 189.
45. Andrew, Chap. 54, *Comm.* 188, citing Dan 7:7–8.

Daniel.[46] The first beast, like a lion, was traditionally understood to represent the Babylonians, the second, the bear, was the Persians, the third, the leopard, was the Macedonians, and the fourth, the most terrible beast, was the Romans. We also see Andrew's reliance on this tradition in his earlier interpretation of Revelation 13:2 in the description of the beast of the sea. "And the beast that I saw was like a leopard, its feet were like a bear's, and its mouth was like a lion's mouth." Revelation 13 describes one beast that combines characteristics of the three animals from the vision in Daniel 7. Andrew writes:

> The leopard means the kingdom of the Greeks, the bear that of the Persians, the lion is the kingdom of the Babylonians over which the Antichrist will rule, coming as king of the Romans, and abolishing their rule when he sees the clay toes of the feet, through which is meant the weak and fragile division of the kingdom into ten.[47]

The devil will be responsible for the destruction of Babylon through the ten "horns" (rulers) because he is a destroyer and he "rejoices at discord."[48] An angel proclaims Babylon's imminent demise: "Fallen, fallen is Babylon the great! She has watered all nations from the wine of desire of her fornication" (Rev. 14:8). Andrew ponders the sin of Babylon and its relationship to the name.

> "Babylon" is the name he significantly gives to the confusion of the world[49] and to the tumult of daily life which, as much as he foretells, is not yet to end. The "wine of desire of fornication" he calls not only the Bacchanalia of idolatry and the alienation of the mind, but also the drunkenness and lack of control which derives from each sin, according to which all those who are unfaithful to God ... will be utterly destroyed.[50]

Even though Babylon conforms to the desires of the devil, the devil will himself direct the "ten horns," ten kings who had previously op-

---

46. Jerome, *On Daniel* 7.1–7, in *Jerome's Commentary on Daniel*, trans. Gleason L. Archer, Jr. (Grand Rapids, Mich.: Baker Book House, 1958), 72–76.

47. Andrew, Chap. 36, *Comm.* 148.   48. Andrew, Chap. 54, *Comm.* 189.

49. This interpretation most likely has its origin in Gen. 11:9, which provides the meaning of the word "Babel" due to the confusion of tongues.

50. Andrew, Chap. 41, *Comm.* 158.

posed one another, to destroy her. The devil "will grant concord to the rebellious ten horns" which will "devastate the densely populated city."[51] The devil "will lead the burning of this city and the cutting-up of human flesh for his own food and it will be [for him] an occasion for rejoicing."[52] Those ruling over Babylon at the time of her destruction will suffer greatly. Andrew comments that it is "unambiguous that [here] is prophesied the sufferings of those holding ruling power during those times."[53] The destruction of Babylon will occur with shocking speed, in "a single day" (Rev. 18:8), meaning "either the suddenness and brevity of time in which, from both the sword and famine, sorrow will come to her, and also from pestilence, to be destroyed and to be 'burnt down by fire.'"[54]

The Devil

Andrew marvels at the character of the devil and how he seeks to destroy both the wicked and the good.

> It is a wonder to me to read how the devil is an enemy and an avenger, because he will operate by directing those "ten horns" himself, on the one hand to put himself in place of the goodness-loving and virtue-loving Christ our God, and on the other hand to devastate the densely populated "city" which has given itself over to fornication from the divine commandments and has diligently served his pleasures, and to fill up with her blood according to the nature of the bloodthirsty beast.[55]

Andrew is very consistent with his identification of "the dragon" with the devil, also known as "Satan." Andrew identifies the beast of the sea with the Antichrist who receives his power and authority from the devil. The beast of the earth is the spokesperson of the Antichrist, hence he is the false prophet. "We think it is not absurd to understand that the dragon is Satan, that 'the beast rising out of the sea' is the Antichrist, and that the one present, according to the opinion of the

---

51. Andrew, Chap. 54, *Comm.* 189.
53. Andrew, Chap. 54, *Comm.* 189.
55. Andrew, Chap. 54, *Comm.* 188–89.
52. Andrew, Chap. 54, *Comm.* 189.
54. Andrew, Chap. 55, *Comm.* 192.

Blessed Irenaeus, is to be understood as the false prophet rising out of the earth."[56]

Oikoumenios, on the other hand, becomes hopelessly confused with the various evil personas. According to Oikoumenios, Satan is the serpent, chief of the demons and the beast of the sea.[57] The beast of the earth is the Antichrist,[58] but the false prophet could also be the Antichrist.[59] Later Oikoumenios says that the Antichrist is simultaneously the Devil who is seen in the beast of Revelation 17.[60] Oikoumenios never clarifies the confusion or resolves the issue and his last attempt is the most muddled explanation of all. He first identifies three separate figures who are to be destroyed in the fire of Gehenna: Satan, the Devil and the Antichrist, classifying Satan and the Devil as *separate* persons.[61] He also conflates the Antichrist with the false prophet, but then immediately identifies Satan as one individual who is also called the Devil and the serpent.[62]

Andrew corrects Oikoumenios and explains the reason for the different titles, revealing that he is aware of the etymologies of those terms. The word "Satan" derives from the Hebrew word for "adversary" and is used because "he is opposed to both the Master and his servants." The Greek word "devil" *diabolos* stems from the verb διαβάλλω, meaning, "I slander" or "I accuse falsely" "because he slanders virtues and those who desire them and [he slanders] God himself to human beings, as he represented him [God] slanderously to Adam." When both terms are used, "it is placed like an overstatement" and not because the "Devil" and "Satan" are two different beings.[63] "Accusation and Slander against human beings are the names the devil had been called, as had been said, which he is."[64]

56. Andrew, Chap. 37, *Comm.* 151.
57. Oik. 7.11.1–2. He is also identified with the serpent by Oikoumenios in 7.3.3.
58. Oik. 8.3.1.
59. Oik. 9.5.2.
60. Oik. 9.11.3–4.
61. Oik. 9.6.2.
62. Oik. 9.6.3.
63. Andrew, Chap. 34, *Comm.* 143, referring to Gen. 3:5.
64. Andrew, Chap. 34, *Comm.* 144.

Andrew introduces traditional background information about the devil in the context of Revelation 12 which describes a "war in heaven." "Michael and his angels fought against the dragon. And the dragon and his angels fought, and they did not prevail, and there was no longer any place to be found for them in heaven" (Rev. 12:7–8). The devil actually had two falls, Andrew explains, and this passage can refer to either or both. It could indicate "the first fall of the devil from the angelic order because of arrogance and envy," and also "his degradation by means of the Cross of the Lord."[65] Andrew reports an ancient Christian tradition and preserves one of the few Papias fragments:

One must know that, as it has been given to the Fathers, after the creation of the perceptible world, this one had been cast down on account of his pride and envy, he to whom had first been entrusted the aerial authority, just as the Apostle said (Eph. 2:2, 6:12). And Papias says in these words: "To some of them, that is, the divine angels of old, he gave [authority] to rule over the earth and commanded [them] to rule well." And then says the following: "And it happened that their arrangement came to nothing."[66]

As Andrew continues his comments on Revelation 12, he expounds on the fall of the devil, what it entailed, and the possibility of the devil's repentance. It was necessary for the devil to fall from heaven, "for heaven does not bear an earthly mentality, because 'darkness has nothing in common with light.'"[67] Furthermore, "the angels are delighted about his ejection 'for there is nothing in common between a believer and an unbeliever.'"[68]

One must know that the fall of the devil that happened after the cross is not that [of] place, [but] as [a fall to] inefficacy from those former [powers], just as he also confessed to Anthony[69].... Therefore, his fall is the annulment of his

---

65. Andrew, Chap. 34, *Comm.* 142. "The ruler of this world is judged" (Jn. 16:11).
66. Andrew, Chap. 34, *Comm.* 142–43.
67. Andrew, Chap. 34, *Comm.* 143, quoting 2 Cor. 6:14.
68. Andrew, Chap. 33, *Comm.* 144, quoting 2 Cor. 6:15.
69. *The Life of Antony*, by Athanasius the Great, relates an incident in which Satan himself visited St. Anthony in his cell and complained to the monk that he had been weakened. *Life of Antony* 41.

evil machinations, after the complete rejection of him from heaven and the rule belonging to him, as it is said.[70]

Since the coming of Christ, the devil's wickedness has worsened; therefore his repentance is virtually impossible. Andrew cites a statement by Justin the Martyr and Philosopher. "It has been said by the blessed Justin the martyr [that] after the coming of Christ and the decree against him [to send him] to Gehenna, the devil is to become a greater blasphemer even [to the extent that] he had never before so shamelessly blasphemed God."[71] Andrew reasons from this statement that the devil cannot be saved since he grows even worse with the knowledge of his impending punishment. If the "expectation of punishment makes him even more evil," how can anyone suppose that the devil or the demons will cease their evil activity? It is simply inconceivable that his punishment would end since their evil actions would never end. "Since they have not attained this [cessation from wickedness], how will they have an end of the punishment against those who have vain thoughts?"[72]

Andrew's discussion of the relationship between the devil and the Church is most extensive in his analysis of Revelation 12, the woman

---

70. Andrew, Chap. 34, *Comm.* 143.

71. Andrew, Chap. 34, *Comm.* 143–44. This quotation of Justin is taken from his lost writings. This exact statement is also quoted by Irenaeus (*Heres.* 5.26.2) and by Eusebius of Caesarea (*E. H.* 4.18.9).

72. Andrew, Chap. 34, *Comm.* 144. The "vain thoughts" Andrew is referring to here are some who believed that, in the end, God will save everyone, even the devil. This belief, known as *apokatastasis ton panton* (ἀποκατάστασις τῶν πάντων, "the restoration of all things"), was denounced as heretical at the Fifth Ecumenical Council in 553, a few decades prior to the composition of this commentary. This belief was attributed to Origen, the greatest teacher of the early Church. As a prolific writer and creative thinker, Origen denied that he ever held the belief that the devil would be saved. Nonetheless, Origen does appear to have held views which were later deemed heretical, including possibly the notion that in the end, all people would be saved. Although Origen was a monumental figure in the early Church and read by virtually everyone for centuries after his death in the mid-third century, the problems created by some of his erroneous ideas and teachings attributed to him, which came to be known as "Origenism," led to the condemnation of both Origen and his teachings at the Fifth Ecumenical Council, some two hundred years after his death. Oikoumenios's inclination toward the idea of universal salvation is discussed in chapter 14.

wrapped in the sun. The woman, who represents the people of God, gives birth to a male child, and when the dragon fails to devour the child, he directs his fury toward the woman, who flees to the desert (Rev. 12:15–16). When he is unable to destroy the woman, he goes off "to make war on the rest of her offspring," the Church (Rev. 12:17). The devil's initial failure occurred when Christ did not succumb to the temptations after his baptism.[73] Then, considerably weakened by the cross and resurrection of Christ,[74] "he armed himself against the holy apostles and was put to shame seeing [that] they found life through death."[75] Next, the devil turned to attack the Church and "began again to persecute the Church, the brave manly people of God having been born and which are being born, those not emasculated by pleasures."[76]

The Church fled to the wilderness, but the serpent pursued her and "poured water like a river out of his mouth after the woman, to sweep her away with the flood" (Rev. 12:15). The river represents "a multitude of ungodly men or evil demons or various temptations" which the devil sends against the Church "that he might enslave her."[77] But the Church is assisted by "the love towards God and neighbor and the helpful providential care of the Crucified One ... and the two testaments" symbolized by the two wings of an eagle, "so that flying away on high into the desert way of life devoid of every dew of pleasure she is to be fed with them."[78] While Andrew would probably not say that an ascetic lifestyle is required for salvation, he certainly seems to suggest that attachment to pleasures is detrimental. Discipline and commitment to the Christian way of life are necessary, implied in his frequent use of metaphors of work and athletics, which are incompatible with laziness and the pursuit of pleasure.[79]

The Apocalypse warns those who are earthly: "Woe to you, Earth and Sea, for the devil has come down to you with great anger, because he knows that he has little time [remaining]!" (Rev. 12:12). The devil,

---

73. Andrew, Chap. 35, *Comm.* 145.
74. Andrew, Chap. 34, *Comm.* 143–44.
75. Andrew, Chap. 35, *Comm.* 145.
76. Andrew, Chap. 35, *Comm.* 145.
77. Andrew, Chap. 35, *Comm.* 146.
78. Andrew, Chap. 35, *Comm.* 145–46.
79. See chapter 11, "Free Will."

Andrew explains, "is now more angered by those who are struggling because of the nearness of his punishment." Therefore, it is appropriate to pronounce a "woe."

"Woe" to those who dwell on the "earth," that is, to those who do not have [dwelling] "in heaven" but have their citizenship on earth. For many of them on the earth are victorious over the enemy and will be victorious.... Wherefore, it is necessary to deplore those who have their "minds on earthly things" and who are tossed by the waves in the sea of life here.[80]

The Antichrist is the beast of the sea, the false prophet is the beast of the earth, but Andrew recognizes that the devil is also referred to as a "beast" in Revelation 17. The use of "beast" for all three members of the "unholy trinity" accounts for Oikoumenios's confusion in part, yet Andrew skillfully navigates through the terms and imagery to correctly identify the beast upon which the harlot sits as the devil. "The beast that you saw was, and is not, and is to ascend from the bottomless pit and goes to perdition" (Rev. 17:8).

The "beast" is the devil "who always seeks to devour someone." This one, having been slain by the cross of Christ, it is said, will again be revived at the end of the world, performing the denial of the Savior in "signs and wonders" of deception through the Antichrist. Therefore "he was" because he was exerting his power earlier than the cross. "He is not" because after the saving passion he had been enfeebled and his power, which he had held over the nations through idolatry, had been displaced. "He will come" at the end of the world in the manner which we have said "rising up out of the abyss," or from where he had been condemned—where the demons cast out had beseeched Christ not to be sent, but instead into the swine—or he will come out of the present life which is figuratively called "abyss" because of the depth of the indwelling of sin which is blown and tossed about by the winds of the passions.[81]

Andrew comments later on the similarity of the description of the evil trio. He concludes that this shows their cooperation.

80. Andrew, Chap. 34, *Comm.* 145, quoting Phil. 3:20 and Phil. 3:19.
81. Andrew, Chap. 54, *Comm.* 184, quoting 1 Pet. 5:8, 2 Thess. 2:9, and alluding to Matt. 8:31, Mark 5:12, Luke 8:32.

That the devil, the Antichrist and the false prophet act in partnership with each other, just as by their deeds, even so by their names, is clearly shown by the things through which each of them is called 'beast.' And from the fact that this "dragon," that is, Satan, manifests seven heads and ten horns with as many diadems placed on him. And the fact that "the beast coming up out of the sea," that is, the Antichrist, appears in the same form additionally confirms [that he shares] this same will and activity for the destruction of the deceived ones.[82]

The Antichrist and the False Prophet

Even though the devil never ceases his warfare against the followers of Christ, during the "one thousand year" era of the Church the devil's power is significantly curtailed. When the eschaton arrives, he will be "loosened," inaugurating a phase of trials that will last three and one half years. The Antichrist "will come carrying Satan in himself, bringing about the ruin of human beings, going to perdition in the future age."[83] As discussed above, Andrew believed that the Antichrist would arise from the empire to which Andrew belonged.[84] Andrew did not identify the Antichrist with any living individual. He had already indicated that the end could not be near since the catastrophes described in Revelation after the opening of the sixth seal had not yet begun to take place and no city held worldwide dominion. Nonetheless, the prophecy was clear: The Antichrist is one of the seven because the seven leading kings represent the entire rule of that kingdom, the last of which is New Rome. Therefore, the Antichrist will come as king of the Romans.

The beast is the Antichrist; as the eighth he will be raised up after the seven kings for the purpose of deceiving and desolating the earth. "From the seven" as one of them he will spring forth. For he will not come from another nation, along [the lines] of the things we have already said, but he will come as King of the Romans.[85]

---

82. Andrew, Chap. 61, *Comm.* 208–9. 83. Andrew, Chap. 54, *Comm.* 184.
84. Andrew, Chap. 54, *Comm.* 187. 85. Andrew, Chap. 54, *Comm.* 187.

Andrew conforms to the traditional theory regarding the origin of the Antichrist. The earliest expression of the belief that the Antichrist would arise out of the tribe of Dan can be found in Irenaeus, who interprets Jeremiah 8:16 as proclaiming this prophecy. Hippolytus repeats this tradition and by the time of Andrew it was firmly established.[86] When the tribes of Israel are listed in Revelation 7, the tribe of Dan "was not included with the rest" of the tribes, "since the Antichrist would be born from it."[87] The Antichrist will come "from the region of the Euphrates."[88] Andrew elaborates elsewhere that he will arise "probably ... from the eastern areas of the land of Persia, where the tribe of Dan originates from the root of the Hebrews, either together with other kings or rulers designated with a royal name, to cross over the Euphrates bringing bodily or spiritual death."[89] The apocalyptic expectation that the Antichrist would arise from the region of Persia, cross the Euphrates with kings and bring death was deeply ingrained in the Christian imagination. At the time this commentary was being composed, Andrew and his congregation were in the midst of a massive invasion by armies from Persia, which would engulf the Empire in a bloody war for twenty years. The Persians had indeed crossed the Euphrates bringing great death and destruction to the entire eastern Empire. Almost everyone was convinced that the end of the world had arrived—except for Andrew. His intelligence, exegetical skill and detached objectivity, especially under such extraordinary circumstances, are truly remarkable and admirable.

The Antichrist will derive his power from the devil, as indicated by descriptions common to both. The beast which rises out of the sea, "with ten horns and seven heads, with ten diadems upon its horns and a blasphemous name upon its head"[90] is the Antichrist "coming out of

---

86. Hippolytus, *Chr. and Ant.* 14.5–6.
87. Andrew, Chap. 19, *Comm.* 106, from Irenaeus, *Heres.* 5.30. 2, who relied on Jer. 8:16.
88. Andrew, Chap. 27, *Comm.* 124.
89. Andrew, Chap. 51, *Comm.* 175.
90. This verse is numbered differently in various versions. Some editions of the Apocalypse number it as 12:17, others as 12:18 and still others as 13:1.

the trouble prone and turbulent sea of this life."[91] "The ten horns with the diadems and the seven heads hint at the union of the devil with him—for these [qualities] were also explained above as belonging to him."[92] The ten horns indicate that the earthly kingdom will be divided. The seven heads connote this world, the "seven day week" of life," as well as the seven ruling kingdoms of this world, through whom Satan works, since he has been called "the ruler of this world" (Jn. 12:31). "The 'blasphemous name' on his seven heads clearly [means] his defenders. For these, since the beginning, have not ceased to blaspheme Christ until the accession of Constantine the Great, after whom Julian and Valens became blasphemers of Christ."[93]

The devil will give his power, throne and authority to the Antichrist (Rev. 13:2). "For Satan, the spiritual dragon, will give to the Antichrist all authority by means of false signs and wonders for the destruction of those unstable [in the faith]."[94] One of the heads will appear to have a mortal wound but it will be healed (Rev. 13:3). This "is either one of the rulers who will be put to death and who will appear to rise again by him through deceitful sorcery" or that the "kingdom of the Romans" which after enduring "some kind of wound by the division will seem to have been healed by the monarchy" similar to the manner in which Augustus unified the Roman empire after war.[95] People will marvel at the beast/Antichrist (Rev. 13:3–4). Through him "the dragon will be worshipped, and it will appear to those whose eyes of the mind are disabled that he is both raising the dead and accomplishing miracles."[96] For three and a half years (42 months), "according to divine allowance" the beast will "have license both for blasphemy against God and the ill treatment of the saints."[97] The beast/Antichrist will be given authority over the entire world, "over every tribe and people and tongue and nation" and everyone will worship it whose name is not written in the Book of Life (Rev. 13:7–8). Devastating plagues will accompany the

91. Andrew, Chap. 36, *Comm.* 147.
92. Andrew, Chap. 36, *Comm.* 147.
93. Andrew, Chap. 36, *Comm.* 147.
94. Andrew, Chap. 36, *Comm.* 148.
95. Andrew, Chap. 36, *Comm.* 148.
96. Andrew, Chap. 36, *Comm.* 149.
97. Andrew, Chap. 36, *Comm.* 149.

three and a half year appearance of the Antichrist, afflicting the earth on a global scale. Two witnesses will be sent by God to oppose the deception of the Antichrist, but he will kill them.

Andrew, like many other Fathers, was also influenced by certain details found in 2 Thessalonians and incorporated them into his end-time scenario, especially the expectation that the "man of lawlessness" (identified with the Antichrist) would sit in the Temple and demand to be worshipped as God. Andrew's tendency is to follow a typical patristic end-time scenario, which combines Revelation and 2 Thessalonians. The expression "man of lawlessness" does not occur in Revelation, nor does Revelation describe the Antichrist as sitting in the Temple. However, Andrew incorporates this traditional expectation into his Apocalypse interpretation. After the symbolic one thousand year period, the time necessary for the preaching of the Gospel, "the son of perdition, the man of lawlessness will come."[98] Just prior to the destruction of all the forces of evil by God, the Antichrist will sit in the Temple to be worshipped as God, "usurping that which is inappropriate for him and 'representing himself as being God.'"[99] Andrew considered it an open question whether the "Temple" would be the Church or "the Judaic one, the old divine temple," which he notes that the Jews expected to rebuild.[100]

The Antichrist would be accompanied by a false prophet who fulfilled the same function as the Forerunner of Christ, John the Baptist, to support the work of the Antichrist and prepare people to receive his deceptions. People will be deceived by the Antichrist and the false prophet who will work wonders by means of sorcery. The false prophet appears as the second beast, arising out of the earth with "two horns like a lamb, and it was speaking like a dragon" (Rev. 13:11). He is the "adjutant" or "right hand man" of the Antichrist. Andrew explains that he arises out of the earth, "that is out of the earthly and groveling way of life"[101] and has "'horns like a lamb,' because he completely

---

98. Andrew, Chap. 63, *Comm.* 212, 2 Thess. 2:3.
99. Andrew, Chap. 63, *Comm.* 214, 2 Thess. 2:4.
100. Andrew, Chap. 63, *Comm.* 214.   101. Andrew, Chap. 37, *Comm.* 151.

covers with sheep's skin the hidden murderous character of the wolf, and because of his appearance of piety in the beginning."[102] He will "'speak like a dragon,' it says, for he will both act and speak the things of the devil, the source of evil."[103] He will receive all the authority of the Antichrist, performing signs and wonders, even bringing fire down from heaven, leading the inhabitants of the earth to worship the first beast (Rev. 13:12–13). "The Forerunner of the rebellious false Christ will perform all things through sorcery for the deception of the people [for them] to consider the Antichrist to be God." "In imitation of the Baptist, who brought believers to the Savior," the false prophet will receive "indisputable glory."[104] "For the lie, to deceive people, strives eagerly to imitate the truth."[105] Together with the devil, the Antichrist and False Prophet will form an unholy trinity which will culminate in destruction.

The Antichrist "shares this same will and activity" with the devil, not only "for the destruction of the deceived ones,"[106] as we have seen, but also for the destruction of the Church. Andrew understands the instruction to measure the temple (Rev.11:1–2) to refer to the persecution of the Church during the era of the Antichrist: "And a reed, like a staff, was given to me, saying: 'Rise and measure the temple of God and the altar and those who worship in it; And exclude the outer courtyard of the temple and do not measure it, for it was given to the nations, and they will trample upon the holy city for forty-two months.'"

The "temple of the living God" refers to the Church and the outside court [is] the gathering place of the unbelieving nations ....[107] The "trampling of the holy city" [is] either the new Jerusalem or the universal Church and the "forty two months" by the nations I think means that the faithful and the ones being tested will be trampled upon and persecuted in the three and a half year appearance of the Antichrist.[108]

102. Andrew, Chap. 37, *Comm.* 151.
103. Andrew, Chap. 37, *Comm.* 152.
104. Andrew, Chap. 37, *Comm.* 152.
105. Andrew, Chap. 37, *Comm.* 152.
106. Andrew, Chap. 61, *Comm.* 201.
107. Citing 2 Cor. 6:16, "For we are the temple of the living God."
108. Andrew, Chap. 29, *Comm.* 131.

Christians hid in the wilderness during Roman persecution and this will occur again. When seventh bowl was poured out, an earthquake divided the great city into three parts, "and every island fled away, and no mountains were found" (Rev. 16:17–20). Through word association Andrew interprets "islands" and "mountains" in this passage to indicate the persecution of the Church and the flight of its leaders: "'Islands' are the churches and 'mountains' are the leaders of them, we are taught to discern from the divine Scriptures. These flee at the time of attack, being foretold [as] we have heard for ourselves from the Lord."[109] Andrew suggests that when the Antichrist arrives on the scene many Christians will again flee, "hiding themselves in the actual physical desert in mountains and caves."[110] Andrew intimates that these would most likely be clergy and monastics. "When the chosen teachers of the Church and those despising the earth have withdrawn to the hardships in the desert ... the Antichrist will declare war against those drafted in Christ in the world.... [F]inding them vulnerable in the occupations of life, he will put them to flight."[111] In the course of these tribulations, the sinners will be "tormented on account of sin," but the righteous will also suffer, "enduring these difficulties patiently in a test of virtue." Not only will they be "tormented by the Antichrist for the sake of Christ," but they will also suffer "in flights and in the miseries in mountains and in caves which, in order to preserve piety, they will prefer to the way of life in the city."[112] Yet even those living "in the world" can be victorious, "and many among them will conquer him because they have genuinely loved Christ."[113] It is important to recognize that in Andrew's eyes "love" for Christ is not sentiment, emotion or a cerebral decision but a genuine commitment which manifests it-

---

109. Andrew, Chap. 52, *Comm.* 179. Here Andrew offers two quotations, the first of which appears to be based on Matt. 24:27. "Then they will flee from the east to the setting sun, and those from the west to the east." This is followed by a second prophecy of the Lord: "For there will be great tribulation which had not happened from the foundation of the world, nor ever will be" (Matt. 24:21, Mark 13:19).

110. Andrew, Chap. 35, *Comm.* 146. 111. Andrew, Chap. 35, *Comm.* 146.
112. Andrew, Chap. 52, *Comm.* 180. 113. Andrew, Chap. 35, *Comm.* 146.

self in deeds and struggles. "Those accused by him … have been victorious over him nonetheless by suffering for Christ."[114]

The Mark of the Beast and the Name of the Antichrist

Andrew notes that those who are deceived by the Antichrist and False Prophet are "those who dwell on earth" (Rev. 13:14). This reinforces his opinion that it is paramount for all Christians to acquire "citizenship in heaven" (Phil. 3:20). They will not be deceived by the Antichrist, "having been made perfectly secure by the prophecy of his coming."[115] They will also refuse to receive his mark "on the right hand in order to cut off the doing of good works, and on the forehead" which will "teach the deceived ones to boldly speak in error and darkness." The faithful have already been "marked with divine light on their faces." The virtuous will suffer for refusing the mark since the false prophet will "make it his business to extend the symbol of the beast everywhere, in both buying and selling, so that a violent death will be suffered from lack of necessities by those who do not receive it."[116]

Although Andrew speaks of the "mark" of the beast, his comments do not necessarily suggest that he considers it a physical mark as much as an indication of spiritual "ownership." One who has the mark is the one who "bows down to the beastly Antichrist and pursues the ungodly lifestyle modeling him, and either in word or in deed proclaims him God—for this can be clear by the mark given on the forehead and hand."[117] The mark of the beast delineates those who worship the beast and stands in contrast with those who belong to God, identified by the "seal" on their foreheads (Rev. 7:3). "[T]his will definitely happen during the time of the coming of the Antichrist, the seal of the life-giving Cross separating the faithful from the unfaithful, [the faithful] without shame and having been emboldened bearing the sign of Christ before the impious."[118] Andrew's sacramental and sacerdotal orientation

---

114. Andrew, Chap. 34, *Comm.* 144–45.
115. Andrew, Chap. 37, *Comm.* 152.
116. Andrew, Chap. 37, *Comm.* 153.
117. Andrew, Chap. 42, *Comm.* 158.
118. Andrew, Chap. 19, *Comm.* 103.

is clearly evident here. In the Eastern Christian practice a new Christian is immediately "sealed" through the sacrament of Chrismation (i.e., confirmation). The sign of the cross is made by the priest with the oil of chrism on the forehead of the newly baptized while the priest proclaims, "The seal of the gift of the Holy Spirit."[119] Chrismation is the bestowal of the Holy Spirit and marks the individual as belonging to Christ. All members of the Church are therefore "sealed" on the forehead with the cross spiritually and literally "separating the faithful from the unfaithful," as Andrew remarks. The seal indicates that "before the bringing of trials the virtuous need to be strengthened through angelic assistance."[120] The doctrine of synergy is still operative: God bestows the grace by 'the seal of the Spirit' which is "given to us," yet also "manifesting our own power according to the amount of work we have put to it."[121]

Andrew declines to speculate about the precise "name" of the Antichrist, the interpretation of 666. "The exact sense of the numerical cipher, as well as the rest of the things written regarding this, time and experience will reveal to those who live soberly."[122] Andrew joins earlier "teachers" in suggesting that "if it were necessary to know clearly such a name, the one who had beheld it would have revealed it. But divine grace was not well pleased to set down the name of the destroyer in the divine book."[123] This had been the explanation given by Irenaeus and Hippolytus for the enigma of 666.[124] Andrew also notes that "many names are to be found contained in this number," some proper nouns and some common nouns. Possible proper nouns that Andrew recounts "according to the blessed Hippolytus and others," are names such as "Teitan," "Lampetis," "Lateinos" and "Benedict," which is interpreted as "blessed" perhaps in imitation of Christ.[125] Common nouns as derogatory appellations could also be formed by the faithful through

---

119. 2 Cor. 1:21–22.
120. Andrew, Chap. 19, *Comm.* 103.
121. Andrew, Chap. 19, *Comm.* 103.
122. Andrew, Chap. 38, *Comm.* 154.
123. Andrew, Chap. 38, *Comm.* 154.
124. Irenaeus, *Heres.* 5.30.3–4 and Hippolytus, *Chr. and Ant.* 50.
125. Andrew, Chap. 38, *Comm.* 154.

their interpretation of 666: "wicked guide," "real harm," "slanderer of old," and "unjust lamb." "[T]hese he will be called by those opposing his deception, rendering the appropriate 'opinion in shame' (Phil. 3:19)."[126] The Antichrist, false prophet and the devil will ultimately be delivered to the fire of Gehenna.[127]

126. Andrew, Chap. 38, *Comm.* 154.
127. Andrew, Chap. 59, *Comm.* 204.

14

DEATH, JUDGMENT, PUNISHMENT, AND REWARD

Death and the Soul

Andrew's comments on death express classic patristic concepts. "There are two deaths; the first is the separation of the soul and the body, the second is being cast into Gehenna."[1] This traditional perspective is based on Romans 6 in which baptism is expressed as being "buried with Christ" and "dying to sin." The specific language of "two deaths" and "two resurrections" is found in the Apocalypse itself.

And I saw thrones, and they were seated on them, and judgment was given to them, and the souls of those who had been beheaded for their testimony to Jesus and for the word of God, and who had not worshiped the beast nor its image and had not received its mark on their foreheads or on their hand, and they came to life, and reigned with Christ a thousand years. And the rest of the dead did not come to life until the thousand years were ended. This is the first resurrection. Blessed and holy is he who has a share in the first resurrection! Over such ones the second death has no power, but they will be priests of God and of Christ, and they will reign with him a thousand years." (Rev. 20:4–6)

Andrew's remarks on this passage reveal not only his views on resurrection and eternal life but also on the state of the soul before and

---

1. Andrew, Chap. 59, *Comm.* 205.

after death. If there are two deaths, then there must be two kinds of life. Andrew explains,

From the divine Scriptures we are taught two lives and two types of deadness, that is to say, deaths. The first life is the transitory and fleshly one after the transgression of the commandment but the other one is eternal life promised to the saints after heeding the divine commandments of Christ. And in like manner, [there are] two deaths: the one transitory of the flesh and the other through sins leading to the full payment in the age to come, which is the Gehenna of fire.[2]

"Death" or "deadness" in this context is not necessarily negative since there are two different kinds of "dead" people. "And we know there is a difference among the dead.... Isaiah says, 'The dead will not see life,' that is, those bringing stench and deadness by [their] conduct."[3] The truly "dead," then, are those who are spiritually dead, a state which they have embraced by their conduct on earth long before their physical death. Devoid of a "heavenly mindset," they may be extraordinarily "sinful," or merely "earthly." On the other hand, the "praiseworthy" ones are those who "'mortify the activities of the body,' who are crucified with Christ and are dead to the world."[4] All will die physically, but those who died 'to the world' "came to life," as the Apocalypse describes, "and reigned with Christ a thousand years. The rest of the dead did not come to life until the thousand years were ended. This is the first resurrection" (Rev. 20:4–5). The "first resurrection," Andrew explains, consists "in the rising out of deadening thoughts and mortifying actions, these are 'blessed.' For the second death will have no power over them, that is, never ending punishment, but instead, they will exercise priesthood and 'reign with Christ.'"[5] When a heavenly voice proclaims the beatitude "Blessed are the dead who die in the Lord" (Rev. 14:13), Andrew observes that the voice "does not bless all

2. Andrew, Chap. 62, *Comm.* 209. The "transgression of the commandment" refers to the fall of mankind in Genesis 3.
3. Andrew, Chap. 62, *Comm.* 209, quoting Isa. 26:14.
4. Andrew, Chap. 62, *Comm.* 210, quoting Rom. 8:13, Col. 3:5.
5. Andrew, Chap. 62, *Comm.* 210.

of the dead, but those 'who die in the Lord,' having been put to death in the world, and who 'bear in the body the death of Jesus' and 'suffer' with Christ."[6] These are the "blessed" dead.

The "rest of the dead" (Rev. 20:5) are "those not 'buried with and raised with Christ, through baptism,' but those remaining in [state of] death by sins."[7] Many who are physically alive are nonetheless spiritually dead. Andrew presumes that everyone who dies will be buried. Upon their physical death, those who are "earthly" will return to earth and remain there since they were born "from the earth only." These "unacceptable dead will not live with him [Christ] until the completion of the one thousand years, that is, the perfect number extending from his first coming until the second in glory ... but having been born 'from the earth' only and not 'by the Spirit,' they will return to the earth."[8] The earthly will not experience eternal life with Christ in the kingdom. They rejected life with Christ here on earth, never acquiring a heavenly mindset and virtuous manner of life, and thus will not enjoy a future heavenly existence after physical death.

Spiritual death can occur in a variety of ways. Generally speaking, sin gives birth to spiritual death.[9] Spiritual death comes to those who "through words or deeds blaspheme the Trinity."[10] It is "the harm of the soul hiding at the end of evil deeds." Those who "had not been sealed with the divine seal on their foreheads and [who do not] shine round about with the enlightenment of the life-giving cross through the Holy Spirit" are subject to spiritual death.[11] Unbelief also results in spiritual death, but behavior is important as well.[12] Those who "do evil to their neighbor will be imprisoned by the devil and will succumb to spiritual death by the satanic dagger."[13] Ultimately spiritual death results "through cowardice and weakness."[14]

---

6. Andrew, Chap. 42, *Comm.* 160, quoting 2 Cor. 4:10 and Rom. 8:17.
7. Andrew, Chap. 62, *Comm.* 210, quoting Rom. 6:4, Col. 2:12.
8. Andrew, Chap. 62, *Comm.* 210.   9. Andrew, Chap. 26, *Comm.* 122.
10. Andrew, Chap. 23, *Comm.* 116.   11. Andrew, Chap. 26, *Comm.* 121.
12. Andrew, Chap. 33, *Comm.* 138.   13. Andrew, Chap. 36, *Comm.* 149–50.
14. Andrew, Chap. 51, *Comm.* 175.

The most common theme is that spiritual death comes to those who refuse to repent,

having renounced neither idolatries nor murders nor fornications nor their thefts, nor the sorceries ... those who worship idols ... who [worship] the creation instead of the Creator ... those who profess to know God, but deny him, first through deeds and then by wearing the appearance of piety but denying its power ... and those who are enslaved by mammon.[15]

Spiritual death will not occur for the faithful, who will experience only bodily death because of their "faith and patient endurance."[16]

So then, since there are two deaths, it is necessary to understand that there are also likewise two resurrections. First, then, physical death, is given as the penalty given for humankind's disobedience; the second, eternal punishment. The "first resurrection" is being brought to life out of "dead works," the second, the transformation from bodily corruption into incorruption.[17]

Those who are reborn in Christ through baptism and the Spirit share the eternal life with Christ now in this life, as the "first resurrection," and to a fuller degree later. Although the point of reference is baptism, Andrew does not attribute this result to baptism as a matter of mere ritual but in terms of its true meaning: "crucified with Christ and dead to the world."[18] Such Christians will never return to "the earth," even though their body will physically be buried.

What is the state of the departed soul prior to judgment according to Andrew? It is clear that true members of the Church are the "blessed dead," not those who were merely baptized but who died and rose with Christ. "For the second death will have no power over them, that is never ending punishment, but instead, they will exercise priesthood and reign with Christ.[19] They are already living and reigning with Christ in the kingdom in some manner during the millennial period. "[N]ot as being then deprived of the kingdom, but as more certainly

---

15. Andrew, Chap. 27, *Comm.* 125.
16. Andrew, Chap. 51, *Comm.* 175.
17. Andrew, Chap. 62, *Comm.* 210.
18. Andrew, Chap. 62, *Comm.* 209.
19. Andrew, Chap. 62, *Comm.* 210.

and very clearly they will possess it by the passage of temporal things and arrival of eternal things."[20]

None of Andrew's comments in his Apocalypse commentary suggest any type of existence after death during the interim period prior to Christ's return for those who are "earthly." They live an earthly life now, therefore when they die they will return to the earth. When Christ returns, they will experience judgment and the "second death," eternal death. Therefore "their [physical] death becomes the beginning of their future punishment."[21] Andrew offers no hint within the commentary that those destined for eternal punishment will experience a "foretaste" of their ultimate lot immediately upon their physical death, even though this is a traditional belief. He expresses his opinion outside of the commentary, however. We have some knowledge of Andrew's opinion regarding the state of the soul after death from a fragment of *Therapeutike*, the only extant writing by Andrew other than the Apocalypse commentary.[22] The fragment preserves his responses to five questions on eschatological themes. The first question concerns where the souls go after leaving the body. Andrew replies that the souls of the dead do not go immediately to a place of reward or punishment nor do they receive a formal declaration of their fate before the judgment. But they will be able to discern their eternal destiny which corresponds to their customary behavior and earthly life.[23]

The opening of the fifth seal reveals the souls under the altar, those who had been slain on account of the word of God and the witness they had made. When the souls cry out to God and ask how long they

20. Andrew, Chap. 62, *Comm.* 210.
21. Andrew, Chap. 62, *Comm.* 210.
22. Franz Diekamp, *Analecta Patristica: Texte und Abhandlungen zur Griechischen Patristik*, Orientalia Christiana Analecta 117 (Rome: Pontifical Institute of Oriental Studies, 1938), 161–72.
23. Franz Diekamp, *Texte und Abhandlungen*, 169. Diekamp notes that because Andrew did not immediately consign the dead to a place of punishment or reward *before* judgment, he was accused of heresy in the Latin West in the year 1252. An anonymous Latin writer pointed to Andrew as the inventor of a "heresy" among the Greeks that that souls enter neither paradise nor hell before judgment (170).

must wait for his judgment, they are each given a white robe and told to rest a little longer until additional martyrs in the future complete their number (Rev. 6:9–11).

Andrew comments that even though they have not received the promise, "they look forward spiritually, having ceased from all earthliness they naturally delight in reposing in the bosom of Abraham."[24] Later in the commentary Andrew also expresses the belief that the souls of the righteous are patiently waiting for the end. Commenting on Revelation 15:8, "No one was able to enter the temple until the seven plagues of the angels finished," he surmises that

> until the divine vexation against the impious is separated from the righteous, in no way are the saints of the heavenly Jerusalem to reach their appointed lot, both worship in the temple of God and repose. For it is necessary, it says, for "the plagues" to be "fulfilled," by which the wages of sin are rendered to the deserving ones, and those who reached a decision chosen by them, whereupon in this way the dwelling of the heavenly capital is to be given to the saints.[25]

Judging from the commentary alone, it appears that Andrew believed the righteous enter paradise immediately, but the souls of those destined for punishment will not experience punishment immediately. Hades is an immaterial place of the dead, he explains, but the dead are "the souls who have pursued deadly deeds 'for the souls of the righteous are in the hand of God.'"[26] But even though the souls of the righteous are presently "in the hand of God," they have not received their full and final reward. They will enjoy the blessings of paradise more fully after final judgment. They "co-reign until his second coming, afterwards enjoying these divine promises to an even greater degree."[27] As for those who are not among the "blessed dead," however, Andrew does not speculate on a "foretaste" of future punishment within the Apocalypse commentary but his view is expressed in *Therapeutike*.

24. Andrew, Chap. 17, *Comm.* 97.
25. Andrew, Chap. 45, *Comm.* 167.
26. Andrew, Chap. 64, *Comm.* 218, quoting Wis. Of Sol. 3:1.
27. Andrew, Chap. 61, *Comm.* 209.

Armageddon, Parousia, and Judgment

Andrew identified the millennium as the period during which the gospel is preached to all nations and Satan's activities are hindered. Afterwards, "when 'Satan is loosed from his prison' he will 'deceive' all 'the nations' and he will arouse 'Gog and Magog' into war for the desolation of the entire inhabited world."[28] The devil and his demons will spread throughout the world since the Church also exists in all parts of the world. This will also be the period of the Antichrist's activity. The Antichrist will sit in the temple and demand to be worshipped as God, "but not for long," according to Andrew.[29] Christ will come with the heavenly armies "to judge the nations impartially."[30]

The beast will join with the kings of the earth to make war against Christ at Armageddon. Andrew interprets the meaning of the Hebrew word "Armageddon" as "deep cut" or "that which is cut in two." The name is appropriate, "for there the nations, being gathered together, being minded to follow and being commanded by the devil, who delights in the blood of people, are to be cut down."[31]

"The false signs which are operated through the demons, [will cause] those persuaded by them to march into war on 'the great and terrible day of God,' 'judge of the living and dead,' over which, having been entirely defeated, those fighting against God in vain will lament, bewailing their prior error."[32]

The devil, the Antichrist, and the false prophet, along with the kings and their armies, will be defeated and "overtaken by divine wrath."[33] Since the Antichrist will be alive at the time of the Parousia, he may not die a physical death, Andrew states, reporting an anonymous Church tradition. The Antichrist will either be thrown directly into the lake of fire without experiencing physical death, or the coming of Christ in glory will destroy him.[34] Christ will deliver the devil "to

---

28. Andrew, Chap. 63, *Comm.* 212.
29. Andrew, Chap. 63, *Comm.* 214.
30. Andrew, Chap. 57, *Comm.* 200.
31. Andrew, Chap. 51, *Comm.* 176–77.
32. Andrew, Chap. 51, *Comm.* 176, quoting Joel 2:11 and Acts 10:42.
33. Andrew, Chap. 59, *Comm.* 204.
34. Andrew, Chap. 59, *Comm.* 204.

the lake of fire together with the Antichrist and the false prophet to be tortured forever and ever."[35]

When Christ arrives with the heavenly armies, the Apocalypse text relates: "From his mouth a sharp sword comes out in order to smite the nations, and he will rule them with a rod of iron, and he will tread the wine press of the fury of the wrath of God the Almighty" (Rev. 19:15). Andrew explains that the "'sword' signifies the torments that will afflict the impious and the sinners in accordance with the just judgment and the command that is proclaimed from the divine mouth, through whom they will be 'ruled' by the unbroken 'rod' of endless torments toward [ensuring] the inactivity of manifold wickedness."[36]

From this interpretation we see that Andrew does not anticipate a prolonged war at Armageddon. Instead, the evil powers will be decisively and instantly defeated as part of Christ's coming in judgment. Christ has been given authority to judge from the Father and he will judge when he returns.[37] After the devil and his accomplices are consigned to the fire of Gehenna, the dead will stand before the throne of God (Rev. 20:12). The "'books' having been 'opened' denote the deeds of each and the consciousness of each [person]. The one book is '[the Book] of Life,' in which are inscribed the names of the saints."[38] Those whose names are not written in the Book of Life will be thrown into the lake of fire and "one must not be amazed," Andrew remarks. In the same way that different levels of reward will be experienced by the righteous, different types of punishment will be meted out. The righteous "will be worthy, the one of a lesser brightness and the other of greater, according to the correspondence of the deeds of each."[39] Just as "there are 'many mansions' in my Father's [house] among those saved, thus, here too, there are different places and manners of punishments, those sharper and those milder, by which those not deemed

---

35. Andrew, Chap. 63, *Comm.* 215.
36. Andrew, Chap. 58, *Comm.* 202.
37. Andrew, Chap. 58, *Comm.* 202, commenting on Rev. 19:15.
38. Andrew, Chap 64, *Comm.* 218.
39. Andrew, Chap. 68, *Comm.* 234.

worthy of the 'Book of Life' will be tried."⁴⁰ God will judge fairly and impartially, but all will receive the punishment or reward which they deserve as chosen by them over the course of their lives. Commenting upon the location of the "wine press," an image of judgment, which is to be trampled on "outside the city" (Rev. 14:20), Andrew concludes that the "city" is the domain "of the righteous." This means that the place of torment for sinners will be separated from existence of the saints. "For in no way is 'the rod of these sinners to be near the inheritance,' according to the prophetic saying. For their habitation will be unmingled [with the righteous], just as their way of life has become."⁴¹

Resurrection and the Renewal of Creation

When the Apocalypse describes the sea giving up the dead within it, along with Death and Hades relinquishing their dead (Rev. 20:13), Andrew explains that "Death and Hades are not living beings ... rather death is a separation of soul and body."⁴² After judgment, when "all were judged by what they had done" (Rev. 20:13c), "death and Hades were thrown into the lake of fire" along with all those whose names were "not found written in the Book of Life" (Rev. 20:14–15).

Andrew offers three interpretations of the destruction of death and Hades. "'Death, the last enemy is abolished,'"⁴³ or "those evil powers [as] the agents of death through sin" are condemned to the fire.⁴⁴ Andrew's third explanation is the most important: "By this is meant that death or corruption will no longer exist, rather that incorruption and immortality will reign."⁴⁵ The rationale he provides is very significant: "For everything which has come into existence by God is 'very good;' things not of that kind that fire will make disappear. It is written 'God

---

40. Andrew, Chap 64, *Comm.* 219, quoting John 14:2.
41. Andrew, Chap 44, *Comm.* 164, quoting Ps. 125(124):3.
42. Andrew, Chap. 64, *Comm.* 218.
43. Andrew, Chap. 64, *Comm.* 218, quoting 1 Cor. 15:26.
44. Andrew, Chap. 64, *Comm.* 218.
45. Andrew, Chap. 64, *Comm.* 219.

did not create death.'"[46] Death and corruption were not created by God nor were they the will of God. Therefore, in the next life neither death nor corruption will exist, but only "incorruption and immortality."[47]

The Apocalypse verse affirms the bodily resurrection of every person. "Each body, it says, from out of those [places] where it is dissolved is recomposed and given back, whether it had been surrendered to the earth or the sea."[48] The "first resurrection" is dying and rising with Christ through baptism and by a lifestyle in which one "dies to the world." "The 'first resurrection' is being brought to life out of 'dead works,' the second, the transformation from bodily corruption into incorruption."[49] Andrew does not discuss the nature of the resurrected body in the Apocalypse commentary. He did affirm the teaching of the Lord, listening to him "saying to the Sadducees that the righteous will be like 'angels of God in heaven,' and to the Apostle who said, 'The kingdom of God is not food and drink.'"[50] By this statement he rejected a sensual interpretation of the resurrected body. But conversely, he did not join with the Origenists in their philosophical interpretation of the resurrected body. In his response to the third question preserved in the *Therapeutike*, Andrew confirmed the resurrection of the entire body. The specific question posed to him concerned the nature of the resurrected body and whether such things as teeth, digestive organs, reproductive organs or even limbs would be present in the resurrected body. Origenists believed that people would be resurrected in spherical bodies, presumably the shape of perfection, since the various body parts we need for this life will no longer be necessary. Andrew rejected the notion of ball-shaped bodies in the *Therapeutike*. Even though the righteous will be "like angels," Andrew stated that the resurrected body would retain all of its parts, even those for which we would presumably have no need in paradise, since all the various parts contribute to the adornment of

---

46. Andrew, Chap. 64, *Comm.* 219, citing Gen. 1 and Wisd. of Sol. 1:13.
47. Andrew, Chap. 64, *Comm.* 219.   48. Andrew, Chap. 64, *Comm.* 218.
49. Andrew, Chap. 62, *Comm.* 210.
50. Andrew, Chap. 63, *Comm.* 211, citing Matt. 22:30 and Romans 14:17 respectively.

the body.[51] Andrew's opinion in *Therapeutike* regarding the nature of the resurrected body is consistent with other statements in the commentary on the renewal of creation. Humans will be transformed but the resurrected body will retain all of its parts because everything God made is "good," and such things will not disappear. When the New Jerusalem is seen "coming down out of heaven from God prepared as a bride adorned for her husband" (Rev. 21:2), Andrew explains that the vision shows "the expression of newness of transformation characteristic of greater joy."[52]

Since God brought creation into existence and it was affirmed as "very good," creation will remain. Death and Hades are to be destroyed because "God did not create death"[53] but creation is to be transformed and renewed. The plagues resulting in the destruction of nature in Revelation are easily explained by Andrew. "Creation, having come into being for us, partakes with us in the afflictions when we are chastised; likewise therefore it will rejoice with the saints who are glorified."[54] That creation itself was adversely affected by the Fall of Adam and that it too will be renewed in the end times was engrained in the patristic tradition and accepted by Andrew. This concept is based upon Paul's statements in Romans. Due to human sin "creation is subject to corruption"[55] and at the end time creation will also be renewed along with us. "Therefore, the creation which came into being for us is to receive with us the way of life changed for the better."[56] The blessings of the future age will be enjoyed not only by humanity but by all of creation. His remarks on Revelation 20:11 are significant: "And I saw a large white throne and him who sat upon it, from whose presence earth and sky fled away. And no place was found for them."

The flight of heaven and earth is their passing away and renewal into [something] better, in which a place of mutability will not be found. For "if creation

---

51. Franz Diekamp, *Texte und Abhandlungen*, 172.
52. Andrew, Chap. 65, *Comm.* 220.   53. Andrew, Chap. 64, *Comm.* 219.
54. Andrew, Chap. 19, *Comm.* 103.   55. Rom. 8:20.
56. Andrew, Chap. 64, *Comm.* 217. See also Chap. 65, *Comm.* 219.

is subject to corruption" on account of us, according to the Apostle, "it will be made anew with us in the glorious freedom of the children of God," being renewed to a more radiant [existence] and remaining, not to a complete disappearance.[57]

Andrew quotes Irenaeus, Antipater of Bostra, Methodios, Isaiah, and the psalms for the concept of the renewal and transformation of the earth rather than the disappearance of creation.[58]

For the Blessed Irenaeus states that "neither the hypostasis nor the substance of creation utterly disappears—for He who composed it is true and certain—but the 'form of this world passes away,' that is to say, in which the transgression occurred and humanity became old in them and because of this, this form became temporary, all things having been foreseen by God."[59]

Andrew cites passages from the psalms and Isaiah, in which God promised that creation would remain and be renewed.[60] He quotes Methodios in his treatise *On the Resurrection* that "the whole world will be consumed in a cataclysm of fire coming down for purification and renewal. It will not come for absolute destruction and ruination."[61] The fire expected by Methodios is a fire of transformation and corresponds with Andrew's expectation for the renewal of creation. It is not a fire of purification which Andrew rejected, discussed below. Creation came into existence for our sakes, experienced corruption after the Fall and suffered through the plagues of the end time. It will be renewed along with us, "not proceeding to non-existence just as neither will we [have no existence] after death."[62]

This is repeated in his comments on Revelation 21:1, "And I saw a new heaven and a new earth. For the first heaven and the first earth passed away, and the sea was no more."

---

57. Andrew, Chap. 64, *Comm.* 216, quoting Rom. 8:20–21.
58. Andrew, Chap. 64, *Comm.* 216–17.
59. Andrew, Chap. 64, *Comm.* 216–17. Irenaeus, *Heres.* 5.36.1, quoting 1 Cor. 7:21.
60. Andrew, Chap. 64, *Comm.* 217, quoting Ps. 104/103:30 and Isaiah 65:17–18 and 66:22.
61. Andrew, Chap. 64, *Comm.* 217.
62. Andrew, Chap. 64, *Comm.* 217.

Here, too, it does not mean non-existence of creation but a renewal for the better, just as the Apostle says, "This creation will be freed from the bondage of corruption into the glorious freedom of the children of God," and the divine melodist, "You will turn them around and they will be changed." For that which has grown old is being renewed, means not a disappearance from existence, but it means the stripping off of old age and wrinkles.[63]

Oikoumenios and *Apokatastasis*

Oikoumenios makes certain comments which suggest at least an inclination toward Origenism. In addition to his Miaphysite statements, his Origenistic tendencies may have prompted Andrew to compose his own commentary. First, Oikoumenios cites and quotes Evagrius, a known Origenist but who was also a highly regarded spiritual writer whom Oikoumenios describes as "all-knowledgeable."[64] Origenism had been condemned at the Fifth Ecumenical Council in 553, a council which Oikoumenios, being a non-Chalcedonian, would not have recognized.[65] This may explain his willingness to cite Evagrius but it does not explain or justify his Origenism. Oikoumenios is inconsistent regarding the matter of eternal punishment. One teaching of Origenism which had led to its condemnation was the *apokatastasis*, "the restoration of all things." This was the belief that in the end all would be saved by God. Oikoumenios struggles with this issue. On the one hand, Oikoumenios expressly aligns himself with the Church and states that punishment must be eternal, because this is the tradition of the Church. Yet on other occasions he hints that perhaps punishment is *not* eternal. Oikoumenios vacillates on the matter of eternal punishment and Andrew's commentary responds to Oikoumenios's unorthodox statements. As a pastor, this is a matter of great importance to Andrew to correct, lest any of his flock become complacent by believing that ultimately no one would suffer eternal punishment.

63. Andrew, Chap. 65, *Comm.* 219, citing Rom. 8:21 and Ps. 102(101):26.
64. Oik. 6.3.12.
65. See chapter 4.

Oikoumenios's interpretation of the fifth trumpet which results in the plague of locusts (Rev 9:1–5), leads him into a discussion about eternal punishment. Using the technique of word association, Oikoumenios had previously concluded that the first trumpet represents the return of Christ.[66] Paul described the Second Coming of Christ as heralded by the blowing of a trumpet,[67] to be followed by the righteous being raised and meeting the Lord in the air. Because Oikoumenios had reached the conclusion that the *first* trumpet was the Second Coming, the subsequent six trumpets and the plagues which they inaugurate *must* represent events after the return of Christ. This means that the sufferings of sinners from the plagues actually describes their suffering in Gehenna, and possibly during an intermittent period prior to the final end. In Revelation 9:1–2 an angel opens the shaft of the abyss. Smoke billows out, which Oikoumenios naturally concludes must represent hell, and the plagues which follow allegorically describe the sufferings of sinners in hell. Immediately this becomes impossibly problematic and results in one of his most unique and theologically troublesome conclusions. The text of Rev. 9:3–5 reads:

And from out of the smoke locusts came upon the earth, and they were given power, like scorpions having power on the earth. They were told not to harm the grass of the earth or any greenery or any tree, but only those people who have not the seal upon their foreheads. They were allowed to torture them for five months, but not kill them, and their torture was like the torture of a scorpion when it stings a man.

Oikoumenios faces two problems with this passage: the reference to those who do not have a "seal upon their foreheads" and the "five months" duration. A distinction is being made between those who are sealed in chrismation/baptism and those who are not. Oikoumenios had already concluded that the righteous were taken up to heaven to be with the Lord when the *first* trumpet sounded. Now Oikoumenios must explain how it is possible that some of those who were sealed re-

---

66. Oik. 5.9.1.
67. 1 Thess. 4:16–17.

mained behind and were not taken up to be with the Lord. Then he must explain why "the sealed" are in hell. He concludes that the previously mentioned sealed ones, who were taken up at the Second Coming, were "holy and pure." They are with Christ "in sight of the divine throne." However, *these* sealed ones are those who were baptized but are "less holy." They have not "gravely defiled themselves." Since they were "midway between good and evil" they will "remain upon earth but escape punishment."[68] Oikoumenios thus divides the situation for humanity after the Second Coming of Christ into thirds: one third is in heaven with the Lord, one third is baptized but not entirely holy and remains on earth, and a final third is those who will go to eternal punishment, consisting of serious sinners and the unbaptized.[69]

This is a unique and fascinating interpretation. Unfortunately, it is not an interpretation which he reaches to solve a problematic passage in the Apocalypse text. Rather, his conclusion developed out of a dilemma which he himself created as a result of his faulty interpretation of the first trumpet. Given the outcome of his interpretation, which he knows to be problematic, Oikoumenios ought to have reconsidered his conclusion that the first trumpet heralds the Second Coming of Christ. But he does not. Instead, Oikoumenios creates a peculiar and permanent "limbo" scenario for the one third who were sealed but not taken up to be with the Lord. They will not be punished in Gehenna and instead will remain on earth. But they also will never be with the Lord. He does not speculate regarding what possible type of existence this might be, mid-way between salvation and damnation, but instead immediately turns to the next problem: that the duration of punishment in this passage is limited to five months.

Oikoumenios repeats his idea of a tripartite afterlife when contemplating Revelation 9:20, "And the rest of humankind who were not killed by the plagues did not repent." This should have been another clue to prompt Oikoumenios to reconsider his interpretation since

---

68. Oik. 5.17.7.
69. Oik. 5.17.9.

the text clearly states that the plagues were sent for the *repentance* of the sinners, not for their punishment. Plagues sent to prompt repentance would have been sent *prior* to the Second Coming of Christ. At this point, Oikoumenios discusses, in a general manner, the need for repentance in this life. But rather than recognizing that the plagues are sent by God for repentance and thus they must occur before the end, he resolves the problem again by allegorizing the passage to refer to the afterlife.[70] Hence, he concludes that those "killed by the plagues" are those *spiritually* dead, that is, in hell. The other third are those who have been caught up into the clouds to be with the Lord. Oikoumenios's thoughts return at the end of this chapter to consider what happened to the "limbo" third, those who were neither saved nor damned according to his analysis. He arrives at no solution and only vaguely remarks that "they eternally live out their life with the wicked, unless of course they will be punished by something worse, which he [John] has prudently passed over in silence."[71]

Oikoumenios's interpretation becomes even more problematic as his commentary continues because the text of Revelation states "The rest of humankind who were not killed by these plagues, did not repent" (9:20). He explains that this does not mean repentance *after* death, which is not possible, but refers to "those who were still living and who did not repent of their various unlawful deeds after hearing and seeing what the future holds."[72] And yet it is clear from his very next sentence that he is still interpreting the images of the pericope to the period of time *after* the second coming of Christ when repentance will not be an option: "By this aforesaid plague, perhaps they will not die the spiritual death—calling punishment death—while they eternally live out their life with the wicked." The text of Revelation unambiguously places the plagues during the time preceding the end so that sinners might repent. Oikoumenios, however, is nonetheless determined to "stay the course" and proceed with the trajectory of his in-

---

70. Oik. 5.25.3.   71. Oik. 5.25.3, FOTC 112: 94.
72. Oik. 5.25.3, FOTC 112: 94.

terpretation regardless of the inconsistencies between his conclusions and the Apocalypse text or between this conclusion and other stated conclusions in the commentary.

It is within the context of this unresolved problem regarding the fate of moderate sinners that Oikoumenios reveals his openness to Origenist ideas. He ponders why "some of the fathers accepted the restoration (ἀποκατάστασις) of sinners, saying they were to be chastised so far but no further, as they had been cleansed by their punishment." He then immediately wonders what position he should take when the majority of the Fathers and the accepted Scriptures say that the punishment is everlasting?[73] As a possible solution he suggests:

One must combine the opinions of both. I say this as a suggestion, not as an affirmation; for I associate myself with the teaching of the church in meaning that the future punishments will be everlasting."[74]

Oikoumenios is conflicted. It is clear that he prefers to believe in *apokatastasis*, however, he is well aware that the consistent ecclesiastical tradition and the Scriptures reject it. Therefore, he returns to his suggestion that a "middle path" be taken between each view, despite the fact that compromises on fundamental doctrinal matters are unthinkable. He states that the "five months" must have a mystical meaning in which "sinners will be most severely punished as if stung by a scorpion; but after this we shall be punished more gently, though we shall certainly not be entirely unpunished, to such an extent that we may seek death and not find it."[75]

Although Oikoumenios affirms that he is inclined to believe the Scriptures and those among the church Fathers who affirm everlasting punishment, we see hints elsewhere of a belief in a "cleansing fire."

---

73. Oik. 5.19.1. Suggit's translation reads "[W]hat is to be done when most of the fathers say this, but the accepted Scriptures say that the punishment ... is everlasting?" FOTC 112:89. The translation's phrasing seems to erroneously imply that Oikoumenios believed that most of the Fathers accepted the restoration and that their opinion contradicted the Scriptures.

74. Oik. 5.19.1–2, FOTC 112: 89.

75. Oik. 5.19.3, FOTC 112: 89–90.

Oikoumenios expresses doubts about everlasting punishment in his comments on Revelation 15, reasoning that the mercy of God will be greater than his wrath at the last judgment. In Revelation 15:2 those who had conquered the beast stand alongside a "sea of glass mingled with fire," which Oikoumenios interprets as a cleansing fire. Both the sinners and righteous will be tested by fire, he states, and the glass is "mixed with fire because of the purging and cleansing of all uncleanness, since even the righteous need to be cleansed."[76]

Another interesting indication of Origenist sympathies can be found in Oikoumenios's explanation of the cup of God's wrath which is pure and unmixed.[77] Ordinarily the pure and unmixed wrath is understood to mean *untempered* anger: no mercy is to be shown. Oikoumenios arrives at the opposite conclusion. The "pure wrath" of God means that, in fact, it *includes* mercy. "For the wrath of God is mixed with loving kindness and goodness; it is purely mixed. For there is no equivalence between his wrath and his goodness, but his loving kindness is many more times abundant."[78] To reconcile this view with his professed concurrent belief in eternal punishment, Oikoumenios surmises that the goodness of God means that people will not be punished according to what they deserve, and they will not suffer physically, but will only be deprived of "a share in God's bounty."[79] Elsewhere, Oikoumenios identifies different levels of punishment in hell, with a more mild punishment for "medium sinners."[80]

No doubt, Oikoumenios's vacillation on the question of eternal punishment and belief in a cleansing fire were factors which motivated the composition of Andrew's commentary. There is no suggestion either in the commentary or in *Therapeutike* of a fire by which everyone must "be cleansed" of sins. This is not surprising. Such a fire would be incongruous with Andrew's many statements in the commentary which indicate that those "blessed dead" are already enjoying para-

---

76. Oik. 8.21.4, FOTC 112: 135.
78. Oik. 8.13.3, FOTC 112: 129–30.
80. Oik. 11.10.12; FOTC 112: 182.
77. Rev. 14: 10.
79. Oik. 8.13.7, FOTC 112: 130.

dise to some degree. In fragments from the *Therapeutike*, Andrew addresses what will happen to those among the righteous who are still alive when Christ returns. They will not die but will be transformed and their works will be tested "by fire."[81] Oikoumenios had concluded that the "sea of glass mingled with fire," before which stood "those who had conquered the beast" (Rev. 15:2) implied a cleansing fire. Andrew, however, interprets the "sea of glass" as "both the multitude of those being saved and the purity of the future condition and the great brilliance of the saints who will shine by means of their sparkling virtue."[82] The "fire" is not present for purification but indicates that the works of each of these saints had been tested. Relying on Paul's statement "the fire will test the type of work of each one" (1 Cor. 3:13), Andrew concludes that the fire "is not inflicted on the pure and undefiled."[83]

Andrew's rejection of cleansing fire is most explicit and undeniable in his specific rejection of Oikoumenios's ideas which support *apokatastasis*. Those standing before the "sea of glass" are described as those who have "conquered the beast." It cannot be a cleansing fire, since the saints are victorious over the devil and do not require cleansing. Andrew explains that since fire has two properties—giving light and burning—it will be bifurcated "into different functions ... both burning the sinners and illuminating the righteous."[84] He also offers an alternative explanation: the fire might also represent "divine knowledge and the grace of the life-giving Spirit."[85]

Andrew's rejection of a cleansing fire in the Apocalypse commentary is consistent with his comments in the *Therapeutike*. Those among the righteous, who have not fought like the perfected saints and have not already triumphed, will "pass through the fire." However their works, for the most part, are like costly stones, gold, or silver. They are similar to dry grass only to a very small extent. Therefore, they will go through this fire without experiencing any harm. Whoever lived in an

---

81. Franz Diekamp, *Texte und Abhandlungen*, 172.
82. Andrew, Chap. 45, *Comm.* 165.
83. Andrew, Chap. 45, *Comm.* 165.
84. Andrew, Chap. 45, *Comm.* 165.
85. Andrew, Chap. 45, *Comm.* 165.

opposite manner will be consumed by fire and will be justly punished forever.[86] Even though they all "pass through" fire, it is not a cleansing fire, since the saved do not require cleansing and will not be affected by the fire. Andrew's repudiation of *apokatastasis* is also evident in his rejection of Oikoumenios's analogy of the human soul with gold, discussed below.

Andrew on Eternal Punishment

Andrew affirms that punishment will be eternal, rejecting the Origenist belief that God will save everyone and Oikoumenios's attempts at "compromise." Andrew's commentary responds in many places to Oikoumenios's assertions that punishment might not be eternal. Oikoumenios's inconsistent opinions and his peculiar conclusions, such as the tripartite afterlife scenario, may reveal not only a lack of exegetical training but possibly also a weakness in theological education, despite his doctrinal statements. If not lacking in theological education, Oikoumenios possibly lacked firm convictions, even though he wished to align himself with the teaching of the Church.[87] He certainly had an inclination toward Origenism.[88] In the opinion of Andrew and "Makarios," Oikoumenios's nontraditional views would certainly contribute to the need for a more orthodox commentary. Andrew's response to Oikoumenios is that God is good but he is also righteous, therefore not all will be saved. Andrew compares this to athletic competitions sponsored by kings. Even earthly kings who host athletic contests know that not all will be crowned victors, but the contest is nonetheless open to all.

86. Franz Diekamp, *Texte und Abhandlungen*, 172.
87. Oik. 5.19.1–2, FOTC 112: 89.
88. Adele Monaci Castagno agrees that Oikoumenios does not demonstrate direct dependence on Origen. However, he is influenced by Origen in a general sense, in terms of a cultural milieu which carries certain sensibilities which led one to discuss and debate the relationship between God's love and his justice, between human freedom and God's economy. Oikoumenios participated in this general spiritual atmosphere and this condition is reflected in the commentary, according to Castagno. "I Commenti de Ecumenio e di Andrea di Cesarea: Due letture divergenti dell' Apocalisse," *Memorie della Accademia delle scienze di Torino II, Classe di scienze, morali, storiche e filologiche* V, Fascicolo IV (1981): 356–57.

Wherefore, those who set the goodness, foreknowledge and power of God as an impediment to eternal punishment, let them also attach righteousness to these [qualities], as being distributive to each of them according to what is due, and in no way will they see an overturning of the divine sentence.[89]

God's express promise to punish the wicked only reinforces the truth that those who will be punished deserve punishment because they "volunteered" for it, having freely chosen to do evil and repeatedly rejecting the compassion and forgiveness offered by God.

But I myself, hearing [of] eternal punishments, I cannot disbelieve what has been declared. Knowing his readiness toward compassion and goodness, I surmise that in no way would he either threaten or strike with endless condemnation those deserving it if the condemned ones had already repented and hated the evil which they freely chose to commit. For it is not through necessity, but voluntarily that they are punished.[90]

Even though God wishes to save all, everyone cannot be saved because they refuse to be saved. Nonetheless, God's goodness and mercy are also undeniable, and are manifested in another way: by lessening eternal suffering later. Even if the sinners for whom the plagues were intended to prompt repentance do not repent, they will nonetheless benefit by suffering a little less in the next life because they suffered somewhat in this one: "towards a moderation, at any rate, of the payment in full by those who had sinned themselves."[91] Even the plagues are evidence of the love and mercy of God. Andrew also suggests elsewhere that punishment here might mean a "milder punishment in the future because they are being afflicted in part here."[92]

Since we are taught by the words in the gospels that the spiritual powers rejoice and celebrate over those who return from repentance to salvation, but grieve over those who turn aside from the straight path, and that they give thanks to God for the punishment of those transgressing against the divine commandments, so that they might make partial payment of their debts, let us make haste, granting them [the angels] joy upon our return.[93]

89. Andrew, Chap. 50, *Comm.* 174.
90. Andrew, Chap. 50, *Comm.* 173–74.
91. Andrew, Chap. 45, *Comm.* 167.
92. Andrew, Chap. 55, *Comm.* 195.
93. Andrew, Chap. 48, *Comm.* 170.

A fire for the cleansing of sin which would be necessary for participation in the future life in the kingdom of heaven is out of the question for Andrew. He rejects the analogy that some made to gold—that people are like gold which contains impurities and needs to be cleansed. "How much more so [would God spare] these if He knew they put aside the filth in the fire, in accordance with the likeness of gold, which some have understood as a paradigm in this situation?"[94] The analogy must be rejected because gold has impurities by its nature, but we "reason-endowed" human beings "intentionally" add the filth to our souls.[95] Since sin has been added by the human, it ought to be removed by him or her. The comparison with gold must be rejected since its impurity is excusable and unavoidable, but the same cannot be said for us. Furthermore, the time for repentance and change is now. There will be no point in having regrets later; it will be too late. In this life we have been given the help of the Holy Spirit to avoid future eternal punishment, but it will not be available to help us later. "For it is necessary that those who have been defeated feel regret for these things and lament in vain, being tormented eternally ... moreover, the help of the Holy Spirit will no more accompany those who have been condemned as it does now."[96]

Andrew directly refutes Oikoumenios and others who insist that eternal punishment will be abolished. The demons are certain to be eternally tormented.[97] There is certainly no hope for the devil, who, fully aware of his impending punishment, has not only refused to cease his evil activity but has intensified it since the coming of Christ. The salvation of the devil is impossible. "[I]f the expectation of punishment makes him even more evil, then how if being punished, either himself or his workers, how are they to be cleansed of the filth of sin in Gehenna through the fire?"[98]

Andrew never retreats from his position that the final punishment is eternal. An angel warns of future eternal torment and the wrath of God directed against anyone who worships the beast and that "the

---

94. Andrew, Chap. 50, *Comm.* 174.
95. Andrew, Chap. 50, *Comm.* 174.
96. Andrew, Chap. 50, *Comm.* 174.
97. Andrew, Chap 27, *Comm.* 124.
98. Andrew, Chap. 34, *Comm.* 144.

smoke of their torment goes up for ever and ever" (Rev. 14:9–11). Andrew remarks that the smoke is the torment of sinners. It "is to 'go up forever and ever' ... that we might learn that it is endless, just as the bliss of the righteous [will be endless] and in like manner also, the torment of the sinners."[99] The same point is made again explaining the description of the destruction of Babylon at whose destruction the smoke ascends "forever and ever" (Rev. 19:3). "And 'the smoke goes up for ever and ever' from the city signifies either the uninterrupted never-to-be-forgotten [nature] of the punishments coming upon her into perpetuity, or the judgments partly rendered to her, to be tormented more fittingly but nevertheless eternally in the future."[100] The Apocalypse text itself confirms that the worshippers of the beast will have "no rest day or night" (Rev. 14:11), which Andrew recognizes as an expression of eternity, not an indication that time will be measured by the sun in the future age. Endless punishment "will fall upon those who commit evil deeds and pronounce the blasphemies of the apostate beast against Christ depicting [the beast] through the deeds they commit and engraving his name on their own hearts as honorable."[101]

Andrew reveals hints of the theological reasoning underlying his insistence upon eternal punishment. Andrew ponders why the afflictions described in Revelation do not encourage repentance by sinners, as they are intended to do, but rather result in more blasphemy against God (Rev. 16:11). He concludes that if eternal hell-fire is not a sufficient deterrent, and terrible plagues on earth do not reform sinners either, punishment must be eternal. If it were not, what would prevent sinners from sinning again? If punishment neither persuades nor dissuades them, then when given the opportunity to sin, sinners will continue to do so. Andrew compares them to prisoners who only cease committing crimes because they are incarcerated and have no opportunity to commit more crimes, not because they have lost the desire or intention to engage in criminal activity.

99. Andrew, Chap. 42, *Comm.* 159.
100. Andrew, Chap. 56, *Comm.* 197.
101. Andrew, Chap. 42, *Comm.* 159.

If those will turn to blasphemy by the application of afflictions ... and if the evil demons through human bodies, which they have used as organs ... nevertheless do not refrain from cursing those who plague [them], one must ponder what, then, is necessary for us to realize about the impious being tormented in the Gehenna of fire. How then is evil so innate to the point that they completely cease from the thought of it, or are they only hindered in the carrying out of evil plans into deed, just as evildoers also are put into prison out of necessity yet [they] do not hold back the intentions to harm others?[102]

Andrew's conclusion regarding the reality of and necessity for eternal punishment accords with his basic assumptions of synergy and human free will. "The 'dead' are the souls which have pursued deadly deeds. Since they willingly chose estrangement from God in the course of their lives, they would likewise freely continue to chose separation from God for eternity. They would not cease their sin in the kingdom of heaven since nothing convinces them to cease in this life. They did not simply sin against God, but they sinned against themselves. The will of God is that "people 'be saved and come to knowledge of the truth' 'and that they return and live,' and on the other hand, secondly [the will of God] is the punishment of those who pursue their own punishment."[103]

The Kingdom of Heaven

Andrew not only insists upon the reality of eternal punishment, but even more so he emphasizes the blessings and delights of paradise. Andrew reminds the reader that pursuing a life of virtue through sacrifices and difficulties of this life is exceeded to an even greater degree by the promised blessings of God. Commenting on the beatitude in Revelation 14:13, "Blessed are the dead who die in the Lord henceforth," Andrew describes those who "die in the Lord."

For those, actually, the exodus from the body is rest from toils, and the consequence of their deeds is the occasion of "unfading crowns" and "rewards of

---

102. Andrew, Chap. 50, *Comm.* 173.
103. Andrew, Chap. 58, *Comm.* 203, quoting 1 Tim. 2:4; 2 Tim. 2:25, 3:7; and Ezek. 18:23, 32.

glory" [which are] the prizes for those winning the contests by a wide margin of victory, [the prizes] which the contestants of Christ our God achieved against the invisible powers.[104]

This life is brief, but the promised rewards are eternal. "For the sufferings of the present time cannot be compared to the future glory to be revealed.'"[105] The blessings of the kingdom of heaven will be so tremendous and extraordinary that all of the difficulties and sorrows of this life will be forgotten. "For by the excessiveness of the unceasing joy and magnitude of the prizes of the rewards in the struggles they will also forget the pains and labors."[106] Andrew frequently encourages his readers with inspirational after-life imagery drawn from biblical motifs. He offers no description of the situation faced by those enduring eternal punishment beyond brief references to torment and fire. However, by contrast, the delights of the faithful are repeatedly referenced, usually expressed in terms of prayerful desire, with the descriptions of paradise preceded by "may we … " often prior to the doxology found at the end of each major section. If believers are diligent and faithful they will enjoy citizenship in the "Jerusalem above,"[107] "the dwelling place of the Royal Trinity—for [the Trinity] dwells in her and walks about in her as it has been promised."[108] They will acquire "the wages, the glory from God, the 'well done, good and faithful servant.'"[109] It will be a place of "blessings"[110] and "reward,"[111] of joy,[112] the "dwelling place of all gladness"[113] and of future eternal "rest" when

---

104. Andrew, Chap. 42, *Comm.* 103, quoting 1 Pet. 5:4, 1 Cor. 9:24–25.
105. Andrew, Chap. 42, *Comm.* 160, quoting Rom. 8:18.
106. Andrew, Chap. 64, *Comm.* 217.   107. Andrew, Chap. 54, *Comm.* 189.
108. Andrew, Chap. 65, *Comm.* 220.   109. Andrew, Chap. 69, *Comm.* 237.
110. Andrew, Chap. 3, *Comm.* 65; Chap. 15, *Comm.* 93; Chap. 18, *Comm.* 99; Chap. 50, *Comm.* 174; Chap. 54, *Comm.* 189; Chap. 57, *Comm.* 198; Chap. 60, *Comm.* 207; Chap. 63, *Comm.* 215; Chap. 66, *Comm.* 222, etc.
111. Andrew, Prologue, 54; Chap. 3, *Comm.* 65; Chap. 9, *Comm.* 80; Chap. 15, *Comm.* 93; Chap. 24, *Comm.* 117; Chap. 27, *Comm.* 124; Chap. 33, *Comm.* 141; Chap. 42, *Comm.* 160; Chap. 62, *Comm.* 210; Chap. 64, *Comm.* 217.
112. Andrew, Chap. 20, *Comm.* 111; Chap. 45, *Comm.* 167; Chap. 57, *Comm.* 198; Chap. 58, *Comm.* 200; Chap. 64, *Comm.* 217; Chap. 65, *Comm.* 220; Chap. 69, *Comm.* 237.
113. Andrew, Chap. 21, *Comm.* 114.

"pain, sorrow and sighing have fled away."[114] They will rejoice, "illumined by 'the light of the countenance of Christ' our God,"[115] and enjoy "the eternal blessings that have been prepared for the saints 'from the foundation of the world.'"[116] It is a place of "heavenly mansions,"[117] of "glory, repose and spaciousness,"[118] where they will "co-reign eternally with Christ."[119] Just as the punishment of sinners differed for each according to the degree and manner of their sin, the rewards of the righteous will also take different forms. "According to the correspondence of the deeds of each" there will be differing degrees of "glory," "some being glorified less and some glorified more."[120]

The kingdom of heaven is nothing short of indwelling with God, human life in communion with the Holy Trinity. It is life with God and in God. There is "no temple" in the heavenly Jerusalem: "For its temple is the Lord God the Almighty and the Lamb" (Rev. 21:22).

For what need is there of a physical 'temple' [in a city] in which God is guard and shelter 'in whom we live and move and have our being'? For he will be this for the saints, both temple and dweller, dwelling in them and moving about just as has been promised, and 'the Lamb,' is the Lamb of God sacrificed for us, which clearly by its essence is placed together with the Life giving Spirit, which he [John] indicated by the river which follows.[121]

In a particularly beautiful passage, Andrew explains the terms used to describe heaven in the Scriptures:

The "supper" of Christ is the festival of those who are saved and the all-encompassing harmony in gladness, of which the blessed ones who will attain [this] will enter together into the eternal bridal chamber of the Holy Bridegroom of clean souls. For the One who promised this does not lie. Many are the blessings in the future age and all surpass understanding, and the participation in these is declared under many names, sometimes the "kingdom of heaven" on account of its glory and honor, sometimes "paradise" because

---

114. Andrew, Chap. 20, *Comm.* 110; Chap. 57, *Comm.* 199; Chap. 67, *Comm.* 226.
115. Andrew, Chap. 57, *Comm.* 199.
116. Andrew, Chap. 54. *Comm.* 189.
117. Andrew, Chap. 27, *Comm.* 124.
118. Andrew, Chap. 36, *Comm.* 150.
119. Andrew, Chap. 20, *Comm.* 110; Chap. 24, *Comm.* 244; Chap. 36, *Comm.* 150.
120. Andrew, Chap. 68, *Comm.* 234.
121. Andrew, Chap. 67, *Comm.* 231, quoting Acts 17:28.

DEATH, JUDGMENT, PUNISHMENT, REWARD   285

of the uninterrupted banquet of all good things, sometimes "bosoms of Abraham" because the repose of the spirits of the dead is there, sometimes as a "bridal chamber" and "marriage" not only because of the unceasing joy but also because of the pure and inexpressible union of God to his servants.[122]

Not surprisingly, the "marriage feast" imagery is especially strong as an expression the union of the saints with God in Andrew's commentary, not only because of its parabolic use by Christ, but also because of its use in Revelation.[123] "[H]aving decorated our beloved souls as for a wedding, we will present them to the king for a union."[124] Andrew encourages the faithful to remain steadfast: "let us enter into the everlasting bridal chamber of joy."[125] "[W]ith joyful torches of the virtuous manner of life, adorned with sympathy, offering ourselves with the clean and blameless wedding garments of holy souls, let us enter together into the bridal chamber of Christ our God."[126] Although marriage is an appropriate image to express union with God, the true nature of life with God is beyond comprehension, Andrew writes. It will be an unimaginable union, "[the] pure and inexpressible union of God to his servants, [a union] so greatly transcending the communion of bodies one with another, as much as light is separate from darkness and perfume from stench."[127]

The New Jerusalem "above" is the Church and the walls are Christ, "high and fit for guarding those in the holy city."[128] The enormous walls measuring twelve thousand stadia (Rev. 21:16) signify its great size, meaning that it contains a large number of inhabitants. The number twelve shows that it was "settled" through the work of the apostles.[129] Its square shape indicates perfection and stability.[130] The size of the walls also reveals that it is a place of safety and security, "the divine sacred enclosure and shelter in which the saints will be protected."[131] And yet, its gates will never be shut (Rev. 21:25). "That 'the gates will not be closed' means ... the security and immutability of her inhabit-

---

122. Andrew, Chap. 57, *Comm.* 198.
123. Rev. 19:7 and 21:2.
124. Andrew, Chap. 9, *Comm.* 80.
125. Andrew, Chap. 45, *Comm.* 167.
126. Andrew, Chap. 51, *Comm.* 177.
127. Andrew, Chap. 57, *Comm.* 198.
128. Andrew, Chap. 67, *Comm.* 224.
129. Andrew, Chap. 67, *Comm.* 226.
130. Andrew, Chap. 67, *Comm.* 226.
131. Andrew, Chap. 67, *Comm.* 232.

ants."¹³² No need exists for protection, since in that city there will be nothing accursed.¹³³ "In this 'tabernacle not made by hands,' there will be neither weeping nor tear. For the Provider of everlasting joy will give the unceasing delight to be seen by all the saints."¹³⁴ The absence of evil or sin in the city means that "'pain, sorrow and sighing have fled away' … the distress of the saints and the arrogance of the impious has met an end appropriate to each of these."¹³⁵

A continuing and developing relationship with God will also characterize life in the kingdom, even though initially the "rewards" distributed will differ. Andrew offers an alternative interpretation of the gates of heaven which will never be shut, which he had previously stated implied safety (Rev. 21:25). The open gates can also mean that "the divine gates of the apostolic teaching are to be open to all for the learning of more perfect things."¹³⁶ Andrew hints elsewhere in the commentary that learning and spiritual growth will continue in the heavenly kingdom. Christ promises "to give the grace of the life-giving Spirit."¹³⁷ Andrew even suggests that "pagans" may be present in the heavenly Jerusalem since the Apocalypse states that the "leaves" of the Tree of Life, are "for the healing of the nations" and for the "purging of ignorance." The citizens of heaven can expect to receive "more perfect knowledge" in the future (Rev. 22:2).

"Leaves of the tree," that is, of Christ, [are] the most superficial understandings of the divine decrees, as his "fruits" [are] the more perfect knowledge being revealed in the future. These "leaves" will be "for healing," that is, for the purging of ignorance of those pagans inferior in the activity of virtues.¹³⁸

As he frequently does, Andrew offers an alternative interpretation of the image. The fruit of the Tree of Life might also mean participation in divinity:

132. Andrew, Chap. 67, *Comm.* 110.
133. Andrew, Chap. 68, *Comm.* 235, referring to Rev. 22:3.
134. Andrew, Chap. 65, *Comm.* 220, quoting Heb. 9:11, 2 Cor. 5:1.
135. Andrew, Chap. 65, *Comm.* 221, commenting on Rev. 21:4b quoting Isa. 51:11.
136. Andrew, Chap. 67, *Comm.* 232. 137. Andrew, Chap. 66, *Comm.* 221.
138. Andrew, Chap. 68, *Comm.* 233.

And one must also understand this differently. "The Tree of Life producing twelve fruits" is the apostolic assembly according to their participation in the true Tree of Life, who, by communion with the flesh, bestowed upon us participation in his divinity. Their fruits are those which have produced a "harvest one hundredfold." The "leaves," [are] those [who bore a harvest of] "sixtyfold, and thirtyfold," those who will bring forth healing from the nations, those lesser, transmitting the radiance of the divine lights which they received through those who bore a fruit harvest one hundred fold. For whatever difference there is between the leaves and fruit, then such is the difference between those who were saved then, some being glorified less and some glorified more, as has been written.[139]

Ultimately, however, Andrew realizes that descriptions of the beauty of the heavenly city can only express concepts and cannot be understood literally since the descriptions are contradictory. The streets are described as transparent gold: "and the wide street of the city was pure gold, transparent as glass" (Rev. 21:21b).

In one example it is not possible to present the exact [nature] of the good things of the heavenly city. Wherefore 'the wide street of the city' on the one hand he viewed as very extravagant and beautifully colored like gold, and on the other hand [it is] clear as crystal, so that for us it is impossible for both [descriptions] to concur in one [image]. The saint saw all these things as he was able. Perfect comprehension of the heavenly city surpasses hearing and sight and thought.[140]

---

139. Andrew, Chap. 68, *Comm.* 234, quoting Matt. 13:23 and Mark 4:20.
140. Andrew, Chap. 67, *Comm.* 231, quoting 1 Cor. 2:9.

15

ANDREW AND THE GREEK APOCALYPSE TEXT

The textual history of the Apocalypse is unique among the books of the New Testament. The commentary of Andrew of Caesarea has impacted the transmission of the text of Revelation itself by creating a text-type of its own, and by stimulating the production of a large portion of the existing Revelation manuscripts.[1] The Apocalypse textual transmission differs from the rest of the New Testament, primarily because the text has been generated along two lines of transmission, one of them entirely outside the stream of the biblical manuscript tradition.

Since the Apocalypse never became part of the lectionary of the Orthodox Church, it was copied far less frequently and a preferred ecclesiastical text type never resulted. Manuscripts containing the Revelation of John are not only found bound with other books of the New Testament but are located among collections of miscellaneous spiritual writings and even with profane literature. For example, one manuscript containing Revelation also holds the *Acts of Thomas* and various theological treatises, with the Apocalypse found between the life of St. Euphrosyne and a treatise by Basil the Great.[2]

---

1. A text-type is a family of manuscripts which derive from a common source and exhibit common characteristics.

2. Caspar René Gregory, *Canon and Text of the New Testament* (New York: Charles Scribner, 1907), 291.

Approximately seven times more manuscripts exist of the gospels than of the Book of Revelation. Half of the manuscripts of Revelation stand alone, whereas other books of the New Testament are consistently found bound together with similar books.³ Metzger made a list of the "Greek Bibles that have survived from the Byzantine period," and noted that the gospels exist in 2,328 copies but Revelation exists in only 287 copies, concluding: "The lower status of the Book of Revelation in the East is indicated also by the fact that it has never been included in the official lectionary of the Greek Church, whether Byzantine or modern."⁴ J. K. Elliott, citing Kurt Aland's 1994 *Liste*, counted 303 manuscripts containing Revelation. He observed that only eleven uncials contain Revelation and only six papyri do, and no papyrus preserves the complete text.⁵ The oldest fragments are P^{98} in Cairo (2nd century), P^{47} third century (Chester Beatty), and P^{18} from the third or fourth century. The oldest complete text is Sinaiticus ℵ)) from the fourth century.⁶ David Aune lists six papyri fragments, eleven uncials and 292 minuscules⁷ as textual witnesses, not including patristic quotations and translations.⁸ Of the 292 minuscules containing Revelation, 98 are commentaries, mostly copies of Andrew.⁹ As can be seen by

---

3. Edgar J. Goodspeed, *The Formation of the New Testament* (Chicago: University of Chicago Press, 1926), 136–37.

4. Bruce Metzger, *The Canon of the New Testament: Its Origin, Development and Significance* (Oxford: Clarendon Press, 1987), 217, citing Kurt and Barbara Aland, *Der Text des Neuen Testaments* (Stuttgart, 1982).

5. An uncial is a manuscript written entirely in uppercase letters. It is also known as a "majuscule."

6. J. K. Elliot, "The Distinctiveness of the Greek Manuscripts of the Book of Revelation," *Journal of Theological Studies*, n.s. 48 (1997): 116–24, 120, citing K. Aland, ed. *Kurzgefasste Liste der Griechischen Handschriften des Neuen Testaments* (Berlin, 1994).

7. A minuscule is a manuscript written with upper and lower case letters.

8. David E. Aune, *Revelation*, 3 vols. Word Biblical Commentary 52A, B, and C, (Nashville: Nelson Reference and Electronic, 1997), 52A: cxxxvi. Although 293 minuscules have been listed as containing Revelation, only 292 actually do. The manuscript identified as number 1277, which has been said to contain Revelation in fact does not. See David E. Aune, *Revelation*, 52A: cxxxix–cxl.

9. David E. Aune, *Revelation*, 52A: cxxxix–cxl. See David E. Aune, *Revelation*, 5252A: cxxvi–cxlvii for a complete listing of Revelation manuscripts. Bruce Metzger, *Canon of the New Testament*, 217. According to Metzger, the Book of Revelation exists in 287 manuscripts and

the figures above, apparently there is no consistent agreement on the number of existing Revelation manuscripts.

A number of peculiarities also exist in the transmission of the actual text of the Apocalypse. First, the reliability presumed for ordinary text-type categories of the New Testament does not apply. Four main text-types can be identified for the Apocalypse: (1) A C Oikoumenios, which is considered the most reliable textual "family,"[10] (2) the textual tradition represented by P^{47} and ℵ (Codex Sinaiticus), (3) the K (or "Koine") text, which Nestle-Aland identifies as M^K, and (4) the Andreas text type, often identified with ℵ^a (the Sinaiticus corrector) and represented in Nestle-Aland siglia as M^A, or the Majority Andreas text-type.[11]

Approximately one-third of the total Apocalypse manuscripts are the Majority Andreas type. Therefore the commentary appears responsible for the existence of one-third more manuscripts than would have existed without the commentary, which is in itself a major contribution toward the understanding and preservation of the Apocalypse text.

The Nestle-Aland edition of the New Testament favors A C Oecumenius as the most reliable textual tradition for Revelation. This conflicts with the usual opinion regarding the reliability of these types in the rest of the New Testament, in which ℵ is preferred and which considers A C to be inferior witnesses.[12] Lachmann and Hort also regarded A as superior to the other uncials of the Apocalypse because it retains many of the Hebraisms of the author, "resulting in wholly ungrammatical Greek, which later copyists tended either to soften or eliminate."[13] All of the text-types can be traced back at least to the fourth century.

---

fragments. Of these, approximately 96 manuscripts contain the commentary of Andrew of Caesarea in its complete form or an abbreviated form.

10. "A" is the text type of *Codex Alexandrinus* and "C" is the *Codex Ephraemi Syri Rescriptus*. Both are fifth century uncials and their Revelation text-type resembles that of Oikoumenios.

11. J. K. Elliot, "Distinctiveness of the Greek Manuscripts," 120.

12. J. K. Elliot, "Distinctiveness of the Greek Manuscripts," 121.

13. R. V. G. Tasker, "The Chester Beatty Papyrus of the Apocalypse of John," *Journal of Theological Studies* 50 (1949): 60–68, 61.

In the twentieth century the work of examining the textual history of the Apocalypse manuscripts was undertaken primarily by three individuals: Hermann Von Soden, Herman Charles Hoskier, and Josef Schmid. Von Soden's work was extremely incomplete, since he only catalogued approximately seventy out of more than two hundred Apocalypse manuscripts known at the time. Von Soden did not seriously study the Andreas textual tradition and came to the conclusion that Andrew created his own text. Von Soden, according to Marie-Joseph Lagrange, by a kind of "juggling act," identified the Andreas tradition with the symbol "I," to indicate Jerusalem, which Lagrange remarked was hardly appropriate for a text created in Cappadocia, as Von Soden had believed.[14]

Hoskier's work encompassed more manuscripts. He divided over 200 manuscripts into about thirty groups, with approximately fifteen remaining which he believed to be unrelated to any family group.[15] However, Hoskier completely excluded the Andreas Apocalypse manuscript family from his project and in fact expressed disdain for the Andreas manuscript tradition.[16] Hoskier was particularly interested in the transmission of the Apocalypse texts "independent of Church 'use' and which owe their freedom from Ecclesiastical standardization to their transmission apart from the documents collected as our New Testament."[17] Hoskier qualified the term 'use' since the Apocalypse does not form any portion of the lectionary of the Greek East. He was referring to Apocalypse texts which were found bound in non-canonical collections, such as with collections of treatises on mystical

---

14. Marie-Joseph Lagrange, *Introduction à l'ètude du Nouveau Testament*, vol. 2, "Critique textuelle, l" Part II "La Critique rationnelle" (Paris: Gabalda, 1935), 579.

15. Herman Charles Hoskier, ed. *Concerning the Text of the Apocalypse*, 2 vols. (London: Bernard Quaritch, 1929), 1, x.

16. In reconstructing the Apocalypse text, Hoskier considered witnesses from Oikoumenios and from a variety of Latin sources, including Victorinus, Primasius, Cassiodorus, Apringius, Tyconius, Beatus, and pseudo-Ambrose, but did not consider Andreas, Arethas, Haymo, or Bede. He expressed a negative opinion of the Andreas manuscript tradition: "There are so many variants in Andreas's commentary manuscripts ... that I have been loth (sic) to cite Andreas or Arethas positively." *Concerning the Text of the Apocalypse*, 1:xxv.

17. Herman Charles Hoskier, *Concerning the Text of the Apocalypse*, 1: xi.

subjects or sermons. He considered those texts particularly valuable because they would presumably serve as a witness to the Apocalypse text which was less impacted by ecclesiastical concerns or interpretations. "Before the official acceptance of the Apocalypse into the Canon … especially by those in the East, it circulated freely from the earliest times among mystical writings, and we find it outside the New Testament included in Collections of Miscellanies."[18] Hoskier noted that more than forty Apocalypse cursives are bound up with other writings, including Hippolytus on Daniel, ascetic sermons of St. John Climacus, ascetic sermons of Ephraim, sermons of St. John Chrysostom on false teachers and on the presence of Christ, the Profession of Faith of 318 Fathers at the Council of Nicaea, the Martyrdom of the Forty Martyrs at Sebaste, and hagiographies of Sts. Nicholas, Elias, Gregory the Armenian, Simeon the Stylite, George and the Holy Archangels.[19]

Hoskier saw the great advantage of having two streams of testimony for the Apocalypse which "never coalesce, but at Athos today side by side we will find the Church standards and the independent texts (in collections of Miscellanies) being copied and re-copied independently."[20] Hoskier states that the double line of transmission of the Greek Apocalypse text provides a "position of superiority as regards our material compared to the other books of the New Testament, because the Apocalypse—admitted somewhat late into the Canon of Scripture—was transmitted on lines independent of ecclesiastical tenets, dogmas and traditions, and is found in the middle of many Miscellanies on mystical subjects," providing an additional means to check other authorities.[21]

Hoskier believed that with the help of Sinaiticus, the large number of cursive manuscripts provide excellent witness to the third century, the time of the Decian and Diocletian persecutions. After separating

18. Herman Charles Hoskier, *Concerning the Text of the Apocalypse*, 1: xxvi–xxvii.
19. Herman Charles Hoskier, *Concerning the Text of the Apocalypse*, 1: xxvii.
20. Herman Charles Hoskier, 1: xxvii. The same point is made by David E. Aune, *Revelation*, 52A: cxxxvi.
21. Herman Charles Hoskier, *The Complete Commentary of Oecumenius on the Apocalypse*, 4.

the Greek manuscripts into their respective families, Hoskier identified "twenty or thirty separate lines of transmission, all converging back to the original source."[22]

In fact and in deed this is very apparent, for we shall not find traces of a mass of copies from which our extant copies were derived, but of one frail witness standing back of them all, for it is very noticeable that in places where this original was faint or difficult to read our principle witnesses falter and labour, and guess at the word, and in these places a variety of half-a-dozen or a dozen variants has resulted, which will be found in our record.[23]

But since Hoskier willfully ignored the Andreas textual tradition, it was left to Josef Schmid to provide the definitive work on the text of the Apocalypse in the mid-twentieth century.[24] After exhaustively examining all of the Apocalypse manuscripts, Schmid identified the main Apocalypse text types as (1) the Andreas text type or—Av (2) the Koine or *K*, (3) A C Oikoumenios, and, (4) the group which includes P[47], Sinaiticus and Origen. Schmid's findings are over fifty years old and need to be updated and reconsidered, but his work on the text of Revelation remains unparalleled. As part of his work on the Apocalypse text, Schmid also created and published the critical text of the *Commentary on the Apocalypse* by Andrew of Caesarea.

Schmid's main concern in editing the commentary of Andrew of Caesarea had been to determine one of the chief text types for Revelation, that of Andrew, which he designated "Av" for Ἀνδρέας. He wanted to determine whether an early text form of the Apocalypse could be accessed by an examination of the Andreas text type.[25] Schmid determined that all of the Av texts go back to one original, either the auto-

---

22. Herman Charles Hoskier, *Concerning the Text of the Apocalypse*, 1: xx.
23. Herman Charles Hoskier, *Concerning the Text of the Apocalypse*, 1: xvi.
24. Josef Schmid, *Studien zur Geschichte des griechischen Apokalypse-Textes*, 3 parts (München: Karl Zink Verlag, 1955–56). Part 1 *Der Apokalypse-Kommentar des Andreas von Kaisareia Text* (1955), Part 2 *Die alten Stämme* (1955), and Part 3 *Historische Abteilung Ergänzungsband, Einleitung*, (1956).
25. Georg Maldfeld, "Zur Geschichte des griechischen Apokalypse-Textes," *Theologische Zeitschrift* 14 (1958): 47–52, 48.

graph of the Andreas commentary or a copy of it.[26] However, he also concluded that the Revelation text in the original Andreas commentary is older than the commentary itself, going back to a previously worked over text,[27] and can be found in the Sinaiticus corrector ℵ[a].[28]

After analyzing the Andreas manuscripts along with the other Apocalypse manuscript types, Schmid rejected Von Soden's assertion that Andrew himself had created the Andreas text-type out of a mixture of several manuscripts.[29] Schmid supported his conclusion not only by his analysis of the relationship between variants found in the texts, but also from the statements of Andrew in the commentary, which indicate that Andrew was following an existing text, as well as his comment regarding the need to respect the text regardless of any violations of proper Attic syntax.[30]

The *K* text exists in a number of archetypes from approximately the ninth century, and can be found in a number of related families. P[47] and Origen are witnesses for the text in the third century and stand in an independent relationship to each other. Where they agree, the presumption is that they preserve a reading older than 200 C.E. They also seem to represent an Egyptian tradition and are associated with Coptic versions. The A C Oikoumenios group contains the best manuscript tradition. The most reliable by far is A, which, although it is from the fifth century, is a better text than Origen's which is two hundred years older.[31]

Schmid concluded that the history of the Apocalypse text can only be traced back to about 200 C.E., and that most of the variants occurred in the first one hundred years of the transmission of the text.[32]

---

26. Josef Schmid, *Einleitung*, 127. G. D. Kilpatrick, "Professor J. Schmid on the Greek Text of the Apocalypse," *Vigiliae christianae* 13 (1959): 1–13, 3. In the terminology of manuscripts and textual criticism, an "autograph" is simply the "original" document written by the author himself.

27. Georg Maldfeld, "Zur Geschichte," 49.

28. G. D. Kilpatrick, "Professor J. Schmid on the Greek Text," 3.

29. Josef Schmid, *Einleitung*, 125.

30. Josef Schmid, 125. See Andrew, Chap. 72, *Comm.* 241–42.

31. G. D. Kilpatrick, "Professor J. Schmid on the Greek Text," 4–5.

32. G. D. Kilpatrick, "Professor J. Schmid on the Greek Text," 5.

No actual text type can truly be traced back before 200. The text of Revelation can be recovered as far back as the middle of the second century, but the gap between this stage and the original text cannot be bridged.[33]

In his review of Schmid's work J. D. Kilpatrick mentions that at least one reason for the many variants in Revelation manuscripts is the language of the Apocalypse. "Even among the writers of the New Testament, some of them with very distinctive styles, the Greek of Revelation stands out. It is eccentric and would invite correction."[34] R. V. G. Tasker, discussing the Chester Beatty papyrus which contains one of the oldest fragments of the Apocalypse (P^{47}), concurred: "It is generally recognized that the text of the Apocalypse, a book which gave some offence in certain quarters of the Greek-speaking Church in the second century, was subject from an early date to a series of attempts to improve the very Hebraic character of its Greek."[35]

Schmid observed that the text used by Andrew was older than even the text which influenced the Codex Sinaiticus and that the Koine text and Andreas type are closely related.[36] However, their transmission was quite different. The archetype of *K* was very questionable in places but Koine was extraordinarily closed.[37] Conversely, the Andreas type splintered and, quite surprisingly, not all manuscripts of the Andreas commentary use the Andreas text type. This is even the case in the most significant commentary which followed Andrew, and the only other patristic exposition of Revelation, the commentary by Arethas, the tenth-century bishop of Caesarea. Although he depended heavily on Andrew for the content of the commentary, either copying Andrew word for word or paraphrasing him, Arethas used a different Apocalypse text, that of the Koine.[38] The Koine text can be found in some Andreas commentary manuscripts, but the Andreas text-type was rarely

---

33. G. D. Kilpatrick, "Professor J. Schmid on the Greek Text," 6.
34. G. D. Kilpatrick, "Professor J. Schmid on the Greek Text," 6.
35. R. V. G. Tasker, "The Chester Beatty Papyrus," 60–61.
36. Josef Schmid, *Einleitung*, 126.   37. Josef Schmid, *Einleitung*, 126.
38. Josef Schmid, *Die alten Stämme*, 96–97.

dispersed apart from the commentary.[39] Therefore, while the Koine text influenced the Andreas text type occasionally, the reverse is not true. The Koine type remained free of influence of the Andreas type.

For Schmid this resulted in a benefit for the analysis of text-types, since Andrew's commentary and the Apocalypse text were almost always copied together. Schmid concluded that the text of both *Av*, and *K* can be determined with certainty.[40] He believed that Andrew himself may have had some influence on the text of the *Av* type, primarily in the strikingly frequent addition of καί.[41] Schmid concluded that Andrew probably added it at least a few times, namely where he concludes a section of commentary and then a section of the text is again inserted.[42] But Schmid also concluded that the Andreas text recension is the work of an earlier man, not Andrew, who had corrected the text through all of the chapters, and that a small portion of the corrections pre-existed this corrector.[43] This text form is inferior to the neutral text of A C Oikoumenios. However, a comparison of the Andreas text with the A C Oikoumenios and the P^{47} is valuable for the production of the Ur-text because it accidentally preserves main witnesses of the neutral text, A C Oikoumenios.[44]

The Andreas manuscripts allowed Schmid to more easily distinguish text-types through their preservation in the commentary. The commentary formed a far better basis than the Apocalypse text alone for researching the text history since through the commentary the influences of other types of the Apocalypse text were distinguishable.[45] The many copies of the commentary not only helped to reconstruct the text used by Andrew, but also helped to determine variations. Through details accidentally preserved in the Andreas commentary transmission, Schmid was able to trace various groups back to an older edition and to a common stem, and to recognize their relationship to older,

---

39. Josef Schmid, *Einleitung*, 126.
40. Josef Schmid, *Die alten Stämme*, 44.
41. Josef Schmid, *Die alten Stämme*, 52.
42. Josef Schmid, *Die alten Stämme*, 52.
43. Josef Schmid, *Die alten Stämme*, 53.
44. Josef Schmid, *Die alten Stämme*, 53.
45. Josef Schmid, *Einleitung*, 128.

no-longer-extant editions.[46] Schmid also concluded that creating a clear family tree for the Apocalypse manuscript tradition is no longer possible.[47]

Recently Juan Hernández Jr. has been engaged in a significant study of the textual history of the Apocalypse, including the contributions of Andrew of Caesarea. He has effectively demonstrated that some manuscript variations are not mere spelling errors but indicate a subtle yet purposeful scribal effort to elucidate the meaning of the Apocalypse text. Attention to such variations is important because they are in fact a type of early "exegesis" or "commentary" on the text.[48] Dr. Hernández continues to make important contributions toward our understanding of Apocalypse interpretation by the study of textual variants.[49]

---

46. Josef Schmid, *Einleitung*, 129.

47. Josef Schmid, *Einleitung*, 129.

48. Juan Hernández Jr., "Codex Sinaiticus: An Early Christian Commentary on the Apocalypse?" *From Parchment to Pixels: Studies in the Codex Sinaiticus*, ed. David C. Parker and Scot McKendrik (London: British Library, forthcoming). See also his "A Scribal Solution to a Problematic Measurement in the Apocalypse," *New Testament Studies* 56 (2010): 273–78, and "Andrew of Caesarea and His Reading of Revelation: Catechesis and Paranesis," *Die Johannesapokalypse: Kontexte und Konzepte*, ed. Jörg Frey James A. Kelhoffer, and Franz Tóth (Tübingen: Mohr Siebeck, 2012).

49. Juan Hernández Jr., *Scribal Habits and Theological Influences in the Apocalypse: The Singular Readings of Sinaiticus, Alexandrinus and Ephraemi* (Tübingen: Mohr Siebeck, 2006).

16

ANDREW'S POSTERITY AND CONTRIBUTIONS

Subsequent Commentaries

In the late ninth or early tenth centuries, Arethas, an episcopal successor of Andrew at the very same see of Caesarea, Cappadocia, wrote a commentary on Revelation.[1] Arethas drew heavily from Andrew's commentary, often quoting him word for word, and in other sections paraphrasing him rather than literally reproducing the passage.[2] Where Arethas copied Andrew word for word, Schmid observes that one can easily recognize the text-type of the Andreas manuscripts which Arethas used.[3] Today, the commentary of Arethas is the second most significant commentary on the Apocalypse in the Greek tradition after that of Andrew.

As discussed in chapter 3, Maximos Kalliopolites created Greek translations of various writings for use by the average laymen and priests in the ἁπλῆ γλῶσα (plain language), or vernacular Greek in the early sev-

---

1. Συλλογὴ ἐξηγήσεως ἐκ διαφόρων ἁγίων ἀνδρῶν, or according to another manuscript, Ἐκ τῶν Ἀνδρέα ... πεπονημένων σύνοψις σχολική, παρατεθεῖσα ὑπὸ Ἀρέθα. Henry Barclay Swete, *Apocalypse of John* cxci. Arethas is printed in J.-P. Migne, PG 106:487–806. See also Josef Schmid, *Untersuchungen zur Geschichte des griechischen Apokalypsetextes I. Der Apokalypse-text des Arethas von Kaisareia und einiger anderer jüngerer Gruppen.* Texte und Forschungen zur byzantinisch-neugriechischen Philologie. Num. 27 (Athens: Verlag der Byzantinisch-neugriechischen Jahrbücher, 1936).

2. Josef Schmid, *Einleitung*, 97.   3. Josef Schmid, *Einleitung*, 97.

enteenth century.[4] The educated classes did not need translations of the ancient authorities, but most spiritual writings were inaccessible to the ordinary person. It is possible that along with his translation of the Apocalypse, Maximos created an accompanying commentary.[5] The identity of the Maximos responsible for the seventeenth-century Apocalypse commentary is disputed. Ernest Colwell believes that the Maximos, author of the seventeenth century commentary, is Maximos "the Peloponnesian" and that he is one and the same individual as Maximos Kalliopolites the translator.[6] Others disagree.[7] Regardless of his identity, Maximos began the commentary as a combination of the best of Andrew and Arethas, but by the time he reached the middle of his exposition he primarily relied on Andrew and only occasionally included additional points taken from Arethas.[8] Anthimos of Jerusalem, who served as Patriarch of Jerusalem from 1788 to 1808, also wrote a commentary on the Apocalypse, the inscription of which indicates its dependence on Andrew and Arethas:

Ἑρμηνεία ὑπὸ τοῦ Ἱεροσολύμων Ἀνθίμου συλλεγεῖσα παρὰ τῶν ἁγίων πατέρων Ἀρέθα καὶ Ἀνδρέου εἰς τὴν ἱερὰν Ἀποκάλυψιν τοῦ ἁγίου, ἐνδόξου καὶ πανευφήμου ἀποστόλου καὶ εὐαγγελιστοῦ Ἰωάννου.[9]

4. There are numerous variations on the spelling, including "Kallipoli," or even "Galliopolite."

5. See Ernest Cadman Colwell and H. R. Willoughby, *The Elizabeth Day McCormick Apocalypse*, 2:4. The *Elizabeth Day McCormick Apocalypse* is one of only four manuscripts which preserve Maximos's Apocalypse commentary.

6. Ernest Cadman Colwell and H. R. Willoughby, *The Elizabeth Day McCormick Apocalypse*, 2:4.

7. Emmanuel Konstantinides states categorically that they are not the same individual. " Μάξιμος Καλλίπολι," Θρησκευτικὴ καὶ Ἠθικὴ Ἐγκυκλοπαιδεία, ed. A. Martinos, 12 vols. (Athens, 1962–68). Both Maximoses knew Cyril Loukaris, both studied in Europe and both lived during the same historical period. At this point with the information we presently have, it is not possible to determine which Maximos is responsible for the commentary on Revelation.

8. Ernest Cadman Colwell and H. R. Willoughby, *Elizabeth Day McCormick Apocalypse*, 2:120: "Maximos began his work with the intention of blending the best of Andreas and Arethas and increasing the scriptural element; that blending decreased as the work progressed, with the result that the dominant source for most of the commentary is that of Andreas." *McCormick Apocalypse*, 2:42. The same observations are made by Josef Schmid who discusses the content and manuscripts of Maximos in *Einleitung*, 97–98.

9. Josef Schmid, *Einleitung*, 99.

Translations of the Commentary

Andrew's commentary was translated into four ancient languages: Latin, Armenian, Old Slavonic, and Georgian. These early translations substantially contributed to the acceptance of Revelation into the biblical canon of the Eastern and Oriental Orthodox churches.

The commentary may have been translated into Latin before the twelfth century, as the description below of a discovery of the commentary in a Latin monastery by an Armenian archbishop seems to suggest. Schmid recounts how the Andreas commentary was translated into Armenian at the instigation of a famous figure in Armenian church history, Nerses of Lampron, Archbishop of Tarsus (d. 1198). Andrew's commentary impacted the New Testament canon for the Armenians by facilitating the acceptance of Revelation.[10] Although Armenian translations of the Apocalypse existed prior to the time of Nerses, Revelation was not widely accepted as Scripture. An epilogue written by Nerses explains the circumstances of his discovery of Andrew's commentary.

I, Nerses, poor in Christ and slothful among the lovers of study, offspring of the last and miserable time, on the reading of the Revelation of John was distressed at not knowing the solution to its amazing words. Hunting here and there for a commentary on the same in our own language, I did not find any. Afterwards I had occasion to visit the great Antioch; and as I was going around the monasteries of the Romans and Franks which were there, this desire burned in my mind. After investigation, I found among the books of the famous monastery of Saint Paul in that city the commentary on Revelation in the Lombard language, in the same script which the Franks use, composed by two authors.[11] Desiring to translate it, I found no one who could turn it from

---

10. Josef Schmid, *Einleitung*, 99.

11. Thomson explains that Nerses had found a copy of Arethas's revision of Andrew's commentary, which Thomson presumes was in Italian. Thomson, *Nerses of Lambron Commentary* 17, n. 80. This is may not be the case, partly because it is highly debatable whether Italian existed as a written language at such an early date. Nerses is clearly identifying Catholics as "Franks," a term very common among the Greeks also. Since Nerses stated that the commentary he discovered was in "the Lombard language," which he then describes as "the same script which the Franks use," this strongly indicates that the manuscript was in Latin. The

that language into Armenian. Then, going out of the city to the holy mountain on the north side, in one of the monasteries of the Romans which is called Bet'ias, I found locked up with one of the reclusive monks called Basil what I desired in the Greek language and script, well written and elegant, which had belonged to Athanasios, patriarch of that city. I requested it with entreaties from that well-disposed man, and on receiving it hastened with the book to the patriarchal throne, to my lord Catholicos, the saintly Grigorios. When he was informed of this he greatly rejoiced, and ordered it to be translated by the metropolitan of Hierapolis, Konstandeay, who was staying there under the auspices of the patriarch. With the help of God and of the holy Lord [Grigorios] we began—he to translate and I to write; and we dedicated this wonderful and divine commentary on Revelation to the studious children of the Armenian church.... This commentary to the divine Revelation was translated in 628 [1179] of the Armenian era.... But it was corrected from the copy in literary style ... by the hand of the humble bishop of that metropolis Tarsus, the miserable Nerses, through the grace and mercy of Christ, who is blessed for ever. Amen.[12]

Nerses's translation of the Andreas commentary bolstered the acceptance of Revelation among the Armenians and the commentary is preserved in approximately one hundred Armenian manuscripts.[13]

Andrew's commentary was also translated at an early date into the

---

Lombards had been heavily involved in the Crusades in and around Antioch and Catholic monasteries were established in Middle East during the Crusader period. It is far more likely that any manuscript discovered in a Catholic monastery would be written in Latin and that Nerses would recognize Latin as a common "script" for both the Franks and the Lombards. Nerses eventually found a Greek copy of Andrew's commentary in a Greek Orthodox monastery, which he calls a "Roman" monastery. Although modern historians may refer to the continuation of the Eastern Roman empire as the "Byzantine" empire, it is an artificial distinction and such a characterization was never part of the consciousness of those who lived in those lands during those centuries. Even to the present time, Greeks from Constantinople still refer to themselves as Ρωμαίοι, or "Romans."

12. Robert W. Thomson, trans., *Nerses of Lambron Commentary on the Revelation of Saint John*, Hebrew University Armenian Studies 9 (Leuven: Peeters, 2007), 17–19. The story is also told by Josef Schmid, *Einleitung*, 107–9.

13. Josef Schmid, *Einleitung*, 100, n. 1. The groundbreaking work in the area of the Armenian text of Revelation was done by Frederick Cornwallis Conybeare. See F.C. Conybeare, *The Armenian Version of Revelation and Cyril of Alexandria's Scholia* (London: Text and Translation Society, 1907).

Georgian language by St. Euthymios (Ekwthime), one of the founders of the Georgian monastery Iwiron on Mt. Athos (d. 1028).[14] Euthymios is also credited with revising the old Georgian gospel text according to Greek manuscripts and completing the Georgian New Testament.[15] Euthymios used a manuscript with the Andreas commentary as the basis for his translation of Revelation and translated both of them into Georgian.[16] This translation is preserved in several manuscripts and the two oldest were probably copied out of the original itself, according to Schmid.[17]

The oldest Georgian copies, which are as old as the oldest Greek copies, may preserve a form of the commentary no longer extant in the Greek tradition. J. Neville Birdsall noted that the Georgian version gave the entire text of Revelation first, followed by a lemmatized version of the commentary, such as the type with which we are familiar in the Greek manuscripts. None of the Greek manuscripts in existence have a prefaced continuous text of Revelation. They only present the text of Revelation in the lemmatized form, section by section, just before Andrew's comments. Birdsall believes that the Georgian tradition preserves an earlier Greek form of the commentary, which must have been in front of Euthymios when he translated the commentary. This is entirely possible since the text of Revelation is already preserved in the lemmata. It is hardly surprising that later copyists would see the prefixed continuous text as superfluous and unnecessary and would prefer to omit making copies which included the prefixed text.[18]

His impact on the acceptance of Revelation in the Slavic tradition can be seen by the fact that the oldest extant Slavic manuscript of Revelation contains a translation of Andrew's commentary in a condensed

---

14. D. M. Lang, "Recent Work on the Georgian New Testament," *Bulletin of the School of Oriental and African Studies* 19 (1957): 82–93, 86.

15. Bruce Metzger, *Canon of the New Testament*, 224.

16. Euthymios's work is not an actual translation but an abbreviated translation or paraphrase of Andrew. See J. Neville Birdsall, "'Revelation' by Euthymus the Athonite," *Beda Kartlisa* 41 (1983): 96–101, 99.

17. Josef Schmid, *Einleitung*, 113.

18. J. Neville Birdsall, "'Revelation' by Euthymus the Athonite," 98.

version, *The Nikol'skij Apocalypse Codex*, dated mid-thirteenth century. To create the abbreviated version many of the patristic quotations were removed as well as the motivational comments and doxologies at the end of each of Andrew's sections. The commentary and text of Revelation follow Andrew's divisions into twenty four main sections and seventy two smaller chapters.[19]

The Old Slavonic translation of the Andreas commentary is available in two printed editions, the latter of which is a literal copy of the older one. The first edition was produced in 1625 and the heading of the older edition reads:

Our holy father Andreas, Archbishop of Caesarea Cappadocia's Interpretation of the Apocalypse of the Holy Apostle and Evangelist of Christ, John the Theologian, from the Greek into the Slavic language has been translated and ordered through the will and the effort and with the blessing of the most worthy and orthodox illustrious father Cyril Zacharais Kopistenskij, through God's grace, Archimandrite of the Cave Monastery in Kiev. Printed for the first time and issued in the Holy Great Cave Monastery at Kiev, of the Stavropege of the holy Ecumenical Patriarch of Constantinople, in the year of the creation of the world 7133, since the appearance of the Word of God 1625 in the 9th Indiction.[20]

Artistic Depictions of the Apocalypse

Andrew's commentary was so influential that it even impacted an unexpected arena: the artistic representations of the Apocalypse. The *Elizabeth Day McCormick Apocalypse* is an illustrated seventeenth-century manuscript of the commentary by the unidentified Maximos. If he is Maximos Kalliopolites, he may have written the commentary to accompany his translation of the Apocalypse in the Greek vernacular. Only four copies remain of the Maximos commentary. One is the *Elizabeth Day McCormick Apocalypse* manuscript, which contains the

---

19. Thomas Hilary Oller, "The Nikol'skij Apocalypse Codex and its Place in the Textual History of Medieval Slavic Apocalypse Manuscripts," (Ph.D. diss., Brown University, 1993).

20. Josef Schmid, *Einleitung*, 114. I am indebted to Dr. John Fendrick for the translation.

most extensive set of Greek images of Revelation, sixty-nine miniature scenes in all. Most titles of the scenes are taken from the chapter headings of Andrew's commentary.[21] Russian-illustrated Apocalypses also reflect influence from the Andreas commentary. The Russian series of scenes were planned and organized to employ the same chapter headings as those of Andrew and to illustrate those headings and divisions.[22] For almost every one of the McCormick miniatures, a thematic counterpart exists in the Russian Apocalypse manuscripts.[23]

Preservation of Early Traditions

Andrew's broad outlook and inclusive style has resulted in a commentary which preserved the entire Eastern tradition of Apocalypse interpretation. He generously reported opinions with which he did not agree.[24] Had Oikoumenios's commentary not survived, Andrew would have preserved many of his opinions as well. Andrew preserves numerous anonymous opinions and traditional views, many of which would have otherwise been entirely lost.[25] Andrew preserved a fragment of Papias regarding the fall of some of the angels,[26] and other patristic comments interpreting Revelation and traditions regarding the end times.[27]

Andrew also preserves Papias as the earliest witness to the tradition of apostolic authorship of the Apocalypse, and cites Papias as one of the authorities who accepted the Johannine authorship of Rev-

21. Ernest Cadman Colwell and H. R. Willoughby, *McCormick Apocalypse*, 2:143–44.
22. Ernest Cadman Colwell and H. R. Willoughby, *McCormick Apocalypse*, 1:160–61.
23. Ernest Cadman Colwell and H. R. Willoughby, *McCormick Apocalypse*, 1:161, citing F. I. Buslaev, *The Russian Illustrated Apocalypse* (in Russian, Moscow, 1884), and *An Apocalypse with Three Exegeses* (Old Believers Printing Shop, Moscow, 1910).
24. See chapter 8.
25. See chapter 10, which lists eighteen unidentified sources or traditional opinions preserved by Andrew.
26. Andrew, Chap. 34, *Comm.* 142–43.
27. For Andrew's preservation of Hippolytus traditions, see Pierre Prigent and Ralph Stehly, "Les fragments du De Apocalypsi d'Hippolyte," *Theologische Zeitschrift* 29 (1973): 315–33, 315–16.

elation.[28] Particularly noteworthy about the list of authorities Andrew provides for the "trustworthiness" of Revelation—Gregory the Theologian, Cyril (of Alexandria), Papias, Irenaeus, Methodios, and Hippolytus—is that it is not a list of those who accepted the book as Scripture, but those who specifically state that the book was composed by John the Apostle and Evangelist. The mention of Gregory the Theologian is at first surprising because Gregory does not list the Apocalypse in his canon, and only cites Revelation on a couple of occasions, something which Andrew must have known. Nonetheless, Gregory is included among those who attest to the "trustworthiness" of the book, because in one of his two references to Revelation Gregory mentions John as the author. It is in this context that the inclusion of Papias on the list is especially important, since Papias's work *Exposition of Dominical Oracles*, which contained many early and apostolic traditions, no longer exists. Andrew had a copy of it, and because he cites Papias as supporting Johannine authorship, through Andrew, we indirectly have the earliest tradition of apostolic authorship of Revelation.[29]

Andrew's commentary is also a witness to the speedy acceptance of the writings of the mysterious author, Dionysios the Aeropagite, or Pseudo-Dionysios, whom Andrew refers to admiringly as "Dionysios the Great" and cites on four occasions.[30] Maximos the Confessor is often credited with reinterpreting and rehabilitating Pseudo-Dionysios (whose theology is highly philosophical) and paving the way for the general acceptance of Pseudo-Dionysios's writings. But Andrew's commentary is strong evidence that Pseudo-Dionysios was already generally accepted by the early seventh century, before Maximos the Confessor even began to produce his writings. Andrew was far more careful than Oikoumenios to use recognized, accepted and uncontroversial ec-

---

28. Andrew, Prologue, *Comm*. 53.

29. This is supported by a Papias fragment prefixed to a manuscript on the gospel of John, which Benjamin Bacon believed to have been originally intended for Revelation, "Adhuc in Corpore Constituto," *Harvard Theological Review* 23 (1930): 305–7. Bacon's arguments are very persuasive.

30. Andrew, Chap. 10, *Comm*. 84; Chap. 28, *Comm*. 128; Chap. 45, *Comm*. 166; Chap. 34, *Comm*. 235.

clesiastical authorities, that is, "Fathers." Andrew presented himself as "more orthodox" than Oikoumenios, not only by his exegetical conclusions but also by the sources he chose to use and those which he intentionally omitted from citation. Unlike Oikoumenios, Andrew avoided Greek pagan sources and any authorities which were questionable in even the slightest degree, such as Shepherd of Hermas, Clement of Alexandria, or Evagrius Ponticus.

Oikoumenios never cites Dionysios, and we cannot know why, but Andrew does and his use of Dionysios is significant. Since Andrew only cites universally recognized authorities, he would never have used Dionysios in his commentary unless he knew that Dionysios was widely accepted within the Church at that time. Maximos the Confessor's writings no doubt contributed to Pseudo-Dionysios's approval, but Andrew's commentary provides strong evidence that Maximos the Confessor was not responsible this widespread acceptance. It is clear that Dionysios was already thoroughly mainstreamed into the patristic tradition by the early seventh century; otherwise Andrew would not have cited him. Furthermore, as the popularity of Andrew's commentary spread, especially in translation, his use of Pseudo-Dionysios alongside other recognizable and universally respected Fathers could not help but promote Pseudo-Dionysios in other parts of the Christian East as a genuine and ancient patristic authority.

Facilitating Acceptance of Revelation into the Canon

The greatest contribution which Andrew made, other than the preservation of Eastern Christian Apocalypse interpretation, was to pave the way for the unanimous acceptance of Revelation into the canon of the Orthodox Church. Andrew's commentary is undoubtedly responsible for the eventual acceptance of Revelation into the New Testament canon of the Churches of Armenia, Georgia, and Russia.

The Nerses translation of Andrew's commentary includes a foreword which recounts the reception of the commentary by an Armenian synod held in Constantinople under "Thetalios" of Constantinople, leading to the acceptance of Revelation into the Armenian canon.[31] The date of the synod is not clear, nor the precise participants, nor the identity of "Thetalios." Nonetheless, the statement of Nerses is quite interesting. He begins the foreword by stating: "On the demand of the general synod held in the God-Preserved city of Constantinople, the Revelation of John was recognized as canonical, but also the investigation about it which happened through the bishops of Caesarea" (no doubt referring to the commentaries of Andrew and Arethas).

Nerses then quotes the words of Thetalios in support of Revelation:

This writing of the Revelation of John has been received among the other apostolic writings which the Church possesses on the basis of the testing and determining of my brothers and holy-collaborating bishops. And it is without mistake and is to be accepted because it contains the wisdom of God which brings the greatest help or usefulness to those who consider it with the eyes of the spirit as a true gift of the Holy Spirit which one may not disregard. It is however, also not un-genuine, as it was supposed by some wicked men. Much more, it is really by the Son of Thunder, that is St. John, because we believe the words of Athanasius of Alexandria, the great patriarch.[32]

Thetalios lists several other patristic witnesses and patristic writings which used or confirmed the Apocalypse, including Basil, Gregory of Nyssa, Gregory the Theologian, Cyril of Alexandria, and Hippolytus. Thetalios continues, saying, "We do not want to make a lot of words, although we have still other witnesses that agree with them among the holy Fathers who confirm that this Revelation is by the Evangelist John," including Irenaeus and others before him, and even the "thrice-ailing Origen."[33] Thetalios then gives his rationale for accepting Revelation:

---

31. Josef Schmid, *Einleitung*, 102, n. 2 states that the name "Thetalios" is found in patristic certifications in an Armenian list of translations published in Constantinople in 1717 of the works of Cyril of Alexandria and that Thetalios is also mentioned in a letter by Nerses.
32. Josef Schmid, *Einleitung*, 102. Translation by Dr. John Fendrick.
33. Josef Schmid, *Einleitung*, 103.

If we approach this Revelation with mistrust then we despise the saints who cleansed the world of bad schisms, and they have made a testimony about it. For if these are seen to be rejected by us then also those who have accepted it would have to be rejected. Far be it to think this! ... Therefore, I also, the poor Thetalios and the holy synod that was with me, have accepted this Apocalypse into the catholic Church with honor as also a true revelation, but that also the examination of the explanation which was composed by Andrew the Archbishop of Caesarea was accepted by this synod, not out of himself but on the foundation of the Fathers he made the construction of his words and whose gift of the Spirit he has taken as his guide and witness in his investigations. Therefore this investigation, which the bishop of Caesarea has made concerning the Revelation, has been taken into our catholic Church on the conclusion and witnessing of the general synod.[34]

As the Nerses foreword continues, Nerses reveals that he did not merely translate Andrew's commentary but considerably reworked it. The title given in the foreword is: "The Apocalypse of the Evangelist John, a short explanation of our holy father Andrew, blessed Bishop of Caesarea, Cappadocia, and with him Arethas, bishop of the same city."[35] Schmid explains that the translated portions are a translation of the Andreas commentary, but also notes those places where Nerses offered his own interpretation in addition.[36] Schmid also observes that although the title mentions Arethas, not a trace of Arethas is to be found in the commentary. Therefore, Schmid concludes that the inclusion of the name of Arethas in the title does not go back to Nerses himself.[37]

As in the case of the Armenians, who did not accept Revelation into the canon until Nerses translated the Andreas commentary into Armenian, the Apocalypse was similarly excluded from the canon of the Georgian Church until the translation of the text of Revelation and the

---

34. Josef Schmid, *Einleitung*, 103–4. Translation by Dr. John Fendrick.

35. Josef Schmid, *Einleitung*, 104.

36. Josef Schmid, *Einleitung*, 109–10. Robert Thomson discusses these features in greater detail in his recent translation and publication of the Nerses commentary, *Commentary on the Revelation of Saint John* (Leuven: Peeters, 2007).

37. Josef Schmid, *Einleitung*, 110.

commentary of Andrew were made to the Georgian language by St. Euthymios (Ekwthime).[38] Euthymios's work on the Book of Revelation would have been completed sometime before 987, which is the date of the earliest known Georgian manuscript of the Apocalypse.[39] According to Robert Blake, the Apocalypse, "strictly speaking, never became canonical among the Georgians."[40] Blake did not explain what he meant by the comment, but if by "canonical" Blake meant "read during Church services," the same can be said of the status of Revelation for all of the Eastern Orthodox Churches since to this day it remains excluded from the lectionary.

In the Slavonic tradition, the second edition of Andrew's commentary, (dated 1768 and bound with homilies by St John Chrysostom), has two forewords. The first is dedicated to the bishop, Gregory Dolmat, but the second is dedicated to the reader.[41] This second foreword discusses the content, the author and the value of the Apocalypse as well as the occasion for the publication of the translation. It presents different views of the Fathers on the authorship of the Apocalypse, and also mentions the ancient opposition to Revelation which claimed it was a forgery by the heretic Cerinthus.[42] The conclusion of the foreword indicates the importance of the commentary of Andrew of Caesarea for the acceptance of the Apocalypse among the Russians:

> The views of those explainers are acceptable to the Church, which holds fast to the authorship of the apostle John. One of these is Andreas of Caesarea. The book was printed so that it might work with the homilies of the blessed John Chrysostom through its content for the Orthodox Church. It is useful then for every Orthodox Christian.[43]

Although Andrew's commentary prompted the inclusion of Revelation into the canons of the Armenian, Georgian, and Russian church-

---

38. D. M. Lang, "Recent Work on the Georgian New Testament," 86.
39. Bruce Metzger, *Canon of the New Testament*, 224.
40. Robert Blake, "The Caesarean Text of the Gospel of Mark," *Harvard Theological Review* 21 [1928]: 287. Bruce Metzger, *Canon of the New Testament*, 224, n. 37.
41. Josef Schmid, *Einleitung*, 116.   42. See chapter 2.
43. Josef Schmid, *Einleitung*, 116. Translation by Dr. John Fendrick.

es, the Book of Revelation remained largely unaccepted in the Greek East even centuries after Andrew's commentary was penned. The first evidence that the tide was beginning to turn in favor of the Apocalypse comes as a notation by the Byzantine historian Nikephoros Kallistos in the fourteenth century.[44] Renewed interest in the Apocalypse was evident in Orthodox circles after the fall of Constantinople in 1453 and the subjugation of Eastern Christians under Ottoman Turkish rule. "[O]nce the Greeks under Turkish rule found themselves in a social and political position comparable to that of the early Christians under Roman rule, their attitude toward the Revelation of John changed entirely. Late-Greek interest in the Christian Apocalypse suddenly became as keen and vivacious as it had earlier been dull."[45] The number of Apocalypse manuscripts sharply increased during this period, followed by a vernacular translation of the Apocalypse by Maximos Kalliopolites into the common Greek of his day.

Certainly, the experience of persecution and martyrdom lived by Greek Orthodox Christians under Turkish rule stimulated interest in the Apocalypse. But that interest alone may not have been enough to result in universal recognition of Revelation as Scripture were it not for Andrew of Caesarea's commentary. Historical circumstances alone would likely not have propelled the Apocalypse, long viewed with suspicion, indisputably into the New Testament canon without support by a patristic authority. Andrew made the Book of Revelation acceptable by providing a sober, sound, and patristic interpretation, entirely orthodox in doctrine, spirituality and style, which led to its ultimate acceptance.

---

44. Ernest Cadman Colwell and H.R. Willoughby, *McCormick Apocalypse*, 1: 93, citing Nikephorus Kallistos, *Ecclesiastical History*, 2.45.

45. Ernest Cadman Colwell and H.R. Willoughby, *McCormick Apocalypse*, 2: 143.

17

CONCLUSION

It is difficult to know which of the accomplishments of Andrew of Caesarea are more impressive or more important: his exposition of the text of Revelation, his contribution toward preserving the past, or the subsequent impact of his commentary.

Extremely impressive are his cool, almost detached, objectivity and his conviction that in spite of the calamities of his times the end of the world had not yet arrived. He based his conclusion on his skillful interpretation of the Apocalypse. Rather than performing *eisegesis*—reading the events of his times *into* the text—he accomplished true *exegesis*, drawing the meaning *out of* the text to offer a very balanced and intelligent commentary free of hysteria, hype, exaggeration or fear-mongering. The commentary was composed in 611, during the horrific circumstances of the early seventh century Eastern Roman empire—plague, earthquake, famine, civil war, and a Persian invasion which decimated the empire, destroying countless leading cities. The climate within the empire was truly apocalyptic and Andrew had received many requests to explain the Apocalypse. But he did not undertake the composition of this commentary until compelled to do so by the mysterious "Makarios," who is most likely Sergius I, Patriarch of Constantinople, the only individual of higher ranking than Andrew in his ecclesiastical jurisdiction and a known patron of writers. During his episcopal tenure

Sergius I had encouraged literary activity, but more importantly, he changed the course of history and saved the empire along with Emperor Heraclius. When the empire was fighting invaders on all fronts and all appeared lost, Heraclius battled the Persians in the Eastern areas while Sergius rallied the people against the Avars and Slavs who were besieging the walls of Constantinople. The considerable strength and resolve of Sergius to fight off the invaders must have found confirmation in the Apocalypse commentary of Andrew of Caesarea. By his knowledgeable and careful interpretation of Revelation, Andrew had concluded that the end of the world was not near in spite of the challenging circumstances the empire was facing and contrary to the prevailing opinions of the day. Andrew would be proven right.

A Greek commentary on the Apocalypse already existed, composed only a few years earlier by Oikoumenios. That commentary was unacceptable for numerous reasons, but it was circulating. Oikoumenios was a Miaphysite who rejected the Fourth and Fifth Ecumenical Councils. Oikoumenios used the commentary to support and promote Miaphysite theological positions. The Book of Revelation was attracting a great deal of attention due to the historical circumstances of the time and the ensuing apocalyptic fervor. Oikoumenios's exposition was the only Greek commentary on the Apocalypse and people were reading it. His interpretation of the Apocalypse and his theological comments required a response by an educated and capable Chalcedonian representative.

Oikoumenios's swipe at Chalcedonian theology was only one of the commentary's flaws. His conclusions were spiritually and pastorally troublesome as well. Oikoumenios wavered on the question of eternal punishment, stating that he accepted the traditional view of the Church, but elsewhere he offered reasons why punishment might not be eternal. Oikoumenios relied on his imagination for many conclusions in his commentary, which certainly fell outside the mainstream of Eastern Christian tradition and methodology. Oikoumenios's commentary also failed to interpret Revelation as prophecy, since he expounded Revelation primarily as symbols from the life of Christ and as allegorical descriptions of suffering in hell, not as actual descriptions of destruction destined to occur at the end times. Oikoumenios also had a peculiar tendency to interpret literally details in Revelation which should have been understood symbolically or theologically, and to allegorically dismiss many important details describing the end, often resulting in odd and even conflicting conclusions. Oikoumenios's commentary neither provided a spiritual response to the current challenges facing the empire nor resolved the pressing question of the day: whether the end of the world had indeed arrived.

Andrew of Caesarea expertly dealt with the symbolic language of Revelation, interpreting literally what was intended to be understood literally, and providing appropriate theological meaning for the symbols. Through Andrew's skilled exegesis, the book unfolded in a consistent and logical manner. As a bishop, Andrew was concerned that his flock not become complacent or spiritually lazy. He also explained why the end was not near for the world, yet it is always near for each of us individually since we never know the day or hour of our death. The commentary is infused with inspirational pastoral advice to engage in the true warfare, against the devil, since defeat by him brings eternal death. The work also radiates with the liturgical and sacramental orientation of the author who sees in the Apocalypse the promise of salvation and eternal life for those who are sealed with the life-giving Cross and who have a heavenly orientation. These are true Christians, sealed and illumined with the divine light on their foreheads, not those who are merely baptized but those who live a virtuous life. They will not escape the trials of the end times, but they will recognize the Antichrist when he comes and will not be fooled by his deceptions. They will refuse to accept his mark and will be persecuted. But through perseverance they will ultimately prevail, if only through death.

Andrew began his work with little existing Apocalypse interpretive tradition in the East preceding him, and no complete Greek commentary other than that of Oikoumenios. Andrew certainly benefitted from having Oikoumenios's commentary before him and he adopted and restated some of Oikoumenios's comments. But Andrew did not rely on Oikoumenios for his commentary since he departed from Oikoumenios on countless occasions and on very important points of interpretation. Unlike Oikoumenios, Andrew's commentary is orderly, disciplined, and logical. Furthermore, Andrew is far more skilled and theologically educated than Oikoumenios, a fact that is obvious throughout commentary. Andrew is aware of different levels of meaning in Revelation and draws them out in an appropriate manner, including the historical meaning, the moral message, which is his most common observation, and the spiritual level of theological insight and the future life in the kingdom of heaven. Andrew analyzes the Apocalypse using the methodology and techniques of a trained interpreter of scripture, including awareness of the author's original purpose, attention to the sequence of events and statements, and the context of a passage. He also demonstrates knowledge of how a word or image was used elsewhere in the Bible and applies that to his interpretation of Revelation where appropriate. As a result Andrew's opinions are sound and consistent within his own commentary, in harmony with the Bible and Revelation itself, and in accordance with theology and tradition of the Church.

It is a great benefit to us and to the history of biblical interpretation that Andrew was tremendously open-minded and remarkably inclusive in his commentary. Even though he had his own opinion as to the meaning of a passage, Andrew freely and generously reported the opinions of others, even when he did not agree. His willingness to share other opinions, usually leaving his own for last, demonstrates confidence in his own abilities and conclusions. Some of the other opinions he shares come to us in the form of nameless "teachers." The most commonly unnamed source, and who is not identified as a "teacher," is Oikoumenios. Respected sources are named, such as Hippolytus, Methodios, and Irenaeus, and Andrew perceives himself as in line with the patristic tradition, echoing those "patristic voices." Indeed he was.

Andrew composed the commentary in the nick of time, during the era which would prove to be the final moments of Late Antiquity. The empire would change forever in the seventh century. Not long after defeating the Persians, the empire would face the Arab and then the Muslim invasions. Countless books were lost forever. Had Andrew not written his commentary when he did, what remained of early Greek Apocalypse traditions might have been lost permanently. Because of his broad style, his willingness to report every known opinion, Andrew preserved virtually the entire Greek tradition. Andrew carefully gathered these scraps of older Eastern Apocalypse interpretation, organized them, and added his own analysis and conclusions to create a beautiful "patchwork quilt" of Greek Apocalypse interpretation which has stood the test of time.

Had Andrew been an exegete of less skill or spiritual experience, he undoubtedly would have read the events of his time into the Apocalypse and concluded that the end was near. Indeed, it was difficult to fix a date for the commentary because Andrew provides few clues to his own times. Had Andrew applied the text to his own times, his commentary would have been a snapshot of a grim era in history. It would also have become irrelevant with the passage of time and it may not even have survived. The commentary has not only survived but flourished, enduring in popularity partly because it rises above its own historical circumstances to present an interpretation of Revelation that is thoughtful, balanced, spiritual, and suits all times.

Eastern Christians who read the commentary recognize in his allusions and quotations the same prayers, sacraments, hymns, liturgy, practices, theology, moral advice that they know in the Orthodox Church today. The topic of the eschaton can be troubling and disquieting, but the commentary feels "comfortable." The language and opinions it expresses are familiar, even "contemporary," quite extraordinary for such an ancient commentary. Andrew expresses classic Orthodox ideas and theology. The Church is one Church, Militant and Triumphant, human and angelic. The liturgy below reflects the ongoing worship in heaven above: altar, incense, sacraments, angels, saints, and hymns.

God, the Lamb and the Holy Spirit offer the promise of eternal life, which is realized through synergy: the cooperation between each human being and God to achieve that individual's salvation. It is not necessary for any soul to be lost, but those who pursue punishment by their manner of life will receive it. It is God's will that all people be saved and come to knowledge of the truth but He never interferes with the exercise of human free will. The dominant description of God, the Holy Trinity, and Christ in Andrew's commentary is also characteristic of Eastern theology: God/Christ is *philanthropos*, the one who loves humankind. Andrew's emphasis on the love of God, even as God sends plagues during the final days for the reformation and salvation of sinners, reflects Andrew's pastoral orientation and his hopes for his own congregation. Also dominant in the commentary are the many reminders of the promised blessings and delights of the kingdom of heaven, descriptions which give the commentary a hopeful and positive tone, even creating an almost optimistic view of Revelation itself in spite of its descriptions of plagues and destruction.

Andrew's final accomplishment, the subsequent impact of his commentary, cannot be overstated. Herman Hoskier, who brought Oikoumenios's commentary to light and published it in a massive work, believed Oikoumenios's contribution to be highly significant, if for no other reason than its rarity. As the first Greek commentary on Revelation, the Oikoumenios commentary is unquestionably important. But Hoskier dismissed Andrew's commentary as "terribly commonplace" and did not even consider the Andreas text-type of Revelation worthy of being catalogued.[1] He failed to recognize that rarity does not necessarily equate with value. Andrew's commentary was "commonplace" because it was popular. Furthermore, it was popular because it was

---

1. "[A]nyone who is at all familiar with Andreas, whose commentary is terribly commonplace, will soon accord to Oecumenius a superior position in these studies. Oecumenius, although most uneven in the value of his expositions, is always vigorous, and at times very interesting." Oikoumenios, *The Complete Commentary of Oecumenius on the Apocalypse*, ed. Herman Charles Hoskier, University of Michigan Humanistic Studies 22 (Ann Arbor: University of Michigan, 1928), 4–5.

recognized century after century as a well done, effective, and thoroughly patristic exposition of a difficult book. In an age before copiers and printers, Andrew's commentary was copied and recopied because it was excellent, meaningful, and relevant. The long hours of arduous labor required to copy texts and the scarcity and expense of the materials meant that copyists invested their efforts on the best and most important texts.

The commentary circulated along with the text of the Apocalypse in a large portion of the Greek Apocalypse manuscripts because it was useful, sensible, orderly, ecclesiastically and theologically sound, and orthodox in thought as well as style. The dramatic disparity between the number of surviving manuscripts of Oikoumenios and Andrew—only one complete manuscript of Oikoumenios versus more than eighty-three of Andrew—is ample demonstration of the quality of Andrew's work, the value it holds in the Christian East and the esteem with which it has been regarded in the Orthodox Church for centuries.

Andrew's commentary is thoughtful and academic, yet also spiritual and ecclesial in demeanor. Andrew exudes an air of episcopal dignity and demonstrates a commendable respect for the text. His division of the commentary into twenty four main sections, each ending in a doxology, along with his emphasis on the spiritual lesson in a passage, gives the work the flavor of a series of sermons. Despite the serious and sober nature of the Book of Revelation and the many descriptions of disasters and punishments, the commentary succeeds in conveying a positive tone of hope and optimism. His emphasis is on the love of God for all humankind and his conviction that everyone is capable of choosing to be saved shines through brilliantly. Ever mindful of his responsibilities as a pastor, he takes the opportunity to offer not only didactic but also paranetic comments aimed at the spiritual edification and improvement of the reader. At times he seems genuinely inspired by the text and in turn he inspires the reader. It has rightly been noted that Andrew's work, for all practical purposes, was the last Greek patristic commentary, since Arethas was heavily dependent on Andrew, and Arethas is considered to be of distant secondary importance. Later commentaries consisted almost entirely of selections taken from Andrew with a few modifications and additions from Arethas.

Andrew's commentary gained a preeminence in the East that remains unparalleled among any Scripture commentaries on Revelation or any other commentary in the Eastern tradition, for that matter, since it is unrivaled in its impact and influence. No single commentary has so decisively impacted the interpretation and acceptance of any single of book of the Bible. In fact, no other ancient commentary on Revelation exists for the Orthodox Church. Its importance for the Eastern Church cannot be overstated. In time, Andrew's commentary led to increased recognition of Revelation and its eventual acceptance into the Georgian, Armenian, and Russian Orthodox canons, and finally, into the canon of the Greek Orthodox Church. Its popularity even influenced the manuscript tradition of the text of Revelation itself, as at least one third of all existing manuscripts of Revelation contain Andrew's commentary. The large number of Andreas' commentary manuscripts helped Josef Schmid define the text of Revelation.

Andrew of Caesarea accomplished all of his goals. Writing in a terrifying age of violence, famine, pestilence, and war, when the genuine fear of an impending end of days loomed in the minds of many, Andrew composed a commentary of wisdom and deep spiritual insight. Andrew wrote his commentary to support the canonical acceptance of Revelation. He wrote to provide an orthodox alternative to Oikoumenios's commentary, motivated either by his own concerns or by those of "Makarios." He wrote to reassure his readers that the end of the world was not near, in spite of their troubling and challenging times. Regardless of the times in which we live, the end of the world will come for each of us soon enough, but God who loves humankind is always present and does everything possible for our salvation. Andrew wrote because he believed that the lessons of Revelation were spiritually beneficial for the faithful. He wrote so the Apocalypse would be read by them, guiding them all to a blessed end. He was far more successful than he could ever have imagined.

SELECTED BIBLIOGRAPHY

Primary Sources

Ambrose of Milan. *Exposition of the Holy Gospel According to St. Luke*, and *Fragments on the Prophecy of Isaiah*. Translated by Theodosia Tomkinson. Etna, Calif.: Center for Traditionalist Orthodox Studies, 1998.

Andrew of Caesarea. *Der Apokalypse-Kommentar des Andreas von Kaisareia*. Edited by Josef Schmid. Vol. 1 of *Studien zur Geschichte des griechischen Apokalypse-Textes*. 3 parts. München: Karl Zink Verlag, 1955–56.

———. *Commentary on the Apocalypse*. Translated by Eugenia Scarvelis Constantinou. FOTC 123. Washington, D.C.: The Catholic University of America Press, 2011.

Antiochus Strategios. *Account of the Sack of Jerusalem*. Translated by F. C. Conybeare. "The Capture of Jerusalem by the Persians in 614 AD." *English Historical Review* 25 (1910): 502–17.

Augustine of Hippo. *Augustine, Sermons on the Liturgical Seasons*. Translated by Mary Sarah Muldowney. Fathers of the Church 38. New York: Fathers of the Church, 1959.

———. *Augustine, Tractates on the Gospel of John*. 4 vols. Translated by John W. Rettig. FOTC 78, 79, 88, and 90. Washington, D.C.: The Catholic University of America Press, 1988–94.

Basil the Great. *On the Six Days of Creation*. In *Basil: Exegetic Homilies*, translated by Agnes Clare Way. FOTC 46. Washington, D.C.: The Catholic University of America Press, 1963.

Chronicon Paschale. Edited by L. Dindorf. Corpus scriptorum historiae byzantinae, 1832.

Chronicon Paschale. Translated by Michael Whitby and Mary Whitby. Translated Texts for Historians 7. Liverpool: Liverpool University Press, 1989.

Dionysios Bar Salibi. *Dionysius Bar Salibi In Apocalypsim, Actus et Epistulas catholicas*. Translated by I. Sedlacek. Corpus scriptorum christianorum orientalium. Scriptores Syri 101. Rome: de Luigi, 1910.

Epiphanios of Salamis. *De duodecim gemmis*. PG 43, 293–366.

———. *The Panarion of St. Epiphanius, Bishop of Salamis*. Translated by Philip R. Amidon. Oxford: Oxford University Press, 1990.
Eusebius of Caesarea. *Eusebius: The Ecclesiastical History*. 2 vols. Vol. 1 translated by Kirsopp Lake. Vol. 2 translated by J. E. L. Oulton. LCL 153 and 265. Cambridge, Mass.: Harvard University Press, 1926 and 1932, repr. 1998 and 1994.
———. *Reply to Hierocles*. In *Contra Hieroclem. Philostratus: Apollonius of Tyana*, translated by Christopher P. Jones. 3 vols. LCL 16, 17, and 458. Cambridge, Mass.: Harvard University Press, 2005–6.
Gregory the Great. *Morals on the Book of Job*. 4 vols. Translated by Members of the English Church. LF 18, 21, 23, and 31. Oxford: John Henry Parker, 1844–50.
Gregory of Nyssa. *Commentary on the Inscriptions of the Psalms*. In *Gregory of Nyssa's Treatise on the Inscriptions of the Psalms*, translated by Ronald E. Heine. Oxford: Clarendon Press, 1995.
Gregory Palamas. *The Homilies*. Edited and translated by Christopher Veniamin. Waymart, Penn.: Mt. Thabor Publishing, 2009.
Hippolytus of Rome. *On Christ and Antichrist*. In *Extant Works and Fragments of Hippolytus: Dogmatical and Historical*, translated by S. D. F. Salmond. *Fathers of the Third Century*. ANF 5. Grand Rapids, Mich.: Eerdmans, repr. 1990.
Irenaeus. *Against Heresies*. In *The Apostolic Fathers with Justin Martyr and Irenaeus*, translated and edited by Alexander Roberts and James Donaldson. ANF 1. Grand Rapids, Mich.: Eerdmans, repr. 1989.
Jerome. *Jerome's Commentary on Daniel*. Translated by Gleason L. Archer, Jr. Grand Rapids, Mich.: Baker Book House, 1958.
———. *Epistles*. In *The Principle Works of St. Jerome*, translated by W. H. Fremantle. Edited by Philip Schaff and Henry Wace. NPNF² 6. Grand Rapids, Mich.: Eerdmans, repr. 1989.
———. *On Illustrious Men*. In *Theodoret, Jerome, Gennadius, & Rufinus: Historical Writings*, edited by Philip Schaff and Henry Wace. NPNF² 3. Grand Rapids, Mich.: Eerdmans, repr. 1989.
John Chrysostom. *Homilies on Matthew*. In *St. Chrysostom: Homilies on the Gospel of Matthew*, translated by George Prevost. NPNF¹ 10. Grand Rapids, Mich.: Eerdmans, repr. 1989.
Justin Martyr. *The Writings of Saint Justin Martyr*. Translated by Thomas B. Falls. FOTC 6. New York: Christian Heritage, 1948.
———. *Dialogue with Trypho*. In *The Apostolic Fathers with Justin Martyr and Irenaeus*, translated by M. Dods and G. Reith. Edited by Alexander Roberts and James Donaldson. ANF 1. Grand Rapids, Mich.: Eerdmans, repr. 1989.
Methodios of Olympos. *The Symposium: A Treatise on Chastity*. Translated by Herbert Musurillo. Ancient Christian Writers 27. Westminster, Md.: The Newman Press, 1958.

Oikoumenios. *The Complete Commentary of Oecumenius on the Apocalypse*. Edited by H[erman] C[harles] Hoskier. University of Michigan Humanistic Studies 22. Ann Arbor: University of Michigan, 1928.

———. *Commentary on the Apocalypse*. In *Oecumenii Commentarius in Apocalypsin*, edited by Marc De Groote. Traditio Exegetica Graeca 8. Louvain: Peeters, 1999.

———. *Oecumenius Commentary on the Apocalypse*. Translated by John N. Suggit. FOTC 112. Washington, D.C.: The Catholic University of America Press, 2006.

Papias. *Fragments*. In *The Apostolic Fathers*, translated by Bart Ehrman. Edited by Jeffrey Henderson. LCL 24 and 25. Cambridge, Mass.: Harvard University Press, 2003.

Pseudo-Dionysios. *The Celestial Hierarchy*. In *Pseudo-Dionysius: The Complete Works*, translated by Colm Luibheid. Classics of Western Spirituality. New York: Paulist Press, 1987.

———. *The Ecclesiastical Hierarchy*. In *Pseudo-Dionysius: The Complete Works*, translated by Colm Luibheid. Classics of Western Spirituality. New York: Paulist Press, 1987.

Sebeos. *The Armenian History Attributed to Sebeos*. Translated with notes by R. W. Thomson. Historical Commentary by James Howard-Johnston. Translated Texts for Historians 31. Liverpool: Liverpool University Press, 1999.

Tertullian. *Against Marcion*. Translated by Peter Holmes. In *Latin Christianity: Its Founder, Tertullian*, edited by Alan Menzies. ANF 3. Grand Rapids, Mich.: Eerdmans, repr. 1989.

Theodore Syncellus, *Homily*. In *Theodore Syncellus*, edited by L. Sternback. *Analecta Avarica*. Cracow, 1900.

Theophanes. *Chronographia*. In *Theophanis Chronographia*, edited by Carl de Boor. 2 vols. Leipzig: Teubneri, 1883, 1885.

———. *The Chronicle of Theophanes*. Translated by Harry Turtledove. Philadelphia: University of Pennsylvania Press, 1982.

———. *Chronicle of Theophanes Confessor*. Translated by Cyril Mango and Roger Scott. Oxford: Clarendon Press, 1997.

Theophylact Simocatta. *History*. In *The History of Theophylact Simocatta*, translated by Michael and Mary Whitby. Oxford: Clarendon Press, 1986.

Victorinus. *Commentary on the Apocalypse*. In *Lactantius, Venantius, Asterius, Victorinus, Dionysius, Apostolic Teaching and Constitutions, Homily and Liturgies*, translated by Robert Ernest Wallis, edited by Alexander Roberts and James Donaldson. ANF 7. Grand Rapids, Mich: Eerdmans, 1975.

Victorin de Poetovio Sur l'Apocalypse, translated by M. Dulaey. Sources chrétiennes 423. Paris: Les Éditions du Cerf, 1997.

Secondary Sources

Ackroyd, P. R., ed. *From the Beginnings to Jerome.* Vol. 1 of *Cambridge History of the Bible.* Cambridge: Cambridge University Press, 1970.

Agourides, Savvas. Ἡ Ἀποκάλυψις τοῦ Ἰωάννου. Ἑρμηνεία Καινῆς Διαθήκης, vol. 18. Thessalonika: Pournaras Press, 1994.

Alexander, Paul. *The Byzantine Apocalyptic Tradition.* Edited by Dorothy Abrahamse. Berkeley: University of California Press, 1985.

Argyriou, Asterios. *Les exégèses grecques de l' Apocalypse à l'epoque turque (1453–1821).* Σειρά Φιλολογική καὶ Θεολογική 15. Thessalonika: Hetaireia Makedonikon Spoudon, 1982.

Aune, David E. *Prophecy in Early Christianity and the Ancient Mediterranean World.* Grand Rapids, Mich.: Eerdmans, 1984.

———. *Revelation.* 3 vols. Word Biblical Commentary 52A, 52B, and 52C. Nashville: Nelson Reference and Electronic, 1997.

Bacon, Benjamin. "Adhuc in Corpore Constituto." *Harvard Theological Review* 23 (1930): 305–7.

Bibliotheca Hagiographica Graeca. 3rd ed. 3 vols. in 1. Edited by François Halkin Brussels: Société des Bollandistes, 1957.

Birdsall, J. N. "The Text of the Revelation of S. John." *Evangelical Quarterly* 33 (1961): 228–37.

———. " 'Revelation' by Euthymus the Athonite." *Beda Kartlisa* 41 (1983): 96–101.

Blake, Robert P. "The Caesarean Text of the Gospel of Mark." *Harvard Theological Review* 21 (1928): 207–404.

Bonneau, Guy. *Prophétisme et institution dans le christianisme primitive.* Montréal: Médiaspaul, 1998.

Bratsiotis, Panagiotis I. Ἡ Ἀποκάλυψις τοῦ Ἀποστόλου Ἰωάννου. Athens: Synodinos, 1950.

———. "'Η Ἀποκάλυψις.'" Θρησκευτικὴ καὶ Ἠθικὴ Ἐγκυκλοπαιδεία. Edited by A. Martinos. 12 vols. Athens, 1962–68.

———. "L'Apocalypse de Saint Jean dans le culte de l'Église Grecque Orthodoxe." *Revue d'Histoire et de Philosophie Religieuses* 42 (1962): 116–21.

Brenneman, James. *Canons in Conflict.* New York: Oxford University Press, 1997.

Bruce, F. F. *The Canon of Scripture.* Downers Grove, Ill.: InterVarsity Press, 1988.

Burrows, Mark S., and Paul Rorem, eds. *Biblical Hermeneutics in Historical Perspective.* Grand Rapids, Mich.: Eerdmans, 1991.

Carroll, Kenneth. "Toward a Commonly Received New Testament." *Bulletin of the John Rylands Library* 44 (1962): 327–49.

Castagno, Adele Monaci. "Il Problema della datazione dei commenti al' Apocalisse di Ecumenio e di Andrea di Cesarea." *Atti della Accademia delle scienze di Torino II, Classe de scienze, morali, storiche e filologiche* 114 (1980): 224–46.

———. "I Commenti de Ecumenio e di Andrea di Cesarea: Due letture divergenti dell' Apocalisse." *Memorie della Accademia delle scienze di Torino II, Classe di scienze, morali, storiche e filologiche* V. Fascicolo IV (1981): 303–424.

Charles, R. H. *A Critical and Exegetical Commentary on the Revelation of St. John*. 2 vols. Edinburgh: T. & T. Clark, 1920.

———. *Lectures on the Apocalypse*. London: Oxford University Press, 1922.

Cheek, John L. "The Apocrypha in Christian Scripture." *The Journal of Bible and Religion* 26 (1958): 207–12.

Chevalier, Jacques M. *A Postmodern Revelation: Signs of Astrology and the Apocalypse*. Toronto: University of Toronto Press, 1997.

Chrestou, Panagiotis K. Πατέρες καί Θεολόγοι τοῦ Χριστιανισμοῦ. 2 vols. Thessalonika: Tehnika Studio, 1971.

———. Ἑλληνική Πατρολογία. 5 vols. Thessalonika: Kyromanos, 1992.

Collins, John, ed. *The Origins of Apocalypticism in Judaism and Christianity*. Vol. 1 of *Encyclopedia of Apocalypticism*. New York: Continuum, 1998.

Colwell, Ernest Cadman. *History and Text*. Vol. 2 of *The Elizabeth Day McCormick Apocalypse*. 2 vols. Chicago: University of Chicago Press, 1940.

Constantinou, Eugenia Scarvelis. "Andrew of Caesarea and the Apocalypse: Studies and Translation." Ph.D diss., Université Laval, 2008.

———. "Apocalypse Patchwork: Finding Lost Scraps of the Ancient Eastern Interpretation of the Apocalypse Preserved in the Commentary of Andrew of Caesarea." In *Exegesis and Hermeneutics in the Churches of the East*, edited by Vahan Hovanessian. New York: Peter Lang, 2009.

———. "Banned from the Lectionary: Excluding the Apocalypse of John from the Orthodox New Testament Canon." In *The Canon of the Bible and the Apocrypha in the Churches of the East*, edited by Vahan Hovanessian. New York: Peter Lang, 2011.

Conybeare, F. C. *The Armenian Version of Revelation and Cyril of Alexandria's Scholia*. London: Text and Translation Society, 1907.

Court, John. *Myth and History in the Book of Revelation*. Atlanta: John Knox Press, 1989.

Cowley, Roger. "The Biblical Canon of the Ethiopian Orthodox Church Today." *Ostkirchliche Studien* 23 (1974): 318–23.

———. *The Traditional Interpretation of the Apocalypse of St. John in the Ethiopian Orthodox Church*. Cambridge: Cambridge University Press, 1983.

Cross, F. L., ed. *The Oxford Dictionary of the Christian Church*. 3rd ed., rev. Oxford: Oxford University Press, 2005.

Dagron, Gilbert. "Toisième, neuvième et quarantième jours dans la tradition Byzantine: Temps chrétien et anthropologie." *Les Temps chrétiens de la fin de l'Antiquité au Moyen âge IIIe–XIIIe Siècles."* Paris: Centre National de la Recherche Scientifique, 1984.

Daley, Brian E. *The Hope of the Early Church*. Cambridge: Cambridge University Press, 1991.
Daniélou, Jean. *The Theology of Jewish Christianity: The Development of Christian Doctrine Before the Council of Nicea*, vol. 1. Translated and edited by John A. Baker. Chicago: Regnery, 1964.
———. "La typologie millénariste de la semaine dans le christianisme primitif." *Vigiliae christianae* 2 (1948): 1–16.
De Groote, Marc. "Die Quaestio Oecumeniana." *Sacris Erudiri*. 36 (1996): 67–105.
Diekamp, Franz. "Das Zeitalter des Erzbischofs Andreas von Caesarea." *Historisches Jahrbuch* 18 (1897): 1–36.
———. "Mittheilungen über den neuaufgefundenen Kommentar des Oekumenius zur Apokalypse." *Sitzungberichte der Königlichen Preussischen Akademie der Wissenschaften* 43 (1901): 1046–56.
———. *Analecta Patristica: Texte und Abhandlungen zur Griechischen Patristik*, 161–72. Orientalia Christiana Analecta 117. Rome: Pontifical Institute of Oriental Studies, 1938.
Dungan, David. *Constantine's Bible*. Minneapolis: Fortress Press, 2007.
Durousseau, Cliff. "The Commentary of Oecumenius on the Apocalypse of John: A Lost Chapter in the History of Interpretation." *Biblical Research* 29 (1984): 21–34.
Edelstein, Ludwig. "Dioscorides Pendanius." In *Oxford Classical Dictionary*, edited by Simon Hornblower and Antony Spawforth. 3rd ed. Oxford: Oxford University Press, 1996.
Elliott, J. K. "The Distinctiveness of the Greek Manuscripts of the Book of Revelation." *The Journal of Theological Studies*, n.s., 48 (1997): 116–24.
Emmerson, Richard, and Bernard McGinn, eds. *The Apocalypse in the Middle Ages*. Ithaca: Cornell University Press, 1992.
Epp, Eldon Jay. "Issues in the Interrelation of New Testament Textual Criticism and Canon." In *The Canon Debate*, edited by Lee Martin McDonald and James Sanders. Peabody, Mass.: Hendrickson, 2002. 2nd ed., 2004.
Every, George. *Misunderstandings between East and West*. Richmond, Va.: John Knox Press, 1966.
Fahey, Michael. *Cyprian and the Bible: A Study in Third Century Exegesis*. Tübingen: Mohr, 1981.
Farmer, William. *Jesus and the Gospel: Tradition, Scripture and Canon*. Philadelphia: Fortress Press, 1982.
Farmer, William, and Denis Farkasfalvy. *The Formation of the New Testament Canon*. New York: Paulist Press, 1983.
Fekkes, Jan. *Isaiah and the Prophetic Traditions in the Book of Revelation. Visionary Antecedents and Their Development*. Journal for the Study of the New Testament

Supplement Series 93. Sheffield, England: Sheffield Academic Press, 1994.
Ferguson, Everett. "Canon Muratori: Date and Provenance." *Studia Patristica* 18 (1982): 677–83.
Feuillet, André. *L' Apocalypse: État de la question.* Paris: Descleé de Brouwer, 1963.
Flusin, Bernard, ed. *Saint Anastase le Perse et l'histoire de la Palestine au début du VIIe siècle.* 2 vols. Paris: Editions du Centre national de la recherche scientifique, 1992.
Foss, Clive. "The Persians in Asia Minor at the End of Antiquity." *The English Historical Review* 96 (1975): 721–43.
———. "Life in City and Country." In *The Oxford History of Byzantium*, edited by Cyril Mango. Oxford: Oxford University Press, 2002.
Fredriksen, Paula. "Tyconius and Augustine on the Apocalypse." In *The Apocalypse in the Middle Ages*, edited by Richard Emmerson and Bernard McGinn. Ithaca: Cornell University Press, 1992.
Freedman, D. N., and M. P. O'Connor. "YHWH." In *Theological Dictionary of the Old Testament*, edited by Johannes Botterweck and Helmer Ringgren. Translated by David E. Green. Grand Rapids, Mich.: Eerdmans, 1986.
Gamble, Harry. *The New Testament Canon: Its Making and Meaning.* Philadelphia: Fortress Press, 1985.
———. "Canon: New Testament." In *Anchor Bible Dictionary*, edited by David Noel Freedman. 6 vols. New York: Doubleday, 1992.
———. *Books and Readers in the Early Church: A History of Early Christian Texts.* New Haven: Yale University Press, 1995.
———. "The New Testament Canon: Recent Research and the Status Quaestionis." In *The Canon Debate*, edited by Lee Martin McDonald and James A. Sanders. Peabody, Mass.: Hendrickson, 2002.
Gerard, Maurice, ed. *Clavis Patrum Graecorum.* 5 vols. Turnhout: Brepols, 1974–80.
Gibson, M. D., ed. *Isho'dad, Commentary on the Epistle of James.* Horae Semiticae X. Cambridge, 1913.
Goodspeed, Edgar J. *The Formation of the New Testament.* Chicago: University of Chicago Press, 1926.
Grant, Robert. "The Fourth Gospel and the Church." *Harvard Theological Review* 35 (1942): 95–116.
———. *The Formation of the New Testament.* New York: Harper and Row, 1965.
———. *Christian Beginnings: Apocalypse to History.* London: Variorum Reprints, 1983.
———. *Augustus to Constantine: the Rise and Triumph of Christianity in the Roman World.* San Francisco: Harper and Row, 1990.
———. *Heresy and Criticism: The Search for Authenticity in Early Christian Literature.* Louisville, Ky.: John Knox Press, 1993.

Gregory, Caspar René. *Canon and Text of the New Testament*. New York: Charles Scribner, 1907.
Guinot, Jean-Noël. *L'exégèse de Théodoret de Cyr*. Paris: Beauchesne, 1995.
Hagner, Donald. *Use of the Old and New Testaments in Clement of Rome*. Leiden: Brill, 1973.
Hahneman, Geoffrey Mark. *The Muratorian Fragment and the Development of the Canon*. Oxford: Clarendon Press, 1992.
Haldon, J. F. *Byzantium in the Seventh Century*. Rev. ed. Cambridge: Cambridge University Press, 1997.
Halkin, François, ed. *Bibliotheca Hagiographica Graeca*. 3rd ed. 3 vols. in 1. Brussels: Société des Bollandistes, 1957.
Hanson, R. P. C. "Interpretation of Hebrew Names in Origen." *Vigiliae christianae* 10 (1956): 103–23.
Harnack, Adolph von. *History of Dogma*, vol. 4. 3rd German ed. Translated by E. B. Speirs and James Millar. London: Williams and Norgate, 1898.
———. *Die Entstehung des Neuen Testaments und die wichtigsten Folgen der neuen Schöpfung*. Leipzig: Hinrichs, 1914.
———. *The Origin of the New Testament*. Translated by J. R. Wilkinson. London: Williams and Norgate, 1925.
Haußleiter, Johannes. "Der chiliastische Schlussabschnitt im echten apocalypsekommentar des Bischofs Victorinus von Pettau." *Theologisches Litteraturblatt* 26 (1895): 193–99.
Hernández, Juan, Jr. *Scribal Habits and Theological Influences in the Apocalypse: The Singular Readings of Sinaiticus, Alexandrinus and Ephraemi*. Tübingen: Mohr Siebeck, 2006.
———. "A Scribal Solution to a Problematic Measurement in the Apocalypse." *New Testament Studies* 56 (2010): 273–78.
———. "The Relevance of Andrew of Caesarea for New Testament Textual Criticism." *Journal of Biblical Literature* 130, no. 1 (2011): 183–96.
———. "Andrew of Caesarea and His Reading of Revelation: Catechesis and Paranesis." In *Die Johannesapokalypse: Kontexte und Konzepte*, edited by Jörg Frey, James A. Kelhoffer, Franz Tóth. Tübingen: Mohr Siebeck, 2012.
———. "Codex Sinaiticus: An Early Christian Commentary on the Apocalypse?" In *From Parchment to Pixels: Studies in the Codex Sinaiticus*, edited by David C. Parker and Scot McKendrik. London: British Library, forthcoming.
———. "Recensional Activity and the Transmission of the Septuagint in John's Apocalypse." In *Die Johannesoffenbarung-ihr Text und ihre Auslegung*, edited by Michael Labahn and Martin Karrer. ABG 38. Leipzig: Evangelische Verlagsanstalt, 2012.
Hill, Charles. *The Johannine Corpus in the Early Church*. New York: Oxford University Press, 2004.

Hoskier, Herman Charles, ed. *The Complete Commentary of Oecumenius on the Apocalypse*. University of Michigan Humanistic Studies 23. Ann Arbor: University of Michigan Press, 1928.
———. *Concerning the Text of the Apocalypse*. 2 vols. London: Bernard Quaritch, 1929.
Joannou, Périclès-Pierre. *Discipline générale antique (IVe–IXe s.)*. 3 vols. in 4. Vol. 2, *Les canons des Pères Grecs*. Pontificia commissione per la redazione del codice di diritto canonico orientale, series fascicolo IX. Grottaferrata (Rome): Tipografia Italo-Orientale, "S. Nilo," 1963.
Jones, A. H. M. *Cities of the Eastern Roman Provinces*. Oxford: Clarendon Press, 1937.
———. *The Greek City from Alexander to Justinian*. Oxford: Clarendon Press, 1940.
Kaegi, W. E., Jr. "New Evidence on the Early Reign of Heraclius." *Byzantinische Zeitschrift* 66 (1973): 308–30.
Kannengiesser, Charles. *Handbook of Patristic Exegesis*. 2 vols. Brill: Leiden, 2004.
Kelly, Joseph F. "Bede and the Irish Exegetical Tradition on the Apocalypse." *Revue Bénédictine* 92 (1982): 393–406.
———. "Early Medieval Evidence for Twelve Homilies by Origen on the Apocalypse." *Vigiliae christianae* 39 (1985): 273–79.
Kelly, J. N. D. *Early Christian Doctrines*. 2nd ed. London: Adam and Charles Black, 1960.
———. *Jerome: His Life, Writings and Controversies*. Westminster, Md.: Christian Classics, 1975.
Kilpatrick, G. D. "Professor J. Schmid on the Greek Text of the Apocalypse." *Vigiliae christianae* 13 (1959): 1–13.
Knox, J. *Marcion and the New Testament: An Essay in the Early History of the Canon*. Chicago: University of Chicago Press, 1942.
Koester, Helmut. *Introduction to the New Testament: History and Literature of Early Christianity*. 2nd ed. 2 vols. New York: De Gruyter, 1995–2000.
Konstantinides, Emmanuel. "Μακάριος." In Θρησκευτικὴ καὶ Ἠθικὴ Ἐγκυκλοπαιδεία. 12 vols. Edited by A. Martinos. Athens, 1962–68.
Kretschmar, Georg. *Die Offenbarung des Johannes: die Geschichte ihrer Auslegung im 1. Jahrtausend*. Stuttgart: Calwer Verlag, 1985.
Krumbacher, Karl. *Geschichte der byzantinischen Litteratur: von Justinian bis zum Ende des oströmischen Reiches, 527–1453*. München: Beck, 1897.
Krupp, R. A. *Saint John Chrysostom: A Scripture Index*. Lanham: University Press of America, 1984.
Kunz, George Frederick. *The Curious Lore of Precious Stones*. New York: Dover, 1913.
La Bonnardière, Anne-Marie, ed. *Saint Augustin et la Bible*. Paris: Beauchesne, 1986.
Lagrange, Marie-Joseph. *Introduction à l' étude du Nouveau Testament*. Vol. 2, *Critique textuelle*, Part II "La Critique rationnelle." Paris: J. Gabalda, 1935.

Lambrecht, J., ed. *L'Apocalypse johannique et l'Apocalyptique dans le Nouveau Testament.* Bibliotheca Ephemeridum Theologicarum Lovaniensium 53. Louvain, 1980.

Lamoreaux, John. "The Provenance of Ecumenios' Commentary on the Apocalypse." *Vigiliae christianae* 52 (1998): 88–108.

Lampe, G. W. H., ed. *A Greek Patristic Lexicon.* Oxford: Clarendon Press, 1961.

Landes, Richard. "Lest the Millennium be Fulfilled: Apocalyptic Expectations and the Pattern of Western Chronography 100–800 C.E." In *The Use and Abuse of Eschatology in the Middle Ages,* edited by Werner Verbeke, Daniel Verhelst, and Andries Welkenhuysen. Mediaevalia Lovaniensia Series 1, Studia 15. Leuven: Leuven University Press, 1988.

Lang, D. M. "Recent Work on the Georgian New Testament." *Bulletin of the School of Oriental and African Studies* 19 (1957): 82–93.

Leipoldt, Johannes. *Geschichte des neutestamentlichen Kanons.* 2 vols. Leipzig: Hinrichs, 1907, 1908. Reprint, Leipzig: Zentralantiquariat der Deutschen Demokratischen Republik, 1974.

Lo Bue, Francesco, ed. *The Turin Fragments of Tyconius' Commentary on Revelation.* Cambridge, England: University Press, 1963.

Lubac, Henri de. *Histoire et Esprit: l'intelligence de l'Écriture d' après Origène.* Paris: Aubier, 1950.

Mackay, T. W. "Early Christian Exegesis of the Apocalypse." *Studia Biblica* 3 (1978): 257–63.

Magdalino, Paul. "The History of the Future and its Uses: Prophecy, Policy and Propaganda." In *The Making of Byzantine History,* edited by Roderick Beaton and Charlotte Roueché. London: Variorum, 1993.

Magie, David. *Roman Rule in Asia Minor.* 2 vols. Princeton: Princeton University Press, 1950. Reprint, Salem, N.H.: Ayer, 1988.

Makrakis, Apostolos. *Interpretation of the Book of Revelation by St. John the Divine.* Translated by A. G. Alexander. Hellenic Christian Educational Society, 1948. Originally published in Greece, 1882.

Maldfeld, Georg. "Zur Geschichte des griechischen Apokalypse-Textes." *Theologische Zeitschrift* 14 (1958): 47–52.

Mango, Cyril. *Byzantium: The Empire of New Rome.* New York: Charles Scribner, 1980.

———. "Le temps dans les commentaries byzantins de l'Apocalypse." *Les temps chrétiens de la fin de l'Antiquité au Moyen age IIIe–XIIIe Siècles."* Paris: Centre National de la Recherche Scientifique, 1984.

———, ed. *The Oxford History of Byzantium.* Oxford: Oxford University Press, 2002.

———. "The Revival of Learning." In *The Oxford History of Byzantium,* edited by Cyril Mango. Oxford: Oxford University Press, 2002.

Martinos, A., ed. *Θρησκευτικὴ καὶ Ἠθικὴ Ἐγκυκλοπαιδεία*. 12 vols. Athens, 1962–68.
Matter, E. Ann. "The Pseudo-Alcuinian 'De Septum Sigillis': An Early Latin Apocalypse Exegesis." *Traditio* 36 (1980): 101–37.
———. "The Apocalypse in Early Medieval Exegesis." In *The Apocalypse in the Middle Ages*, edited by Richard Emmerson and Bernard McGinn. Ithaca: Cornell University Press, 1992.
Mavromatis, Georgios B. *Ἡ Ἀποκάλυψις τοῦ Ἰωάννου μὲ Πατερικὴ Ἀνάλυση*. Athens: Apostolike Diakonia, 1994.
McDonald, Lee. *The Formation of the Christian Biblical Canon*. Peabody, Mass.: Hendrickson, 1995.
———. "Identifying Scripture and Canon in the Early Church: The Criteria Question." In *The Canon Debate*, edited by Lee Martin McDonald and James A. Sanders. Peabody, Mass.: Hendrickson Publishers, 2002.
McDonald, Lee, and James A. Sanders, eds. *The Canon Debate*. Peabody, Mass.: Hendrickson Publishers, 2002.
McGinn, Bernard, ed. *Apocalypticism in Western History and Culture*. Vol. 2 of *The Encyclopedia of Apocalypticism*. New York: Continuum, 1998.
Metzger, Bruce. *Textual Commentary on the Greek New Testament*. 3rd ed. Stuttgart: Biblia-Druck, 1975.
———. *The Canon of the New Testament: Its Origin, Development and Significance*. Oxford: Clarendon Press, 1987.
———. *The Text of the New Testament: Its Transmission, Corruption and Restoration*. 3rd ed. New York: Oxford University Press, 1992.
Meyendorff, John. *Christ in Eastern Christian Thought*. Washington, D.C.: Corpus Books, 1969.
———. *Byzantine Theology*. New York: Fordham University Press, 1974.
———. *Imperial Unity and Christian Divisions*. Crestwood, N.Y.: St. Vladimir's Seminary Press, 1989.
Milavec, Aaron. *The Didache. Faith, Hope, and Life of the Earliest Christian Communities, 50–70 C.E.* New York: The Newman Press, 2003.
Miller, John. *The Origins of the Bible: Rethinking Canon History*. New York: Paulist Press, 1994.
Mondésert, Claude, ed. *Le Monde grec ancien et la Bible*. Paris: Beauchesne, 1984.
Morin, Germain. "Le Commentaire Homilétique de S. Césaire sur l'Apocalypse." *Revue Bénédictine* 45 (1933): 43–61.
Nassif, Bradley. "Antiochene Θεωρία in John Chrysostom's Exegesis." In *Exegesis and Hermeneutics in the Churches of the East*, edited by Vahan Hovanessian. New York: Peter Lang, 2009.
———. "'Spiritual Exegesis' in the School of Antioch." In *New Perspectives on Historical Theology*, edited by Bradley Nassif. Grand Rapids, Mich.: Eerdmans, 1996.

Nautin, Pierre. "Hippolytus." In *Encyclopedia of the Early Church*, edited by Angelo Di Berardino. Translated by Adrian Walford. 2 vols. New York: Oxford University Press, 1992.

Nock, Arthur Darby. "A Feature of Roman Religion." *Harvard Theological Review* 32, no. 1 (1939): 83–96.

Obolensky, Dimitri. *The Byzantine Commonwealth: Eastern Europe, 500–1453*. New York: Praeger Publishers, 1971.

Oden, Thomas, ed. *Greek Commentaries on Revelation*. Translation, Introduction, and Notes by William C. Weinrich. Ancient Christian Texts. Downers Grove, Ill.: InterVarsity Press Academic, 2011.

Oller, Thomas Hilary. "The Nikol'skij Apocalypse Codex and its Place in the Textual History of Medieval Slavic Apocalypse Manuscripts." Ph.D. diss., Brown University, 1993.

Olster, David. "Byzantine Apocalypses." In *The Encyclopedia of Apocalypticism*. Vol. 2, *Apocalypticism in Western History and Culture*, edited by Bernard McGinn. New York: Continuum, 1998.

Ostrogorsky, George. *History of the Byzantine State*. Translated by Joan Hussey. New Brunswick, N.J.: Rutgers University Press, 1957.

Pelikan, Jaroslav. *The Christian Tradition: A History of the Development of Doctrine*. 5 vols. Vol. 2, *The Spirit of Eastern Christendom*. Chicago: University of Chicago Press, 1974.

Pirot, Louis. *L'Oeuvre Exegetique de Theodore de Mopsueste*. Rome: Sumptibus Pontificii Instituti Biblici, 1913.

Podskalsky, Gerhard. "Représentation du temps dans l'eschatologie impériale byzantine." In *Les temps chrétiens de la fin de l'Antiquité au Moyen âge IIIe–XIIIe Siècles.* Paris: Centre National de la Recherche Scientifique, 1984.

———. "Virtue." In *Oxford Dictionary of Byzantium*, edited by Alexander Kazhdan. 3 vols. New York: Oxford University Press, 1991.

Prigent, Pierre. *Apocalypse 12: Histoire de l'exégèse*. Beiträge zur Geschichte der Biblischen Exegese 2. Tübingen: Mohr (Paul Siebeck), 1959.

———. "Hippolyte, commentateur de l'Apocalypse." *Theologische Zeitschrift* 28 (1972): 391–412.

———, and Ralph Stehly. "Les fragments du De Apocalypsi d'Hippolyte." *Theologische Zeitschrift* 29 (1973): 315–33.

———. "Citations d'Hippolyte trouvées dans le ms. Bodl. Syr. 140." *Theologische Zeitschrift* 30 (1974): 82–85.

Quasten, Johannes. *Patrology*. 4th ed. 4 vols. Westminster, Md.: Christian Classics, 1988.

Robertson, J. N. W. B., trans. *The Acts and Decrees of the Synod of Jerusalem*. London: Thomas Baker, 1899.

Sarris, Peter. "The Eastern Empire from Constantine to Heraclius." In *The Oxford History of Byzantium*, edited by Cyril Mango. Oxford: Oxford University Press, 2002.

Schmid, Josef. "Der griechischen Apokalypse-Kommentare." *Biblische Zeitschrift* 19 (1931): 228–54.

———. *Studien Zur Geschichte des grieschischen Apokalypse-Textes*, 3 parts. Part 1, *Der Apokalypse-Kommentar des Andreas von Kaisareia*. Part 2, *Die alten Stämme*. Part 3, *Historische Abteilung Ergänzungsband, Einleitung*. München: Karl Zink Verlag, 1955–56.

Simonetti, Manlio. "Andrew of Caesarea." In *Encyclopedia of Early Christianity*, edited by Everett Ferguson. New York: Garland Publishing, 1990.

———. *Biblical Interpretation in the Early Church*. Translated by John Hughes. Edinburgh: T. & T. Clark, 1994.

Souter, Alexander. *The Text and Canon of the New Testament*. New York: Charles Scribner, 1913.

Steinhauser, Kenneth B. *The Apocalypse Commentary of Tyconius: A History of Its Reception and Influence*. Peter Lang: Frankfurt am Main, 1986.

Stendahl, Krister. "The Formation of the Canon: The Apocalypse of John and the Epistles of Paul in the Muratorian Fragment." In *Current Issues in New Testament Interpretation*, edited by William Klassen and Graydon Snyder. New York: Harper, 1962.

Stephanidis, Vassilios K. Ἐκκλησιαστικὴ Ἱστορία. 3rd ed. Athens: Aster, 1970.

Stiernon, Daniel. "Caesarea, Cappadocia." In *Encyclopedia of the Early Church*, edited by Angelo Di Berardino. 2 vols. Translated by Adrian Walford. Cambridge: James Clark, 1992.

Stonehouse, Ned Bernard. *The Apocalypse in the Ancient Church*. Goes, Holland: Oosterbaan and Le Cointre, 1929.

Stratos, Andreas. *Byzantium in the Seventh Century*. 5 vols. Translated by Marc Ogilvie-Grant. Amsterdam: Hakkert, 1968.

Sundberg, Albert C., Jr. "Canon Muratori: A Fourth Century List." *Harvard Theological Review* 66 (1973): 1–41.

Swete, Henry Barclay. *The Apocalypse of St. John*. London: MacMillan, 1906.

Symes, John Elliotson. *The Evolution of the New Testament*. London: John Murray, 1921.

Tasker, R. V. G. "The Chester Beatty Papyrus of the Apocalypse of John." *Journal of Theological Studies* 50 (1949): 60–68.

Ternant, Paul. "La θεωρία d'Antioche dans le cadre des sense de l'Écriture." *Biblica* 34 (1953): 135–58, 354–83, and 456–86.

Thompson, Steven. *The Apocalypse and Semitic Syntax*. Cambridge: Cambridge University Press, 1985.

Thomson, Robert W., trans. *Nerses of Lambron Commentary on the Revelation of Saint John*. Hebrew University Armenian Studies 9. Leuven: Peeters, 2007.

Torjesen, Karen Jo. *Hermeneutical Procedure and Theological Method in Origen's Exegesis*. New York: de Gruyter, 1985.

Treadgold, Warren. *A History of Byzantine State and Society*. Stanford: Stanford University Press, 1997.

Vaporis, N[omikos] M[ichael]. *Translating the Scriptures into Modern Greek*. Brookline, Mass.: Holy Cross Orthodox Press, 1994.

―――. "The Last Phase of the Translation Controversy." In *Rightly Teaching the Word of Your Truth: Studies in Faith and Culture, Church and Scriptures, Fathers and Worship, Hellenism and the Contemporary Scene*, edited by Nomikos Michael Vaporis. Brookline, Mass.: Holy Cross Orthodox Press, 1995.

Wainwright, Arthur. *Mysterious Apocalypse*. Nashville: Abingdon Press, 1993.

Weidmann, Frederick. *Polycarp and John*. Notre Dame: University of Notre Dame Press, 1999.

Weinrich, William, ed. *Revelation*. Ancient Christian Commentary on Scripture 12. Downers Grove, Ill.: InterVarsity Press, 2005.

Westcott, Brooke Foss. *The Bible in the Church*. 6th ed. London, 1855. Reprint, Grand Rapids, Mich., 1980.

Whitby, Michael. *The Emperor Maurice and His Historian: Theophylact Simocatta on Persian and Balkan Warfare*. Oxford: Clarendon Press, 1988.

Willoughby, H. R. *A Greek Corpus of Revelation Iconography*. 2 vols. Vol. 1 of *The Elizabeth Day McCormick Apocalypse*. Chicago: University of Chicago Press, 1940.

Wutz, Franz. *Onomastica sacra: Utersuchungen zum Liber interpretationis nominum hebraicorum des hl. Hieronymus*. Leipzig: Hinrichs, 1914–15.

Zahn, Theodor. *Die Offenbarung des Johannes*. 2 vols. Leipzig, 1924 and 1926.

SCRIPTURE INDEX

Genesis
  1: 268n46
  2.21: 229n67, 229n67
  3: 260n2
  3.5: 245n63
  11.9: 243n49

Exodus
  9.7-28: 218n13
  25.9: 140
  36.15-21 (LXX): 199n78
  39.8-14: 199n78

Deuteronomy
  25.5: 132n25

Psalms
  7.1: 213n154
  7.2: 213n154
  32(31).9: 217n5, 231n76
  45(44).10: 115n17
  64(63).3: 218n12
  102(101).26: 271n63
  104(103).30: 270n60
  119(118).71: 225n52
  125(124).3: 225n50, 225n51, 267n41
  140(139).3: 218n12

Song of Songs
  8.11-12: 238n28

Wisdom of Solomon
  1.13: 268n46
  3.1: 264n26
  11.16: 210n132

Isaiah
  1.14: 174
  6.3: 163, 182
  6.9-10: 164
  14.12: 167-68
  26.14: 260n3
  51.11: 286n135
  61.1-2: 188
  61.2: 200n84
  65.17-18: 270n60
  66.22: 270n60

Jeremiah
  8.16: 251

Ezekiel
  39.9: 174
  18.23: 209n124, 282n103
  18.32: 209n124, 282n103

Daniel
  7.1-7: 243
  7.7: 174n69, 242, 243
  7.7-8: 242
  7.9: 134
  7.20: 174n69

Joel
  2.11: 265n32

Micah
  7.18: 205n112

Matthew
  5.16: 213n154
  6.13: 208n123
  6.24: 196n52, 216n3
  7.13: 222n35
  7.14: 197n61, 219n20, 221n28
  8.2: 166
  8.3: 249n81
  9.28: 198n63
  11.26: 209n124
  11.28: 231n76
  13.13-15: 164n32
  13.18-23: 219n20, 221n28
  13.23: 287n139
  13.30: 226n53
  13.46: 200n81
  20.16: 219n20, 221n28
  22.1-10: 155n7
  22.14: 219n20, 221n28
  22.30: 235n15, 268n50
  24.2: 177n83
  24.20: 221n32
  24.21: 255n109
  24.27: 255n109
  24.36: 109n26
  24.42: 108n23
  24.43: 108n23
  24.44: 108n23
  24.50: 108n23
  25.1-13: 155n7
  25.34: 231n76

Mark
  4.12: 164n32
  4.14-20: 219n20, 221n28
  4.20: 287n139
  5.12: 249n81
  12.25: 235n15
  13.4: 177n83

334 SCRIPTURE INDEX

Mark (cont.)
13.19: 255n109
13.20: 221n32

Luke
4.21: 188
8.5-15: 219n20, 221n28
8.32: 249n81
12.35: 213n154
12.37: 231n76
16.13: 196n52, 216n3
20.36: 235n15
21.7: 177n83
22.30: 198n63

John
1.1: 154
6.35: 118
6.48: 118
7.38: 118, 132
9.4: 234
10.9: 200n81
12.2: 198n69
14.2: 226n53, 267n40
14.6: 200n81
12.2: 198n69
21.11: 146n91
21.23: 172n63

Acts of the Apostles
1.7: 109n26
10.42: 265n32
17.28: 284n121
28.24-25: 164n33

Romans
3.1-7: 156n10
6.4: 238n26, 261n7
8.13: 238n26, 260n4
8.17: 261n6
8.18: 283n105
8.20: 269n55
8.20-21: 270n57
8.21: 271n63
14.17: 235n15, 268n50

1 Corinthians
1.21-22: 257n119
2.9: 287n140

3.9: 205, 231n75
3.13: 277
7.21: 270n59
9.24-25: 283n104
10.13: 212n140, 224
11.31: 226n54
11.32: 225n52
15: 152n1
15.24: 231n76
15.26: 267n43
15.28: 231n76

2 Corinthians
1.12: 208n123
2.15: 195n45
4.10: 261n6
5.1: 286n134
6.1: 207n120, 230n69
6.14: 246n67
6.15: 246n68
6.16: 254n107

Ephesians
2.2: 246
2.14: 194
2.18: 199n73
6.12: 212n140, 246

Philippians
2: 186
3.19: 213n152, 249n80, 258
3.20: 213n152, 213n153, 249n80, 256

Colossians
2.12: 261n7
3.5: 216n3, 238n26, 260n4

1 Thessalonians
4.16: 159, 167
4.16-17: 272n67
5.2: 108n23

2 Thessalonians
2.3: 238n28, 253n98
2.4: 253n99
2.9: 249n81

1 Timothy
1.16: 196n50
2.4: 209n124, 209n125, 236n19, 282n103
2.25: 282n103
3.5: 216n3
3.7: 282n103

2 Timothy
2.5: 212n140
3.5: 196n51
4.2: 212n140

Titus
1.16: 216n3

Hebrews
1.14: 148n96, 202n94
9.11: 286n134
12.13: 231n75

1 Peter
1.19: 208n123
5.4: 283n104
5.8: 249n81

2 Peter
2.19: 223n38
3.10: 108n23

Revelation
1: 189
1.1: 54, 60, 98, 138,
1.2: 188
1.3: 14n2, 14n3, 14n5, 72n3, 233
1.4: 123-24, 154, 163, 180, 182, 183, 190
1.8: 35n1, 61, 154
1.11: 190
1.15: 118, 122, 150
1.17: 227
1.18: 33
2: 132, 138, 189
2.13: 116, 177
2.17: 118
2.28: 167
3: 132, 138, 189
3.4: 117

SCRIPTURE INDEX

3.7: 128, 163, 181
3.10: 224
3.10-11: 139
3.14: 97
3.19: 229
3.20: 207
4.20: 95, 122, 133, 134, 138, 183, 184
4.1: 149
4.3: 179
4.4: 92n13, 155
4.6: 92n13, 170
4.7: 20n24
4.8: 182
5: 185
5.1-5: 188
5.7: 195
6: 157, 177
6.1-2: 189
6.3-4: 189
6.5-6: 189
6.7-8: 190
6.9: 157
6.9-10: 172, 190
6.9-11: 264
6.12: 190, 232
6.12-13: 163, 165
6.12-17: 177
6.14: 122, 145
7: 117n32, 118, 198, 251
7.1: 197
7.2: 3n6, 3n9
7.3: 119, 256
7.9: 155
7.11: 117
7.14: 97n35, 155
7.16: 115
7.17: 118
8: 3n6, 159
8.3: 195, 218
8.5: 195
8.5-6: 217
8.7: 159, 167, 203n99
8.7-13: 138,
8.8: 172
8.8-9: 219
8.9: 91
8.11: 232
8.12: 222

8.13: 204
9: 3n6, 124, 138, 221
9.1-2; 272
9.1-4: 119
9.1-5: 272
9.3-5: 272
9.5; 167, 221
9.6: 221
9.7: 212n139
9.13-16: 64n46
9.13-19: 203n101
9.20: 273, 274
9.20-21: 138n47, 167, 215
10.11: 172
11: 159, 227
11.1-2: 254
11.2: 221, 224
11.3: 221
11.3: 134
11.3-4: 173
11.3-10: 159
11.15: 159
12: 119, 138, 139, 159, 188, 198, 246
12.1: 180
12.1-2: 159
12.2: 139
12.3-4: 159
12.4-6: 159
12.5: 224
12.6: 221, 224
12.7-8: 246
12.7-9: 160
12.11: 225
12.12: 213n152
12.13-16: 212
12.13-17: 160
12.15-16: 248
12.17: 200n82, 248, 251n90
12.18: 251n90
13: 25n41, 243
13.1: 251n90
13.1-2: 134
13.2: 243, 252
13.3: 176, 252
13.3-4: 252
13.5: 221
13.7-8: 252

13.10: 197
13.11: 173, 253
13.12-13: 254
13.14: 256
13.14-17: 176
13.20: 222
14: 196, 198
14.1: 198
14.3: 207
14.8: 98, 243
14.10: 276n77
14.9-11: 281
14.11: 281
14.12: 197, 200n82, 223
14.13: 72n3, 212, 260, 282
14.18-20: 222, 225
14.20: 210, 267
15: 196, 276
15.1: 216
15.2: 276, 277
15.6: 129
15.8: 215, 264
16: 3n5
16.2: 217
16.7: 148
16.8-9: 217
16.10: 160
16.11: 281
16.12: 64n46
16.13: 160
16.15: 72n3
16.17-20: 255
16.19: 196
16.21: 218
17: 99, 149, 245, 249
17.1-3: 239
17.2-3: 149
17.6: 240
17.8: 249
17.10: 193, 238
17.18: 241n41
18.8: 244
18.21: 173
19.3: 281
19.6: 174
19.9: 72n3
19.7: 285n123
19.12-13: 184, 185
19.15: 266

Revelation *(cont.)*
  19.17: 209n124
  19.20: 160, 174
  19.21: 174
  20: 5, 133, 161, 166, 188
  20.1-3: 193, 236
  20.2-3: 160
  20.2-5: 26
  20.3: 161
  20.4: 3n8, 166, 193, 236
  20.5: 166
  20.4-5: 161, 260
  20.4-6: 259
  20.5: 261
  20.6: 72n3, 237
  20.7-8: 174, 193, 237
  20.11: 269
  20.12: 266
  20.13: 267
  20.14-15: 267
  21:179
  21.2: 3n7, 269, 285n123
  21.3: 140
  21.4: 286n135
  21.6: 229
  21.9: 228
  21.12: 199
  21.13: 199n74
  21.14: 175, 199
  21.16: 285
  21.17: 199
  21.19: 199n77
  21.19-20: 146
  21.21: 200n81, 287
  21.22: 284
  21.25: 285, 286
  22.1: 118
  22.2: 200n84, 286
  22.3: 286
  22.6: 14n2, 72n3
  22.7; 234
  22.10: 14n2
  22.11: 211
  22.14: 72n3, 200
  22.16: 168
  22.17: 206
  22.18: 14n4
  22.18-19: 129
  22.19: 14n2, 20n22

GENERAL INDEX

Acts of Andrew, 31n58
Acts of John, 31n58
Acts of Paul, 30
Acts of Peter, 176
Acts of Thomas, 288
Acts of the Apostles, 6, 15, 30, 72n3, 164,
Afflictions, 108, 111, 167, 203, 204, 223, 224, 228, 229, 232, 269, purpose of, 215–18, 223, 225–27, 230, 280–81; extent of, 221–23; nature of, 218–20, 223. *See also* torment; punishment; suffering
After-life, 283. *See also* eternal life
Agourides, Savvas, 37n7
Akolouthia. See Sequence
Alexander the Great, 241
Alexandria: church of, 16, 26, 33, 68n55, 70n61, 145; city of, 81n34; school of, 26, 145
Allegory and allegorical interpretation, 3, 25, 26, 91, 107, 115n18, 128, 138–39, 140, 142–43, 145–47, 152, 153, 162, 166, 167, 174, 218–19, 221, 272, 274, 313
Alogoi, 22, 23, 26
Ambrose of Milan, 10, 88n2, 88n4, 171, 291n16
Ambrosius Autpertus, 4n13, 6, 89n5
Amphilochios of Iconium, 28, 34
Anagoge 136, 142, 143, 147–48, 152, 154–55, 156, 157, 162. *See also* spiritual sense
Andrew of Caesarea: accused of heresy in the West, 263n23; assigned to write commentary, 48, 72–73, 74, 76, 87, 104; believed end was not near, 83, 85, 108–10, 232–33, 234, 238, 250, 251, 311–13; believed forbidden to seek time of the end, 109, 135; believed we cannot know the end, 108, 135; on the benefit of reading the

Apocalypse, 95, 105, 107, 110–11, 112, 153; considers Apocalypse inspired, 18, 105, 131, 136; contribution to Apocalypse text, x, 288–89, 293–96, 316; corrects Oikoumenios, 89–91, 107, 123–25, 129, 133, 169–70, 180, 182–83, 187, 312–13; defends the Greek of the Apocalypse, 129–31; date of episcopal reign, 47–49; division of commentary, 18n14, 120–21, 303–4, 317; does not apply Apocalypse to his own times, 108–10, 251, 253, 311, 315; does not rely on Oikoumenios, 89–91, 133, 135, 169, 178, 314; doxologies, 120–21, 283, 303, 317; easily misunderstood, 81n36, 109, 123–125, 233, 234n9; ecclesiology, 194–97; eschatology, ix, x, 64, 80, 81n36, 85, 109, 156, 160, 172, 175, 177, 188, 190, 192–93, 195, 197, 203, 205, 212, 217, 219–21, 223, 224–25, 232–58, 263–64, 269–70, 312–15; exegetical training and knowledge, ix, 48, 91, 109–110, 126–51, 178, 278, 312, 314; follows patristic traditions, ix-x, 18, 25, 82, 90, 119, 122–23, 124n60, 127, 129–36, 145–47, 162, 170, 172–73, 177, 178–80, 183, 194, 234, 236, 239, 240, 242, 253, 259, 269, 304, 306, 307–308, 309, 314; historical milieu, 77–85, 311–12, 314–15, 318; importance of commentary, ix-x, xiii, xiv, 36, 39, 78, 305, 306–10, 311; influence of commentary, x, xiii, 9, 12–13, 44, 85, 111, 296, 303–10, 316–18; knowledge of Hebrew terms, 132–33, 168, 176; knowledge of manuscript variations, 128–29, 130; life, 47–48; liturgical orientation, 114–17; motivation, 8, 72–74, 77–78, 81–83, 85, 87–88, 103, 104–7, 112; other works, 47; pastoral concerns, 107, 108, 110–11, 112–13,

337

Andrew of Caesarea (cont.)
233, 271, 313, 316, 317; preserved Eastern Apocalypse interpretive tradition, x, xiv, 9, 18, 127, 170–75, 179, 246, 304, 315; purpose of commentary, 88, 92, 104–111, 112, 144, 233; purpose of afflictions, 167, 203, 204, 215–18, 225–27, 230, 280–81; purpose of life, 209, 211; purpose of punishment, 113, 138, 153, 204, 216, 218, 219, 222–23, 225, 226–27, 228, 229–30; purpose of the Apocalypse, 110, 112, 144, 151, 153, 219, 314; rank as Archbishop of Caesarea, 48, 74, 76, 311; recognizes three levels of Scripture, 127–28, 152, 314; reluctant to interpret Apocalypse, 73, 76, 87, 104, 135, 149; reports opinions of others, ix, 8, 89, 91, 114, 122–23, 127, 178–79, 235, 304, 314, 315; responding to Oikoumenios, ix, 8, 51, 58, 89–91, 103, 107–8, 111, 113, 114, 154, 180, 219, 245, 271, 278, 314, 318; sacramental orientation, 117–20, 195, 256, 257, 313, 315; sources 8, 11, 12, 69, 89–91, 122–23, 127, 169–80, 191, 201, 304n25, 306, 314; spiritual quality of the commentary, 46, 85, 105, 110, 113, 136, 144–45, 149, 151, 233–34, 310, 315, 317, 318; spiritual purpose of commentary, 83, 105, 107, 111, 126, 128, 129, 133, 144–45, 153, 233–34, 313, 317; structure of commentary, 120–21; style, 9, 104–5, 112–14, 120, 121–25, 127, 168, 169–70, 218–19, 311, 314, 316–18; success of commentary, ix, xiii, xiv, 85, 86, 317–18; theology, xiv, 46, 48, 58, 163–65, 182–87, 205–14, 278–87, 312–16; treatment of the text, 121–23; use of Scripture, 127, 168, 169; view of history, 189–93; view of prophecy, 81n36, 105, 135, 138, 158, 166, 187–89; why the first Greek patristic commentary, xiv; writes out of obedience, 73–74, 76, 104–5. See also bishops, civic duties; historical milieu; Therapeutike Angels, 64n46, 97, 109n26, 116–17, 124–25, 129, 148, 150, 163, 167, 173, 179n88, 182, 185, 191, 194–95, 201–5, 212n139, 216–17, 220, 222, 223, 226, 228, 229, 235, 236, 243, 246, 264, 268, 272, 279, 280, 304, 315

Anthony, St., 246

Antichrist, 19, 24, 43n29, 81n36, 108, 140, 143, 160, 172, 173, 174, 188, 212, 213, 215, 217, 223, 224, 225, 226, 233, 235, 236, 238, 239, 242, 243, 244, 245, 249, 250–58, 265–66, 313. See also beast of the sea

Anti-Montanists, 20, 24, 26. See also Montanism/Montanists

Antioch, 1n2, 20, 47, 64, 68n55, 80, 146, 300

Antiochean exegesis and School, 33, 140n58, 146–47, 148n98, 149n99

Antiochus IV, "Epiphanes," 140, 175

Antiochus Strategos, 66n51

Antipas, martyr, 116, 177

Antipater of Bostra, 178, 270

Apocalypse Commentaries: ix-x, xiii, 1, 2; Greek/Eastern 1, 2, 5, 7–12, 48–50, 52, 58, 77, 82, 86, 90, 92n14, 94, 107, 178, 298, 310, 312–13, 315, 316–18; Latin/Western 1, 2–6, 9–13

Apocalypse of John: authorship of, xiii, 18–27, 29, 30–32, 42, 97, 130n17, 131, 178, 304–5, 309; in the Canon of Scripture, ix, x, xiii-xiv, 2, 5, 9, 15–17, 25, 27–34, 35–46, 86, 97, 131, 292, 300, 305, 306–10, 318; dual interpretive tradition, 10–13; Greek of, 129–30; inspiration, 14, 17, 18, 30, 97, 105, 131, 162, 317; interpretation of, ix, x, xiv, 1–13; in the lectionary, xiii, 9, 40, 288, 289, 291, 309; as prophecy 1, 14, 17, 19, 21–22, 23–24, 26–27, 60, 64, 67, 80, 98n41, 105, 107, 108–9, 126n3, 129–30, 135, 137, 138, 144, 153, 156, 162, 172, 174, 187–89, 208, 219, 225, 240, 244, 250, 256, 267, 312; spiritual benefits of reading, 95, 105–6, 112, 145, 153; spiritual purpose of, 138, 144, 153, 312, 318; trustworthiness, 18, 130, 178, 305. See also Apocalypse in the Orthodox Church; Attic syntax; patristic interpretation; manuscripts

Apocalypse in the Orthodox Church: ix, x, xvn2, 45, 87, 300–301, 306–308, 309, 318; Armenian, ix, x, xvn2, 45, 87, 300–301, 306–8, 309, 318; Georgian ix, 45, 308–9, 318; Greek, ix, xiii, 16–17, 40–43, 46, 48, 49, 50, 52, 77, 82, 86, 90, 92n14, 107, 178, 295, 298, 302, 303, 304, 310, 312, 313, 315, 316, 317, 318; Slavic/ Russian, ix, x, xiii-iv, 45, 46, 302, 303, 304, 309–10, 318

Apocalypse of Peter, 30

Apocalyptic expectations ix, xiv, 38, 39, 58,

GENERAL INDEX 339

64, 80–81, 83, 85, 107–10, 111, 251, 311–12, 318. *See also* eschatology
Apocalyptic genre, ix, 24, 82, 111, 162–63, 177
Apocalypse of Peter, 30
Apokatastasis, 56, 211, 247n72, 271, 275, 277, 278
Apostle John. *See* John, Apostle
Apostle Paul. *See* Paul, Apostle
Apostles, 19, 29, 108, 135, 189, 197–200, 205, 242, 248, 285
Apollonius of Hierapolis, 20, 21
Apollonius of Tyana, 176
Arbaces of Medes, 241
Arethas, Archbishop of Caesarea, 11, 36, 37, 42, 50n7, 291n16, 295, 298, 299, 300n11, 307, 308, 317, 318
Argyriou, Asterios, 38n11
Arianism, 16, 97, 178, 186, 240
Armageddon, 265–66
Armenian Orthodox Church. *See* Apocalypse in the Orthodox Church; manuscripts of the commentary; translation of the Apocalypse
Armenian, revolt, 62, 70n62, 78
Assyrians, 174, 193, 241
Athanasius, the Great of Alexandria, 16, 27, 28, 33, 75, 88n4, 101n57, 246n69
Athletic imagery, 211, 248, 278
Attic syntax, 129n14, 130, 175, 294. *See also* Apocalypse of John
Augustine of Hippo, 5, 5n17, 6, 10, 11, 10n35, 12, 17, 28n49, 88n4, 89, 123, 1289, 132n24, 132n25, 146n91, 171, 172n63, 192, 193
Augustus, Caesar, 252
Aune, David, 39n13, 289, 292n20
Avars, 80, 81n34, 84, 312
Averky, Archbishop, 124n58

Baptism, 110, 117–19, 192, 195, 196, 235, 237, 259, 261, 262, 268, 272; of Christ, 173, 248
Barbarians, xiv, 61, 70, 79n25, 82, 108–10, 113, 218, 220, 233
Babylon, 61, 62, 98–99, 173–74, 192, 238–44, 281. *See also* harlot
Babylonians, 175, 193
Basil, the Great, 33, 34, 88n2, 101n57, 145, 178, 288, 307
Beast: 25n41, 142, 149, 159, 160, 174, 176, 239, 240, 243, 244, 249–50, 252, 254, 256, 265, 281; mark of the
beast, 217, 220, 256, 259; those who conquered the beast, 276, 277; worship of 217, 220, 256, 259, 280–81. *See also* Antichrist; beast of the earth; beast of the sea
Beast of the earth, 173, 244, 245, 249, 253. *See also* False Prophet
Beast of the sea, 134, 243, 244, 245, 249–50, 251, 252. *See also* Antichrist
Beatus of Liebana, 4n13, 6n24, 89n5, 291n16
Bede, the Venerable, 4n13, 89, 291n16
Birdsall, J. Neville, 45n36, 302
Bishops, civic duties of, 67–68, 70–71, 76, 85
Book of Life, 197, 252, 266–67
British Bible Society, 40
Bruce, F. F. 31n59
Bubonic plague, 62, 78, 80–81, 82, 108, 110, 311
Bulgars, 80
Byzantine Empire, 35, 37–39, 47–48, 78, 289, 300, 310. *See also* Roman Empire

Caesarea, Cappadocia, xiv, 47–49, 61, 63–71, 80, 145, 146, 298
Caesarea, Eusebius of. *See* Eusebius of Caesarea
Caesarius of Arles, 4n13, 6, 89n5
Canon of Scripture, 14–17, 20–21, 23, 25, 27–34, 35–36, 37–38, 40, 42, 43–44, 96n32. *See also* Apocalypse of John
Cassiodorus, 4n13, 6, 89n5, 291n16
Castagno, Adele Monaci, 54, 56, 59n34, 91, 92n14, 96n30, 98n41, 98n43, 101, 102n58, 102n59, 102n61, 103n64, 109, 110, 127n6, 127n7, 157n13, 179n87, 187, 188n20, 233, 234n9, 234n10, 278n88
Catholic Church. *See* Roman Catholic Church
Cerinthus, 23, 24, 26–27, 309
Chiliasm, 3, 4–5, 4n14, 7, 24, 25–26, 30, 89n5, 234–35. *See also* millennialism; millennium
Chalcedon, Council of. *See* Ecumenical Councils
Chalcedonian theology and Christians, 56, 57, 58, 83, 92, 96, 99–103, 164, 181–84, 186–87, 312

Cherubim, 115, 117, 292. *See also* angels
Chrismation, 119, 195, 257, 272
Chronicon Paschale, 67, 71n63, 76, 77, 80n30, 80n31, 81n34, 84n39, 84n40
Chrysostom. *See* John Chrysostom
Church Fathers. *See* patristic interpretation
Civil war, 62, 65, 78, 79–80, 81, 82, 108, 110, 311
Clement of Alexandria, 1, 96, 306
Constantinople: 35, 36, 40, 41n22, 43, 45, 47n1, 48, 56n29, 65, 67, 68n55, 70n62, 74, 76, 77, 78, 79, 79n21, 79n25, 80, 80n26, 83, 84, 85, 96n34, 104, 242, 300n11, 303, 307, 311, 312; fall to Crusaders, 37–38; fall to Ottoman Turks, xiv, 38, 39, 310; knowledge of Latin there, 10n34, 10n35, 11n36. *See also* Ecumenical Patriarchate
Constantine the Great, 193, 238, 241, 252
Contest, life as, 211–12, 278
Context, 114, 116, 124, 137, 151, 152, 163, 165, 166, 167, 168, 169, 219, 246, 275, 314
Councils. *See* Ecumenical Councils, and individual councils by name
Council of Laodicea, 28, 44
Council of Hippo, 28n49
Council of Jerusalem, 43–44
Council of Trent, 37
Council of Trullo, 36
Councils of Carthage, 28n49
Chrestou, Panagiotis, 49n4, 51n9, 53n16
Colwell, Ernest Cadman, 38n10, 38n12, 40n17, 42, 43n27, 299, 304n21, 304n22, 304n23, 310n44, 310n45
Conybeare, F. C. 66n51, 301n13
Creation, 95, 97, 100, 145n90, 174, 186, 191, 201, 209, 216, 246, 262, 269–71
Cross of Christ, 66, 67n54, 81n34, 119, 157n14, 158, 195, 208, 229, 246, 248, 249, 251, 256, 257, 261, 313. *See also* True Cross
Crown(s), 111, 194, 198, 211, 212, 213, 278, 282
Crusade of 1204. *See* Fourth Crusade
Cyprian of Carthage, 1, 132n24
Cyril of Alexandria, 27, 28, 33, 101n57, 102, 178, 182, 301n13, 305, 307
Cyril of Jerusalem, 33
Cyril Loukaris, Patriarch, 40, 42–43, 44n30, 299n7
Cyrus of Persia, 175, 241

Daley, Brian, 81n33
Damasus, Pope, 28n49
Daniel, 19, 24, 47n1, 95, 126n5, 140, 174n69, 188n20, 240, 242, 243
Daniélou, Jean, 192
Darius of Persia, 175
Date of the commentary, ix, 7, 49–50, 51, 58, 61–71, 72, 74, 315
De Groote, Marc, 7n28, 54–55, 56, 57, 87, 89–90, 194, 183n7
Death: 62, 64, 78, 166, 172, 175, 177n82, 189, 190, 195, 212, 215, 217, 219, 221, 224, 251, 256, 260–63, 265, 267, 269, 274, 275, 313; to be despised, 105, 111, 112, 141, to be destroyed, 267, 269; for Christ, 111, 198, 225, 261, 313; of Christ 157n14, 158, 207, 229, 261; Christ's authority over, 129; faithfulness until, 111, 198, 225, 248; not created by God, 267–68, 269; second death, 237, 259–63; of sinners, not desired by God, 227; spiritual death, 223, 237, 251, 259, 261–62, 274; time of ours unknown, 234, 313; two kinds of, 259–60
Demons, 113, 148, 153, 160, 176, 179n88, 193, 198, 203n101n, 205, 209, 212, 237, 245, 248, 249, 265, 280, 282
Desert, 39, 150, 212, 248, 255. *See also* wilderness
Devil, 111, 160, 161, 172, 179n89, 188, 193, 212, 223, 228, 235–36, 239, 243–44, 244–50, 251–52, 254, 258, 261, 265–66, 277, 280, 313. *See also* Dragon; Satan
Didache, 30
Didymus the Blind, 28, 33
Diekamp, Franz, 47n1, 49n5, 50, 51, 263n22, 263n23, 269n51, 277n81, 278n86
Diocletian, Emperor, 2, 80, 178, 240, 292
Dionysios Bar Salibi, 24n38
Dionysios, Bishop of Alexandria, 2, 26–27, 29, 31n59, 32, 33, 130, 176
Dionysios the Aereopagite. *See* Pseudo-Dionysios
Dobschütz, Ernst von, 31n59
Domitian, Emperor, 53, 157, 158n15
Donatists and Donatism, 3, 5, 12, 89
Dragon 159, 160, 188, 244, 246, 248, 250, 252–54. *See also* Devil; Satan
Dungan, David, 31n59

GENERAL INDEX   341

Earthquakes, 80, 108, 110, 151, 156, 162, 165, 190, 217, 255, 311
Eastern Christianity, x, xiii, xiv, 5, 8, 9–12, 13, 15, 16n7, 25, 27, 29, 33, 34–46, 85, 88, 90, 111, 115, 116, 119, 127, 154n3, 169, 186, 187, 205n113, 206, 208, 210, 229, 234, 236n19, 257, 300, 304, 306, 309, 312, 315, 316, 318. *See also* Orthodox Church
Ecumenical Councils: 36–37, 56, 57; Chalcedon, 53n15, 312; Nicaea I, 16, 292; Ephesus, 57, 96n34; Fifth, 36, 53, 56, 96n34, 247n72, 271, 312; Sixth, 36; Trullo, 36
Ecumenical Patriarchate, 40, 76, 43n29, 303
Ecumenios. *See* Oikoumenios
Edessa, 63, 70
Egypt, 26, 70n62, 80, 139, 160, 294
Eighth day, 192
Eighth king, 250
Ekwthime, St. *See* Euthymios, St.
Elders. *See* twenty-four elders
Elizabeth Day McCormick Apocalypse, 38n10, 38n12, 40n17, 42n23, 42n24, 42n26, 43n27, 299n5, 299n8, 303–4, 310n44, 310n45
End of the world, ix, 80, 81, 83, 108, 159, 195, 217, 232, 234n9, 249, 251, 311, 312, 313, 318. *See also* apocalyptic expectations; end times
End times, 24, 38, 64, 81n36, 85, 107–9, 111, 172, 175, 188, 190, 203, 205, 212, 219–20, 223–25, 232–33, 238, 253, 269, 270, 304, 313. *See also* apocalyptic expectations; end of the world
Enoch and Elijah, 126n5, 134, 173, 226, 227
Epilogue of the commentary, 49, 76, 106
Epiphanios of Salamis, 22n32, 23n36, 28, 33, 146, 178, 179
Ephesus, Church of, 170
Ephesus, Council of. *See* Ecumenical Councils
Epistle of Barnabas, 30, 191, 192
Epistles of John, 15, 23n33, 25, 30, 33n65, 34n71
Epistles of Peter 15, 30, 33n65, 34n71, 223n38
Epp, Eldon Jay, 16n7
Eschatology. *See* Andrew of Caesarea; end of the world; end times
Eternal life, 111, 192, 209, 230, 239, 259, 260, 261, 262, 313, 316. *See also* after-life

Eternal punishment. *See* punishment, eternal
Eucharist, 97n35, 118, 155
Euphrates River, 63, 64, 65, 203, 226, 251
Eusebius of Caesarea, 2, 7, 19n19, 20n25, 20n26, 20n27, 21n29, 22n30, 22n31, 23n34, 23n36, 25n39, 25n40, 26–34, 62, 63, 130n17, 132n25, 175–76, 179n89, 188n20, 190, 247n71
Euthymios, St., 45, 302, 309
Evagrius Ponticus, 53, 56, 57, 96, 271
Every, George, 10n35, 12n39
Ezekiel, 126, 174

False Christ, 208, 254. *See also* Antichrist; pseudo-Christ
False prophet, 160, 173, 174, 217, 244–45, 249, 250, 253–54, 258, 265, 266. *See also* beast of the earth
False prophets 21, 22
Famine, xiv, 61, 62, 78–80, 82, 108, 110, 175n75, 190, 244, 311, 318
Farkesfalvy, Denis, 17n10, 17n11
Farmer, William, 17n10, 17n11,
Fathers of the Church. *See* Patristic interpretation
Flavius Josephus. *See* Josephus
Figurative sense, 98, 136, 139, 141, 142, 143, 144. *See also* tropologia.
Fire/flame: 92, 113, 177, 195, 215, 217, 220, 244, 254, 276, 277, 283; bifurcated, 277; of Caesarea, 65, 68, 69, 71, 79n25; of cleansing or purification, 209–10, 219, 270, 275–76, 277–78, 280; eternal, 281; of Gehenna, 229, 245, 258, 260, 266, 280, 282; lake of 160, 174, 265–66, 267; punishment by, 62, 201, 217, 267; tests works of people, 198, 276, 277–78; of transformation, 267, 270
Foss, Clive, 65n49, 78n15, 79n22, 80n27
Four horsemen, 138, 189–90, 198
Four Living beings, 95, 122, 133, 134, 149, 170, 171, 185, 207, 267
Fourth Crusade, 37–38
Free will, 205–7, 209–10, 216, 282, 316. *See also* synergy

Gaius, anti-Montanist, 22–23, 24, 26, 30, 31n59, 33

Gamble, Harry, 16n7
Garment(s) 117, 155, 285. *See also* robes
Gates of heavenly Jerusalem, 198–200, 285, 286
Gehenna, 125, 179n89, 203, 219, 229, 245, 247, 258, 259, 260, 266, 272, 273, 280, 282
Gog and Magog, 64n46, 174, 175, 193, 237, 265
Gold, 138n47, 206, 287; analogy to the soul, 210, 277–78, 280
Goodspeed, Edgar, 14n4, 27n45, 28n49, 31n59, 34n71, 36n3, 36n4, 289n3
Gospel According to the Hebrews, 31
Gospel of John, 20, 22, 23, 24, 25, 27, 30, 98, 118, 130n17, 171n53, 172n63, 305n29
Gospel of Luke, 72n3, 132, 188
Gospel of Mark, 164
Gospel of Matthew, 132, 164, 192
Gospel of Matthias, 31n58
Gospel of Peter, 31n58
Gospel of Thomas, 31n58
Grant, Robert, 27n45
Greek Commentaries. *See* Apocalypse, commentaries
Greek Fathers. *See* patristic interpretation
Greek language, 2, 9–10, 11, 12n39, 39, 40–43, 53, 55, 58, 75, 90, 107, 113n9, 115n18, 128n11, 130, 150, 152, 245, 298, 301, 303, 310
Greek manuscripts. *See* Manuscripts, Greek
Greek of the Apocalypse, 129–31, 175–76, 290, 294n26, 295. *See also* Attic syntax
Greek pagan sources, 8, 180, 187, 306
Greek Orthodox Church. *See* Orthodox Church; Eastern Christianity
Greek New Testaments, xiii, 40–42, 289
Greek thought, 96, 97, 171n51
Gregory, Caspar René, 39n16, 288n2
Gregory of Nyssa, 34, 101n57, 128n10, 145, 307
Gregory the Armenian, 292
Gregory the Theologian of Nazianzus, 28, 34, 35n1, 88n4, 101n57, 178, 184, 305, 307
Gregory the Great, 11n36, 81, 132n24, 171
Gregory Palamas, 38

Hades, 128–29, 264, 267, 269
Haldon, J. F., 65n47, 65n48, 65n49
Harlot, 149, 50, 239, 249. *See also* Babylon
Harnack, Adolf von, 17n9

Harvest: of the faithful, 237, 287; as judgment, 203, 222, 225. *See also* judgment; wine press
Haußleiter, Johannes, 4n14
Hebrew language, 40n19, 133–34, 168, 245, 265
Hebrew people, 140, 251
Hebrews, Book of, 15, 30
Hermogenes, 20
Hernández Jr., Juan, 91, 127, 129, 297
Hezekiah, 174
Hierocles, 176
Historical sense/*historia*, 137–40, 144, 152. *See also* literal sense
Holy Spirit, 3, 19, 115, 118, 119, 124n60, 149, 164n33, 165, 257, 261, 280, 307, 316. *See also* Life-giving Spirit
Holy Trinity. *See* Trinity, Holy
Horse(s), 203, 210, 215, 216, 220, 222, 230
Hymns, 84, 114, 115, 116, 117, 182, 183, 186, 194, 195, 196, 202n95, 315. *See also* Trisagion hymn.
Hebrew language, 40n19, 133, 134, 168, 245, 265
Hebrew people, 140, 251. *See also* Jews
Hebrews, Book of, 15, 30
Heraclius, Emperor, 65, 77, 80, 81n34, 83–85, 312
Hilary of Poitiers, 10
Hill, Charles, 24n33, 31n59
Hippolytus, 1, 3, 9, 12, 24, 30, 173, 178, 188n20, 191, 193, 239, 242, 251, 257, 292, 304n27, 305, 307, 314,
Hoskier, H. C., 7n28, 94, 291–93, 316
Huns, 80

Incarnation of Christ, 53n15, 59, 60, 161, 166, 173, 184, 186, 189, 227, 228, 235, 236, 237
Irenaeus of Lyon, 1, 2, 12, 19–20, 22–23, 134, 171, 173, 174n69, 178, 179n89, 188n20, 191, 245, 247n71, 251, 257 ,270, 305, 307, 314
Isaiah, 19, 97, 126n5, 163, 164, 168, 174, 182, 260, 270
Isauria, 52, 53

James, Book of, 15, 30
James, St. /Brother of the Lord, 126n5
Jeremiah, 126, 251

Jerome, St. 2n1, 3n3, 4, 5, 6, 10, 17, 88n4, 89, 132n25, 242, 243n46
Jerusalem: City of, 175, 177, 196, 291; destruction of 49, 61, 66–67, 69, 70n61, 71, 81n34; heavenly 106, 140, 146, 179, 198–200, 201n90, 229, 231, 264, 283, 284, 285, 286; new, 3, 21, 133, 148, 254, 269, 285
Jerusalem, Council of. *See* Council of Jerusalem
Jews, 70, 97, 140, 158, 194, 196. *See also* Hebrew people
Johannine writings, 22, 23, 24, 31n59, 33n67. *See also* Gospel of John; Epistles of John
John, Apostle/Evangelist: 14n4, 18–19, 20, 21, 23, 24, 24n38, 25, 27, 29, 30, 38, 50, 53, 60, 92n13, 98, 99, 130n17, 132, 134, 137–38, 140, 149, 153, 155n5, 156, 159, 162, 172, 177, 180, 187, 188–91, 193, 227, 228, 239, 274, 284, 304, 305, 307, 309
John Baptist and Forerunner, 126n5, 253
John, Catholikos, Armenian Patriarch, 70n62
John Chrysostom, 33, 88n3, 109n26, 116, 117, 123, 131n18, 140n58, 152, 156n10, 292, 309
John Climacus, 292
John of Damascus, 35
John, Epistles of. *See* Epistles of John.
John, Gospel of, See Gospel of John
John, Patriarch of Alexandria, 70n62
John, presbyter, 27, 29, 131
Jones, A. H. M., 68n55
Josephus, Flavius, 175, 177
Judgment, 116, 117, 161, 165, 166, 187, 190, 192, 195, 203, 205, 215, 218, 222, 225, 226, 233, 259, 262, 263, 264, 265–67, 276; See also harvest and wine press
Jude, Book of, 15, 30, 33n65, 34n71
Julian, Emperor, "The Apostate," 178, 240, 252
Julius Africanus, 132n25
Justin Martyr and Philosopher, 1, 11, 18–19, 178, 179, 247,
Justin II, Emperor, 62n45
Justinian, 11n36, 62, 68n55, 78, 101

Kannengiesser, Charles, 7n29, 51–52
Kelly, J. N. D., 101n55
Khosrov II, King, 62n45, 69

King of the Romans, 81n36, 239, 240, 243, 250
King, God as, 115n17, 115n18, 117, 228, 285
Kings: of the earth/nations, 64n46, 241, 265, 278; of the east, 64n46, 251; Persian, 62n45, 69, 81n36; "pious," 67n53, 193, 237; Roman, 140, 170, 193. *See also* seven kings; ten kings
Kingdom: of the Antichrist/Beast, 160, 216; of heaven, 117n32, 118, 147, 148, 155, 192n32, 193, 211, 228, 234, 235; literal, earthly, 234, 235, 261, 262, 268, 280, 282–86, 314, 316; Roman, 240–42, 252; of the saints, 239; seventh, 239, 241. *See also* successive kingdoms; seven kingdoms
Koester, Helmut, 16n7
Konstantinides, Emmanuel, 41n22, 75n8, 299n7

Lake of fire. *See* fire, lake of
Lamb: Christ as the, 97n35, 118, 134, 155, 185, 186, 188, 194, 196, 198, 229, 284, 316; False lamb/Antichrist, 253, 258
Lamoreaux, John, 54, 55, 56, 58–60
Lang, D. M., 45n35, 302n14, 309n38
Laodicea: Church of, 230; city of, 18
Laodicea, Council of. *See* Council of Laodicea
Latin: of the Apocalypse text, 19–20, 291; knowledge of in East, 10–12; language, 9–10; rise of patristic literature in, 10–11, 13
Latin Apocalypse interpretation, 2–7, 9–13, 89. *See also* Apocalypse Commentaries
Latin Fathers, knowledge of Greek 10–11
Latin translation of the commentary. *See* translation of the commentary
Laval, Université, x
Lectionary, Apocalypse in, xiii, 9, 17, 40, 288, 289, 291, 309
Letter of the Churches of Lyon and Vienne, 19
Life, earthly 191, 213, 263
Life, eternal. *See* eternal life
Life, future, 147, 192n32, 280, 314. *See also* eternal life
Life: of the Church, 115, 141, 165, 197, 202; manner of/way of, 141, 142, 148, 195, 207, 213, 224, 225, 248, 253, 255, 261, 267, 269,

Life (cont.)
  285, 316; present life/this life, 90, 91, 192n32, 205, 211, 212, 213, 215, 226, 227, 230, 234, 239, 243, 249, 252, 262, 268, 274, 280, 282, 283; two kinds, 260, 268. See also book of life; eternal life; purpose of life; sea of life; spiritual life; tree of life; water of life; Andrew of Caesarea; life of Christ; life with Christ
Life of Andrew of Caesarea. See Andrew of Caesarea
Life of Christ, 66, 107, 157, 158–61, 166, 172, 173, 177, 180, 188, 189, 228, 235n13, 313
Life with Christ/God, 261, 262, 284, 285. See also eternal life
Life-giving Spirit, 120, 277, 284, 286. See also Holy Spirit
Literal sense, 128, 137–40, 141–42, 144, 147, 150, 151, 153, 287, 313–14. See also historia
Literalism/literalist interpretation, 24–26
Logos, 22n32, 53n15, 102, 154, 163, 181, 184, 229
Lombards, 80, 300n11
Love of God/Christ for humanity, 97, 113, 165, 198, 205, 216, 225, 226–31, 278n88, 279, 316, 317. See also philanthropia
Love of angels for humanity, 201, 203, 204
Love of money, 196, 216
Love for Christ/God, 72n3, 208, 213, 225, 248, 255
Luke, see Gospel of Luke

Maccabees, 175
Macedonians, 193, 241, 243
Magdalino, Paul, 81n36
Magog. See Gog and Magog
Makarios, commentary recipient, 59, 72–76, 82–83, 87, 104–7, 110, 131, 135, 136, 278, 311, 318. See also Sergius I
Makarios of Jerusalem, 74
Maldfeld, Georg, 293n25
Male child, 188, 248
Mango, Cyril, 170n48
Manuscript variations, knowledge of. See Andrew of Caesarea
Manuscript variations in the Apocalypse text, 19, 128–29, 158, 293–95, 296–97
Manuscripts of the Andreas commentary: x, xiv, 39, 45–46, 85, 87, 288–97; in Armenian 301; in Georgian, 302; in Latin, 300; in Old Slavonic/Russian 45–46, 302–4
Manuscripts of the Apocalypse, 8–9, 38–39, 288–89, 288–97, 302–4
Manuscripts of the Oikoumenios commentary, 50, 59, 87, 94, 99, 182
Marcion, 21, 132n24
Marcus Aurelius, 19
Mark of the beast. See beast, mark of
Mark, Gospel of. See Gospel of Mark
Marriage: 21, 117, 132n25; kingdom as, 285; of the Lamb, 198, 229
Martyrs/Martyrdom, 2, 19, 25, 38, 43, 97n35, 116, 126n5, 155, 157, 158, 161, 162, 166, 172, 177, 189, 193, 212, 225, 239–40, 242, 264, 292, 310. See also saints
Mary, Virgin. See Mother of God; Theotokos; Virgin Mary; woman wrapped in the sun
Matthew, Gospel of. See Gospel of Matthew
Matthias, Gospel of. See Gospel of Matthias
Maurice, Emperor, 62n45, 69n56, 79, 81
Mavromatis, Georgios, 49n4
Maximin, Emperor, 175, 190
Maximos the Confessor, 35, 305–6
Maximos Kalliopolites, 42–44, 298–99, 303, 310
Maximos the Peloponnesian. See Maximos Kalliopolites
McDonald, Lee 14n1, 16n7, 17n23
Medes, 193
Melito of Sardis, 1, 20
Metaphor, 107, 138, 142–43, 147, 150, 151, 211, 248
Methodios of Olympos, 1, 25–26, 30, 75, 95 96n30, 178, 180, 188n20, 189, 270, 305, 314
Metzger, Bruce, 16, 17n8, 28n47, 30n56, 31n58, 31n59, 33n63, 34n71, 45n34, 45n35, 200n82, 289, 302n15, 309n39, 309n40
Meyendorff, John, 101n55, 103n63, 103n64
Miaphysite, as a term 53n15
Miaphysite theology, ix, 51, 52, 53, 54, 56–57, 59, 83n38, 92, 100–103, 114, 163, 181–83, 271, 312. See also non-Chalcedonian
Michael, Archangel, 160, 246
Michael the Syrian, 79n24
Millennialism 2, 3, 5, 18–19, 23, 24, 26, 29, 34, 234–38. See also chiliasm; millennium

GENERAL INDEX   345

Millennium 5, 11, 19, 21, 23, 26, 162n28, 173, 193, 234–38, 259, 260, 261, 262, 265. *See also* chiliasm; millennialism; one thousand years
Minge, xiv
Monophysite theology. *See* Miaphysite; non-Chalcedonian
Montanists/Montanism, 2, 7, 21–23, 25, 26, 31n59. *See also* anti-Montanists
Mother of God, 84. *See also* Theotokos; Virgin Mary; woman wrapped in the sun
Moral sense of scripture, 138m 141–43, 148, 314. *See also tropologia*
Morning star, 167–68
Moses, 95, 126n5, 140, 154; Law of, 119, 141
Muratorian Canon, 132n24
Muslims xiv, xiii, 35, 37, 315

Name(s): of the Antichrist, 19, 256–58; of the apostles, 199; of Babylon, 243; of the Beast, 149, 250, 251, 252, 281; of Christ, 185, 186, 198; of Christian, 196; of the devil, 245; for kingdom of heaven, 284; Makarios, 72, 74–75; of Oikoumenios 50n7, 51–52, 58–59, 88, 100, 113; of Theophilus, 73; of the saints, 266, 267; of the twelve tribes, 106, 133, 198–99; of the twenty-four elders, 134 *See also Onomastica*; Andrew of Caesarea
Nassif, Bradley, 140n58, 148, 149n99
Nebuchadnezzar of Babylon, 241
Nepos of Arsinoe, 26, 29
Nero, Emperor, 19
Nerses of Lampron, xvn2, 45, 300–301, 306–8
Nestorians/ Nestorianism, 53n15, 100, 102, 155
New heaven and earth, 270
New Prophecy. *See* Montanists/Montanism
New Rome, 193, 239, 240, 241, 250. *See also* Constantinople
New Testament, 9, 14, 15, 17, 28, 30, 34, 36, 39–46, 168, 205, 288, 289, 290, 291, 292, 295, 300, 302, 306, 310
Nicaea, Council of. *See* Ecumenical Councils
Nicolaitans, 144
Nikephoros Kallistos, 38, 310
Nikephoros, Patriarch of Constantinople, 35–36
Nikol'skij Apocalypse, 46, 303

Nino of Assyria, 241
Nock, Arthur Darby, 17n8
Non-Chalcedonian Orthodox, 53, 96n34, 100–101, 103, 181, 187, 271. *See also* Oriental Orthodox; Miaphysite; Eastern Christianity
Non-Chalcedonian theology, 53, 57, 96n34, 99–103, 181, 187, 271. *See also* Miaphysite theology
Norris, Frederick, 49n4
Nous, 95

Obolensky, Dimitri, 84
Oecumenius. *See* Oikoumenios
Oikoumenios, commentary author: Commentary's flaws, ix, 82, 86, 87–89, 91–98, 99, 103, 107, 117–19, 124, 133–34, 138–39, 156–62, 165, 166–67, 219, 221, 245, 249, 272, 275, 313–14; Date of commentary, 7, 8, 50, 53–54, 58–61, 74, 96n34; Division of commentary, 93–94, 137; first Greek commentary, ix, xiii, xiv, 7, 50, 58, 86; his confusion, 160, 245, 249; identity and affiliation of, 7, 51–61, 92–93, 96, 97; inconsistencies, 98–99; knowledge of manuscript variations, 128, 158; lack of exegetical training, ix, 97–99, 132, 133–135, 143, 152, 162, 180, 278; limited influence of commentary, ix, 13, 57–58, 86, 87–88; non-Chalcedonian ix, 51–52, 54, 56–57, 59, 83n38, 92, 99–103, 114, 163, 181–83; orientation, 94–96; Origenism, 92, 95, 96, 247n72, 271, 278; originality, 92, 133, 312; philosophical background, ix, xiv, 92–96, 112, 143; problematic conclusions, 7, 119, 156–57, 158–59, 161, 167, 272–73, 274–75, 278; problems with sequence, 98n43, 158–61, 272–73, 274; readability of the commentary, 93–94; style, 9, 82, 92, 93–95, 97–98, 112; treatment of the text, 93–94, 97–98; understanding of prophecy, 96, 98n41, 107, 127, 162, 180, 187, 188n20, 219, 312; use of Scripture, 93–94; use of sources, 8, 56, 96, 127, 134, 175, 177–80, 306; as source for Andrew, 12, 50, 88–89, 91. *See also* non-Chalcedonian theology; Manuscripts of the Oikoumenios commentary; Miaphysite; *Trisagion* Hymn

Oikoumenios, Count, 51–53, 54, 55, 58, 59
Oikoumenios, tenth century Bishop of Trikki, 7, 51, 52
Old Testament, 35n1, 40n19, 92n13, 128n11, 140, 141, 144, 154n3, 158, 163, 166, 168, 172
Oller, Thomas, 46n37, 303n19, 144, 196, 198
One thousand years. *See* thousand; thousand year reign of Christ; chiliasm; millennium
Onomastica, 133
Order: in heaven, 201, 202, 203; of creation, 195, 221
Orders, angelic, 195, 246
Oriental Orthodox Church, x, 53n15, 300. *See also* non-Chalcedonian Orthodox; Miaphysite; Eastern Christianity
Origen, 1, 3, 24–26, 53, 56, 56n29, 95, 128, 136–37, 145, 189n20, 247n72, 307; text of, 293, 294
Origenism, 57, 83n38, 92, 95, 96, 96n30, 137, 211, 247n72, 268, 271, 275–76, 278. *See also Apokatastasis*
Orthodox Church, x, xii, xiv, 9, 36–38, 40–46, 81n34, 84, 85, 103, 115, 115n17, 116, 116n22, 117, 120, 177n82, 205, 209, 288, 300, 306, 309–10, 315, 317, 318. *See also* Eastern Christianity
Ostrogorsky, George, 77n13, 78n15, 79n25, 81n34
Ottoman Turks, 37, 38, 43, 65n49, 310

Papias of Hierapolis, 3, 18, 29, 32, 178–79, 246, 304–5
Paul, Apostle, 95, 99, 100, 159, 164, 167, 195n45, 205, 269, 272, 277, 300
Pauline writings, 15, 30, 96n32, 99, 132
Patristic commentaries. *See* Apocalypse commentaries
Patristic interpretation: ix, 1, 2, 8, 9–12, 20n26, 24, 33, 34, 36, 92n13, 95, 96, 101, 122–23, 124n60, 127–31, 132, 133–34, 136, 140, 141, 142, 145 – 47, 155, 162, 165, 178–80, 182, 191, 211, 236n19, 239, 240, 241, 242–43, 246, 253, 259, 269, 275, 295, 306, 307; Greek influence on Latin 9–13; Latin influence on Greek 10–13. *See also* Apocalypse commentaries; allegory; anagoge; *historia*; sequence; *theoria*; *tropologia*; word association

Pelikan, Jaroslav, 101n55, 101n56, 101n57, 103n64
Peltanus, Theodore, xv
Pergamum, 81n34, 116, 177
Persecution. *See* Roman persecution
Persian Empire, 175, 193, 240, 241, 243
Persian invasion, 49, 62–71, 76–77, 79, 80–81, 84, 251, 311, 312, 315
Persian occupation and destruction of Caesarea, 61, 62–63, 65–66, 67–72, 80, 110, 170
Persian destruction of Jerusalem, 49, 61, 66–67, 69, 70n61, 71, 81n34
Pestilence, 61, 244, 318. *See also* plagues, and bubonic plague
Peter, Apostle, 176–77
Peter, Epistles of. *See* Epistles of Peter
Peter, Gospel of. *See* Gospel of Peter
Peter, Apocalypse of. *See* Apocalypse of Peter
Pharaoh, 218
Philadelphia, Church of, 163, 182, 224
Philanthropia, 204, 226, 229–31, 316
Phocas, tyrant, 65, 69n56, 79–80
Photios the Great, 36, 132n25
Plagues, 61, 108, 130, 138n47, 175n75, 187, 191, 195, 196, 197, 203, 216, 217–18, 220, 221, 225–28, 238, 252, 264, 269, 270, 272, 273–74, 279, 281, 316. *See also* bubonic plague; pestilence.
Prayer(s), 105, 114, 115, 116–17, 148, 153, 164, 165, 194, 195, 201, 202, 208, 209, 218, 229, 236n19, 283, 315
Precious stones, 106, 133, 146, 179, 199
Primasius of Hadrumentum, 4n13, 6, 291n16
Printing Press, xiii, 39
Prophets: 19, 24, 35n1, 105, 126, 144, 158, 227, 242. *See also* False prophets
Prophecy, 21–22, 96, 127, 166, 174, 180, 187, 189, 251, 255. *See also* Apocalypse
Protestant Christianity, 40–41
Proverbs. *See tropologia*; moral sense
Psalms, Book of, 270
Pseudo-Christ, 227. *See also* False Christ; Antichrist
Pseudo-Dionysios, 35, 49, 75, 75n9, 178, 201, 202, 305–6
Punishment: 20, 112, 113, 138, 139, 153, 201, 203, 204, 210, 216, 219–20, 222, 225, 226–27, 228, 229, 263–64, 274, 283, 317; of

the devil, 247, 249, 280; eternal, 50, 211, 218, 230, 247, 260, 262–63, 271–73, 275–76, 277–82, 283, 312; is self chosen, 209, 210–11, 212n139, 218, 219–20, 222–23, 266–67, 279–80, 282, 316. *See also* afflictions; suffering; torment

Quasten, Johannes, 9n33, 10n34
Quinisext Council, 36

Recapitulation, 3, 156, 157
Recipient of the commentary. *See* Makarios
Renewal of creation, 186, 209, 267–71
Repentance, 110, 113, 138, 153, 167, 203–205, 207, 216–18, 226, 227, 229, 230–31, 246, 247, 274, 279, 280, 281
Repose: God's throne as, 116–17; of the saints, 191, 192, 193, 264, 284, 285. *See also* rest, eternal
Rest, eternal: 175, 191–92, 231, 282, 283; holy powers do not rest, 184; worshippers of beast will have none, 281; *See also* repose of the saints
Resurrection: bodily, 268; of Christ 157, 186, 192, 193, 208, 248; Church of the, 66; defended against Philosophers, 96; false resurrection, 176; first resurrection, 235, 237, 259, 260, 262, 268; of the saints, 234; two resurrections, 234, 237, 259, 262; universal, 219, 234, 235, 259
Return of Christ, 19, 159, 193, 26, 263, 266, 272, 277. *See also* Second Coming of Christ
Return of Apostle John, 172
Return of sinners to God, 204, 209, 217, 223, 227, 279, 282
Reward for the Churches, 167, 168
Reward for writing the commentary, 105
Rewards of the righteous, 24, 107, 112, 159, 211, 212, 226, 227, 228, 231, 234, 235, 239, 260, 263, 264, 266, 267, 269, 282–84, 285, 286
Revelation, Book of. *See* Apocalypse
Robes: 97, 117, 155, 200n82; white, 117, 155, 194, 264. *See also* garments
Roman Catholic Church, 17n8, 37, 40, 300n11
Roman Empire, 31n59, 38, 47, 61–65, 66n50, 69–71, 78–79, 81, 108, 174, 175n75, 177, 189, 193, 224, 238, 239, 240, 242, 243, 252, 311. *See also* Byzantine Empire
Roman persecution, 156, 177n82, 189, 255, 310
Rome, city of, 10, 19, 24n38, 28n49, 99, 173–74, 239, 240, 241. *See also* New Rome
Romulus of Rome, 241
Russian illustrated Apocalypses, 304
Russian Orthodox Church. *See* Apocalypse in the Orthodox Church; Eastern Christianity; Orthodox Church

Sabbath of future rest, 175, 190, 191, 192. *See also* seventh day
Saints: around the throne, 117; co-reign with Christ, 193, 234, 236, 237, 260, 262; display patient endurance, 196–97, 223; helped by angels, 197; in union with God, 285; life of, 174, 177, 202, 204n111, 223, 259, 260, 313; persecution of, 240, 252; pray for chastisements, 218; pray for the end, 190, 195; prayers like incense, 201; rejoice at destruction of Babylon, 218; sing hymns to God, 196; spiritual experiences of, 135, 149, 202; suffer for Christ 223–25; victorious over the devil, 277; virtue of, 277; virtues are hidden 197; were tested by trials 277; will be separated from the sinners, 267; worship with angels, 117, 195, 315. *See also* martyrs; repose of the righteousness; rewards of the righteous
Salvation: 100, 138, 148, 157n13, 198, 202, 203, 204, 205–7, 209–12, 226, 229, 248, 273, 279, 313, 316, 318; of the devil, 280. *See also* Apokatastasis; will of God
Samaritans, 196
Sanders, James, 16n7, 17n13
Sardis, 1, 20, 81n34, 117
Satan: 244–46, 250, 252, 265; binding of 161, 236–3, 265; fall of 159, 168; meaning of word, 133. *See also* devil and dragon
Schaff, Philip, 2n1, 3n3, 109n26
Schmid, Josef, xiv, xivn1, xvn2
Sea: destruction of, 219; disappearance of, 270; of glass, 196, 276; of life, 90, 91, 213, 249, 252; surrenders the dead, 267. *See also* beast of the sea
Sebeos, historian, 66n52, 69n56, 70, 71n64
Seal: fifth 157, 158, 172, 190, 263; first, 157n14,

Seal (cont.)
  189, 198; fourth, 157n14, 190; second, 157n14, 189; seventh, 191; sixth 156, 157n14, 158, 165, 177, 190, 232, 250; third, 157n14, 189. See also seven seals
Seal of the Spirit, 209, 257
Sealing of the faithful, 119, 195–96, 197, 256–57, 261, 272, 273, 313
Seals, seven, 153, 156, 157, 158, 172, 180, 188, 189, 191
Second Coming of Christ, 159, 161, 167, 193, 203, 237, 264, 272, 273, 274. See also return of Christ
Second death, 237, 259–63
Sennacherib, 174
Septuagint, 40n19, 41, 128n11, 168
Sequence, 3, 151, 152, 155–62, 165, 167, 172, 187, 221, 314
Seraphim, 103, 117, 163–65, 182. See also angels
Severus of Antioch, 51, 52, 53–54, 54–55, 59, 60, 61, 100, 163
Sergius I, Patriarch of Constantinople, 76–77, 82, 83–85, 104, 311–12. See also Makarios
Seven, symbolism of, 99, 132, 146, 175, 190, 191–92, 216, 252
Seven ages, 192, 241
Seven angels, 191, 216
Seven beatitudes, 72n3
Seven bowls, 156, 191, 203
Seven churches, 90, 93, 99, 132, 189, 190
Seven heads, 25n41, 149, 150, 250, 251–52
Seven hills, 239, 241
Seven kingdoms, 241, 250, 252. See also successive kingdoms
Seven kings, 193, 241, 250
Seven millennia. See seven ages
Seven plagues, 129–30, 191, 195, 216, 264
Seven seals, 153, 156, 157, 158, 172, 180, 188, 189, 191
Seven spirits, 123, 124n60
Seven trumpets, 138, 157, 159, 195, 203
Seventh age, 190–193, 216, 252
Seventh day. See seventh age
Shahin, 64, 70
Shahrbaraz, 64, 66, 70
Shepherd of Hermas, 30, 96, 306
Simon Magus, 176

Simonetti, Manlio, 3n10, 7n27, 49n4, 233, 234n9
Sinaiticus, Codex, 200n82, 289, 290, 292, 293, 294, 295, 297n48
Six, symbolism of, 191–92
Six ages, 191–92, 235, 616, 19–20
666, 19–20, 134, 146, 257, 258
Sixth day, 191–92
Sixth seal. See seal
Skopos, 111, 152–53, 157, 162
Slavery: by the devil, 223; by Persians, 66, 70n61, 71n63, 80; to mammon, 196, 216, 262; to sin, 212, 216
Slavs, 80, 81n34, 84, 312
Slavic acceptance of Apocalypse. See Apocalypse in the Orthodox Church
Slavonic translation of Commentary. See translation of the commentary
Slavonic translation of Apocalypse. See translation of the Apocalypse
Smyrna, Church of, 111
Soul: after death, 220, 259–64, 267; illness of, 139, 150, 220, 231; not filthy by nature, 210, 278, 280, 282; relationship with Christ/God, 207, 284, 285, 316
Souls under altar, 157, 158, 172, 190, 263
Souls of the slain, 161
Souter, Alexander, 28n48, 28n49
Spirit. See Holy Spirit
Spiritual death, 220, 223, 251, 260–62, 274
Spiritual life, 105, 111, 112, 115, 116, 141, 234
Spiritual powers, 204, 279. See also angels
Spiritual sense of scripture, 5, 25, 143–45, 147–49, 150, 151, 220, 223, 257, 314. See also anagoge; *theoria*
Spiritual suffering, 220
Spiritual warfare, 211–12
Spiritual worship, 194, 202
Steinhauser, Kenneth, 3n4, 4n12, 5n18, 5n19, 6n20, 6n21, 6n23, 6n24, 6n26, 89n5
Stonehouse, Ned Bernard, 5n15, 5n17, 21n28, 27n45, 31n59, 33n66
Stratos, Andreas, 11n36, 65n48, 70n57, 70n62, 79n21, 79n24, 85
Successive kingdoms, 81n36, 134, 193, 238–43, 252
Sufferings, beneficial 220, 223, 225. See also punishment; afflictions; torment

Suggit, John, 7n28, 55–56, 94–95, 161, 205n113, 275n73
Swete, Henry Barclay, 3n3, 6n23, 11n37, 33n66, 298n1
Symbolic language, 99, 107, 133, 139, 146, 147, 151, 163, 220, 236, 238, 253, 313
Symes, John Elliotson, 17n12
Synergy, 205–9, 211, 215, 257, 282, 316. See also free will
Synoptic gospels, 23, 24

Tabernacle, 140, 286
Teacher, Christ as, 198
Teachers of the Church, ix, 88, 127, 159, 170, 172, 173, 174, 240, 247n72, 255, 257, 314
Temple, Church as, 67n54, 253; heavenly, 129, 215; of Jerusalem, 253; pagan, 236
Ten horns 149, 150, 174, 240, 242, 243, 244, 250, 251, 252
Ten kings, 240, 243. See also ten horns
Tertullian, 1, 9, 21, 132n24
Textual transmission of Apocalypse, x, 9, 39, 129–30, 288–97
Text Types of the Apocalypse, x, 39, 288–98, 316
Theodore of Ioannina, 43n29
Theodore of Mopsuestia, 33
Theodore Syncellus, 84n39, 84n40
Theodoret of Cyrus, 33
Theophilus of Antioch, 1, 20
Theophylact Simocatta, 76, 77n12
Theoria 143, 145, 146–51, 152. See also spiritual sense
Theotokos, 84, 159, 180
Therapeutike, 47n1, 263, 264, 268–69, 276–77
Thomas, Acts of. See Acts of Thomas
Thomas, Gospel of. See Gospel of Thomas
Thessalonika, 75n29, 81n34m 84
Thomson, Robert, 45n33, 45n34, 67n24, 300n11, 301n12, 308n36
Thousand year binding of the devil, 161, 188, 250, 253
Thousand year reign of Christ. See millennium; chiliasm; millennialism; one thousand years
Thousand, interpretation of, 175, 191, 193, 235, 236, 237, 238, 285

Thyatira, Church of, 167, 168
Three and a half years, 173, 221, 224, 235, 252, 253, 254
Three levels: of prophecy, 96, 127; in Scripture, 106–7, 127–28, 136–37, 140, 147; typology, 140
Three parts: of a human being, 120, 136, 137; of Jerusalem, 196, 255
Throne: of the apostles, 161, 198; of the beast, 142, 252; episcopal, 74, 145, 170 301; of God, 20, 23, 92n13, 95, 116–17, 118, 123, 139, 149, 179, 185, 186, 194, 202, 224, 266, 269, 273; of judgment, 161, 259; Persian, 62n45, 69n56; Roman, 65, 69n56, 79, 80n26; of twenty-four elders, 126, 161
Tiberius II, Emperor, 57
Translation of the Bible, into Georgian, 45, 302; into Modern Greek, 9, 40–42, 299
Translation of the Apocalypse: into Armenian, 45, 300, into Georgian, 45, 308–9; into Modern Greek, 42–43, 303, 310; into Slavonic, 302–3
Translation of Commentary: into Armenian, x, xvn2, 45, 87, 300–301, 306–8; into English x, 18n14; into Georgian, ix, x, 45, 87, 302, 308–9; into Latin, xv, xvn2, 87, 300; into Lombard, xvn2, 300; into Slavonic, x, 45–46, 87, 302–3, 309–310
Treadgold, Warren, 10n35, 62n43, 62n45, 65n47, 65n48, 68n55, 78n16, 78n17, 78n18, 78n19, 78n20, 79n21, 79n23, 80n26, 80n29
Tree of Life, 130, 200, 286, 287
Tribe of Dan, 251
Tribes of Israel. See Twelve Tribes
Trinity, Holy, 114n15, 115, 117n29, 120, 123, 124, 154, 163, 180, 182, 183, 184, 194, 199, 261, 283, 284, 316
Trinity, "unholy," 249, 254
Trisagion Hymn, 103, 114n15, 117, 163–65, 180, 181–83
Tropologia, 141–43, 148, 152. See also figurative sense
Tropos. See tropologia
True Cross, 66, 81n34. See also Cross of Christ
Trullo, Council of. See Council of Trullo
Trumpets. See seven trumpets
Twelve precious stones, 133, 146, 179, 199, 200

Twelve tribes, 106, 133, 135, 146, 198–99, 251
Twelve symbolism, 199–200, 285, 287
Twenty-four elders, 92n13, 106, 117, 120, 126, 134, 138, 139, 155, 194, 197–98.
Twenty-four sections. *See* Andrew of Caesarea
Two deaths, 259–60, 262
Two kinds of life. *See* life
Two resurrections, 234–35, 259, 262
Two witnesses, 134, 159, 167, 172, 173, 226, 227, 253. *See also* Enoch and Elijah
Tyconius, 3, 4n12, 5, 6, 6n20, 6n21, 6n23, 6n24, 6n26, 11, 12, 13
Typology, 140–41, 152

Universite Laval, x

Valens, Emperor, 252
Victorinus of Pettau, 2–6, 13, 89n5, 132n24, 156, 291n16
Virgin Mary, 139, 159. *See also* Mother of God; Theotokos
Virtue, 105, 133, 141, 170–71, 196, 197, 199, 201, 213, 223, 224, 228, 233, 244, 245, 255, 277, 282, 286
Visigoths, 80
Vulgate, 17

Wace, Henry, 2n1, 3n3,
Wages, 210, 211, 223, 264, 283; *See also* rewards of the righteous
Wainwright, Arthur, 6n22, 6n25, 11–12
Walls: of Caesarea, 69; of Constantinople, 84, 312; of heavenly Jerusalem, 179, 199, 285
War: against the Church, 248, 255, 265, 266; against demons, 212; civil, 62, 65, 78–80, 81, 82, 108, 110, 311, 318; in heaven, 160, 246; Jewish, 177; with Persia, 62, 70, 81, 83, 251, 311, 318. *See also* Armageddon; spiritual warfare

Water of life, 115, 118, 206, 230
Wedding imagery, 285. *See also* bridal chamber
Week, symbolism, 192, 252. *See also* seven
Weinrich, William, 49n4, 54, 55, 124n58
Western Christianity, 300, 301
Whitby, Michael, 76–77. *See also Chronicon Paschale*
White robes, 117, 155, 194, 264
White hair, 134
White horse, 189, 198
Willoughby, H. R., 38n10, 38n12, 40n17, 43n27, 304n21, 304n22, 304n23, 310n44, 310n45
Wilderness, 140, 149, 150, 224, 248, 255. *See also* desert
Will of God, 208, 209, 268, 282
Wilderness, 140, 149, 150, 224, 248, 255
Wine press, 222, 225, 266, 267; *See also* judgment; harvest
Witnesses. *See* two witnesses
Woe(s), 204, 213, 248, 249
Woman on the beast, 149–50, 239, 241. *See also* harlot; woman wrapped in the sun, 119, 138, 139, 159, 160, 180, 188, 198, 224, 247–48
Word association, 151, 159, 162–68, 183, 255, 272
Work, imagery of, 211, 248
Works: dead, 262, 268; good, 195, 198, 205, 208, 209, 229, 231, 234, 256, 257; in heaven 201, 205; to be tested, 277
Worship: of God, 115, 116, 194, 264, 265, 315; of the beast/demons, 138n47, 176, 217, 220, 252, 254, 256, 259, 280, 281; demanded by Antichrist, 253, 265

Zacharias, Patriarch of Jerusalem, 66, 67n54, 71n63
Zechariah, 126n5
Zion, Mt., 196, 198

www.ingramcontent.com/pod-product-compliance
Lightning Source LLC
Chambersburg PA
CBHW022027290426
44109CB00014B/780